# ROBERT OWEN
## Prophet of the Poor

*Essays in Honour of the Two Hundredth
Anniversary of his Birth*

# ROBERT OWEN
## Prophet of the Poor

*Essays in Honour of the Two Hundredth Anniversary of his Birth*

Edited by
**SIDNEY POLLARD**
and
**JOHN SALT**

*With an Introduction by Sidney Pollard*

Macmillan

Selection and editorial matter © Sidney Pollard and John Salt 1971

First published 1971 by
THE MACMILLAN PRESS LTD
London and Basingstoke
Associated companies in New York Toronto Dublin
Melbourne Johannesburg and Madras

SBN 333 00926 6

Printed in Great Britain by
WESTERN PRINTING SERVICES LTD
Bristol

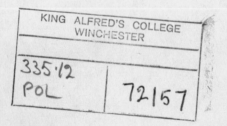

# Contents

# Introduction

## SIDNEY POLLARD

ON 14 May 1971 it will be two hundred years since the birth of Robert Owen. There will be celebrations to mark the anniversary in England, in Wales, the country of his birth, and in Scotland, where he achieved his greatest triumph as a factory manager and community builder. Owen will also be commemorated in many other countries outside Great Britain. This volume is part of the tribute which men all over the world will feel to be the due of one of the truly creative spirits of his age.

Although Owen lived to a ripe age, his main work was over before he reached his sixtieth year. His active lifetime thus spanned the momentous years of the industrialisation of Britain, the rise of liberal democracy in France, and the transformation of the United States from a dependent colonial society to a promising industrial power. It was an age of giants in many fields, yet there were few among them whose memory will be cherished as much, in so many parts of the world, as Robert Owen's. We must ask ourselves to what he owed that influence in his own lifetime, and the continued respect and interest in ours.

Some men achieve great practical success, or create a system of thought which pioneers new ways of insight and marks out the path on which others may travel forward. Neither of these applied to Owen. Though he was a successful cotton spinner for many years, in the end he lost control over his New Lanark Mill; his community experiments all failed and so did the trade union and labour exchange organisations with which he was associated; and his efforts to influence governments and constitution-makers could scarcely be taken seriously. Similarly, there could not be any claim to intellectual pioneering, for he has often been accused, and not without cause, of being a man of a single idea, and that not very original. Nor would the theory in its extreme form as propagated by Owen, that men's characters are exclusively the products of their circumstances, be widely accepted anywhere.

Where, then, does his power lie, to move earlier generations and ours too? In some measure, the answer is to be found in his many-sidedness, in the wide range of the human experience to which he applied his energies. He might have started out with a single basic idea, but it enabled him to look with new and critical eyes on much that was generally accepted in his age, and to propose novel solutions to its problems. In some respects he might have been old-fashioned in his own day – he has been characterised as a belated propagator of the Enlightenment – but in others he was far ahead of his time. In the field of education, for example, or on the economy of high wages, it took several generations before the Western world caught up with his insights, and in other respects, as in the best form of urban living, we might find ourselves still moving towards his position. Yet, in spite of the wide sweep of time commanded by him, he himself was concerned exclusively with problems of his own time in a severely practical manner, and could not be ignored by his contemporaries on such issues as unemployment, poor relief, or methods of cultivating the land. Here is one reason why his ideas are being studied as having particular relevance to the developing countries today.

Thus the epithet 'utopian' was particularly inappropriate, and often his ideas were worked out in relation to specific times and places, and in acres, in bushels, and in pounds, shillings and pence. And if we are tempted to smile at his naïve optimism about human nature, the one true utopian streak in his make-up which allowed him to believe that employers and governments, rich men and diplomats, would flock to his support as soon as the correctness of his views was explained to them, we should remember with humility his own patience with his opponents and his unwillingness to impute base motives to others, be-cause of his own essential kindness. There are not many figures who have made their mark on world history, yet who at the same time were happier in the company of children than of adults, and were as humble as Robert Owen in the company of those whom the world would unequivocally have denominated their inferiors.

It is, in part, with this many-sidedness in mind that we have assem-bled the contributions to this volume. His active life spanned an amazing range of specialisms. The experts of today on Owen as cotton spinner, as socialist, as social reformer, as social scientist and economist, as educator, as community builder, as trade union leader and as one of his several other parts may no longer be able to converse with each other professionally, but each can evaluate Owen's contribution to his own field, and gain an understanding of his wide appeal by considering his impact on so many others.

We have attempted to stress Owen's many-sided appeal not only by the content of the different contributions, but also by their form. Some of the papers are the fruits of recent detailed original research, seeing the light of day for the first time. Others are attempts to synthesise the studies of a lifetime. Others still take a broad sweep and a distant view, or represent bibliographical and other summaries of work done over the generations by large numbers of politicians, social reformers and scholars. For Robert Owen still fascinates and enriches the young scholar and the old, the co-operator or socialist, the teacher and the psychologist. We had originally intended to include also a bibliography of recent writings on Owen, but desisted, in part because of lack of space for such a massive undertaking, but largely because we have been anticipated by the very full list in J. F. C. Harrison's *Robert Owen and the Owenites in Britain and America* (1969) pp. 263-369.

Finally, the catholicity of Owen's influence is also reflected in the presentation of the work of scholars from France, Germany and Japan, besides those of Great Britain, and at least two who might be called Anglo-American. It is our regret that limitations of space forbid the inclusion of work from a wider range of countries still, for Owen's memory is honoured not only in the industrialised world, but is revered even more in the developing continents, where his gospel of co-operation finds an echo in societies that have many similarities in structure with the society in which Owen's ideas ripened in the first instance.

Owen's appeal survives, in part, because it is directed to so many different interests, at so many different levels, and at so many different stages of social development. Each aspect is enriched by the originality of his approach to the others. Yet, in the end, it is a single individual who combined them all, by all accounts a well-balanced individual, happy in his personal relationships and firmly of the belief that he held a unitary, all-embracing philosophy of life. Part of the power of Owen's appeal must also lie in the consistency, in the single focus of his ideas.

Owen himself believed that the key to all his ideas was the recognition of the infinite malleability of human character, particularly in childhood, and of the infinite power of society, i.e. the human environment, to mould it. A century and a half later, however, this tenet, important though it was to him, appears to be merely a rationalisation which does not fit all his pronouncements, nor does it form the true base of those which it does fit. The foundations of Owen's world lie much deeper than in such dubious psychology. The single thread which runs through all of Owen's ideas, colouring them and imparting their direction to them, is his humanity. His is not the humanism of the Renaissance, or even that of the Enlightenment, which proceeded on the powerful, if always unspoken assumption that the full development to the rounded and free human being was thinkable only in terms of a privileged minority. What was new and revolutionary in Owen was the belief, made possible for the first time in history by precisely the economic revolution in which he played such a striking part in his younger years, that the right to a full humanity was to be available to all, even to the humble peasant and cotton spinner and street sweeper. The contrast with his predecessors could not be sharper, though it is well hidden by the form of words. For the Enlightenment also appears to concern itself with 'man' as such, and with the elevation and the rights of 'men'. But when any of its spokesmen turn from philosophy to economics, as did Hume and Adam Smith, for example, we can see at once, by the role which they assign to labour (and usually by their attitude to universal suffrage), that they simply did not consider as full members of civil society those who were condemned to struggle somewhere near the subsistence minimum, and to spend their day in monotonous toil. Not that these eighteenth-century philosophers had no compassion: it is just that they could not conceive of equality with the lower orders.

The break in continuity occurs with Owen. One of the very few successful self-made manufacturers of the Industrial Revolution, he looked upon the poor, the peasantry and the proletariat not merely as the fit objects of philanthropy, but as members of the same society as he himself belonged to. It was true that he treated his workpeople at New Lanark and the co-operative and trade union leaders of the 1830s as children who had to be led and instructed; it is also true that he alone, among the middle-class reformers of his own day, looked upon them as his own children who would one day grow into man's estate, and not as children of some paupers without the gate, always destined to remain there. This is the common thread running through his life, from the management of his early workshops and his success in the tedious and troublesome fine cotton spinning, which put great strain on the workers, to the moulding of a rabble into a progressive community in New Lanark, and on to his educational innovations, his attitude to organised religion, to Factory Acts, to trade unions and to communal settlements. No one doubted his honesty when he declared that he would gladly end his life as an ordinary member of one of his proposed communal settlements. At each stage it was his recognition of workmen (and their children) as full citizens and full human beings which marked him off from his contemporaries.

What was unique in Owen's day has since become commonplace. At the same time the process of accepting the classes formerly outside the full membership of the nation was a painful one, and it would not be too much to say that it has dictated the shape of the social history of the Western world in the past century and a half. Owen is of interest still today because his critique and his positive ideas foreshadow the stresses of that period and are more relevant to them than almost any other contemporary writings, both in fields in which he proved to be right and in those in which he turned out to be wrong.

Today, when another section of humanity is knocking at the doors, demanding the full rights of world citizenship, hitherto reserved for white men alone, while at the same time passing through a phase of social development not unlike that lived through by Owen, his flashes of insight may still help to light the path of humanity. Two hundred years after his birth, Robert Owen's heritage is being extended from the Western world, which alone formed the basis of his experience, to become, fittingly, a part of the heritage of the whole human race.

# CHAPTER ONE

# A New View of Mr Owen

## J. F. C. HARRISON

THE paradox of Robert Owen has a continuing fascination. Why has he remained a central figure in the English socialist tradition even though Owenite institutions failed and his version of socialism was already outmoded before his death? How was it that Friedrich Engels could condemn Owen's socialism as utopian and yet concede that 'every social movement, every real advance in England on behalf of the workers links itself to the name of Robert Owen'?[1] What were the circumstances in which 'the father of English socialism' was not a working man seeking to raise his class, but a self-made industrialist turned gentlemanly philanthropist? The enigma – and charm – of Owen, which so attracted his contemporaries, casts its spell on succeeding generations of reformers. And as with another popular figure in the pantheon of the English Left, William Morris, each generation discovers in its hero what it most wishes to find. His work and ideas became surprisingly 'relevant'; he has a lesson or a message for the times. A good part of the English socialist tradition is in fact a series of reinterpretations of enigmatic figures from the past. For each age there is a new view of Mr Owen.

It is a pity that none of Owen's closest surviving friends or disciples (William Pare, Henry Travis, Robert Dale Owen, George Jacob Holyoake) wrote a full-scale study of his life. The only biography by an Owenite is Lloyd Jones's *Life, Times and Labours of Robert Owen*, 2 vols (London, 1889–90), which is disappointingly uninformative. The first batch of biographies, which appeared in the 1860s, was therefore limited to outsiders' impressions and heavily reliant on Owen's autobiography.[2] Holyoake was the first to attempt an interpretation of Owen's work by successfully annexing it to his own propaganda for consumers' co-operation and, to a lesser extent, secularism. This was the more acceptable in that many old Owenites were associated with these movements in the 1860s and 1870s. Owen became the patron saint of the British Co-operative movement – though in his lifetime he had shown but little interest in 'mere trading associations'. The climax

of this phase came around the turn of the century, with the erection
of a memorial to Owen in Kensal Green Cemetery, London, and the
restoration in 1902 of his grave in Newtown by the Co-operative
movement.[3]

The next interpreters of Owen were the Fabians. They found him to
be a sympathetic though misguided reformer, and in Owenism they
recognised a native socialist theory which owed nothing to Marx.
Frank Podmore's two-volume *Robert Owen: A Biography* (London,
1906) was the first scholarly work on Owen and Owenism, and has
remained the most useful standard source. Podmore was a founder-
member of the Fabian Society and was also closely associated with the
Society for Psychical Research. Perhaps it was because of his dual
interest in socialism and spiritualism that Podmore found the theme of
Owen's biography so congenial. He was acquainted with the eccentric
Rosamund Dale Owen, Robert Owen's granddaughter, who was also
an early Fabian. Podmore was able to use a collection of Owen's
papers which, after disappearing for a generation, were rediscovered
and passed on to Holyoake, who deposited them in the archives of the
Co-operative Union in Manchester. At the same time biographies of
Owen were published in France and Germany.[4]

Another interpretation of Owen was provided by the Marxists.
In the *Communist Manifesto* and in Engels's pamphlet, *Socialism,
Utopian and Scientific*, Owen was commended for his critique of
existing society but condemned for his failure to realise the significance
of class antagonisms. The disparaging epithet 'utopian' was fastened
upon Owenite socialism, which, it was argued, was bound to be futile
because it did not lead to revolutionary class action. For many years
Marxist theories were little known in Britain; but after 1888 cheap
editions of Marxist works in English changed this state of affairs. The
label 'utopian' was widely applied to Owenism, and perpetuated as
a description of pre-Marxian socialism, a term that originated as a
criticism by contemporary polemicists. Even historians who were not
Marxists found it a convenient way of categorizing Owen and his
disciples.

A second generation of Fabian historians, with some assistance from
Marxists, in the inter-war period integrated Owen into the history of
the British working-class movement and this continued to be the
usual treatment of Owenism until the 1960s. Owen was accorded a
niche in the standard histories of British labour and socialism, and
Owenism was seen as a link in the continuous chain which stretched

from 1789 to the present-day Labour movement. G. D. H. Cole's biography, *Robert Owen* (London, 1925) was the most important of the new contributions to the study of Owen.[5] It did not repeat the details of Owen's life which Podmore recorded, but added valuable new material on education and trade unionism. Cole touched only lightly on the communities, America, and Owen's later career; and could make little sense of the millenarian and spiritualist elements.

Outside this English neo-orthodoxy were other interpretations. The Welsh, anxious to claim Owen as a native son (though he did not maintain much connection with his birthplace of Newtown), honoured him in several biographies and articles from time to time. In America Owenism has been treated as part of the communitarian tradition from John Humphrey Noyes's *History of American Socialisms* (New York, 1870) to Arthur E. Bestor's scholarly and definitive study, *Backwoods Utopias* (Philadelphia, 1950). New Harmony, Owen's first community in America, was investigated in George B. Lockwood's *New Harmony Movement* (New York, 1905) and has continued to exercise a fascination for essayists, novelists and writers of popular history. The concept of utopia has been used on both sides of the Atlantic as a framework in which to include Owenism, but has usually resulted in over-emphasising the quaint and curious. American labour historians have interpreted Owenism as a warning example of how working men can be misled by socialist theoreticians who seek to use the trade union movement for their own ends.

Clearly there is by now no shortage of views of Mr Owen. Many facets of Owen and Owenism have been examined, and there is now a considerable body of knowledge on which we can draw.[6] Most of these interpretations are still current, to the extent that they are repeated in standard histories of the nineteenth century and accepted as valid by the historians of socialism. The danger at present is that we may be content to accept these verdicts as final, and confine ourselves to a little extra documentation of what we already know or a little speculation about the more obscure parts of the accepted views. In this bicentenary year it is perhaps appropriate to take stock of the state of Owen studies, so that we can see where our strengths and weaknesses lie and what should be the tasks for the future. The remainder of this chapter will therefore attempt to show what has been done and how well, what are the gaps, and what needs to be done next.

Beginning with Owen himself, we have as full a biographical coverage as we are probably ever likely to get. Podmore and G. D. H.

Cole between them present the main outlines of Owen's career and personality, and there are useful supplementary studies by Margaret Cole and Rowland Hill Harvey.[7] The chief limitation here is the paucity of original material relating to Owen's early and middle years. The main collection of his correspondence, the Owen papers in Manchester, begins in 1821, and the bulk of it is from the two decades 1830–40 and 1848–58. This has meant that Owen's biographers have had to rely heavily on his account of his early years as given in the autobiography, published in 1857–8 as the *Life of Robert Owen, Written by Himself*, 2 vols (London), eked out with material from contemporaries, especially his eldest son, Robert Dale Owen.[8] The autobiography ends where the surviving manuscript collection begins, i.e. around 1821, and it may be that these papers were collected for another volume of the autobiography which Owen did not live to complete. Although the *Life* is much the most readable book that Owen wrote, it has to be used with caution. It was published when Owen was a very old man. Parts of it had appeared earlier, and the volume was to some extent a compilation of autobiographical fragments written at various times from 1817 onwards. Like all autobiographers Owen sees his early life through the distorting glass of later interests and experiences: subconsciously he hides part of himself and exaggerates those elements which he thinks substantiate his own self-image. Thus his formative intellectual development is glossed over in an unanalytical fashion, while his religious views at the age of nine or ten are precocious to the point of incredibility. Other passages, however, are more revealing, such as the famous account of his interview with Peter Drinkwater in 1792 when Owen applied for the position of manager in Drinkwater's mill.

Efforts to find more about the crucial period of Owen's life in Manchester, when he was a young man in his twenties, have not yielded very much.[9] Speculation on the intellectual formation of his ideas has gone on for a long time. Whether he 'borrowed' his ideas from Rousseau, Bentham and Godwin, or was influenced by contemporaries in Manchester, has been discussed in his biographies with somewhat inconclusive results. Perhaps a more profitable approach is to consider Owenism as part of the whole complex of ideas in the late eighteenth and early nineteenth centuries. The hypothesis underlying this is that the ideas of a period are contained within a framework and have a certain unity based on common assumptions and attitudes. Owenism thus becomes a cluster of social ideas drawn from several sources united within an overall intellectual boundary. In this context both the originality and limitations of Owen's ideas become apparent.

It seems unlikely that we shall be able to learn much more about Owen's personality without either some fresh material or a psychological reinterpretation of the existing material. Surprises, however, are always possible. No one, for instance, has so far suggested that Owen was a poet. Yet a tantalising clue has turned up in the Kooperativa Forbundet in Stockholm: three poems in Owen's handwriting, entitled 'Sonnets for Slaves', which it seems he may have composed.[10] Owen's private life is difficult to glimpse behind the public façade which he did so much to promote. Robert Dale Owen's memories of life at Braxfield provide the most vivid account of Owen's family life, but there are many things left out which we would like to know – especially about his relations with his wife, Caroline, who, one suspects, was a rather sad and lonely figure. The Owen family itself would be well worth a serious study, and the recent collection and consolidation of the family papers at New Harmony should provide a convenient starting-point. The 'New Harmony story' has attracted a succession of writers in the past, but there is room for a serious history which would treat the family as a social unit extending across several generations.[11] Three of Owen's four sons made their mark in America (the second son, William, died prematurely in 1842), and their descendants have included a high proportion of unusual people, ranging from Rosamund Dale Owen to the present members of the family engaged in an imaginative renaissance of New Harmony.

Turning next to Owen's public career, the areas in which most has been done are labour and socialist history, co-operation and education. Owen's image as the founder of English socialism and the inspirer of great working-class movements for reform in the 1820s and 1830s is based on a considerable body of research and disseminated by many secondary works. In its original form this view probably owes most to the work of G. D. H. Cole,[12] with assistance from scholars such as Max Beer[13] and R. W. Postgate.[14] Some recent writers, notably E. P. Thompson, have made their own reassessment of Owen's role in the working-class movement;[15] others, with less originality, have been content to repeat earlier views.[16] Whether there is much more to be mined from this particular seam would appear doubtful. Without substantially improved sources it is difficult to see how we can get beyond Cole's *Attempts at General Union, 1818–34* (London, 1953) and the usual accounts of working-men co-operators in the 1820s. A more fundamental difficulty with the working-class movement approach to Owenism is that it has become part of a Labour version of the Whig view of history. Owenism is a chapter or phase in the long and glorious evolution of the present-day Labour movement.[17] This is altogether too restricting to make full use of the sources, and is based on certain narrow assumptions about the nature of social history, the relation of ideas to society and the process of social change. With this caveat, we may say that Owenism as part of the early English socialist and trade union traditions has been fairly well explored.

The same is also true of Owen and the Co-operative movement. After Holyoake's death in 1906, the historians of the Co-operative movement – J. J. Dent, T. W. Mercer and W. H. Brown – continued to probe into Owenite origins when they were writing their monographs on individual societies and pioneers; and in his *Century of Co-operation* (Manchester, 1944) G. D. H. Cole defined clearly and fully the nature of the connection between Owen and the early co-operators. Since then, further work has been done by R. G. Garnett and Sidney Pollard.

Cole was also the first modern scholar to draw attention to the centrality of education in Owenite schemes. 'The basis of Owenism', he wrote, 'was his [Owen's] theory of education'. Recently there has been a revival of interest in Owen as an educationist. Harold Silver's *Concept of Popular Education* (London, 1965) examines the pedigree of Owen's educational ideas as well as the schools at New Lanark;[18] and W. A. C. Stewart and W. P. McCann's *Educational Innovators, 1750–1880* (London, 1967) has important new material on Owenite schools and teachers. There are, however, certain weaknesses and gaps in the accounts of Owenite education. The tendency has been to get stuck in two grooves: an obsession with where Owen could have got his educational ideas from (hence the tracing of intellectual pedigrees), and over-concentration on the educational institutions at New Lanark which so impressed contemporary visitors. Practically all accounts of Owenite education rely on the same few sources, and these are by no means adequate. They are all written by sympathetic teachers, visitors or Owen himself. As with most popular education, the views of the pupils are entirely lacking. It is surely odd that if the schools and adult classes at New Lanark were the great success that Owen claimed, there should not have been a single ex-pupil who later in life wrote a tribute to the benefits he had received there. Or have we overlooked some possible sources – local records, memoirs, the Glasgow and Lanarkshire press – which could throw light on the matter? The problem is connected with another mystery: what happened to New Lanark after Owen left? There is an almost complete dearth of information about New Lanark from 1825 to 1881, when it was acquired by Henry Birkmyre from Charles Walker. A critical account by W. Davidson, *History of Lanark and Guide to the Scenery* (Lanark, 1928) admitted that Owen's absence was deeply regretted and that it was felt that the prosperous days of New Lanark were over; but a visitor in 1839 found that the schools were still much the same as in Owen's time, and that some of the old teachers remained.[19]

Our ignorance about New Lanark, alas, is not confined to the post-1825 period, but extends to many aspects of Owen's management there. Virtually all contemporary accounts of New Lanark, including Owen's, concentrate on the social and philanthropic aspects, and neglect the business side of the operation. Only a few of the business records of the mills survive, and unless these records can be supplemented by new sources, such as court records, it will remain impossible to write a complete economic history. We have thus no means of accurately assessing Owen's stature as a businessman. Beyond his own general statements about the profitability of the mills, and the obvious respect of his contemporaries, we do not know how successful a capitalist employer he was. It may have been, as Podmore suggested, that Owen's commercial success was largely an accident of the time: with the margin of profit so wide (enterprising manufacturers could make 20 per cent on their capital) he could hardly fail to show a respectable return. Certainly in later life any business acumen he may have possessed seems to have deserted him – or at any rate he subordinated it to his enthusiasm for his social schemes. Until this gap can be filled, one whole dimension of Owen and his work is lacking.

Studies of Owen's followers have until recently been somewhat limited.[20] Podmore's biography contains useful information about various Owenites; but with the exception of the leaders of the working-class co-operators and trade unionists and those writers who could be classified as Ricardian socialists, little has been known about the people who were attracted to the New View of Society. They were for the most part very minor figures, for whom biographical and other data are scarce; but a more significant reason for their neglect is that certain aspects of Owenism (notably philanthropy, communitarianism, millennialism, spiritualism) have been ignored or misunderstood. It is an interesting comment on the usual British historiography of Owenism

that it was too narrow to allow these aspects to be fully appreciated.
The poor Owenites were not allowed to speak for themselves, to be
taken seriously, because they did not fit in with a certain prevailing
orthodoxy. They were misguided, utopian, cranky, or just plain mad.
Our task now is to try to rescue them, as E. P. Thompson has so aptly
put it, 'from the enormous condescension of posterity'.

How is this to be done? In general by broadening the whole approach
to Owenism. Instead of considering Owenism as an aspect of this or
that social or intellectual development, we have to examine its role in
the total context of early nineteenth-century industrial civilisation.
Nor can this be confined to Britain, for American and French experience is also relevant. Instead of asking what Owenism contributed to
the making of the English working class, or how it related to American
frontier conditions and westward expansion, we have to examine the
points of contact or similarity in British and American social experience
which made Owenism attractive in certain situations. When this is
done we shall find our sights focused on developments which previous
interpretations paid little attention to, and involving people who have
not hitherto appeared as part of the Owenite story, such as millenarians, communitarians, phrenologists and sectarians of various kinds.
The relation of Owenism to other social experiments and reform
movements needs to be explored as a means of identifying certain
aspects of Owenism itself.

The further progress of Owen studies along these lines is dependent
on work in other separate but related fields. Three examples may be
taken to illustrate the point: the family, millennialism and sectarianism.
It is unfortunate that while we have a great many studies of political
parties, trade unions and religious bodies, there is not a single history of
the basic social institution of British life, the family. Most historians
take it for granted that the family as an institution was subjected to very
considerable pressures in the nineteenth century, and that as a result it
began to change. But what the exact nature of this change was we do
not know. Contemporaries frequently expressed concern about the
family, but we have no means of evaluating this comment until we
have examined seriously such questions as the relations between
parents and children, the regulation of sexual mores, the authoritarian
role of the father, and the difference between the ideal of home and
family and the reality. Yet the role of the family in early nineteenth-
century society is crucial to an understanding of Owenism. It supplies
the otherwise missing link between anti-capitalism, communitarianism

and rejection of the class struggle.

Owen saw the family as the main bastion of private property and the guardian of all those qualities of individualism and self-interest to which he was opposed. The disharmony which Owenites deplored in competitive society they attributed largely to the institution of the private family. It isolated people and served as an organ of tyranny by which the wife was subjected to, and in fact made the property of, her husband. Owen regarded the family as a fundamentally divisive force, much more so than class. Hence he attacked the family and refused to regard class divisions as primary. Community was the alternative to the private family; and education of infants from the age of two was a logical step towards undermining family influence. The Owenites' championing of feminism, divorce and birth control also stems from this root. But before we can take this new view of Mr Owen much further we need to know many things about the family which at present are only surmise.

A similar situation exists for millennialism, although the portents here are more hopeful as several social historians have become aware of the importance of millenarian movements. The older generation of historians of Owenism, with the exception of Podmore, had difficulty in taking millennial manifestations seriously, or indeed of treating religious themes as genuinely relevant to social movements. The basic fact is, however, that Owenism originated and flourished entirely within the grand era of evangelical ascendancy (c.1800–60), and the doctrines, attitudes and assumptions of enthusiastic religion permeated society at many levels. Millennialism was one aspect of this wider culture of evangelicalism, which spilled over into secular as well as religious forms. The implications of millennialism become much clearer when viewed from the American side – mainly, one suspects, because American historians have done more work in this field than their British counterparts; for there is little doubt that similar effort could uncover the social springs of popular religion in Britain.[21] In the American context the connection between millennialism and communitarianism is well established, and the significance of this for Owenism is soon apparent. Owenism developed in an Anglo-American matrix of millennialism, and in this, as in some other respects, a comparative approach seems indicated. Owen's millennial statements have long puzzled (not to say embarrassed) sympathetic historians, while his millenarian followers have been dismissed as a lunatic fringe. Sadly we are told that Owenism degenerated into a mere sect – as if that were the end of the matter.

In fact an examination of the nature of sectarianism might provide valuable clues about some obscure aspects of Owenite history. Sect is not a pejorative term but a type of social organisation which may be well adapted to the pursuit of certain desired goals. Except for a brief period of a few months in 1833–4 when Owen put himself at the head of the mass trade union movement, the Owenites were a millennial sect. This was not because they had tried to be something else (such as a political party or a mass movement of the proletariat) and had failed, but because the sect was the institutional form which best fitted the values and goals of Owenism. To contemporaries this was clear: in the *Cyclopledia of Religious Denominations* (London and Glasgow, 1853) the chapter 'Socialism, by Robert Owen' is sandwiched between chapters on the Shakers and the Mormons. But before this clue can be followed very far we need a social history of sectarianism in the nineteenth century, and there is no sign that this is likely to be forth-coming just yet.[22]

The present state of Owen studies can be summarised thus: a substantial body of scholarship devoted to the labour–socialist–co-operative view of Owenism, a renewed interest in Owenite education, the beginnings of serious investigation of the millenarian, sectarian and communitarian aspects, and some big gaps in business history and the history of the family as a social institution. There seems little doubt that in the future the books and articles on Owen will continue to come out. The search will be for some concept or frame of reference within which Owen and Owenism can be fitted. So far the interpretation in terms of the labour-socialist-co-operative syndrome has been dominant, though in America the emphasis has been mainly on communitarian-ism. For a new view of Mr Owen we need to build on this substantial body of material, while broadening our social perspective until it becomes possible to see Owenism as a contemporary comment on the civilisation of the early nineteeth century.

## NOTES AND REFERENCES

1. Friedrich Engels, *Socialism, Utopian and Scientific* (1880); L. S. Feuer (ed.), *Marx and Engels: Basic Writings* (New York, 1959) p. 80.

2. William Lucas Sargant, *Robert Owen and His Social Philosophy* (London, 1860); Frederick A. Packard, *Life of Robert Owen* (Philadelphia, 1866); Arthur John Booth, *Robert Owen, the Founder of Socialism in England* (London, 1869).

3. And in fairness it should be added that the Co-operative movement has remained the most consistent and generous of all the supporters of schemes to honour Owen's memory.

4. Édouard Dolléans, *Robert Owen, 1771–1858* (Paris, 1905); Helene Simon, *Robert Owen, Sein Leben und seine Bedeutung für die Gegenwart* (Jena, 1905).

5. Other Fabians who wrote on Owen included B. L. Hutchins, Sidney and Beatrice Webb, Graham Wallas, J. L. and Barbara Hammond, C. E. M. Joad and Margaret Cole. On the bibliographical, as on other aspects of Owenism dealt with in this chapter, further details are given in my *Robert Owen and the Owenites in Britain and America* (London, 1969).

6. At least 150 secondary works on Owen and Owenism, 90 articles and 20 unpublished theses.

7. Margaret Cole, *Robert Owen of New Lanark* (London, 1953); Rowland Hill Harvey, *Robert Owen, Social Idealist* (Berkeley and Los Angeles, 1949).

8. Robert Dale Owen, *Threading My Way* (London, 1874).

9. See W. H. Chaloner, 'Robert Owen, Peter Drinkwater and the Early Factory System in Manchester, 1788–1800', *Bulletin of the John Rylands Library* (Manchester), XXXVII (1954–5); and E. M. Fraser, 'Robert Owen in Manchester, 1787–1800', *Memoirs and Proceedings of the Manchester Literary and Philosophical Society*, LXXXII (1937–8).

10. Walter Sjolin, 'New Light on Robert Owen: Poetic Vein in the Reformer's Personality', *Co-operative Review*, XXIX 2 (Feb. 1955).

11. See Shigeru Goto, 'The Family Tree of Robert Owen', *Review of Economics and Political Science* (Meiji University Press, Tokyo) XXXVII 5–6 (1969). [In Japanese and English.]

12. In addition to the works already cited, his widely-read *Short History of the British Working-Class Movement, 1789–1947* (London, 1925, 1948) and his (with Raymond Postgate) *Common People, 1746–1938* (London, 1938 and later editions) should be mentioned.

13. Max Beer, *History of British Socialism* (London, 1919 and later editions).

14. Especially in his *Builders' History* (London, 1923).

15. E. P. Thompson, *The Making of the English Working Class* (London, 1963).

16. e.g. George Lichtheim, *The Origins of Socialism* (London, 1969).

17. A good example, even to the title, is Francis Williams, *Magnificent Journey* London, 1954).

18. See also Brian Simon, *Studies in the History of Education, 1780–1870* (London,

1960); and J. F. C. Harrison (ed.), *Utopianism and Education: Robert Owen and the Owenites* (New York, 1968).

19. *New Moral World*, 13 Apr. 1839.

20. But in recent years the situation has begun to change, thanks to the researches of W. H. G. Armytage, A. E. Bestor, R. G. Garnett, J. F. C. Harrison, E. P. Thompson, Mrs Eileen M. Yeo and others.

21. See G. F. A. Best, 'Popular Protestantism in Victorian Britain', in R. Robson (ed.), *Ideas and Institutions of Victorian Britain* (London, 1967).

22. In the meantime see Bryan R. Wilson's valuable *Sects and Society* (London, 1961).

# CHAPTER TWO

# Robert Owen and Revolutionary Politics

## CHUSHICHI TSUZUKI

ROBERT OWEN had little sympathy with political reform and held aloof from all the popular movements of the day for political democracy. He has been described as a consistent upholder of the *status quo* in politics, hostile to all reforms.[1] Some of his contemporaries regarded it as 'an absurd idea' that he should hope to establish Co-operative principles 'with the aid of a plundering aristocracy'.[2] Even evil designs were attributed to him – 'some collusive scheme with the government' to entice the workers from their endeavours for political emancipation by 'the witcheries of Co-operation'.[3] The last remark was elicited by the discussion which took place soon after the passage of the Reform Bill of 1832 on the relative merits of political action and Owenite co-operation, the ending of which was reported to have been 'irregular, irrelevant, and stormy'.[4] Shortly before, 'a Grand Junction' of the working-class radicals and the Owenites had been proposed, and Owen replied to this, bluntly and indeed tactlessly, by comparing the English radicals to the French republicans, who gained little from the July Revolution.[5] Here, it seems, is the genesis of various later views of Owen's attitude towards popular politics and political revolutions. The following is an attempt to evaluate this attitude in its historical context as well as in the light of his social philosophy.

At the time when Owen rejected the proposal for the 'Grand Junction', he was making an attempt to set up branches of his Labour Exchange, and in this campaign, as on many similar occasions, he solicited the patronage of wealthy philanthropists as well as the support of the working-class masses. Glimpses of his propaganda work from this time onward can be obtained from the numerous letters that he wrote to Thomas Allsop and his wife Anna and which were collected by John Burns.[6] These letters appear to throw some new light upon Owen's later life, except, unfortunately, for the early period of Chartism, materials relevant to which are lacking in the correspondence. It is also part of the object of this study to consider these letters in relation to his 'political' interests.

Allsop, a Lincolnshire landowner and disciple of Coleridge, who acquired considerable skill on the Stock Exchange during the early period of railway construction, became one of Owen's wealthy supporters. In November 1832, Owen wrote to Allsop on his reception at Birmingham, where 'a real desire prevails among the working classes to establish a branch bank [of the Labour Exchange]'.[7] 'The thick clouds are everywhere dispersing', he wrote from Barnsley a year later; 'the real producers of wealth are beginning everywhere to discover their true position and & are preparing to act upon it'. He was reporting the progress of the eight-hour agitation which constituted part of his militant trade union movement. He was going to see 'a dozen of the principal manufacturers' of Barnsley in the hope of converting them to his views.[8]

Shortly after the collapse of his trade union, Owen proclaimed the imminent advent of the millennium.[8A] Such a proclamation was not new, but with it Owenism shed much of its reformism, and Owen emerged as a Socialist critic. Though repetition did much to blunt its edges, his millenarianism, armed with a 'science' of society, provided a pungent theory of social transformation with which he was to criticise what he regarded as the shortcomings of all the contemporary popular movements for political change, especially of Chartism and the European revolutions of 1848.

Owen devoted the rest of his life to the propagation of socialism among 'all classes of all nations', a phrase which appeared in the original title of the society he founded in 1835.[9] For the next few years, however, his work was mainly carried out among the working classes of his own country. This phase of Owenism coincided with the heyday of Chartism, and the coincidence had much to do with the widespread distress during the trade depression of 1836–42 which affected both the employers and the workers. Many of the Chartist leaders had been associated with Owenism at its various stages, while the Owenite 'social missionaries' went among the rank and file of the Chartists, seeking to win them over to socialism. Hence there was friction as well as mutual influence between the two movements, as had been witnessed during the Reform agitation of the early thirties. Chartism was a mass working-class movement, but Owenism remained elitist, and its middle-class leaders and their working-class lieutenants endeavoured to impress the Chartist masses, or rather their chiefs, with socialist ideas.

At the time when the Chartist Convention opened its proceedings in February 1839 amidst great hopes and enthusiasm, the Owenites pleaded with them for unity of action, though their appearance of goodwill was weakened by their somewhat arrogant assertion that the establishment of communities was 'the shortest . . . way to secure "equal rights" to all'.[10] When the Convention moved to Birmingham in May, the Owenites held their annual conference in the same city, and issued an address drafted by Owen, who now tried to persuade the Chartists of the futility of a political revolution. The party which enjoyed political power would not relinquish it to the uneducated and inexperienced workers except through physical force. 'In such warfare', he went on,

which must be most murderous and dreadful, success is doubtful, and many suppose you could not succeed.

But, suppose you triumphed over every obstacle, and that you had wrested political power from your opponents, who now possess it. The victory must have been achieved by physical force, and some individuals must thereby attain the political power now possessed by the aristocracy of this country. Who the parties acquiring this power, after such a revolution, might be, no man can know, probably some more fortunate military chiefs.

You will have succeeded in giving political power to a new set of men, who have been trained from their birth in as much error as those you would have displaced.

It is true, the error may be different in character, but it is doubtful which class of errors, when in power, will produce the most misery to the mass of the people.[11]

Evidently Owen had a horror of a violent revolution which would lead only to another kind of irrational rule. Here is the keynote of his opposition to all the popular movements for political change which, under the circumstances, could be achieved only through violence.

Meanwhile, the Chartist Petition was rejected in the House of Commons in July, and inconclusive discussions over the 'ulterior measure' brought confusion even among the Chartists who advocated the use of physical force. The outbreak of isolated disturbances culminated in the riot in Newport in November. Throughout this period the Owenites were actively engaged in their work. According to Lloyd Jones, one of their missionaries, the socialists 'considered it a duty to go among the Chartists to beg of them not to risk the cause of progress by an outbreak, which could only end in failure and needless bloodshed'.[12]

The Owenite campaign seems to have had some effect. The discovery that 'the working classes, under present arrangements, are feeble & powerless' led a young Chartist to accept 'the great scheme of Industrial Co-operation'.[13] John Finch, a Liverpool merchant and Acting Governor of the Queenwood Community which had been launched in the summer of 1839 partly as an Owenite alternative to the Chartist agitation, now wrote to Owen on the imprisonment of Bronterre O'Brien, asking him to exert his influence on the members of the Royal family so as to secure the release of all the political prisoners 'on their own recognizances that they will never more advocate the obtaining their rights by physical force'. O'Brien, he added, 'is entirely with us and I know he is sick both of politics and his party. Lovett is also with us and many others'.[14]

In 1840 Chartism slowly recovered from the débâcle of the previous year. The National Charter Association was founded in July, but the Chartists were divided by the 'new moves'. Lovett's 'Knowledge Chartism', one of these, apparently derived sustenance from his Owenite background, and O'Brien, too, began to place more emphasis on social power, of which political power, he now declared, was only a consequence. The socialists, for their part, strengthened their effort to narrow the gap between themselves and the Chartists by persistent attempts to encourage the moral-force Chartists and to force the social issues upon the Chartists as a whole. A fresh interest in socialism was also aroused about this time by the attack made by the Bishop of Exeter on Owen and Owenism. The *Northern Star*, the Chartist organ, admitted that the great meetings held almost every night in various parts of London 'evince the vast increase which has taken place in the disciples of Socialism since the . . . memorial attack' of the Bishop.[15]

The 1841 annual congress of the Owenite society sent an address to the Chartists, pleading for 'a free and friendly communication with the leaders of your party'.[16] 'Governments were the effect of the social system, and the energies of the working men ought to be directed towards a change of that system', declared an Owenite orator in the North-east in a debate with a Chartist leader. The case of America served his purpose, for thousands of working men there were unemployed – 'men possessing the franchise'.[17] At the Social Institution at John Street, the new Owenite centre in London, the discussion on socialism and Chartism attracted a large crowd and created great excitement. Here Alexander Fleming, editor of the Owenite *New Moral World*, was prominent: he maintained that the Charter would not eliminate the influence of class prejudices and class interests, and advised the Chartists not to regard man merely as 'a husting animal' and 'a Parliament animal'.[18] His paper emphasised 'a marked improvement among the Chartists', who were more willing than before to discuss the questions connected with land, labour, machinery and capital,[19] and welcomed the 'New Phase of Chartist Agitation' when a meeting of the Chartist lecturers in the North recommended the consideration of such problems as 'a just distribution of the produce of labour' and the possible incompatibility of private property with the Charter.[20] The Owenites were indeed helping to bring the social problems to the fore.

Chartism, on the other hand, elicited a rival programme of social transformation from Owen, who apparently was much impressed by its striking recovery, and sought, in his turn, to influence the Convention now in session. In April 1842 he issued a 'Transition Charter' from the Queenwood Community: its 'Nine Points' were 'a graduated property tax', the abolition of all other taxes, 'national employment', 'national education', freedom of speech, 'home-made national money based on nationally secured property and the credit of the nation', 'home colonization', 'laws of divorce', and superior circumstances in general.[21] This was followed by an address 'To the Chartists of the British Isles', in which he declared that 'if it [the People's Charter] were to be obtained to-morrow, and its workings known, there are no parties who would be more disappointed with the effects which would be produced than the Chartists themselves'. The enactment of the Charter 'will make all petty politicians'. Moreover, none of the Six Points went to the root of the evil. He advised the Chartists to follow the lead given by those who had 'the universality of experience' rather than their present leaders, who were 'men of small experience', of one class and one kind of action.[22]

The Chartist Petition of May 1842 was preceded by a statement of the social and economic grievances of the workers, but it was killed once more by the combined forces of the Tories and Whigs. The workers' resistance to wage cuts, which had formed the background to the Chartist revival, also led to the widespread strike movement, and the Plug Riots in the summer 'converted the busy manufacturing hives of the north into the resemblance of towns in a state of siege or civil war'.[23] Owen now issued an address to the trade unionists, 'turn-outs', and others who suffered from 'the present irrational mode' of production and distribution. 'The immediate cause of your sufferings', he declared, 'is the amount of productive power throughout society, and especially in Great Britain, opposed to the value of your labour. . . . It is this new power misunderstood, and most irrationally applied, that has caused your late and present suffering.' It was easy 'with a little more knowledge' to make this power their slave, instead of their master, to produce wealth and happiness for all.[24] The irrational society also brought sufferings to Queenwood, where shortage of funds led to Owen's resignation from responsible offices connected with the experiment.

Shortly after his resignation, Owen wrote a remarkable essay entitled 'A Peaceful Revolution of Society' in which he dwelt on the irrationality of society, the combination of 'force and fraud' as he called it. This society revolved around money, a 'deception' to exploit the producers, and encouraged 'classes, sects, and parties' to oppose each other in order to secure their permanent subjection. He now looked back upon his many years of struggle, and confessed that the overwhelming system of falsehood

> has compelled me to occupy my time in various measures, in various places, to remove the great quantity of rubbish created by the priesthood, warriors, statesmen, political economists, lawyers and commercial men, before anything like a firm foundation could be attained. . . . Often have I been under the necessity to convince impatient parties that this foundation had not been arrived at, by letting them try some partial attempt. . . .

Even the experiment at Queenwood, he admitted, was 'a partial measure of this character', and what was really required was the general acceptance of the true principle, the science of circumstances, principles being 'the basis of society'.[25]

Meanwhile, Chartism stood helpless after the failure of the second petition, and a trade recovery further sapped its strength. O'Connor now turned to a Land Scheme; his National Land Company was conceived as the means by which the working-class shareholders of the company would eventually be enabled to return to the land, and had nothing to do with socialism. Yet it appears that it owed something to Owen's teaching and the Owenite agitation.[26] Indeed, the Owenites welcomed O'Connor's plan for 'home colonization' and his 'wholesome conclusion' about political power and social happiness,[27] but their interest in the scheme quickly faded because of O'Connor's hostility to socialism.

Friedrich Engels, who had come to Manchester shortly after the strike movement of 1842, paid a tribute to the socialism of his host country, saying that the German communists of his school agreed 'much more with the English Socialists than with any other party':

> Their system, like ours, is founded upon philosophical principles; they struggle, as we do, against religious prejudices. . . . Although our fundamental principles give us a broader base, inasmuch as we received them from a system of philosophy embracing every part of human knowledge; yet in every bearing upon practice, upon the *facts* of the present state of society, we find that the English Socialists are a long way before us, and have left very little to be done.[28]

Engels soon retracted much of his tribute. Writing about a year later, he commented that 'English Socialism arose with Owen, a manufacturer, and proceeds therefore with great consideration toward the bourgeoisie and great injustice toward the proletariat in its methods'. Moreover, the English socialists were so 'dogmatic' that success by their method of winning over public opinion was 'utterly hopeless'. They recognised no historical development and were unaware of the 'class hatred' of working men as an element of progress. They accepted 'only a psychological development, a development of man in the abstract. . . . Hence they are too abstract, too metaphysical, and accomplish little.' The socialists must 'condescend' to come round to the Chartist standpoint, which, though theoretically less developed, was genuinely proletarian. 'The union of Socialism with Chartism' would make the working class 'the true intellectual leader of England'.[29] It was only after the European revolutions of 1848, however, that Engel's hopes were realised, and then in part, in the movement for 'The Charter and Something More' led by the 'Socialist–Chartists'[30] such as George Julian Harney and Ernest Jones. But by that time Owenite socialism had disintegrated between secularism and the Co-operative movement, and Owen himself emerged as a critic, although still a socialist critic, of the Red Republicans.

Owen left for America on 23 August 1844, and stayed there more or less continuously[31] until the summer of 1846. Consequently he had no direct knowledge of the enthusiastic reception given by his followers in London to Wilhelm Weitling, 'the founder of German Communism', who had come to England after imprisonment and persecution on the Continent; nor had he any direct contact with the international movement that arose in its train. Instead, he plunged into an international movement of his own. It also happens that Owen's extant correspondence with the Allsops, which had been interrupted for many years apart from a few occasional notes, became active and frequent about this time, and from now on our account will depend largely on this source.

In October 1845, Owen wrote from New York: 'since my arrival I have held the World Convention here', which 'terminated much to my satisfaction. . . . I have now to form at my pleasure a Society of my own choosing & I shall be very particular in this selection.'[32] His next letter covered the same ground but was informative:

> I remained in New York until my 'World Convention' terminated & which it did exactly to my wishes & left the invitation & power of future measures entirely with me, after I had ascertained by that Convention that there were no parties on this side the water more than on yours who possessed a knowledge of the extended theory & practice necessary to accomplish this great change while every step of the progress is as plain before me as a map. I have now to form a new Society of picked men & women in these States who are the best calculated to aid to effect our object.[33]

Early in the following year, he wrote from Washington: 'I am trying how far the Washington City papers will venture to go with me. I am truly suprised they have so readily gone so far as they have done. I have some more M.S. in advance prepared for them & if they insert these I shall be pretty confident of no distant ultimate success.' He was also drafting a New Constitution of the State of New York, 'no ordinary constitution, but a model one for the world'.[34]

While in America, Owen was entrusted by his son, Robert Dale Owen, then a Congressman, to put pressure upon the British Government so as to avoid a crisis in the Oregon boundary dispute, which had considerably strained the Anglo-American relationship. In April 1846 he returned to England, interviewed Lord Aberdeen, wrote a letter to Robert Peel, and in May sailed again for the States. From Boston he proceeded to Albany where he gave 'a kind of conversational lecture' on the New Constitution to the President and members of the State Convention. But the Oregon business hurried him to Washington where he 'called upon the President, all the Secretaries & our minister

Mr Parkenham with whom I had a long conversation respecting the
Oregon treaty & urged him to bring it to a speedy termination'.[35]
When the two Governments consented to a compromise over the
boundary, Owen was convinced that he had contributed to the cause
of peace by his skilful intervention. 'The Oregon question', he wrote in
June, 'was finally settled & on the principle which I recommended &
the details will scarcely vary from my proposals to both governments.'[36]

Owen's method for effecting political change was a permeation of
the existing governments with his views. Thus he was concerned,
first of all, to create a favourable public opinion through the press on
the one hand and the propaganda work of an elite society of men of
wealth and intelligence on the other. These would also work directly
upon the governments. Although his attempt to form such a society in
America does not seem to have been successful, he must have felt that
the satisfactory conclusion of the Oregon dispute had proved the
effectiveness of his method.

Thus, on his return to England, he found himself 'in the midst of a
bold attempt to interest British Statesmen in [his] views'.[37] His first
attempts seemed propitious, and he was hopeful: 'I had yesterday
afternoon a most gratifying interview with the Earl of Clarendon
[Lord Lieutenant of Ireland] who, as well as Mr McGregor [secretary
of the Board of Trade], Viscount Palmerston & Lord Brougham, is to
be my correspondent. *This between ourselves*'.[38] He was much more
interested in guiding the opinions of the great statesmen than influenc-
ing the vote of the electors. When he stood for Parliament at Marylebone at the General Election of 1847, he was strongly advised to do so
by William Pare, his loyal disciple and formerly a prominent member
of the Birmingham Political Union, who believed that his candidature
would provide an opportunity for 'a cheap popular agitation'.[39] So in
his election address, he was able to recapitulate the points he had already
made in the 'Transition Charter', and in another address issued about
the same time, he stressed 'the irrational condition, degraded &
miserable' of Ireland, which, together with the progress of productive
power in Britain, 'applied in opposition to manual labour', would
render 'a change . . . imperative'.[40]

The severe distress in Ireland during the great potato famine in the
latter half of the forties did much to intensify class antagonism and
seemed to threaten a revolution. Owen visited Ireland in the autumn of
1847 and was much depressed by the religious division of the country,
which aggravated the crisis:

I find *all parties* more in mental bondage now than they were twenty years ago when I came first among them. Those then the most advanced & full of hope, are now despairing of any good being done with such rampant superstition as pervades the island & the contests & hatred existing between both religious & political partisans.

He hoped, however, that 'Ireland will force the change upon Great Britain & the world. The miseries of Ireland will be the immediate cause of the happiness of nations'.[41]

At the time, Owen was staying as a guest of his old friend Lord Cloncurry at his house at Maretimo overlooking the Bay of Dublin. Lord Cloncurry and his son Cecil, an M.P., were attentive to his wishes:

> I frequently go with the former in his carrier to Dublin, distant about 5 miles, to attend public meetings, & to make such calls upon the editors and others whom I wish to see & at other times I am allowed to write quietly in my own room for the *London Mercury* &c. . . . But Ireland & the working classes in England call for the exertion of all my time & faculties to devise the means to terminate the severe suffering of both, but to effect this change I must in a great measure fight single handed. None are sufficiently independent in position to express their real sentiments or wishes.[42]

In his five letters on 'the Permanent Relief of Ireland', published in the *London Mercury*,[43] Owen proposed the establishment of parishes as Owenite communities on each side of the railways that were to be constructed, and even suggested 'a military governor of superior abilities . . . aided by the requisite subordinates' as a possible form of government to weather the difficulties of transition. But it was not the Irish nation and the English workers alone that appeared to be calling for his assistance.

Owen was preparing an address to Queen Victoria on the existing social system of 'falsehood', when a student demonstration and an insurrection of the workers actually precipitated a revolution in France.[44] He soon wrote a similar address 'to the Men and Women of France', stating the familiar conditions of 'a new government based on truth alone': beneficial employment, universal education, freedom of speech and thought, graduated property tax, 'rational association', local self-government, 'non-interference by any foreign power except as mediator to stay hostilities', and an armed nation for self-defence; for

practical purposes 'the American Government in principle with some
essential modifications in their practice' was recommended as 'a good
present model with which to commence'. He urged the Frenchmen to
be moderate and merciful.[45]

Meanwhile, the decree issued by the Provisional Government on
25 February 1848, promising work to all citizens and ordering the
immediate establishment of *Ateliers Nationaux*, ('National Workshops'),
encouraged Owen and his followers as it discomforted the English
bourgeoisie. 'Surely the good sense of the people of England will not be
blinded by this Abbé Sieyèsism applied to labour', wrote the Paris
correspondent of the *Morning Herald*. 'Do not hope', he went on, 'by a
revival of the New Harmonies of Robert Owen, of Lanark, to effect
what the nature of man must render impossible.'[46] William Pare, on
the other hand, welcomed what he called 'an Industrial Revolution',[47]
while John Finch believed that the French revolution was a fulfilment
of Owen's prophecies.[48]

Towards the end of March, Owen went to Paris, and shortly after
his arrival he paid a visit to Louis Blanc, President of the Government
Commission for Labour, known as the Luxembourg Commission,
which had been set up to deal with the conditions of the working
classes. On the following day, probably 31 March, he wrote to Allsop:
'Today I have breakfasted & spent two hours talking over the labour
question, and finance with him [Louis Blanc] & Albert & a dozen of
their friends.' He handed over to Vidal, the socialist author and secretary to the Commission, a copy of his address, perhaps the one referred
to above, that had been adopted at an Owenite meeting in London.[49]
In a letter to Mrs Allsop dated 1 April, Owen referred to the external
affairs of the Republic:

> Say to Mr Allsop that I do not think there is any desire on the part
> of the Provisional Government to go to war with England & they
> will avoid unless the English Aristocracy shall force it upon the
> French nation. But there are such discordant elements in action in
> France & throughout Europe that no one can say what will happen
> next day, except this, that old prejudices & state of society are
> destroyed & no power can restore them.[50]

On 2 April he had an interview with Lamartine, the Minister of
Foreign Affairs, who, in spite of his visions of a 'grand national
republican synthesis' revolving around the working-class masses,[51] had
a genuine horror of a popular uprising. From his conversation, Owen

seems to have received the impression that there was a real danger that 'violent Republicans with much less consideration & good feeling than the Provisional Government' might get into power, and he hoped that 'the present men will be reappointed'.[52]

He often visited Étienne Cabet, the author of *Voyage en Icarie*, whose preaching of peaceful communism seemed very much in his own line. Cabet was then 'at the head of a large Socialist party here', the *Société Fraternelle Centrale*, one of the popular clubs that flourished in Paris when the Provisional Government proclaimed the people's right to free assembly. 'I last night attended one of his new weekly public meetings', he reported:

> More than 6000 were present. . . . It was a splendid meeting in a splendid building beautifully lighted up. . . . I had the honour of the right hand seat to the Chairman, the Vice President. . . . M. Cabet introduced me to the meeting in the most flattering terms & I was received by the whole assembly with French enthusiasm; on leaving I would scarcely escape from their caresses & tokens of regards.

Although the situation seemed unsettled and fluid, he felt that 'Socialism will be sure ultimately, if not immediately, to prevail'.[53]

On the morning of 5 April, Owen had another meeting with Louis Blanc over breakfast and found him 'entirely with me in principle & much inclined to take my advice' which he was to prepare in writing. On the same morning he called upon 'the Irish delegates', the representatives of the Young Irelanders, who had, as it was generally believed, been soliciting arms from the Republic for a civil war against England, and who, according to Owen, 'have been very properly rebuked in their wild schemes by the [Provisional] Government'. Lamartine, who administered the rebuke, 'is a first rate man & will do whatever is possible to effect our great change in peace. He & Louis Blanc are men raised up for this critical period'. In accordance with Lamartine's wishes, Owen started preparing a series of short lectures for the Paris press 'with a view to instruct the French nation in what it should do in this crisis'.[54]

Allsop apparently was much pleased with what he was told by Owen. 'My heart is with you in your really holy and sacred work', he wrote back.[55] He also reminded Owen of the latter's own maxim that 'it was as impossible to unite the living & the dead as to conjoin the old & new Systems of Society'. So 'the Revolution must be accomplished. Private Property must be at once & for ever annihilated and then, when all men are equal, the desire to elevate all, self being included, would lead to the realising some one or other of those forms of Socialism or communism which seem destined to heal the wounds of old Society'.[56] It appears from this that Allsop was perhaps less sectarian than Owen himself, and in fact he supported most of the causes associated with progress in his days. Thus he was a link between Owen and O'Connor, being 'the most trusted adviser' of the latter. It was he who cautioned O'Connor against a rash action on the eve of the third Chartist Petition in London.[57]

On that day, 10 April 1848, a great crowd assembled at Kennington Common, but they were advised by O'Connor to disperse, and the Petition was carried to Parliament in cabs instead of by the scheduled great procession, which was cancelled: the dreaded revolution, for which the Government and the propertied classes had made elaborate preparations, did not take place. On the following day, Owen wrote from Paris: 'All is quiet – confidence is gradually re-establishing itself among the capitalists & the funds are rising – & yesterday having passed off quietly in London – will, it is said, give more confidence to the capitalists & advance them still more'.[58] Allsop, in his turn, informed Owen that the Chartist Convention had met 'in spite of the authorities and dispersed when they had obtained their object'. He was satisfied that 'all are approaching a very great era', although he feared that 'it will be sanguinary also'.[59] However, 'it is well that Monday [10 April] passed off so quietly', wrote Owen in his reply:

> Had a revolution of violence occurred, it would have been premature & before any parties knew what to substitute for the present & all would have been disorder & confusion; for it is to me most evident that no parties among any class, yet know how to form a government. It is better that Great Britain & Ireland should wait to see what France can do. No nation or people ever had so promising an opportunity to establish a good government & a superior society as the French people at this crisis in their history. I do not intend to lose an hour before the elections of the National Assembly or before its meeting in preparing the public mind here for the important event.[60]

Owen carried on his self-appointed crusade among the politicians of the Republic. On 12 April he was again at the Luxembourg, but found Louis Blanc 'so overwhelmed with deputation after deputation from different sections of the working classes that there was no time for any conversation'.[61] By the end of the month, however, he was getting twenty-two lectures, which he had delivered at a hall in Paris, translated, and also making arrangements with his French friend Goupy for the translation of his *Report to the County of Lanark*.[62]

On 23 April, the elections for the Constituent Assembly took place under universal suffrage, and the result was a confirmation of the strength of the social reaction that had already begun. 'It matters not who may be elected', wrote Owen characteristically, shortly before the announcement of the final returns, 'the practical result of the revolution will be to establish "The New System of Society" in its purity & full extent'.[63] On the following day he visited Cabet and found him 'much frightened': 'M. Cabet . . . says there will be a reaction & much bloodshed with a massacre of the Communists. On the contrary I think the present position of all parties the most favourable for a change to the Rational System'. As for the new Assembly elected, Owen said, 'it will be to all appearance a good assembly on which to make an impression in the right direction'.[64]

From London, Allsop advised Owen to see such men of the Left as Lamennais, Guinard, Flocon, and Ledru Rollin, and also Lamartine. As for Lamartine, he said, 'the aristocrats there, doomed as they are, cling to Lamartine and . . . if he harkens to them, he is lost'. 'This is sheer folly', he added,

> but it is well to know the purpose of a party & a class who have power & money which they are using secretly &, I think, *with effect*. . . . I tell you *advisedly* that money is being used lavishly . . . to produce a reaction. . . . If Property-Capital ever gets its hook into the Public nose again the Revolution is lost for this generation. I believe that the only hope is in the utter, the *immediate* destruction *or* division of Capital as such & the making public property of real immovable wealth at an early period. Where one man is rich & another poor, the motto of the French Republic is a falsehood, a fraud – stark staring nonsense, a self-contradiction.[65]

'Go on, my admirable, revered & excellent friend', he wrote again. 'Finish your course as you have begun, the greatest friend to Humanity.'[66]

It appears that Owen was receiving financial assistance as well as general advice from Allsop. Acknowledging the receipt of a cheque, he reported that 300 copies of one of his pamphlets[67] had been sold in four days at Cabet's office, and he had written another proclamation to the French nation. Newspapers in Switzerland and Spain were 'canvassing my views', and Eugène Sue had published 'a long article on New Lanark & my proceedings'. Louis Blanc's *exposé* of his views in the *Democratie Pacifique*, edited by the Fourierist Considérant, was said to be 'my ideas in his language'. Only the Parisian newspapers were 'afraid of my writings & will not insert my letters; the food is too strong yet for their digestion'.[68]

The Assembly began work on 4 May amidst great expectations. 'This great movement no longer depends on individuals', declared Owen. 'The truth has gone forth & no men can now stay its course. The French – the world – must have Liberty, Equality, & Fraternity, & no fraud will now prevent these terms becoming a reality.'[69] As for the Assembly, 'it is evident that the majority have the right spirit. Now that they have said A to B, I will take care that France shall say the whole alphabet.'[70] Owen, however, failed to grasp the full meaning of 'A to B', for a new Labour Committee set up by the Assembly had already got up opposition to Louis Blanc and the Luxembourg, and Louis Blanc was resigning his post in the Commission. On 11 May, the delegates to the Luxembourg refused to take part in the festivities planned by the Government, and their postponement made the National Guards, who were arriving from the provinces for the occasion, uneasy and clamorous. Owen now realised that the French nation were 'not calm, thinking, persevering philosophers' but 'a people of impulse, of quick decision & action'.[71] The events of 11 May were a prelude to the demonstration of 15 May, which had originally been arranged by the clubs in favour of the oppressed nations, the Poles, the Irish and the Italians, but developed into an insurrection led by Blanqui and Barbès, and its failure greatly strengthened the hands of reaction.

Allsop now hoped that Owen would 'cultivate Louis Blanc',[72] whose position, however, had been further weakened after 15 May. Owen, for his part, made a study of the republican politics:

The three parties are gradually developing themselves. The too advanced, the too retarding & the medium. The first precipitates forward movements without having a knowledge of public opinion or how to guide it. The second is ignorant of human nature & society. The third better knows human nature but is also ignorant how to make society conform to it. But fear not. The progress onward is substantially good & matters here will daily improve. The great mass is looking for the means to improve the condition of society on true principles. . . . You shall see I will effect what they cannot do here by violence – & what is done here will be sure to be followed in England.[73]

He had 2000 copies of his 'Proclamation au Peuple Français, aux militaires et aux civiles' on the walls of Paris.[74] 'You would see by the newspapers,' he wrote to Allsop, 'that the Committee is proceeding with the New Constitution & to make it a Democratic Republic. Both the Committee on the Constitution & on work are proceeding very much on my views & I have no doubt will continue to do so without telling the public.'[75]

On 3 June, Owen suddenly left Paris for London.

Before he went to Paris in March, Owen had issued a proclamation warning the British Government that it was 'reposing on a barrel of gunpowder'.[76] He was satisfied, as we have seen, that 10 April had passed quietly, and he welcomed the sudden change of policy on the part of O'Connor, who now openly advocated an alliance with the middle-class radicals in their 'Little Charter' movement. 'I am glad', he wrote to Allsop, 'to see that Feargus has joined Cobden, Hume &c. & agitate, agitate, agitate is what is required & above all union between the workers & middle classes if it can be now effected'.[77] A certain amount of disturbance and unrest, however, followed the events of 10 April, and joint demonstrations of the Chartists and the Irishmen, which took place in the North and in Ireland, seemed ominous and threatening. It was under these circumstances that Owen wrote another address to the Queen, stressing her 'delicate, difficult, and dangerous' position. The Ministers of the Crown had ignored his repeated request for an investigation of his proposals. 'The time has arrived when the public will require it of them or it will undertake the task for them.'[78] These were strong words indeed for Owen.

Now he hastened back to Paris, where he arrived on 16 June to find many letters awaiting him, including one from Corbon, President of the Labour Committee, inviting him to explain his system before its members.[79] Yet it was in the Labour Committee and the Ministry of Public Works that action both open and underhand had been taken against the National Workshops. The decision made at last on 21 June to abolish the workshops, which were in fact wasteful organisations keeping hundreds of thousands of workers idle, and to send these men either into the army or to the provinces, led to a rising, which began on 23 June and lasted three days. On the 26th Owen reported from his lodgings at the Boulevard des Capucines on the state of siege in which Paris had been placed. He felt safe now that 'the military force of the government already is, & it is hourly increasing, so immense & well sustained in spirit, that it must overwhelm the deluded mass opposed to them'. 'It is greatly to be regretted', he added,

> that this conflict could not have been avoided & so many lives saved & the good feelings of parties maintained, for if the insurgents had had patience, & made their applications in a legal form, they would have gained from the new government all that men ought now to desire. It appeared to me that a strong party in the government were determined to have a Constitution & government favourable to the permanent interests of the masses, & would have succeeded if they had not been thus interfered with.

During the June days, absolute power was given to General Eugène Cavaignac, a moderate republican, who commanded the troops that quashed the insurrection. 'Most parties speak well of him [Cavaignac],' Owen went on, '& I am sure when the power of the state is centered in one that it will not be more easy to effect a great beneficial change than when the power is divided.'[80] He thought that Allsop had been right to expect a dreadful outbreak in Paris – 'instigated by the English Aristocracy & Russian & English gold, as all here believe'. A civil war, an actual revolution by force with its horrors and alarms, was a new event for Owen, and 'one is quite sufficient to confirm me in the belief that all are now most irrational'.[81] Yet he hopefully believed that even the most irrational state of society was providential, and everything pointed to the final acceptance of his system. He was sorry that the socialists had antagonised public opinion by their wild schemes and actions:

> There is great error in the proceedings of the parties who advocate the cause of the working class, here as well as in England & in both countries they create enemies when they might with ease [create] friends. They alarm & frighten the ill informed & timid & thus build walls against which to break their own head.[82]

For some time after the June days Owen seems to have gained access to some of the Parisian newspapers, such as the *Courrier de Paris*, which had his open letter to Thiers, declaring that it should be possible to assure 'un emploi constant et utile' to all the workers,[83] and the *Corsaire*, which serialised his article on social principles.[84] The gagging laws passed in July and August, however, dealt a final blow to his hopes

that the French Government would accept his views. Owen left Paris
some time in August.[85]

From Paris, his friend Goupy tried to attract Owen's attention to
the rise of Louis-Napoleon Bonaparte, whose 'name is more in favour
with the army and the people', and advised him to 'see whether he
[Napoleon] is disposed to enter in some Socialist ideas'.[86] Owen
seemed duly impressed. In December when Napoleon climbed the
ladder to imperial glory by being elected as the President of the Republic with a large majority of the popular vote, Owen prepared an
address to this 'remarkable man'. He sought to advise the future
emperor to be on guard against the factions around him and to 'ignore
all limited schemes which are connected with particular interests'.
'Declare to Europe', he went on,

> that you desire to introduce immediately into France that transition
> [to the true social system] and you will be supported by the elite of
> the European peoples because they are sick and tired of that inter-
> minable and useless war between Aristocracy and Democracy, having
> discovered that both are incapable of governing well, not knowing
> how to create a superior character for the human being or to
> produce an abundance of wealth for all the world.[87]

In London Owen had chances to see Louis Blanc and Considérant who
were now in exile, but he took little interest in the final acts of the
struggle in France between the party of order and the shrinking army
of the Left.

All through these years, Owen found a willing correspondent and a
warm hostess in Mrs Allsop, who provided him with a home to retire
to from his 'little work of changing the world' – 'from all the errors of
its thoughts & practices & particularly Mr Allsop, Mr Feargus O'Connor & Julian Harney', as he cheerfully wrote to her.[88] In May 1849 he
told her that he was preparing 'a publication for the upper & middle
classes who do not yet understand my view', which was to be accompanied by a cheap edition for the people 'to please Mr Allsop'.[89] This
was most likely *The Revolution in the Mind and Practice of the Human Race*,
which Marx later described as 'Owen's very important work in which
he gave a résumé of his whole doctrine'.[90] This book is also important
as it contained Owen's critical remarks on revolutionary politics,
especially on the European revolutions of 1848.

In the preface, Owen dissociated himself from 'the Red Republicans,
Communists, and Socialists of Europe' who, under the false notion that

man was a free agent, accepted violence. Until they possessed the true knowledge of 'the three great objects of life' – useful character, desirable employment, and superior associations for all – all attempts to bring about revolutions would be useless: 'for, when successful, they will only increase the miseries of the mass, and make democrats into aristocrats, and thus keep society in a continual circle of contention and turmoil'.[91] He believed, however, that revolutions were inevitable, and his reasons for this belief appeared almost Marxian, in so far as he touched upon social system and productive power, as he had already done in his analysis of the labour unrest of 1842, though his principles remained largely moral and psychological. Under the present false system of society, he wrote, 'those incalculable new powers for producing wealth and happiness' were 'so misapplied as to produce all manner of evil', and it was the 'impulse to overcome evil' that was 'the true cause' of the February Revolution, and indeed of all the revolutions that had ever taken place.[92] In short, a revolution, 'the change in the system', would be effected 'not through any patronage, but through irresistible necessity'.[93]

His whole system hinged upon an acceptance of the principle that man was made by 'nature and society' and was not responsible for what he was made to be. In order to put this principle into practice, he proposed the establishment of 'townships', each 'self-educating, self-employing, self-supporting, and self- governing',[94] on land to be purchased by the government. These townships would eventually be federated and extended over Europe and the whole world, 'uniting all in one great republic, with one interest'.[95]

'The difficult corner from irrationality to rationality' could only be turned by reason. The 'glorious change for humanity' could not be achieved by class or party, nor by any favoured nation or individual, but by 'a just and pure equality, gradually extending over the human race, under a refined parental democracy'.[96] A revolution was a necessity, but peaceful and rational revolution required the leadership of reason, the benevolent leadership of the intellectuals, which would go beyond classes and parties.

In Owen's new townships, there should be no private property, for it was 'one of the great demoralising and repulsive powers arising from the laws of men' and exercised 'an isolating and individualising influence upon each'. Finally, there should be no election to offices, for elections were 'demoralising to the electors and the elected'. Political functions were to be exercised only by direct democracy, all the members of a township being capable of participating fully in the affairs of its government.[97] It would not be too difficult to discern elements of an Anarchist Utopia in his account: in spite of his revolutionary millenarianism, his Godwinian belief in enlightened reason as well as his 'science' of circumstances led him to teach peace and decry violence.

This was perhaps the last important account of his mature thought. Owen was then nearly seventy-nine years old, and found it increasingly difficult to cope with events as they arose. 'Busy as I am', he wrote to Mrs Allsop, 'I cannot keep pace with public events & public opinion as I wish. Both are running wild for want of calm & wise direction.'[98] Yet he was indefatigable, and his patient and persistent labours continued.

The Great Exhibition of 1851 stirred Owen's imagination with its gospel of industry and peace. He hoped that the exhibition would become 'the pacifier of all contending interests' and prepare for that millennium, the materials of which, he believed, were at hand except for the 'pure spirit of charity'.[99] He met Mazzini, Louis Blanc and Francis Place in an effort to organise 'a powerful demonstration . . . towards changing the present system without bloodshed or violence'.[100] He thus tried to 'convert leaders of parties', but it proved to be 'a difficult task'.[101]

A public meeting was held at the John Street Institution in May 1851 to celebrate Owen's eightieth birthday. He addressed an audience of nearly a thousand, and in his speech he again urged 'the leaders . . . of the innumerable petty reforms' to direct their combined efforts to 'well-educate, well-employ, well-place, and cordially unite, the human race'.[102] 'I do not recollect ever addressing an audience with more evident effect,' he wrote to Mrs Allsop, '& the feelings of the meeting were enthusiastic & unanimously expressed.'[103] Marx, who had settled in London after the failure of the European revolutions, sat among the audience. 'In spite of fixed ideas', he wrote to Engels, 'the old man was ironical and lovable.' Marx, however, was shocked when he saw Owen actually recommending an organ of the German refugees, who were opposed to Marx, simply because he was told by one of its partisans present that the paper contained his own principle.[104]

In the summer of the same year, Owen told Mrs Allsop that he was determined 'to effect my revolution & to be beforehand with the revolutionaries of violence'.[105] He seemed very much concerned about

ROBERT OWEN AND REVOLUTIONARY POLITICS        33

the arrival in England of the Hungarian revolutionary Louis Kossuth. In a letter to Allsop, who was then in America, he remarked that Kossuth had 'produced most extraordinary feelings throughout the entire population elevating the power of the people & depressing the aristocracy in the same proportion'. 'Although his address exhibits extraordinary talent, tact, & elo[quence]', he went on,

> it is evident from them that he is himself only an advanced man on the old wornout notions of an insane state of society. Yet he is an important agent, in the progress of nature to bring up those less advanced than himself to where he is & thus is he preparing himself & them for the new order of things which is rapidly in progress & in a fair way of stepping in between democracy & aristocracy & giving speedily peace & prosperity to the human race.[106]

In the summer of 1852 Owen moved to 'plain but good farmhouse' at Sevenoaks. 'From early in the morning I am deep in my philosophy & statesmanship until past noon; in the afternoon reading & looking over & enjoying the air of Park Farm, not sure but I may become a bit of a farmer. . . .'[107] Yet he was still trying to 'compel the authorities of the world' to abandon the irrational system.[108] Writing to a young correspondent, possibly Allsop's son, he explained that his views went 'far beyond the establishment of a single community' and that his object was 'to change the public opinion of the world for which I have made a life time of preparation'.[109]

Soon an interest in spiritualism crept into his correspondence. Yet it was a tribute to his unflagging energy and a reminder of his attitude towards politics and society that in the last year of his life he sought to set up two organisations, one called 'The Society of Social Science Chartists' for the working classes, and the other 'The Social Science Society' for the middle and upper classes. The six points of the Charter would be useless except when 'united with the superior natural formed character and with permanent beneficial occupation'.[110] This was the gist of his social science and the epitome of his attitude towards political socialism.

Owen's attitude towards popular politics was largely determined by his views on social classes. A child of the eighteenth-century Enlightenment and a model employer whose whole life was devoted to the welfare of the working classes, Owen felt himself to be beyond the limits of a social class, while his own analysis led him to believe that classes were the embodiment of the false principle of division in the old society. His attitude towards classes, however, was more that of a realist than that of a millenarian visionary. In order to transform an irrational society, a class society, into 'the Rational System, in which, ultimately, there will be but one class', he would have to depend heavily upon the class that was best qualified to direct this transformation. That was the middle class, which 'possess the greatest breadth of useful knowledge within its circle to form a Rational Community'. They would be assisted by the upper class, 'with their trained perceptions of the principles of governing and of being governed'. Under their direction the working class would execute such work as they have been accustomed to. The children of all the classes should be trained to attain superiority physically, mentally and morally. But

> it is not practicable that the adults of the working class can be made, in this generation, more than working class members. . . . Their language, habits, manners, limited ideas, and ignorance of the world, make it impossible to put them, until their mind shall be born again, to be equal with those whom education and station have made unequal.[111]

In fact, Owen's socialism, as Engels pointed out, was largely a bourgeois affair fraught with the prejudices of his own class, though his observation on the classes contained valuable grains of truth. His apparent indifference or even hostility to democratic reforms can also be seen in this light.

His Association of All Classes of All Nations, which embodied the first organised socialist movement in England, was not a miniature classless society, but an elite army ordered according to the wealth and intelligence of its members.[112] He firmly believed that 'the existing governments, aided by the most intelligent and influential of all classes', should be capable of directing a revolutionary change without violence.[113]

As an elitist movement, socialism did make an impact on Chartism, though Owen's rejection of democratic methods alienated many possible allies among the Chartists. Peter McDouall, one of the most forceful of the physical-force Chartists, recalled that 'the principles of Socialism or Communism, have been already adopted [by the Chartists] from 1840, after a general discussion with Robert Owen and the other Communists'. Owen's system, however, did not appear to them democratic enough: so 'they have adopted the principles, without

adopting any system'.[114] Indeed, Owen and his followers could claim
some credit for the widening of the Chartist outlook that broadened
from political to social issues after the failure of the National Petition
of 1839.

The 1848 revolution presented a dilemma to Owen. As a social
revolution, he saw in it a great opportunity to persuade the revolutionary governments to adopt his system of education, employment
and association, that in his view would finally abolish the distinction
of classes. At the same time, he abhorred a political revolution by
violence, an attempt to subvert the existing system by force which
would only lead to bloodshed and human misery, and most likely to
an aristocracy of a new species.

In fact, he was not upholding the *status quo* in politics, for he was
not a supporter of any particular political form. He believed that all
the political forms tried in history – despotism, aristocracy and democracy – were based on the principles of repulsion and warring interests.
He only sought to permeate the existing governments, whatever they
might be, with his 'Rational Socialism', his principles of solidarity of
interests.

The principles you have established are those which must be adopted
or the world will never have peace as it never yet has had peace or
internal harmony. It is thus that time winnows out the chaff from the
grain, and it would seem that only by time and thro' time can the
People slowly, very slowly emerge from the slough of ignorance &
absurd irrational habits and practices.[115]

A worthy tribute from a worthy disciple.[116]

NOTES AND REFERENCES

1. Ralph Milliband, 'The Politics of Robert Owen', *Journal of the History of Ideas*, xv 2 (Apr. 1954).
2. Henry Hetherington in *Poor Man's Guardian*, 14 Jan 1832.
3. *Poor Man's Guardian*, 29 Sep 1832.
4. *Crisis*, 6 Oct 1832.
5. *Poor Man's Guardian*, 22, 29 Sep 1832.
6. John Burns Papers, vol. LXIV, Add. MSS. 46344, British Museum (hereafter cited as JBP).
7. Owen to Allsop, 20 Nov 1832, JBP. See also *Crisis*, 1 Dec 1832.
8. Owen to Allsop, 21 Nov 1833, JBP.

8A. 'The time is . . . arrived when the foretold millennium is about to commence, when the slave and the prisoner, the bond-man and the bond-woman, and the child and the servant, shall be set free for ever, and oppression of body and mind shall be known no more: *New Moral World*, 1 Nov 1834

9. His Association of All Classes of All Nations became the Universal Community Society of Rational Religionists in 1839 and the Rational Society in 1842.

10. *New Moral World*, 2 March 1839.

11. Ibid., 25 May 1839.

12. Lloyd Jones, *The Life, Times and Labours of Robert Owen*, 2nd ed. (1895) p. 347.

13. James Dodd to Owen, 22 Nov 1839, Manchester Collection.

14. John Finch to Owen, 8 Apr 1840, Manchester Collection.

15. *Northern Star*, 2 May 1840.

16. *New Moral World*, 12 June 1841.

17. A debate between Gamsby, secretary of the Sunderland branch of Owen's society, and Morgan Williams, a member of the Chartist Executive, *New Moral World*, 3 July 1841.

18. *Northern Star*, 30 Oct, 6, 13 Nov 1841.

19. *New Moral World*, 6 Nov 1841.

20. *Northern Star*, 24 July 1841; *New Moral World*, 31 July 1841.

21. *New Moral World*, 23 Apr 1842.

22. Ibid., 30 Apr 1842.

23. Ibid., 20 Aug 1842.

24. Ibid., 17 Sep 1842.

25. Ibid., 22 Oct 1842.

26. Frank Podmore, *Robert Owen: A Biography* (1906) p. 565.

27. *New Moral World*, 22 Apr 1843.

28. Ibid., 18 Nov 1843.

29. Engels, *The Condition of the Working-Class in England in 1844* (1845; English ed. 1892, reprinted 1936) pp. 236–8. A writer in *The Times* (29 Dec 1843) reported that Owen was regarded by many of the German communists as so 'unpractical' that he 'writes down as much visionary and absurd stuff in his works as a German professor'. Quoted in *New Moral World*, 6 Jan 1844.

30. A. R. Schoyen, *The Chartist Challenge* (1958) p. 181.

31. Owen returned to England for a few weeks in the summer of 1845 and again in the spring of 1846.

32. Owen to Allsop, 25 Oct 1845, JBP.

33. Owen to Mrs Allsop, 13 Nov 1845, JBP.

34. Owen to Mrs Allsop, 26 Feb 1846, JBP.

35. Owen to Mrs Allsop, 12 June 1846, JBP.

36. Owen to Allsop, 23 June 1846, JBP.

37. Owen to Mrs Allsop, n.d. [12 Aug 1846], JBP.

38. Owen to Allsop, 16 Aug 1846, JBP.

39. William Pare to Owen, 12 July 1847, Manchester Collection.

40. Owen, 'To the Electors of the Borough of Marylebone'; 'Address of Robert Owen to the Electors of Great Britain & Ireland', 24 July 1847, Manchester Collection.

41. Owen to Mrs Allsop, 1 Dec 1847, JBP.

42. Owen to Mrs Allsop, 17 Nov 1847, JBP.

43. *London Mercury*, 23 Oct, 13, 20, 27 Nov, 4 Dec 1847.

44. Owen, 'To her Majesty Victoria, Queen of the British Empire', 22 Feb 1848, Manchester Collection.

45. Owen, 'To the Men & Women of France', 27 Feb 1848, Manchester Collection.

46. *Morning Herald*, 29 Feb 1848.

47. Pare to Owen, 2 Mar 1848, Manchester Collection.

48. Finch to Owen, 7 Mar 1848, Manchester Collection.

49. Owen to Allsop, n.d. [31 Mar 1848], JBP. Owen did not speak French, but 'I have an excellent interpreter in Mr Thomas Doherty & now another when Mr D. is busy in his own affairs in Captain Price who is one of our old Socialists', he wrote in the same letter.

50. Owen to Mrs Allsop, 1 Apr 1848, JBP.

51. Georges Duveau, *1848* (Eng. trans. 1967) pp. 84–5.

52. Owen to Allsop, 4 Apr 1848, JBP.

53. Owen to Allsop, 4 Apr 1848, JBP.

54. Owen to Allsop, 5 Apr 1848, JBP.

55. Allsop to Owen, 6 Apr 1848, Manchester Collection.

56. Ibid.

57. G. J. Holyoake, 'Thomas Allsop', *Dictionary of National Biography*.

58. Owen to Allsop, 11 Apr 1848, JBP.

59. Allsop to Owen, 12 Apr 1848, Manchester Collection.

60. Owen to Allsop, 14 Apr 1848, JBP.

61. Owen to Allsop, 12 Apr 1848, JBP.

62. Owen to Allsop, 29 Apr 1848, JBP.

63. Owen to Allsop, 28 Apr 1848, JBP.

64. Owen to Allsop, 29 Apr 1848, JBP.

65. Allsop to Owen, 3 May 1848, Manchester Collection.

66. Allsop to Owen, 5 May 1848, Manchester Collection.

67. *Dialogue sur le Système Social de Robert Owen.*

68. Owen to Allsop, 4 May 1848, JBP.

69. Owen to Allsop, 5 May 1848, JBP.

70. Owen to Allsop, 7 May 1848, JBP.

71. Owen to Allsop, 12 May 1848, JBP.

72. Allsop to Owen, 22 May 1848, Manchester Collection.

73. Owen to Allsop, 24 May 1848, JBP.

74. Bill of Imprimerie Centrale des Chemins de Fer, Napoléon Chaix & Cie, 29 July 1848, Manchester Collection.

75. Owen to Allsop, 29 May 1848, JBP.

76. *Reasoner*, IV 17, pp. 232–3.

77. Owen to Allsop, 28 Apr 1848, JBP.

78. Owen, 'To her Majesty the Queen of the British Empire', London, 13 June 1848, Manchester Collection. The letter was published in *Douglas Jerrold's Weekly Newspaper*, 17 June 1848.

79. Owen to Mrs Allsop, 18 June 1848, JBP; A. Corbon to Owen, 6 June 1848, Manchester Collection.

80. Owen to Allsop, 26 June 1848, JBP.

81. Owen to Mrs Allsop, 27 June 1848, JBP.

82. Owen to Allsop, n.d. (1848), JBP.

83. *Courrier de Paris*, 10 July 1848.

84. *Corsaire*, 29 June, 4, 7, 10, 14 July 1848.

85. Henry Price to Owen, 5 Aug 1848, Manchester Collection.

86. Goupy to Owen, n.d., Manchester Collection.

87. Owen's address to Louis-Napoleon Bonaparte, Manchester Collection.

88. Owen to Mrs Allsop, 25 Dec 1849, JBP.

89. Owen to Mrs Allsop, 26 May 1849, JBP.

90. Marx to Engels, 8 Aug 1877, in Marx–Engels, *Werke*, Bd. 34, p. 68.

91. Owen, *The Revolution in the Mind and Practice of the Human Race* (1849) p. xxv.

92. Ibid., pp. xix–xx.

93. Ibid., p. 27.

94. Ibid., p. 43.

95. Ibid., p. 65.

96. Ibid., p. 77.

97. Ibid., pp. 111, 125–6.

98. Owen to Mrs Allsop, 28 Mar 1850.

99. Owen, 'To the Men of All Nations who have come to the World's Fair in the Palace of Glass', *Robert Owen's Journal*, 25 Jan 1851.

100. Owen to Mrs Allsop, 6 Mar 1851, JBP.

101. Owen to Mrs Allsop, 2 Apr 1851, JBP.

102. *Robert Owen's Journal*, 7 June 1851.

103. Owen to Mrs Allsop, 25 May 1851, JBP.

104. Marx to Engels, 21 May 1851, in *Werke*, Bd. 27, p. 263.

105. Owen to Mrs Allsop, 12 Aug 1851, JBP.

106. Owen to Allsop, 25 Nov 1851, JBP.

107. Owen to Mrs Allsop, 10 Aug 1852, JBP.

108. Owen to Mrs Allsop, 31 Aug 1852, JBP.

109. Owen to (?), 17 Feb 1853, JBP.

110. *Millennial Gazette*, 3 Apr 1858.

111. Owen in *New Moral World*, 10 Feb 1844.

112. See its Constitution art. 3–8, *New Moral World*, 7 Mar 1835. Its members had to undergo a series of examinations on their Owenite intelligence and to pay increasingly higher fees as they advanced to become the 'brothers and sisters of the New Moral World'.

113. *New Moral World*, 18 July 1840.

114. McDouall in *Le Populaire*, 19 Aug 1843, trans. by John Watts for *New Moral World*, 25 Nov 1843.

115. Allsop to Owen, 23 Dec 1855, Manchester Collection.

116. Allsop, 24 years younger than Owen, was able to assist the Communard refugees in 1871 and was attracted to Marx and Engels for their work in the International. 'Aiming now and always at the *perfect* solidarity of the People, the End sought will ever be a recompence, a reward and a solace,' he wrote in one of his letters to Engels. (Allsop to Engels, 11 Dec 1878, International Institute of Social History, Amsterdam). Allsop died in 1880.

CHAPTER THREE

# Robert Owen and the Community Experiments*

## R. G. GARNETT

ALTHOUGH Robert Owen's behaviour as the leader of the Owenite movement must continue to remain largely inexplicable, an analysis of the community experiments associated with his name should help us to place him in clearer perspective, as 'community' was both the process and purpose of transforming society into the new moral world.

A study of the communities should also add to our awareness of working-class aspirations, belief and organisational experience, and highlight the problem of leadership: landed gentry, industrialists and social reformers were just as closely involved in community planning and operation as were representatives of the working classes. An investigation of the experience of the communities therefore promises to clarify the relationship between Owen and his disciples and sympathisers, widen our appreciation of the impact of maturing industrialism, and lead us to speculate on the aftermath of Owenism and its permeation into latter-day social idealism and development. Perhaps most of all a comparative investigation of the Owenite communities should tend to correct the disparagement of posterity that Owenites were mostly cranks and the value of their community experiments largely illusory.

Community experiments were the main preoccupation of the Owenites, whose strength was not in their numbers, which were far exceeded by the members of friendly societies, Chartists and trade unionists, but in their intense social questioning. We cannot claim much consistency for their social remedies, but this does not diminish their

---

* This paper is restricted to an investigation of the Owenite communities in Britain. Robert Owen's experience at New Lanark is not here considered relevant, as New Lanark was really a capitalist enterprise with an infusion of business ethics and paternalism: indeed part of the confusion seen in Owen was in his attempts to translate New Lanark into a model for replacing or outmoding the capitalist system.

importance which lies elsewhere in the permeation of their ideas, and in their conviction that drastic reform of society need not call for politically revolutionary methods. Perhaps the most apposite lesson modern society can learn from the Owenites is through a study of their community experience of dealing with the problem of reconciling individual incentive and participation with efficient decision-making in the democratic process. Ralph Waldo Emerson commented on the problem of power:

> Philanthropic and religious bodies do not commonly make their executive officers out of Saints. The Communities hitherto founded by the socialists . . . are only possible by installing Judas as steward. The rest of the offices may be filled by good burgesses.

He later added:

> Of the Shaker society it was formerly a sort of proverb in the country, that they always sent the devil to market. . . . It is an esoteric doctrine of society, that a little wickedness is good to make muscle. . . .[1]

Owenism largely equated with community experiments in Britain during the second quarter of the nineteenth century. This poses certain queries: Why did these experiments take root during this particular period? Why should such social aspirations coalesce into movements only at certain times and in certain forms such as Owenism between 1825 and 1845? Why did Owenism have a stronger and more lasting appeal than the individual call to conversion of millenarial cults such as the Southcottians?[2] Answering that Owenism was infinitely more sensible and practical is partly begging the question – fanaticism will always appeal more to those with fanatical tendencies. It seems feasible to argue that the Owenite appeal had a more lasting impact just because it promulgated a social programme and an institutional framework, whereas the millenarians were content with personal salvation. There are, of course, exceptions – the Shakers and Mormons (the latter gaining many emigrant converts in Britain during the 1840s), and other sects who congregated their elect into communities; but the distinguishing feature of Owenism was that it thought of its mission in terms of a redemptive society rather than a redeemed elect.

The period 1825–45 covers the main events: Orbiston community was established in 1825 and the last Owenite settlement at Queenwood broke up in 1845, bringing about the virtual disruption of the Rational Society and so ending any further concerted Owenite activity. But

1825 to 1845 is also appropriate on other grounds: by the mid-nineteenth century industrialism had so matured that working-class institutions, and to a lesser extent working-class attitudes, were compelled to come to terms with the economic realities of capitalism, once working men eschewed the revolutionary alternative. Before 1850 it was possible at least to visualise the Owenite solution; after 1850 the success of Owenite questions and remedies could only be in their percolation into other minds and measures. Early Victorian England had much social optimism despite the uncovering of many social problems: emancipating slaves or providing cheap lodging-houses, public baths and libraries were all thought to be within the competence of middle-class good works. The age was distinctly amateur in its approach, especially when dealing with matters of social reform: Owenism differed only in the implicit comprehensiveness of its proposals. After 1850 society came more predominantly under the influence and control of specialists and professionals. Social inquisitiveness remained but uncovered problems so extensive that no one could contemplate such sweeping remedies as would be needed to overlap sectors of health, housing, education and employment within an urban environment.

The communitarians believed their plans to be perfect. They did not, however, pay sufficient attention to the devising of means for achieving their ends: financial support from official sources was not forthcoming; hence communities could only be established on self-generated capital and there were no precedents for the accumulation of large funds by working-class institutions. The communitarians were too optimistic of their powers of dissemination of knowledge, of conversion and of discernment of social principles and motivation. They could not achieve either sufficient isolation from or integration with the outside economy and still retain their identity as communities.

From 1840 there was a confusing proliferation of terms with varying connotations of the general theme of socialism.[3] The word 'communitarian' and its associated 'communitarianism' came into use to identify both the ideology of those who planned communities and the actual community experiments themselves: 'communitarianism' denoted a system of small co-operative land settlements, with 'communitarian' either an advocate of the community ideal or a member of such a community experiment.[4]

Communitarian and its lesser-used alternative 'communionalist' had a short life and passed into oblivion after the collapse of Queenwood in

1845. Although the word did not exist before 1840, it is possible, with some discretion of definition, to use 'communitarian' to encompass the whole range of aspirations and community experiments. A modern revival of communitarian would supersede the looser term 'utopian socialist' with its disparaging overtones and would enable 'pure' communism to describe systems based on complete community of possessions – in fact, most 'communistic' experiments have been communitarian in form, and this feature has been more significant than compliance with the theory of property-in-common, a theory generally vague and incompletely applied.

The benefits of community were to be so self-evident that the world would follow by emulation – for the community idea was the law of nature re-established. Providence was good; property was theft; institutions of government were evil.

The basis of communitarian thought was equality – economic rather than political – in that the labourer had a right to the full value of the product of his labour. It was believed that communities would create their own perfect markets in sharp contrast to the imperfectly competitive conditions prevailing outside, where 'the more employers and distributors . . . the less business is there for each; and the less business they have, the greater profit do they require to support them'.[5] It was co-operation in place of competition because competition bred inequality, and it was apolitical because it ignored or rather treated the state and the establishment as neutral.[6] In 1840 a branch society of the Owenites stated:

> The plans of the Socialists will be carried on under entire obedience to the laws of the State. . . . The Socialists take no part in the agitation for political changes, as they are convinced that permanent prosperity and happiness can be gradually secured for every human being under any form of government which recognises the principle of toleration.[7]

Capitalism could follow if it wished, and in the interim demonstration of the communal good life there would be no expropriation of property, merely a reorganisation of production and distribution so that the benefits of division of labour would not be wasted.

The communitarians were never wholly consistent in their economic thought and policy. They confused economic with social and political issues, but if pressed they would argue that radical changes in society were the critical aims of their programmes and economic reorganisation was an ancillary to social transformation.

The small community was an experiment with all that an experiment implies: it was limited, its environment was controlled, and its forces manipulated, not necessarily to give a final answer, but to provide evidence on which an eventual answer could be formulated. Nor did they insist on refined material; part of their purpose was to distil out impurity – they set out to overcome ignorance, poverty and vice, and they did not seek to excuse their failure by pointing out that many of the subjects of their experiments were ignorant, poor, vicious. The communities followed no set blueprint. They were liable to fail but they *could* learn from their errors. Their real weakness was that they refused to learn from their weaknesses.

## ORBISTON (1825–7)

Orbiston is important irrespective of the extent of its Owenism because it was the first communal experiment on British soil with a view to emancipating the working class through a transformation of the economic system. The community was planned to integrate agriculture with industrial production on the assumption that it would attract funds from sympathetic capitalists who would receive adequate dividends in the interim period until communal assets were eventually taken over by the tenants on an amortisation basis out of expected surplus.

Orbiston is also noteworthy as a piece of social engineering; it had no precedent for its comprehensive provisions for communal living, work and leisure. The first buildings in Britain specifically designed for working-class habitation, in fact the first buildings to be directly associated with the working-class movement, were at Orbiston.

The preliminaries to its setting-up can be explained largely in terms of the leading personalities associated with the experiment: Robert Owen; A. J. Hamilton, the son of General Hamilton, a Lanarkshire landowner; and Abram Combe, an Edinburgh tanner.

Owen, dissillusioned over the lack of Parliamentary support for his proposed communities as outlined in the *Report to the County of Lanark*, turned to other forms of sponsorship. The British and Foreign Philanthropic Society, which included many notable names, was intended by Owen to raise £100,000 for a community experiment but met only once – in June 1822. Many potential supporters refused to accept Owen's proposal that there should be absolute equality and common property in any forthcoming land colony. It also appears that Owen was beginning to prevaricate over the original plans for a community at Motherwell, as he left for Ireland during the autumn of 1822 to propagate his views before the Irish landlords. He wrote from Ireland in December to the President of the Edinburgh Practical Society, 'I have not for a moment lost sight of Motherwell, Sir, it is my intention to commence there at the earliest practical period. I hope this spring'.[8]

Robert Owen had purchased 660 acres of the Motherwell estate from General John Hamilton for £14,756, but by 1825 Abram Combe and A. J. Hamilton were no longer in agreement with Owen's plans; they wanted a system of individual reward for labour with economic equality later; they also preferred to begin a community on a smaller scale. General Hamilton therefore sold to Abram Combe, as trustee, part of the remaining estate of 291 acres at Orbiston, one mile west of the earlier proposed Motherwell site, for £20,000 by feu disposition on 13 May 1825. A letter from Robert Dale Owen to A. J. Hamilton on 17 March clarifies the position:

> In reply to your letter of 13th we now understand that you have purchased from us on behalf of Mr Owen the Lands of Motherwell as acquired by him from your Father at £14,756 14s 9d and to relieve him of his obligation for payment of the debt affecting the same due to your Father.
>
> It is further understood that this price is to bear interest at 5 per cent from Whit Sunday 1825 when your entry to the land is to commence and that you are to pay any sums that may be advanced by Mr Owen on account of the lands after that date including the expense of conveying them: and to relieve Mr Owen of his obligation to the servants and others engaged on the land. In short you just go into Mr Owen's place as regards these lands.[9]

It is therefore apparent that Owen resold the Motherwell estate to A. J. Hamilton on behalf of his father General Hamilton.[10]

William Maclure and Richard Flower visited Owen in Scotland in 1824 and imbued him with ideas which led to his leaving for America[11] at the end of the year and severing any connection with the proposed community at Orbiston, which he did not visit until 1827 – although his wife and daughters remained in residence at Braxfield House in nearby New Lanark.

The first meeting of A. J. Hamilton with Owen had been in 1816. After the unfortunate reception of Owen's *Report to the County of Lanark* by the county commissioners of supply in May 1820, A. J. Hamilton proposed to the Justices of the Peace that he was prepared to let 500 to 700 acres to facilitate the establishment of an Owenite settlement. Owen disagreed with Hamilton. He thought it preferable to provide a community for relieving the unemployed rather than the improvident and indolent. With some modification to the proposals he believed the community arrangements could be made applicable to 'middling and higher classes of society; being calculated to increase, in an extraordinary degree, the benefits now derived from any given expenditure'.[12] The landowners and justices finally abandoned the scheme after its criticism in the House of Commons on 26 June 1821 and rejection of the motion of the M.P. for Renfrewshire that Parliament should appoint a Commission of Inquiry into Owen's proposals.

A. J. Hamilton and Abram Combe eventually decided to establish their community at Orbiston on 18 March 1825 without any support from Owen. The community would be secure from any injury:

> On the contrary a similar establishment erected in our immediate neighbourhood will increase the comfort of the inhabitants and the value of both properties at the same time. A third and a fourth will still add to those advantages; and the value of the whole will continue to increase with their number, till the world shall be saturated with wealth.[13]

The prospects were therefore cheering:

> We shall have no enemies, we shall have the powerful aid of Government, as soon as out exertions exhibit their natural tendency to increase the peace and prosperity of the country; and we shall have the friendly aid of the Church as soon as we exhibit the absence of vice and immorality, and the presence of the spirit of True Religion.[14]

Orbiston was duly purchased from General Hamilton for £19,995 and the trustees given power to raise loans on the security of the estate. To acquire the land Abram Combe had borrowed £12,000 on bond from the Scottish Union Insurance Company, £4995 from General Hamilton and £3000 from a private source.

Combe was undoubtedly right in not thinking of New Lanark as a model community:

> New Lanark, however, bears no resemblance to the proposed village of unity and mutual co-operation. It will be impossible for one of

these villages to be a year in existence, without EITHER convincing the world of their incalculable utility, OR proving that the plan is utterly impracticable. One or other of these results must invariably follow; and be the result what it may, the sooner it is known the better.[15]

Although the language is that of Robert Owen, it should be noted that the latter was unaware of the existence of the community until some months after its inception.[16]

The community survived precariously for two years, short of capital, with little success in production, and violently divided over methods of internal government and distribution of income. Soon after Abram Combe's death in August 1827, the Orbiston Company of Proprietors decided to suspend all proceedings and dispose of the property. The last issue of the *Orbiston Register* was printed on 19 September 1827. A. J. Hamilton's failing health only allowed him to reside at Orbiston until shortly after Combe's death. Hamilton thought at the time that the residents were not sufficiently interested in the desired success of the experiment. He later ascribed the break-up of the community to mischievous influences brought to bear on tenants by local relatives and friends, the clergy, and 'the bad times of 1826', when the rate of interest, previously $3\frac{1}{2}$ per cent, was raised to 5 per cent; 'this alone added more than £1 per acre to the rental of the land'.[17]

Owen was in America during the dissolution of Orbiston whilst his wife and family were residing at Hamilton 'in a house belonging to John Allen, the Grocer'.[18] Alexander Campbell wrote to Owen in 1828 from Hamilton gaol, where he was imprisoned as a debtor for the plant and materials advanced to the Orbiston manufactory, and the letter confirms that Owen did on a single occasion visit the Orbiston iron foundry.[19]

Why did Orbiston fail? Certainly insecurity of funds was a factor. There was also strong local antagonism, and there was no consensus among the members over the basic issues of individualism versus egalitarianism, either of effort or reward. But present-day sociologists would be surprised not so much that Orbiston collapsed, but that it survived for as long as it did, given its crude attempts at social engineering. Orbiston was the first of the Owenite communities; but the subsequent experiments at Ralahine and Queenwood learned nothing from the experience. The Scottish community was bedevilled by the demise of its founder-manager, Abram Combe, but his death was the occasion rather than the cause of the collapse of the experiment.

Ultimately Orbiston failed because it was attempting a radical change in social attitudes and cohesion without any of the preconditioning necessary for converting members for the New Society. The dilemma was how to accommodate a radical change of human nature as both a precondition and a resultant. Orbiston was important because it showed the working class as agents rather than as objects of social reform, as they had been previously. In one sense, entering a community was the equivalent of emigration to a new land without radical upheaval from home ties and resettlement in a strange and often hostile environment.

The blindness of the early Owenite experimentalists was not in seeking unattainable ends but in misjudging the effort that would be required to prepare people for communal living: ingrained social habits are at least as hard to break as individual ones. A resolution of the problems of communal conflict could not be anticipated by drawing up paper constitutions. The communitarians learned on the job (Combe was a firm exponent of the value of experience), but in the end the job became too complicated to understand or control with the primitive knowledge of social science at their disposal. In economic terms, communities were in a quandary: they could aim to become self-sufficient, which was hardly possible as enclaves in a sea of capitalism, or they would have to reconcile themselves to compete as producers with the outside world. Orbiston could not provide an answer to the problem.

At the 3rd Co-operative Congress held in London in 1832, Owen argued that Orbiston failed because his advice had been repudiated: 'That society was not the one-tenth part of a community; it was not formed upon community principles, but in direct opposition to them, and that from beginning to end.'

RALAHINE (1831–3)

Ralahine community in County Clare cannot be fully understood either in purely Owenite or in communitarian terms; one must also know something of Irish land history. Of the three leading Owenite communities, Ralahine was the most parochial in its settlement plans and architecture; it was also the experiment with the strongest agricultural basis. As was the case with Orbiston, there were two leading

personalities – a landed proprietor, John Scott Vandeleur, and a
working-class Owenite organiser, E. T. Craig.[20] The Irish community
is no less remarkable because it was the most successful of the early
co-operative land schemes, after one has taken into consideration the
prevailing conditions of livelihood for Irish land workers compared
to those in England.

An estimate of the wage for Irish agricultural labourers in 1830 was
given as 10*d*. a day.[21] But Sir George Cornewall Lewis thought that
only one-third of labourers had the benefit of all-year-round employment:

> If every labourer in Ireland could earn eight pence per day for 310
> days in the year, we should probably never hear of Whiteboys. It
> is the impossibility of living by wages which throws him upon the
> land; it is the liability of being driven from the land and the con-
> sequences of having no other resource that makes him a Whiteboy.[22]

Robert Owen had first visited Ireland in 1822 when he stayed as a
guest of Lord Cloncurry, but there is scant evidence that he grasped the
nature of Irish land problems. Ireland was for Owen the first staging-
post in his transfer to a community in the New World. Perhaps he
thought that the dire economic condition of Ireland, which was less
industrially developed than either England or Scotland, would be more
suitable for a social improvement plan based on the provision of
adequate agricultural employment. He held a series of public meetings
in Dublin in 1823: the first launched into economics but then drifted
into criticism of religion before it broke up; subsequent meetings were
confined to discussion of improvement schemes.[23] Owen wanted the
Government to be the agent for his proposed reforms, but the Select
Committee on Employment of Poor in Ireland reporting in 1823
flouted this, and the Hibernian Philanthropic Society, which Owen
set up on the model of the British and Foreign Philanthropic Society to
solicit funds from private sympathisers in the absence of government
support, was just as moribund as the parent society. The wonder of
Owen's reception in Ireland was that he got a hearing at all from Roman
Catholics when in his scheme 'there was to be no public worship – no
avowed recognition of God, no belief of responsibility to a higher
tribunal than man's'.[24] But it was reported that Owen did attempt to
clear the ground by visiting Maynooth and giving an assurance that he
was not interested in the spread of Protestantism in Ireland: 'Hence his
subsequent operations in Ireland were never interfered with by the

clergy.'[25] There is, however, other evidence showing that the final disenchantment came as a result of Owen's extended tour of Ireland after the Dublin meetings:

> In his journey to Limerick and Clare, his principles more plainly unfolded themselves, and then his visit to Ireland caused a feeling of horror and of awe in those whose opinion he would probably wish to conciliate.[26]

Probably Owen visited John Scott Vandeleur during his itinerary, which included County Clare. The Vandeleurs had first settled in Ireland from the Netherlands during the seventeenth century. When John Scott Vandeleur came to inherit the Ralahine property he found it divided into a number of smallholdings, except for a portion of home farm. Vandeleur had another estate of some 700 acres elsewhere in County Clare, but at Ralahine he personally directed operations. He had the opportunity of frequent talks with Owen during the Dublin meetings and was deeply impressed with Owen's account of New Lanark, whose benefits Vandeleur thought could be transposed on to an agricultural basis in order to achieve higher rents, adequate interest on capital and also to provide better facilities for labourers. Ralahine in many ways was to become the agricultural equivalent of New Lanark. In fact it was to have more in common with New Lanark than with the other co-operative experiments at Orbiston and Queenwood. Vandeleur became the truest disciple of Owen the mill manager: both sought and achieved a buoyant level of profits, but Vandeleur turned out to be not quite so autocratic as Owen – at Ralahine profit-sharing was at least contemplated, unlike New Lanark.

Early in 1831 Vandeleur visited England to seek help, as he foresaw difficulties in the way of implementing improvements for his labourers as a member of the landed classes in the riotous situation prevailing in County Clare. The Irish landowner first met E. T. Craig in a Manchester hotel and Craig later wrote of the meeting:

> It was . . . the work I had done in Manchester that Mr Vandeleur heard of, through John Finch of Liverpool, that induced him to come to Manchester, where I had an interview with him at the Talbot Hotel, which existed at the bottom of King Street before the improvements were made.[27]

Craig's imagination was stirred by the desire of Vandeleur to provide improved conditions for his farm workers, and he wrote to Owen:

Mr J. S. Vandeleur of Ralahine has invited me to Ireland to assist in his arrangements. I shall go there with pleasure, as my whole heart is with the cause. As the success of the experiment will mainly depend upon its management I should feel a pleasure if you could furnish me with any suggestions, especially respecting the machinery of Infant Schools. . . .[28]

Craig could not claim to have any intimate knowledge of agriculture at this time. He never became a farmer; he was an organiser, a manager, and the parallel situation of Craig in 1831 is that of the young Owen showing all the qualities of leadership when he took over the management of Peter Drinkwater's mill in Manchester with negligible experience, but with a will to learn.

The inspiration for the Ralahine experiment can be traced to Owen's Dublin meetings, but the actual planning and direction was the work of Vandeleur and Craig who were the only persons at Ralahine conversant with Owen's principles. If this shows anything, it indicates that provided members of a community agree to be governed in the first instance by officials, 'it is not absolutely necessary at the beginning that every member should be thoroughly acquainted with all the principles and duties of our system'.[29] The agreement between Vandeleur and his tenants was drawn up in November 1831. The level of rent payable was fixed in terms of farm produce. Vandeleur would gain directly from any rise in market price of produce as the tenants were required to supply a notional quantity which at the average price levels ruling in 1830–1[30] would sell for £900: hence if prices rose the tenants had to supply the same physical corn-rent, but they were relieved of anxiety over price falls and could concentrate on increasing their output. Any surplus would accrue to wages and repayment of interest on capital. Ralahine was not, however, an example of a *métayer* system, because Vandeleur received rent in kind; under the *métayer* system there was a fixed percentage of actual annual produce in rent, but at Ralahine there were fixed quantities irrespective of actual output or price change. The stipulated rent was paid in full by the residents during the two years of the life of the community, in addition to investment in more buildings and some land reclamation.

A system of labour notes was introduced, which in contrast to other Owenite ventures worked successfully. Labour notes in fact enabled Vandeleur to support members without having to make cash advances. It would have been difficult to have over-valued the labour notes in terms of the input–output ratio of the community's resources, given the low regulation wage of 8*d*. a day at Ralahine. The notes were exchanged at the communal store, but as the quantity and rates of corn-rent were fixed, the actual marketable value was immaterial to the members. Indeed the labour-note system was a method of strictly regulating the level of purchasing power. Nevertheless there had to be some currency transactions with the outside world because Ralahine was never wholly self-sufficient; in these cases Vandeleur acted as sole intermediary – he supplied cash for outside supplies, and all saleable produce from the community passed through his hands – otherwise the labour-note system with its inherent weaknesses of leakage and depreciation when involved in outside exchange transactions would not have worked so smoothly.

Attention was drawn to Ralahine during the summer of 1833 by William Pare and Robert Owen, who saw possibilities of using the community as a source of agricultural produce for the Owenite labour exchanges in England. Owen made plans to meet the trustees of William Thompson's estate in County Cork, and also visit 'Mr Vandeleur's infant community, ascertain in what way it can be made available to promote the Equitable Labour Exchange'.[31] The inference must be drawn that Owen at this stage was more interested in labour exchanges than communities, as he had first visited Lord Wallscourt's estate before arriving at Ralahine – which is indicative of his casual attitude to the importance of the experiment, although it should be noted that he did compliment Vandeleur as being

> the only gentleman in Ireland who has made experiments on a large scale to try the effect of our principles. . . . Mr Vandeleur is quite pleased with his tenants, and on both sides they confess to be doing much better by these plans of co-operation than they could otherwise do.[32]

As is well known, Ralahine collapsed as a result of the bankruptcy of Vandeleur who wagered his fortune and estate in the Dublin clubs during the autumn of 1833.

Ralahine was regarded at the time and during the rest of the nineteenth century as the most successful of the experiments in agricultural co-operation.[33] Certainly there were improved relations between landlord and labourer, land improvements, encouragement of thrift, and an increase in self-respect. Vandeleur received prompt payment of a higher rent and interest on his investment; hence he did not need to face the risk of allowing his Owenite sympathies to run away with his self-interest. The prerequisites for success at Ralahine were, first, a homogeneous local peasantry with everything to gain from co-operative effort and use of capital – significantly, the only failures at Ralahine were a handful of over-zealous outsiders; secondly, a proprietor who was a hard bargainer with power of expulsion of members during the first year of community. Vandeleur was in effect a sponsoring capitalist who insisted on maintaining his legal ownership of the land, so that the community dwellers were licensed residents with a contractual obligation to pay rent in perpetuity. Ralahine was a most successful experiment in communal living and social equality, but it was not a self-generated co-operative, and it would have been unlikely that the heirs of John Scott Vandeleur would have conceded their land entitlement to erstwhile peasants. Seen in terms of co-operation, the most unfavourable interpretation that can be put on Ralahine is to treat it as a variation, albeit in a more efficient and improving form, of agrarian feudalism, with strong incentives for the members to improve their productivity and maintain communal discipline. The distinction between governor and governed was too wide for Ralahine to be a true example of co-operative ownership. Paradoxically Owen would have found the Ralahine system much more akin to his views on community management than his more personal creation of a community at Queenwood.

OWENISM DURING THE 1830S

Owen was thus little involved in the first two leading community experiments in Britain associated with his name. Rather he had a vision of a perfect community and criticised his followers for precipitate action, constantly emphasising that his views were misinterpreted and misapplied:

> Such communities as I have recommended, have never yet been in existence – have never been attempted – and therefore have never failed. . . . I was directly opposed to Orbiston, because I saw that the arrangements were not according to the circumstances which would ensure success. It is as necessary that individuals should be trained for a Community; as it is necessary they should be trained for any trade; and this can only be done by proper arrangements for the

purpose. These are – the due proportion of labour applied to production, distribution, education and police. There is as certainly a
science of society as there is of mathematics. . . . I have sought far
and wide for an individual who understands Society but without
success.[34]

Having deserted business, Owen was always preaching the merits of
businesslike attitudes when dealing with the organisation of social
programmes. After New Lanark he never completed any other practical experiment. Owen's was a temperamental weakness; he was
psychologically incapable of consistent leadership. G. D. H. Cole has
said that Owen could lead but could not follow; the truth is surely that
after leaving New Lanark Owen could neither lead nor follow. He
was an isolate, but one who somehow could infuse his disciples with
dedicated allegiance; yet whenever they reached a point where a policy
decision had to be made, he could never follow through its practical
implications. Not once but on each occasion when a community was
to be launched, Owen reneged or otherwise absented himself.

In seeking a stage-development analysis for Owenism in the period
after the first flush of co-operative store-keeping (1829–31), one must
interpose the halls of science and communitarian phase between the
labour-exchanges (1832–4) and the culmination and dénouement of
Owenism at Queenwood in the 1840s to which we must now turn.[35]
The succession of Owenite bodies during the second half of the 1830s
– the Association of All Classes of All Nations (1835), the Community
Friendly Society (1836), the National Community Friendly Society
(1837), the Universal Community Society of Rational Religionists
(1839), the Home Colonisation Society (1840) – all show in their
titles this bias towards community.

QUEENWOOD (1839–45)

In 1838 Owen showed his hand at the 3rd Congress of the Association
of All Classes of All Nations concerning the suitability of the poorer
elements of the working classes for admission to community: it was an
earnest endeavour of the Owenite association to improve the conditions of such people, 'but to effect this, funds were needed; and the
operations of the Society could not be clogged by these parties in the

meantime'.[36] Owen wanted a capital of not less than £1 million and
thought the first community should be situated within thirty miles of
London, but not less than ten miles from the City. His proposals were
now contemplating two estates: one an agricultural and educational
community, the other to be a combined manufacturing and agricultural
settlement. There would be a need for men with a superior education:
'The middle classes are, by position, the business classes of the world.'
Owen was later to crystallise his views even more sharply on the qualities of middle-class leadership:

> Now, the middle class is the ONLY efficient DIRECTING class in Society,
> and will, of necessity, remain so, until our system shall create a NEW
> class of very superior DIRECTORS as well as OPERATORS; a class very
> superior to any men or women who have ever yet lived. . . . The
> working class never did DIRECT any permanent successful opera-
> tions.[37]

A discussion followed at the May 1839 Congress over the appointment of a first Governor for the proposed community in 'the South of
England', the site of which the estates subcommittee of the Central
Board had visited. Owen announced plans to visit members of his
family in America during the ensuing autumn for the purpose of
putting his personal affairs in order in the expected event of his early
decease. He could then devote attention to the proposed communica-
ties on his expected return to England in the spring of 1840. In spite of
Owen's coincidental decision to renew family acquaintanceship
precisely at the time of inception of the first model Owenite community, and after he had preached social salvation for almost a quarter
of a century, the delegates at the 4th Congress felt they could not
dispense with Owen as titular head, even if he had evaded their expectation of his active leadership.

A draft lease for the Tytherley estate in Hampshire of I. L. Goldsmid
was drawn up and forwarded to W. H. Ashurst, an eminent City
solicitor, colleague of Rowland Hill and legal adviser to Robert Owen,
for his professional advice. Ashurst pointed out that Goldsmid, the
landlord, 'objects to your buying down the rent below £200 . . . an
indisposition on his part to vacate during his lifetime his position as
landlord of the property'. There were also other hazardous contingen-
cies: with some prescience, Ashurst warned, 'suppose the Bishop and
Clergy of the diocese wish to crush you, they would buy the head lease,
enforce all the covenants rigidly, and if they could not work a for-

feiture, would work a pretty considerable lot of inconvenience and annoyance'.[38]

The admonitions of Ashurst went unheeded and the Central Board of the Owenites proceeded with the legal formalities to lease the Goldsmid property, the majority of their members unaware of the slender rights of proprietorship that could be claimed over what were intended to be the first socialist acres in Britain. In August and again in September 1839 the Central Board wrote to Owen who was in Scotland and pleaded with him to return to England to speed up the arrangements for setting-up the long-awaited community experiment.[39] Some weeks later at a Central Board meeting on 27 September 1839 it was announced that Owen had given notice of resignation from the office of Governor, just four days before date of possession (1 October 1839) on the grounds that Tytherley would be merely 'a preliminary working community adapted to the views and habits of the better-conditioned of the working classes' rather than 'a community according to his ideas of a community, calculated for the general population of a country'. Owen would, however, recommend Finch, Green and Aldam as suitable persons to direct community operations.[40]

Queenwood was therefore the only community to have official sponsorship from the central body of the Owenite movement.[41] Although both Orbiston and Ralahine received more attention from contemporary observers and historians than did Queenwood, the Hampshire community survived for a much longer period than either of its predecessors.

The first residents arriving at Queenwood had to face considerable problems of estate management with negligible resources at their disposal. They must have found it hardly reassuring that Owen had already resigned as Governor. It is difficult to explain Owen's dramatic turning away from his followers. He seemed incapable of meeting and dealing with crucial issues. Whatever qualities of sound management he had demonstrated at New Lanark were somehow inverted and subsequently he could never keep his plans within the bounds of available finance. When faced with intolerable situations which he himself had largely brought about through imbuing his followers with grandiloquent images of community life, Owen could always evade responsibility and action by pointing out that his disciples had not followed his precepts. In the last resort he could claim that only he could visualise the new society, and on these almost logical positivist terms no one could prove him wrong.

Hence the actual responsibilities of governing Queenwood devolved on John Finch and two nominal assistants. Finch was soon appointed Acting-Governor with Heaton Aldam as director of agricultural operations. The change in calendar at Queenwood to Year One of the Millennium (CM.1) was not sufficient to solve the problems of farm management; the handful of colonists who were sponsored mainly by Owenite branches in the industrial North had little experience of agriculture, nor were they satisfied with the dilapidated state of the farm buildings which had to serve in the first place for accommodation.

The Central Board members looked to Owen for guidance over the affairs at Queenwood, but he was hardly forthcoming: he was written to in December 1839 that the Central Board wanted to 'go ahead' immediately with a school, 'and we much want your advice on the subject'.[42] Finch also wished to see Owen to discuss a proposed constitution for the colony and the erection of workshops.[43] Owen had lately visited New Lanark and met again the builder and the architect responsible for Owen's mill extensions there – 'the only persons in existence who have anything like accurate knowledge of what is required in practice to constitute a community such as I have always had in contemplation'.[44]

The Hampshire community soon drew opprobrium from the clergy. The presentation of Robert Owen to the young Queen Victoria was thought highly reprehensible, and the Tories lost no time in making political capital out of Lord Melbourne's indiscretion.

Owen argued at the 1840 Congress that the Central Board should cease drafting any members to Queenwood who were not expected to be capable of earning their maintenance; it would be cheaper to hire labour locally than to use that of members who were willing but unskilled.[45] He further suggested the completion of communal arrangements before any further admission of residents: 'As, however, with their present limited means, they could not do this, they must exercise the strictest vigilance in all they did.' Owen then went on to lecture delegates on his plan for a £600,000 community from whose towers 'would be reflected at night, by powerful apparatus, the new koniophostic light, which would brilliantly illuminate its whole square'.[46] According to Owen, the experiment at Queenwood would serve as a normal school 'in which working classes would be properly fitted to carry out more enlarged and perfect arrangements'. G. A. Fleming brought Owen's listeners down to earth, as 'he believed they would all agree with him in thinking the plan was far too extensive for them to adopt. . . .' Owen remained in the clouds; he disparaged the efforts of his followers: 'All community plans and experiments were uninformed'; in effect Owen had given up hope for the present generation. Some indication of his evacuation is given in a reported lecture at Nottingham:

> Were you in any way connected with Orbiston? Answer – 'No'. Was Gray's Inn Labour Exchange of your contrivance? Answer – 'No'. Was New Harmony an attempt to carry out your principles? Answer – 'My principles have never been carried out'. He [Owen] then commenced his lecture, produced plans for the building of houses and every requisite for a Community, in which capitalists may invest their money, and realise more than 100 per cent.[47]

Owen had despaired of converting the working classes as he conceded that ingrained environmental constraints were too strong to overcome except through the education of a new generation. He appealed for rich backers, and in this period when the survival of Queenwood was becoming more precarious he was eminently more successful in raising funds than at any previous time – when his proposals at least had the merit of being untried and therefore could be regarded as potentially sound investment propositions or charitable endeavours.

At the 1841 Congress William Galpin explained that he had been called to a meeting of the Central Board during August 1840 to consider the growing estrangement between Owen and his colleagues on the Central Board; after several days' discussion, Owen

> declared that he went forth alone to the world for the prosecution of larger plans that the Central Board contemplated. He [Mr Galpin] together with Mr Travis and several other gentlemen in London formed the provisional committee of an association called the Home Colonisation Society.[48]

In August 1841 a foundation stone was laid by Owen at Queenwood for a building which was to be named Harmony Hall and which was destined to take such a disproportionate share of the declining contributions to Owenite funds. Owen acclaimed: 'I have named our new Establishment "Economy" and the new parish "Harmony".'[49]

In January 1842 a baby born in community was named by Owen, Primo Communist Flitcroft, or the 'first born in Community': 'It is a lovely child and all are fond of it.'[50]

The £15,000 of loans from the Home Colonisation Society were put

at the personal disposal of Owen with a proviso that he should not
overspend these resources. Building operations had to be suspended,
however, when he could not locate any new source of loans. William
Pare, as auditor, stated that £18,000 had been expended to 31 March
1842.[51] By August, a special congress had to be convened as 'It had
however very recently become known that the Governor of Harmony
had been proceeding with practical operations faster than the means of
the society would warrant. . .'.[52] Owen had previously resigned as
Governor in July 1842, 'solely that new energies may be given to some
of your friends possessing many valuable qualities to direct in some of
your departments, but who are unequal in other respects to the task
which is now to be performed'.[53] A rider was added by Owen that he
had not met with a single person with the right qualities to direct so
difficult a task. Several delegates were prepared to excuse Owen's
irresponsibility. Alexander Campbell exclaimed that 'All he had failed
in was a paltry matter of finance'. Another delegate thought that one
might just as well have expected that Napoleon at the height of his
military career would have been stopped by a failure in the supply of
ammunition.

When pressed over his attitude towards increased democracy, Owen
was guilty of deviancy at the 1843 Congress. A delegate complained
that 'many in the branches had not confidence in the operations of Mr
Owen now. . . . He [Mr Owen] had been used to carry on such
extensive operations, that he could not work on a small scale; he could
not keep within the means placed at his disposal'.[54] Notwithstanding
these criticisms Owen was then elected President and Governor in
place of John Finch, but William Pare continued to run the affairs of
Harmony Hall as Deputy Governor.

The situation was deteriorating rapidly. After four years of endeavour the per capita cost of settling a member in community was in
the region of £700, and with a standard of living, if not of physical
accommodation, much below that of the old immoral world – at least
for those colonists who were skilled artisans and perforce were reduced
to the level of agricultural labourers.

William Pare, as expected, was re-elected Acting-Governor by the
1844 Congress. Owen addressed the delegates regarding the decision:
'He [Owen] could not accept office in connection with the Society
unless he could have full authority, without reference to previous
resolutions of Congress.' The *carte-blanche* was refused and Congress
agreed 'that the resignation of Mr Owen as President of the Society be

accepted'. John Buxton from Manchester was then elected in his place; the antagonism between Owen, supported by his middle-class sympathizers from the Home Colonisation Society, and the working-class members from the branches of the Rational Society, was now acute. William Pare refused to continue in office as Acting Governor under Buxton. In Podmore's standard biography of Owen there is no mention that Pare acted as Governor of Queenwood for a longer and more difficult period that Owen himself, or indeed of any of the succession of Governors between 1839 and 1845 – including Finch, C. F. Green and James Rigby. This omission from the fullest published account of Harmony Hall has undoubtedly diminished the importance of Pare in the history of Owenite co-operation.[55]

After the inevitable dismemberment of Harmony Hall in 1845 there was little bitterness among the Owenites. Some of the innate honesty and incomprehension of the residents is seen in a postscript: 'There were receipts for sums amounting to £14,000 advanced by the Home Colonisation Society entered in a sixpenny pocket-book – and many of them in pencil,'[56]

Characteristically Owen had left for America during the summer of 1844, but was reported back in England on 13 June 1845 when he announced that 'he should be able to do as much good in one year in America as he could do in England in ten'.[57] His return visit was short – on 20 July 1845 he sailed once more for the New World.

The obvious weakness at Harmony Hall was financial, but the deeper malaise was in the confused aim of the experiment: its implicit purpose was to demonstrate whether labour, irrespective of whether it was manual, skilled or managerial, could become so united and rewards so distributed as to prevent excessive wealth and poverty from remaining a prevailing element of an economic system. Successful operation of a farm, school or boarding establishment *per se* would not have been a sufficient realisation or vindication of this aim.

The communitarian solution was little heard of after Harmony Hall. The idea of home colonies survived simply as a method of alleviating urban unemployment. But the broad issues of the land question remained in continuous debate throughout the second half of the nineteenth century: land nationalisation schemes and single-tax Henry Georgeism underwrote the basic fears of the harmful consequences from excessive urbanisation and a lessened dependence on the soil.

In terms of community development Ralahine learned nothing from Orbiston and Queenwood nothing from either of its predecessors.

Each of the communities studied was largely unique and yet all three suffered from an amalgam of blind fate and internal dissension rather than from adverse outside pressures. The three experiments failed, but the final question is not whether they would have survived if fate had treated them more kindly, but how protracted would have been their eventual demise? They were certainly out of context in early nineteenth-century Britain. Perhaps the community idea as a solution for social atomism and deprivation was also bound to fail because of incompatibilities between its ethos and its structure. Granted that communities were to be proliferated, a charismatic leader would no longer be required – indeed a Robert Owen would become an increasing liability: the role of a community leader is more important than his personal contribution and it is even more important that provision is made for corporate succession. Owen had a glimpse of this problem when he saw Queenwood as a seminary for training a cadre of community organisers, but he could never accept the inevitability of his own extinction as a policy-maker. Community dwellers must be given freedom to develop their inchoate communities, otherwise a community will disrupt or atrophy.

This study of the Owenite community experiments has shown the need for some reappraisal of the character of Robert Owen as seen in his activities during the post-New Lanark years. Owen made theatrical appearances before his followers but not always with a due sense of timing: the influence of Owen was nevertheless immense, almost in spite of his actions. G. J. Holyoake was probably nearest the truth when he said: 'He never acted on the maxim that the working class are as jealous of each other as the upper classes are of them. All that he did as a manufacturer, he omitted to do as a founder of communities.'[58]

Owen acted as if money had already been dispensed with, especially in his relationships with communities. He believed that a paternalist system of management was all that was necessary to organise resources and distribute the real surplus created by labour. He never really emancipated himself from the idea of poor-law colonies; his later plans for rural retreats for the middle classes, although on a smaller scale and not as necessary socially, were not far removed from his first views. Eventually the new moral world would be ushered in by a newly-constituted working class hardly distinguishable from the contemporary middle class.

Owen was not really interested in community development, nor was he at heart capable of co-operation. His name should remain indissolubly linked as he would have wished with New Lanark rather than with any of the community experiments.

NOTES AND REFERENCES

1. R. W. Emerson, 'Power', in *Collected Essays* (1908 ed.) p. 362.

2. An account of Joanna Southcott and her sect is given in E. P. Thompson, *The Making of the English Working Class* (1968 ed.) pp. 420–6, and W. H. G. Armytage, *Heavens Below: Utopian Experiments in England 1560–1960* (1961) pp. 68–70.

3. The term 'communionist' was first used in the *Co-operative Magazine* (Nov 1827) p. 509: 'The chief question on this point, however, between the modern (or Mill and Malthus) Political Economists, and the Communionists or Socialists, is, whether it is more beneficial that this capital should be individual or in common.' In November 1841, John Goodwyn Barmby set up the 'Universal Communitarian Association' and issued a journal *The Promethean or Communitarian Apostle*. The contribution of Barmby is merely etymological in the history of socialist vocabulary. For other contemporary examples of the term 'communitarianism', see Rev. E. Miall, *Nonconformity* II (1842) 809: 'Your communitarians, or societarians of modern days who seem intent on fashioning a new moral world by getting rid of all individual feeling.' See A. E. Bestor, Jr, 'The Evolution of the Socialist Vocabulary', *Journal of the History of Ideas*, IX 3 (June 1948).

4. In this paper, the term 'communitarianism' will be reserved for social secular ideology and experiments with a community basis. 'Millenarianism' will be understood to denote chiliastic, apocalyptic cults which may or may not have developed settlement programmes (contrast the Shaker and Mormon communities with the Southcottians who had no plans for community experiments).

5. Abram Combe, *Sphere of Joint Stock Companies* (1825) p. 23.

6. 'We have now before us', said Robert Owen, 'a plan of improving society. . . . We are now I think in a position to command it from the hands of the Government; and why? because they do not know how to relieve the community from a state of wretchedness and poverty, and we will show them the means of creating a Paradise' (*Report of Second Co-operative Congress*, Oct. 1831, p. 11). A decade earlier Owen had stated: 'My aim is therefore to withdraw the germ of all party from Society' ('An Address to the Inhabitants of New Lanark', reprinted in G. D. H. Cole (ed.), *A New View of Society and Other Writings of Robert Owen* (1927) p. 106).

7. *Statement submitted to Marquis of Normanby relative to Universal Community Society of Rational Religionists by Branch A.1 London* (Feb 1840) pp. 7, 14.

8. Letter of 29 Dec 1822, from Robert Owen in County Cork to Mr Wilson, President of Practical Society, Infirmary Street, Edinburgh, in Hamilton Papers (Motherwell Public Library).

9. Letter in Hamilton Collection.

10. Alex. Cullen's account in *Adventures in Socialism* (1910) p. 182, is wrong in assuming that Owen kept this Motherwell land for an indefinite period, and F. Podmore, *Robert Owen* (1906) p. 355 n., is confused on this issue.

11. For Robert Owen and the New Harmony Community, see bibliography in A. E. Bestor, *Backwoods Utopias: The Sectarian and Owenite Phases of Communitarian Socialism in America 1663-1829* (1950).

12. 'Report to the County of Lanark', in Cole (ed.), *A New View of Society*, p. 66.

13. A. Combe, *Sphere of Joint Stock Companies*, p. 5.

14. Ibid., pp. 6-7.

15. A. Combe, *Observations on the Old and New Views and their effects on the Conduct of Individuals as manifested in the proceedings of the Edinburgh Christian Instructor and Mr Owen* (1823) p. 15.

16. *The Register for the First Society of Adherents to Divine Revelation at Orbiston in Lanarkshire*, 9 (12 Jan 1826) p. 70.

17. A. J. Hamilton, 'The Soldier and the Citizen of the World with Reflections on Subjects of Intense Interest to the Happiness of Mankind' (MS., n.d.) p. 201. MS. in possession of Lord Hamilton of Dalzell and kindly lent to author.

18. Letter from Alexander Paul at Orbiston to A. J. Hamilton, Geneva, 17 Aug 1829, Hamilton Collection.

19. Letter from Alexander Campbell, 3 Oct 1828, *Robert Owen Correspondence*, no. 85. For other evidence of Owen having visited Orbiston, see letter no. 1148 from Alexander Paul, 25 Aug 1848, and letter no. 2713, 6 May 1856, from Alexander Campbell.

20. R. G. Garnett, 'E. T. Craig: Communitarian, Educator, Phrenologist', in *The Vocational Aspect of Secondary and Further Education*, xv (1963).

21. *Report of Select Committee on State of Poor in Ireland* (1830).

22. Sir G. C. Lewis, *Irish Disturbances* (1836) p. 313. (Sir George Cornewall Lewis was Chancellor of the Exchequer 1855-8.)

23. See *Report of Proceedings of Several Meetings held in Dublin* (Dublin, 1823), also *Letter to Nobility, Gentry and Clergy of Ireland*, Robert Owen, 1 March, 1823, and *Letter to Nobility, Gentry, Professions, Bankers, Merchants, Master Manufacturers of Ireland*, Robert Owen, 21 March, 1823, in National Library of Ireland.

24. W. Urwick, *Biographic Sketches of James Digges La Touche* (Dublin, 1868) p. 166.

25. J. F. Hogan, 'Early Modern Socialists, II', *Irish Ecclesiastical Record*, xxvi (1909) 24.

26. Urwick, *Biographical Sketches*, pp. 160-1.

27. E. T. Craig, 'Early History of Co-operation', *Co-operative News*, 7 Jan 1888, p. 16.

28. Letter of E. T. Craig, 69 Hanover Street, Manchester, 1 Sep 1831, in *Owen Correspondence*, no. 143.

29. John Finch, letter no. 2, *Liverpool Mercury*, 24 Mar 1838. (Finch wrote a series of fifteen letters on Ralahine, which he visited during the spring of 1833.)

30. The quantity of each crop-rent was fixed on the average produce of Ralahine during the three years before the community and at average prices ruling at Limerick market 1830-1. The rent was payable on six named products: wheat,

barley, oats, beef, pork, butter.

31. *The Crisis*, 22 (8 June 1833,) p. 170.

32. Letter of Robert Owen, ibid., 23 (15 June 1833) p. 178.

33. L. Goupy, *Quaere et Invenies* (Paris, 1853); W. Pare, *Co-operative Agri-culture: A Solution of the Land Question as exemplified in the History of Ralahine Co-operative Agricultural Association* (1870); E. T. Craig, *The Irish Land and Labour Question illustrated in the History of Ralahine and Co-operative Farming* (1882); C. W. Stubbs, *The Land and the Labourers: A Record of Facts and Experiments in Cottage Farming and Co-operative Agriculture* (1884); A. R. Wallace, *Studies, Scientific and Social* (1900).

34. *Report of Second Co-operative Congress* (Oct 1831) p. 14.

35. S. Pollard, 'Nineteenth Century Co-operation: from Community Building to Shopkeeping', in Asa Briggs and John Saville (eds.), *Essays in Labour History* (1960).

36. *Report of Proceedings of 3rd Congress of All Classes of All Nations and 1st Congress of National Community Friendly Society, May 1838*, p. 36.

37. *New Moral World*, VI 38 (11 July 1839) 595.

38. Letter to Director of National Community Friendly Society, Birmingham, from W. H. Ashurst, 6 July 1839. *Owen Correspondence*, no. 1126. See also R. J. Reid, *Exposure of Socialism* (1845) p. 23: 'No wonder Sir Isaac Lyon Goldsmid, to accomplish his purpose became a Socialist of Branch A.1 London and paid £5 of his two shillings weekly subscriptions in advance.'

39. Letters of Henry Travis to Robert Owen, 29 Aug and 5 Sep 1839, *Owen Correspondence*, no. 1151.

40. *New Moral World*, VI 50 (5 Oct 1839) 799. Also letter to Robert Owen to Central Board, 27 Sep 1839, *Owen Correspondence*, no. 1166.

41. There were other spurious community experiments with some support from local Owenite branches at Pant Glas and Manea Fen: Owen had no con-nection with either of these experiments.

42. Letter of Henry Travis, 6 Dec 1839, *Owen Correspondence*, no. 1194.

43. Letter of John Finch, 5 Dec 1839, *Owen Correspondence*, no. 1198.

44. *New Moral World*, VI 61 (21 Dec 1839) 976.

45. Supplement to Report of 5th Congress, May 1840, ibid., VII 87 (20 June 1840) 1331.

46. Ibid., pp. 1332–3.

47. Ibid., VIII 3 (18 July 1840) 36.

48. *Report of 6th Congress, May 1841*, p. 353.

49. *New Moral World*, X 12 (18 Sep 1841) 95.

50. Ibid., X 29 (15 Jan 1842) 231.

51. 'Address of Congress to Members of Rational Society', 6 Aug 1842, ibid., XI 7 (13 Aug 1842) 57–8.

52. 'Proceedings of Special Congress, August 1842', ibid., XI 6 (6 Aug 1842) 41.

53. Ibid., p. 43.

54. 'Report of Congress, May 1843', ibid., XI 50 (10 June 1843) 406.

55. R. G. Garnett, *Ideology of Early Co-operative Movement* (1966), First Annual Co-operative Endowment Lecture, University of Kent; 'William Pare: A Non-Rochdale Pioneer', *Co-operative Review* (May 1964). See also J. F. C. Harrison, *Robert Owen and the Owenites in Britain and America* (1969), and A. E. Musson,

'Ideology of Early Co-operation in Lancashire and Cheshire', in *Transactions of Lancashire and Cheshire Antiquarian Society*, LXVIII (1958) 117–38.

56. *New Moral World*, XIII 57 (26 July 1845) 465.
57. Ibid., XIII 56 (19 July 1845) 459.
58. G. J. Holyoake, *Life and Last Days of Robert Owen* (1871) p. 19.

CHAPTER FOUR

# Owen's Reputation as an Educationist

## HAROLD SILVER

IN this study we are concerned more with how people have seen Robert
Owen in relation to education than with his ideas and efforts in themselves. In very general terms it can be said that his reputation in this
field, after the early interest generated by his work, suffered a hiatus
from the mid-1820s until (among socialists) the 1880s and (among
educationists) the twentieth century. Certainly at the height of his
fame at New Lanark Owen's work could win enormous acclaim as a
system 'both in point of theory and practice, new, and unrivalled'. His
system at that time was considered to be 'adequate to the great purposes of forming the character of individuals and collective bodies,
civil, moral and religious, of nations and empires'.[1] Yet, at the beginning of the twentieth century, Owen's most important biographer was
to regret that 'the name of Robert Owen is little known to the present
generation as an educational reformer'.[2]

It is, of course, easiest to follow through influences and reputations
when they have been upheld by such obvious end-products as legislation, administrative apparatus or collected works. The value and
relevance of the work of Brougham and Kay-Shuttleworth, for instance, has been consistently upheld. Owen's reputation, however,
has needed rescue operations, and on this point it is perhaps important
to bear in mind that the national reputation which Owen established
whilst at New Lanark, based on both the success of the mills and the
authority which this success lent to Owen's views, was being eroded
even before his actual connection with New Lanark ended in the
period 1824-9. Central to this process of erosion was, of course, Owen's
attack, in keeping with a social philosophy of which 'educational'
ideas were an integral part, on established religion. But the process
itself was of a complex nature.

The first New Lanark mill had been completed by David Dale, in
association with Richard Arkwright, in 1785. A description written
before Owen came from Manchester to assume full managerial control
in 1800 explained that 'the spinning of cotton yarn is carried on to a

greater extent, than at any other place in Scotland, or probably in Britain'. Over 400 children were employed, and were not 'neglected with regard to their health, education, or morals, every exertion being used for the accomplishment of these purposes, which, as yet, have been attended with a degree of success hitherto unprecedented at any other public works in this kingdom'.[3] Owen (who acknowledged in his *New View of Society* the foundations Dale had laid) improved vastly on the conditions and facilities, but it was his educational arrangements in particular which were enthusiastically and internationally praised. Dr Macnab, investigating New Lanark on behalf of the Duke of Kent, 'was at once thrown into an ecstasy of admiration; his unpractised pen was sorely taxed to depict the feelings with which he was inspired. . . . The Duke at once professed himself a disciple'.[4] For Macnab, the Duke, deputations, visitors and the onlooking world Owen had 'proved he is an extraordinary man'.[5] Macnab, it should be remembered, was extolling this 'proof' some two years after Owen had publicly denounced religion and set out along the road that was to bring upon him widespread abuse for his infidelity and socialism.

The New Lanark schools were too overwhelming a piece of evidence for Owen's standing as an educationist to be undermined at once. George Combe, phrenologist and secularist educator, unsympathetic to Owen's views generally, visited New Lanark in November 1820 and described the Institution for the Formation of Character, opened some four years earlier. The children were admitted at the age of two, 'three women watch them until they are four years old; they then go to school. . . . We saw them romping and playing in great spirits. The noise was prodigious, but it was the full chorus of mirth and kindliness.' He describes the children dancing and 'singing three or four songs of the sweetest melody and merriest measure'. Owen had ordered £500 worth of 'transparent pictures representing objects interesting to the youthful mind' so that children could 'form ideas at the same time that they learn words'. The greatest lessons Owen wished the children to learn were 'that life may be enjoyed, and that each may make his own happiness consistent with that of all the others'. Combe's most revealing comment, in this period of monitorial education, was that 'the teachers had studied the dispositions and faculties of the children more than any teachers I had met with'.[6]

Combe's testimony is important in showing the close working relationship and sympathy of aims of Owen, who built and shaped the schools, and his teachers. There is clear evidence from this period of the amount of time Owen spent in the schools, and of the children's affection for him. One of them, writing to Owen at the age of twenty-one, referred to 'the very condescending politeness with which you are pleased to regard those in an humble sphere of life and the amiable disposition you have always preserved towards, such: especially those who are more imediately under your charge'. Owen was 'the cause from which I learned to think and act'.[7] A deputation from the Leeds Poor Law Guardians in 1819 considered that the most remarkable thing about the education of the children was 'the general spirit of kindness and affection which is shown towards them'.[8] Owen's reputation, based on the evidence of such humanity, and on the educational programme of *A New View* into which it could be seen to fit, remained unshaken in the early twenties. A meeting held in 1822 of a society to promote community settlements as advocated by Owen since 1817 had as imposing a list of vice-presidents and members as had the committee set up in 1819 to investigate his plan. The Earl of Blessington, as ecstatic as Macnab, referred to Owen's 'humane and enlightened mind' and his plans which had 'been brought into successful practice'. The public were indebted to him 'for the most valuable collection of facts and successful experiments that have ever been attended to in the cause of suffering humanity'. Sir Walter de Crespigny, M.P., had at New Lanark seen little children playing 'with a degree of harmlessness, of fondness, and of attention to each other, which we do not often witness in this country'. The chairman, Lord Torrington, declared that 'no language can do justice to the excellence of the arrangements in that establishment'.[9]

Nevertheless, Owen's reputation *was* being undermined. He was not at this or any other point concerned about his own social standing. 'In after life,' commented Holyoake, 'Mr Owen was really reckless of his own fame. No leader ever took so little care in guarding his own reputation.'[10] After the public meetings in London in 1817 opposition began to mount, though most of it at first combined criticism with sympathy. Major Torrens, for all his recognition of Owen's 'disinterested labours and perfect benevolence', was attacking his views in the *Edinburgh Review* in 1819,[11] echoing the general resistance of the political economists to Owen's community plans. *Blackwood's*, in 1821, was insisting that it was necessary to discriminate between Owen the New Lanark philanthropist and Owen the system-builder. New Lanark was 'a pattern for manufacturing establishments' and Owen disseminated 'contented cheerfulness among the grown population under his charge, and application and study among the fine children, whose education, almost step by step, he superintends'. Everyone who had been to New Lanark, the writer continued, knew that Owen's life was passed at his mills, and that in superintending their details, displaying these to visitors, and caressing the children at his school, scarcely all the hours of the day are sufficient for him'. Owen's notion that character was formed by circumstances was 'opposed both to reason and to revelation', and the practice at New Lanark was quite unrelated to Owen's theories.[12]

In view of the essentially unitary nature of Owen's thought, it was perhaps inevitable that attempts to distinguish between what was 'educational' and what was 'social' could only pave the way for a more general opposition. A. J. Booth in the 1860s saw the position clearly: Owen's 'claims to our gratitude as an educational reformer are now almost forgotten. His fame as a philanthropist is obliterated by the notoriety he subsequently acquired as the exponent of Socialism, a system of society not generally regarded with favour'.[13] The truth was that, in so many fundamental ways, Owen's message was regarded as unacceptable or even irrelevant in the rapidly advancing, achievement-orientated industrial society of the mid-nineteenth century. Apart from the fact that Owen was never again associated with an educational enterprise that appeared to offer the same degree of positive 'proof' that New Lanark had done, the breadth of Owen's optimism was unacceptable in an age of deep-seated uncertainty and confusion. 'Man has walked by the light of conflagrations', pronounced Carlyle in 1831, 'and amid the sound of falling cities; and now there is darkness, and long watching till it be morning'.[14] Owen was one of those who had been imbued with a sense of moving through the long watch towards brighter things. There were others, like Thomas Pole, a Quaker and early infant education enthusiast, whose language could be as visionary as that of Owen himself: 'Man is now emerging from the deep shades of ignorance, and the light of a celestial morning is breaking forth with unprecedented splendour since the commencement of the nineteenth century.'[15] The people who made and preserved reputations in high Victorian England were attempting to move away from the state of mind in which such enthusiasms and visions were perpetrated.

One element in the memory of Owen, therefore, was a sense of indignation at the vastness of his projects. At its most tolerant, this opinion of Owen was as a 'sanguine old projector, who, through an almost innumerable succession of baffled projects, hopes on as fervently

as ever'[16] – a tone of voice met frequently in mid-century comments on
Owen. To be a man of panaceas in the Victorian 'Golden Age' was to
be irrelevant. To be a man of 'one idea' was even more intolerable to
the Victorians than it had been to Hazlitt,[17] and only a small number of
prominent non-Owenites managed to combine irritation at this aspect
of Owen with a certain sympathy: they included Harriet Martineau and
Charles Bradlaugh (who described Owen as 'a good, pure, one-idead
man'.[18] The one idea was, of course, consistently defended by Owen's
supporters. William Pare, for example, on the centenary of Owen's
birth, recalled that 'it has been said that Owen was a man of one idea. If
so, the idea was at once grand, catholic, and comprehensive.'[19] Lloyd
Jones compared Owen's one idea with St John's constant cry of 'Little
children, love one another'. Owen had spent fifty years, Jones pointed
out, being concerned about the importance of a sound education as a
means of securing justice and humanity, and it was 'natural, therefore,
that his persistence in urging this view upon the attention of others,
should be irksome to those who differed from him'.[20]

Another point is that, after his return from America in 1829, Owen
became associated with working-class movements whose educational
efforts were in general deprecated by those who were engaged from
the 1830s in an attempt to strengthen the administrative process represented in the Committee of Council on Education or the voluntary
efforts which were aimed at making that intervention unnecessary.

A crucial milestone was being passed. The Committee of Council
symbolised the growing conviction that the battles to legitimise
education (even if not to agree on its control) had been largely won.
There were no longer, as Macnab had pointed out in 1819, men
persecuted 'for advocating the right of the poor to education'.[21] The
Dean of Durham, in 1848, told Mechanics' Institute members of 'an
almost obsolete prejudice against institutions such as yours'.[22] But the
'legitimising' of education involved the appearance of the 'legitimate
educator', who, among other things, must not advocate the provision
of too much education. As the historian of a later period of English
education has pointed out, debates about the appropriate amount of
education continued right through the century. Discussion of the
Revised Code, for example, reflected the continuing belief 'that too
much education was undesirable', and he quotes the opposition of *The
Times* in 1880 to Mundella's attempt to revise the Code: the danger was,
it was suggested, that 'education might turn the heads of ploughboys
and make them look down on their destined walks in life'.[23]

It was clearly important to the legitimate educator that his work must not be considered socially subversive. Owen is not mentioned in the reports from 1840 in the Minutes of the Committee of Council (his name is also absent from such contemporary journals as the *Quarterly Journal of Education*, the *Quarterly Educational Magazine* and the *London Scholastic Journal*), but a comment in one inspector's report for the year 1840-1 is revealing. The mechanical teaching of reading and writing with a little arithmetic, and the dogmatic inculcation of Scripture, were, in his view, inadequate, because, 'if the legitimate educator does no more than this, there are those that will do more: the Chartist and Socialist educator – the publisher of exciting, obscure and irreligious works – he who can boldly assert, and readily declaim upon false and pernicious dogmas and principles'.[24] Ten years later the same inspector was horrified at the extent of the sales of 'Chartist and infidel' newspapers 'of an immoral nature, hostile to the existing state'.[25] Such a view, it must be emphasised, coloured educational history as well as policy. In 1845 another inspector explained in a report to the Committee of Council how 'desultory individual efforts' had been outstripped since the first infant schools were established, largely through the efforts of the Home and Colonial Infant School Society: 'previous and even subsequent to the date of its formation, some of the promoters of infant schools appear to have considered them merely as asylums for healthful amusement'.[26] Owen was expunged from the record partly because of the need to cleanse the newly emerging national educational machine of unacceptable influences. He could not now be safely accepted as a 'legitimate educator'.

Owen's reputation had not been based, then, on the combination of features which made that of, say, Lancaster and Bell, Brougham and Kay-Shuttleworth, Herbert Spencer and Matthew Arnold more secure. There were no schools, societies, Parliamentary Bills (the 1819 Factory Act has to be discounted in this connection) or administrative machineries to associate with him. His ideas were too entangled with vast schemes of social reorganisation for them to continue to feature for long in educational debate, as did – in a later generation – those of Spencer on the curriculum or Arnold's on payment by results. The very problems Owen was trying to solve were unacceptable, in the form he approached them, to 'legitimate' opinion from the 1830s onwards. Even Owen's earlier writings did not appeal, for these reasons, to Victorian England. His *New View of Society*, a document of considerable stature in the 1810s and 1820s, is scarcely mentioned in educational and social debate afterwards, and has only very recently become part of the canon of educational texts.[27] The nature of the requirements for a firm reputation in Victorian Britain, and the way in which any form of radical or secularist ingredient distorted the educational record, are confirmed in the case of George Combe, who was by the 1840s one of the most important, and subsequently one of the least remembered, figures in British education. There are many parallels between the careers of Owen and Combe (both of whom, it was suggested in 1842, had 'the same type of mind'.[28] Combe was not in any sense a socialist or radical of the Owenite stamp, but his phreno- logical panaceas and educational secularism played a similar part in the decline of his reputation to the ones we have traced in the case of Owen. Combe's reputation as a pioneer of the teaching of social studies, health education and science did not survive, when that of, for instance, Spen- cer and Huxley did. One of the few attempts to revive interest in Combe (since Jolly's massive edition of Combe's writings in 1879) laments the lack of reference, or scant reference, to Combe in twentieth- century histories of education, a neglect traced back to the fact that 'as a leader of the "Secularists" he was subjected to much misrepresen- tation and obloquy'.[29]

It is not difficult, then, to see why Owen's reputation wilted, and that of, for example, Samuel Wilderspin and the Mayos did not. Owen was only the founder of the first infant school, which had an important relationship to a wide set of ideas; Wilderspin was the founder of the first infant-school movement, and he and the Mayos brought infant education into an unambiguous relationship with the existing educa- tional order.

Considerations such as these define not only the nature of reputation, but also the type of historical writing in which it is to some extent regulated. The Victorian history of education measured importance in terms of the permanency of institutions or the continuing utility of ideas (the most valiant, but largely isolated, attempt to approach popular education with wide terms of reference being George Bartley's *The Schools for the People*).[30] One of the first historical pamphlets in the field of popular education was, symbolically, a summary of 'the education question in Parliament'.[31] A review of Quick's *Essays on Educational Reformers*, when it appeared in 1868, emphasised the diffi- culty a teacher would have in gratifying a desire 'to know about the various educational experiments that have been now and then made, or about the men who have most influenced the methods and work of

education. There is a lamentable deficiency in our literature of works
that deal with the history of education or educationists'.[32] The tradition
of 'institutional history', confirmed in books like Craik's *The State in its
Relation to Education* (1884), which does not mention Owen, was the
dominant one until well into the twentieth century. Quick's book
(published in a first edition of 500 copies and for twenty years out of
print) did not mention Owen, and in a chapter on Froebel added for a
later edition he refers to the early history of infant schools and the
way in which this Continental idea was 'taken up by James Buchanan
and Samuel Wilderspin'.[33] Gill's *Systems of Education* and Leitch's
*Practical Educationists* were both published in 1876, both merely mention
Owen in passing, and both devote their main attention in the field of
English infant education to Wilderspin.[34] The President of the Education Department of the National Association for the Promotion of
Social Science in 1875 mentioned, among early contributors to popular
education, Raikes, Bell and Lancaster, and believed that Wilderspin
gave us 'our first Infant School in 1824'.[35] Wilderspin had in fact
promoted the idea that he was the founder of infant schools, and the
historians were glad to follow the lead he gave. Typical of the approach
was Holman's *English National Education* (1898), which mentioned
Owen in parenthesis to both Wilderspin and Buchanan – 'another hero
of popular education was Samuel Wilderspin', whose interest in infant
education was due to his friendship with Buchanan, 'who had come
from Robert Owen's infant school at New Lanark – the first established
in Great Britain'.[36]

Although, as we have seen, Owen's stature as an educationist was
considerably diminished after the mid-1830s, it was never totally
swept away. One factor in all this was the continuing importance of
the 'proof' represented by New Lanark. As we have suggested, there
is a particular problem about Owen's reputation as the founder of
infant schools. There is no need for us to examine this controversy in
detail, but it is useful to glance at the attitudes it reveals.[37] Wilderspin
tried to retract the indebtedness he expressed to Owen in the first
edition of *On the Importance of Educating the Infant Children of the Poor*
(1823). Owen was probably less than fair in his disparaging remarks
about Buchanan in his autobiography. We have already seen evidence
of the high quality of the New Lanark schools and of Owen's teachers in
general, and also Owen's deep personal involvement in the life of the
schools. The nature of the record in the 1830s and 1840s can easily be
illustrated. The Central Society of Education, for example, published

an article in 1838 ascribing the success of the New Lanark infant school to Buchanan, 'partly with the assistance of Mr Owen'.[38] The *Westminster Review* interested itself in Buchanan's role, on the grounds that 'it is not so much those who with philanthropic objects establish a school, as he who first introduces the plan which makes a school succeed, to whom the country is chiefly indebted'.[39] Wilderspin was telling a Select Committee in 1835 and *The Times* in 1846 that Buchanan brought from New Lanark a system which amounted to a 'mere assemblage of children . . . a refuge for destitute children . . . but not Infant Schools conducted upon the system now known as the Infant School System'. He denied the contention that 'Oberlin, Fellenberg, or Robert Owen was the Founder of the present Infant School System, with its various arrangements, details, and implements'.[40]

Wilderspin was, of course, right that by his definition Owen was not the founder of infant schools; it is his definition that is interesting, reinforcing the view of infant education we have already seen through inspectorial eyes. The move to assert Buchanan's role as a teacher was important, but it overreached itself in suggesting that Owen himself was not deeply responsible for and involved in all aspects of school planning and activity at New Lanark.

The controversy was not one-sided, and there were educationists who came to his defence, especially Brougham, who in response, for example, to Wilderspin in Select Committee and *The Times*, was deferential to Owen and his role in the history of the infant school. Frederick Hill in 1836 was admitting, on the subject of infant schools, 'the high honour of originating and first bringing into successful operation this important instrument of human improvement and happiness is due to Mr Robert Owen'.[41] A writer in the *National Instructor* in 1850 explained that it was at New Lanark that 'the Infant School originated, and from which all the others have sprung'.[42] Even Sargant understood that 'the infant school system was an inevitable consequence of Owen's doctrine, as to the vital importance of surrounding human beings with circumstances favourable to their development'. Owen's 'claim to the invention remains unimpeached'.[43]

T. H. Huxley, not otherwise known for any attraction towards Owenism, was invited to take the chair at an Owen centenary commemoration in 1871, and declined in most interesting terms:

> I think that every one who is compelled to look as closely into the problem of popular education, must be led to Owen's conclusion, that the infant school is, so to speak, the key of the position; and that

Robert Owen discovered this great fact, and had the courage and patience to work out his theory into a practical reality, is his claim, if he had no other, to the enduring gratitude of the people.[44]

There is no clearer testimony to the way in which Owen's reputation endured outside of, and in spite of, the official record.

The memory of Owen's doctrine of character formation was indeed clearly linked with the 'proof' offered by New Lanark. In 1877, for instance, Charles Bradlaugh declared that 'society now adopts the view which Robert Owen was the first to popularise – although not the first to enunciate – that man is better or worse according to the conditions surrounding the parent . . . and those which surround the infant itself. . .'. Owen had 'set an example to all Britain by introducing infant schools in his New Lanark village'. Like John Stuart Mill, Bradlaugh saw how important, if oversimplified, Owen's doctrine of character formation had been: 'the formula that man's character is formed for him, and not by him, does not express all the truth, but expresses much more than is taught by those whose dogma it is that man may will, uninfluenced by events'.[45]

The Owenites, of course, commented persistently on Owen's role as the pioneer of infant education, which they saw as a necessary preliminary to the advance towards a new society. The tone of their comments can be judged from an example in a letter to Owen, written in 1854 when Owen was planning to use a 'panorama' the following year to demonstrate how the human mind could be formed from birth:

How extremely necessary it is that the epoch which commenced infant teaching as a science should be represented in the panorama; therefore your Colony of New Lanark, exhibiting the infant school teaching, begun by yourself, surrounded with those superior conditions, as far as the state of things and of times could permit, should be the starting point. . . .[46]

Within the Owenite movements, and within those working-class and radical movements which owed any kind of debt to him, his educational message was pervasive. It would be impossible here to consider the relationship between Owen's educational views and, for instance, the later Owenite activities, the London Working Men's Association and Chartism, and the educational ideals of co-operation, trade unionism and the labour movement in general.[47] Between the climacteric of Chartism in 1848 and the new socialist organisations of the eighties, Owen's reputation in the labour movement was keenest among Chartists, ex-Chartists and co-operators. The best-known example from the later days of Chartism is Hetherington's 'Last Will and Testament', dated 21 August 1849. In it he bids farewell to a loathsome social system, expressing his 'ardent attachment to the principles of that great and good man – Robert Owen. I quit this world with a firm conviction that his system is the only true road to human emancipation.' Owen's system was one which 'makes man the proprietor of his own labour and of the elements of production – it places him in a condition to enjoy the entire fruits of his labour and surrounds him with circumstances that will make him intelligent, rational and happy'.[48] Hetherington was one of the pioneer, heroic figures of Chartism. Thomas Cooper, a later recruit to Chartism, considered himself a friend of Owen's,[49] and in 1850 was on the margin of Chartism and publishing *Cooper's Journal*. In that year he published a short article entitled 'Reflections Suggested by the 79th Anniversary of the Birth-day of Robert Owen', by a young Owenite called Thomas Shorter. It reminds readers that Owen

> was the founder of the first and most efficient institution ever established in this country for the purpose of infant training. . . . Education and employment, – equal rights and liberty of conscience, – the development of all man's faculties and the supply of all man's rational wants: these have been the great objects of his unceasing exertions, and to which his life has been consecrated. His theory of the power of education and surrounding circumstances in the formation of character were submitted by him to the test of practical experiment . . . and the wonderful success of that experiment has been attested by evidence of the most incontrovertible character.[50]

This testimony of 1850 (in terms little different from those of, for example, Macnab thirty years earlier) is as revealing in the story of the labour and radical movements as is that of Huxley for educational opinion twenty years later.

In the Co-operative movement Owen's educational work was a recurring memory. When A. J. Booth published his *Robert Owen, the Founder of Socialism in England* in 1869, *The Co-operator* published both a short notice of the book and a letter from Booth explaining that he had included a chapter on the early history of co-operation, and that he would be pleased to present a copy to Co-operative libraries.[51] Throughout the late sixties and into the seventies the same journal contained extensive reference to Owen. An exchange of correspondence between Thomas Hughes and George Storrs on the utility of Owen's works to co-operators took place in 1867–8. Robert Harper contributed two articles on Owen in 1868 (declaring that 'scarcely one of the superior methods of ameliorating human suffering, but was either invented or adopted by him'). Alice Wilson contributed a long poem on Owen in 1868. Henry Travis contributed a series of five articles on 'Education on the Principles of Social Science' (based very largely on Owen's own writings) in 1868, one on 'Education as a part of the Co-operative Social System' in 1869, and another on Owen in 1871. There is a sense throughout of Owen as major educator, including as 'originator of the rational infant school system', and of New Lanark as the 'greatest of all steps in the onward progress of the human race'.[52]

The revival of interest in Owen's educational work was a feature of the increasing part played by collective social solutions in the national consciousness of Britain in the later decades of the century. The reform, radical and socialist movements helped increasingly after the mid-sixties to confirm the move away from *laissez-faire* modes of thought. H. S. Foxwell in the late nineties made the points that Owen had in England 'brought socialism down from the study to the street, and made it a popular force', and that popular education and other aspects of social improvement 'either originated in, or were powerfully reinforced by, the Owenite agitation'.[53] Beatrice Webb was only one of those making similar points in the nineties. Describing Owen as the father of English socialism (a distinctively English socialism, she argued, defined in typically Fabian terms), she associated him with 'beneficent legislation forcing the individual into the service, and under the protection of the State'. The Education Acts are one of her examples.[54] Among educationists, Michael Sadler showed a special awareness of Owen's position in this respect, and in at least three places between 1905 and 1907 he used Owen as the main example of the 'collectivist and authoritarian' nineteenth-century alternative to the 'individualist and radical' current (of the first the 'great figure' was Owen, of the second – Bentham, Brougham and Place).[55] J. F. C. Harrison has rightly argued that too much emphasis has been placed on the view of Owen as socialist pioneer, and by exploring more fully the millenarian and sectarian significance of Owen and Owenism has provided an important corrective to 'over-concentration on a few selected years'.[56] It is also important, however, to establish to what extent outside immediate Owenite circles Owen's reputation (we have been exploring, of course, only one dimension of it) was kept alive in the period between the contraction of his mass base in the late thirties and the revival of interest in the final decades of the century. Interestingly, the writings of both John Stuart Mill and Harriet Martineau reflect a willingness critically to consider the relevance of Owen's views in the light of the increasing need for 'collectivist' solutions to social problems.[57]

We have suggested that clues to Owen's reputation in the fifties and sixties can be found in such places as the late Chartist publications, Co-operative and other journals, and A. J. Booth's book of 1869. They can be found also in the writings of Marx and Engels. Both were keenly interested in Owen and in the education at New Lanark, Marx principally seeking confirmation of his views on the combination of productive labour and instruction.[58] Engels, in a passage published in German in the seventies, and in English in 1892, described Owen as 'the inventor of infant schools' where the children 'enjoyed themselves so much that they could hardly be got home again'. In fact, considered Engels, 'all social movements, all real advances in England in the interests of the working class were associated with Owen's name'.[59]

Owen's standing as an educational reformer in twentieth-century British eyes owes most, however, to the relentless enthusiasm with which the Fabians went out of their way to rehabilitate him. Socialists and radicals in the seventies and eighties (including Joseph Cowen and Annie Besant)[60] had begun the process, but it was the Fabian effort that counted. One of the founding fathers of the Fabian Society, and author of its motto,[61] was Frank Podmore, whose *Robert Owen* is probably the greatest landmark in Owen studies. A pamphlet committee elected in 1884 included Rosamund Dale Owen, Owen's granddaughter.[62] The Society's main work on Owen came after the turn of the century, though indications of the scale of renewed interest can be seen in its, and other, work in the nineties. Beatrice Webb's *Co-operative Movement in Great Britain* appeared in 1891; a Co-operative pamphlet on the history of social conditions in Huddersfield affirmed in 1894 that 'when Robert Owen first directed attention to the early education of infants, he advocated a method of training human character, which our statesmen at length wisely and completely adopted'.[63] Leslie Stephen's famous article on Owen in the *Dictionary of National Biography* in 1895 expressed the certainty that Owen would 'be recognised as one of the most important figures in the social history of the time'.[64]

Of course, not all Fabian writers were equally interested in the restoration of Robert Owen's reputation as an educationist. Sidney

Webb, for instance, eager to establish Owen's role in the history of collectivism and socialism, was attracted by that aspect of Owen which related to the growth of state and municipal forms of collective responsibility. But Owen's specifically educational work (apart from his proposals for a national system of education) were not of great interest to Webb himself. To the Fabians generally, however, this was not the case. It was after the turn of the century that interest grew. In 1901 a tract entitled *What to Read* recommended Owen's autobiography and Lloyd Jones's book on Owen (a further list in 1906 added Podmore's biography, published in the same year). Between 1908 and 1917 six Fabian tracts were either about Owen or commented significantly on him. Mrs Hylton Dale's *Child Labor under Capitalism* (1908) considered that Owen 'more than any educationist before or since, recognised that children are like plants, in that they want more than care and attention; they want love'. Mrs Townshend's *Case for School Nurseries* (1909) described Owen's work in infant education as an 'illusory dawn' – with England 'deep in the trough of *laissez-faire* . . . one need not wonder that here Owen's preaching fell on deaf ears and produced no permanent results'. B. L. Hutchins's tract on *Robert Owen, Social Reformer* was published in 1912, and C. E. M. Joad's tract on *Robert Owen, Idealist* came five years later. St John Ervine in 1912, in a tract on *Francis Place*, considered that Owen and Place together 'made it possible for democracy to be in England', and Colwyn Vulliamy, in a tract on *Charles Kingsley and Christian Socialism* (1914), turned aside from the main theme to comment on 'the wonderful, almost quixotic, romance of the New Lanark mills, raised wages, reduced hours, free education and amusements . . .' and Owen's 'magnificent schemes for the general organisation of industries and the free instruction of the whole community'.

It was from starting-points such as these that the educational work of Owen came to be built into labour history. From Ramsay MacDonald's *Socialist Movement* (1911), for example, through the work of Max Beer on the history of socialism (his edition of Owen's *Life* appeared in 1920, his *History of British Socialism* in 1919, and *Social Struggles and Thought* in 1925) and that of G. D. H. Cole, emphasis was laid on Owen's part in making it 'impossible for men to refuse to ponder over great fundamental social changes'.[65] The main burden of most of this analysis of Owen as pioneer socialist was not only that he had helped to build a labour movement but that his message had managed to be woven into the fabric of responses to social problems.

Thomas Frost, for instance, reflecting in 1880 on the communitarian experiments he had known, commented that though socialism was at that period little heard of, 'the results of its teaching are everywhere around us, and its fundamental tenet, 'man is the creature of circumstances', may be recognised in all the legislation of the last quarter of a century'.[66] Holyoake, when summarising Owen's central doctrine, expressed the view that 'nobody doubts this now'.[67]

There was a growing sense, however, that Owen's specifically educational reputation was inadequate. Podmore's admission that Owen was 'little known' as an educational reformer was echoed two years later by Joseph Clayton, who noted that 'Robert Owen, the founder of infant schools in Great Britain, is still but the shadow of a name, even in circles where Pestalozzi is honoured; and the work Owen wrought for education at New Lanark, unsurpassed in the years that have followed, is still to be apprized at its true value'.[68] This appraisal in educational history was to come with a widening of the 'institutional history' of education to incorporate a social-historical approach.

It is an interesting fact that the 'new educationists' of the late nineteenth and early twentieth centuries did not rediscover, or at least did not acknowledge, Owen as part of their tradition. The reason, no doubt, is that his Enlightenment rationalism placed him outside their interests; he was within a tradition which had not broken with reason as the foundation on which to build educational practices. There is a passage in *Democracy and Education* in which Dewey explains the shortcomings of Locke and Helvétius. Their approach to education, including the improvements they advocated in learning processes, remained over-intellectual. At the call of reason 'practice was not so much subordinated to knowledge as treated as a kind of tag-end or aftermath of knowledge. The educational result was only to confirm the exclusion of active pursuits from the school, save as they might be brought in for purely utilitarian ends'. Even object lessons excluded 'the natural tendency to learn about the qualities of objects by the uses to which they are put through trying to do something with them'. The educational reform effected by rational-empiricist theories' was confined mainly to doing away with some of the bookishness of prior methods; it did not accomplish a consistent reorganization'.[69] Although much of this would be inapplicable to Owen – particularly to the infant school as he created it – he derived his overall theory from the tradition of Locke and Helvétius, and the fact may explain the absence of reference to him in the work of the late-century progressivists.

There is no apparent, and perhaps no real, bridge between them.

The position of Owen's reputation in the literature of education depended finally, therefore, on the historians who, in the wake of socialist, and especially Fabian, rehabilitation, attempted to redefine educational history in terms of broader social processes and the history of ideas. Although works like David Salmon and W. Hindshaw's *Infant Schools: Their History and Theory* (1904) helped in the process, it was probably A. E. Dobbs, using a very limited range of sources, who nevertheless contributed most to a new approach to nineteenth-century education. In *Education and Social Movements 1700-1850* (published in 1919) he saw education as part of a wider process of social development, and accepted as a legitimate field of inquiry the many relationships between schools and other types of formal and informal education, on the one hand, and social attitudes and realities on the other hand. Both Combe and Owen are given serious attention, and in a chapter entitled 'Education by Collision' Dobbs looks at the educational impact of social movements and programmes. Owen's role as educator was now accessible in a whole new historical environment. J. W. Adamson's *English Education, 1789-1902* (a better book than most of its successors) appeared in 1930, with Owen featuring in a chapter entitled 'Educational Opinion'. The following year came Frank Smith's *History of English Elementary Education 1760-1902*, which bases a summary of Owen's educational work on such sources as Owen's *Life* and *A New View*, Robert Dale Owen, Podmore and Cole. What Dobbs and Smith, for example, had to say about Owen was in no sense original, but it was necessary and influential, as can be judged from the fact that the Hadow Reports on *The Primary School* (1931) and *Infant and Nursery Schools* (1933) both made emphatic reference to Owen, whose infant school at New Lanark 'had a great influence on the development of infant education'.[70]

Owen's reputation as an educationist in Britain has to be seen, then, in terms of a pattern of educational development, and an accompanying set of historical inclusions and exclusions. Its fate shows how sharply nineteenth-century reputation-makers were able rapidly and effectively to readjust the direction and focus of their lens to suit their educational ideology. It is doubtful whether, as Holyoake appears to suggest, Owen's reputation would have met with any different a fate if he had been more careful in guarding it. It was not Owen's lack of attention, but the administrative system, the 'legitimate educators', the historians of institutions, and various kinds of Victorian indignation in response to Owen's views and activities, that demoted him. It was a new set of social policies and attitudes, radical and socialist revivals, and a wider interpretation of the history of education that rehabilitated him.

## NOTES AND REFERENCES

1. Henry Gray Macnab, *The New Views of Mr Owen of Lanark Impartially Examined* (London, 1819) pp. 214–16.

2. Frank Podmore, *Robert Owen: A Biography* (London, 1906) p. 102.

3. James Denholm, *The History of the City of Glasgow and Suburbs*, 2nd ed. (Glasgow, 1798) pp. 265–6.

4. Arthur John Booth, *Robert Owen, the Founder of Socialism in England* (London, 1869) p. 81.

5. Macnab, *New Views of Mr Owen*, p. 214.

6. Charles Gibbon, *The Life of George Combe* (London, 1878) 1 131–2.

7. Letter of 20 Sep 1828, from John Williamson, Co-operative Union Library collection, no. 111. Original spelling and punctuation retained.

8. 'Report of a Deputation from Leeds', reprinted in *A Supplementary Appendix to the First Volume of the Life of Robert Owen* (London, 1858) p. 254.

9. Quoted in Lloyd Jones, *The Life, Times and Labours of Robert Owen*, 6th ed. (London, 1919) pp. 106–8.

10. G. J. Holyoake, *Life and Last Days of Robert Owen, of New Lanark*, centenary ed. (London, 1871) p. 19.

11. *Edinburgh Review* (Oct 1819) p. 454.

12. *Blackwood's Edinburgh Magazine* (Apr 1821) pp. 88–92. See also ibid. (Mar 1823) p. 339. The writer was 'Christopher North' (John Wilson).

13. Booth, *Robert Owen*, p. 67.

14. Quoted from 'Characteristics', in Walter E. Houghton, *The Victorian Frame of Mind 1830–1870* (New Haven, 1957) p. 27.

15. Thomas Pole, *Observations relative to Infant Schools* (Bristol, 1823) p. 11. For the millenarian background to Owenism see J. F. C. Harrison, *Robert Owen and the Owenites in Britain and America* (London, 1969).

16. John Hill Burton, *Political and Social Economy* (Edinburgh, 1849) p. 225.

17. Owen features in Hazlitt's essay 'On People with One Idea'.

18. Charles Bradlaugh, *Five Dead Men whom I Knew when Living* (London, 1877) p. 6.

19. *Report of the Proceedings of the Festival in Commemoration of the Centenary Birthday of Robert Owen* (London, 1871) p. 7.

20. *Life, Times and Labours*, p. 438.

21. Macnab, *New Views of Mr Owen*, p. 213.

22. The Dean of Durham, *Sentiments Proper to the Present Times* (Gateshead, 1848) pp. 3–6.

23. R. W. J. Selleck, *The New Education 1870–1914* (London, 1968) p. 68.

24. Seymour Tremenheere 'Report on the State of Elementary Education in

the County of Norfolk', *Minutes of the Committee of Council on Education, 1840–1* (London, 1841) p. 437.

25. Quoted in W. L. Burn, *The Age of Equipoise* (London, 1964) p. 111.

26. Joseph Fletcher, 'Report on Infant Schools on the Principles of the British and Foreign School Society,' in *Minutes* (1845) p. 217.

27. The Cambridge series 'Landmarks in the History of Education', for example, did not include Owen, and only in a new series has it been introduced in 1969 – the first time it has been reprinted in Britain as an *educational* document.

28. *Aberdeen Banner*, 31 Dec 1842 (MS. copy in University of London, Pare Collection 578, no. 112).

29. Alan Price, 'A Pioneer of Scientific Education: George Combe (1788–1858)', *Educational Review* (June 1960) pp. 219, 227.

30. George C. T. Bartley, *The Schools for the People* (London, 1871). The garbled reference to Owen and New Lanark does not detract from the value of this important book.

31. J. C. Buckmaster, *The Education Question in Parliament. Being a Digest of Proceedings, from 1816 to the Publication of the Revised Code* (London, n.d.).

32. *The Museum, and English Journal of Education*, 1 Aug 1868, p. 176.

33. Robert Herbert Quick, *Essays on Educational Reformers* (London, 1904 ed.) p. 409.

34. J. Gill, *Systems of Education: A History and Criticism of the Principles, Methods, Organisation and Moral Discipline advocated by Eminent Educationists* (London, 1876); James Leitch, *Practical Educationists* (Glasgow, 1876). For Leitch the line of tradition runs through Locke, Pestalozzi, Bell, Lancaster, Wilderspin, Stow and Spencer.

35. Sir Charles Reed, in *Transactions of the National Association for the Promotion of Social Science, 1861* (London, 1862) p. 71.

36. H. Holman, *English National Education: A Sketch of the Rise of Public Elementary Schools in England* (London, 1898) p. 41.

37. For twentieth-century commentaries on this controversy see Robert R. Rusk, *A History of Infant Education*, 2nd ed. (London, 1951); T. Raymont, *A History of the Education of Young Children* (London, 1937), and Harold Silver, *The Concept of Popular Education* (London, 1965).

38. Central Society of Education, *Second Publication* (London, 1838) p. 376.

39. See *Westminster Review* (Oct 1832) p. 407; (Oct 1846) pp. 220–2; (July 1847) pp. 484–5.

40. MS. copy of letter to *The Times*, Aug 1846, Pare Collection, no. 144.

41. Frederick Hill, *National Education; its Present State and Prospects* (London, 1836) p. 169.

42. 'Memoir of Robert Owen', *National Instructor*, 22 June 1850, p. 76.

43. William Lucas Sargant, *Robert Owen and His Social Philosophy* (London, 1860) p. 107.

44. *Report of the Proceedings*, p. 5.

45. Bradlaugh, *Five Dead Men*, pp. 4–5.

46. Letter from Robert Pemberton, 27 Nov 1854, Co-operative Union, no. 2305. See also no. 1083 (letter from Lord Wallscourt, 1839) and other examples in Harold Silver, *Robert Owen on Education* (London, 1969) pp. 31–2.

47. For the twenties and thirties see Silver, *The Concept of Popular Education*;

for the Owenite movement (although there is little directly on education) see
Harrison, *Robert Owen and the Owenites*; for Chartism see Brian Simon, *Studies in
the History of Education 1780–1870* (London, 1960).

48. Quoted in Ambrose G. Barker, *Henry Hetherington 1792–1849* (London,
n.d.) pp. 59–60.

49. See *The Life of Thomas Cooper written by himself* (London, 1872) p. 128.

50. *Cooper's Journal*, 15 June 1850, pp. 370–1.

51. 'Robert Owen. – A Liberal Offer', *The Co-operator*, 1870, p. 104.

52. Ibid., 15 Nov 1867, 22 Feb 1868, 21 Mar 1868, 11 Apr 1868, 11 July 1868,
7 Nov 1868, 14 Nov 1868, 28 Nov 1868, 5 Dec 1868, 19 Dec 1868, 2 May 1869,
4 Mar 1871, 27 May 1871. There is an item on Owen and agricultural co-operation
in 12 Dec 1868, and a reprint of an article from the *Beehive* on 'Robert Owen as
a Practical Man' in 30 Oct 1869. The quotations are from Travis, 5 Dec 1868.

53. H. S. Foxwell, Introduction to Anton Menger, *The Right to the Whole
Produce of Labour*, 1st English ed. (London, 1899) pp. lxxxvi, xciv.

54. Beatrice Potter, *The Co-operative Movement in Great Britain* (London, 1891)
p. 16.

55. M. E. Sadler, *Continuation Schools in England and Elsewhere* (Manchester,
1907) p. 5. See also 'The School in some of its Relations to Social Organisation
and to National Life', *Sociological Papers*, II (1906) 124, and *Owen, Lovett, Maurice,
and Toynbee* (London, 1907).

56. Harrison, *Robert Owen and the Owenites*, p. 3.

57. See J. S. Mill, *Utilitarianism* (London, 1954 ed.) pp. 52–3; *Autobiography*
(London, 1955 ed.) pp. 104–6, 141–6. Also see H. Martineau, *Autobiography*, 3
vols (London, 1877) I 232.

58. See Karl Marx, *Capital*, reprint of English ed. of 1887 (Moscow, 1954) I
483–4.

59. Friedrich Engels, *Herr Eugen Dühring's Revolution in Science*, reprint of 1934
ed. (London, n.d.) pp. 288–90. This passage occurs in the part of the book (published in German in 1878) which appeared separately in English as *Socialism:
Utopian and Scientific* in 1892.

60. See Silver, *Robert Owen on Education*, pp. 37–8.

61. See M. Beer, *A History of British Socialism* (London, 1948 ed.) p. 274.

62. See Margaret Cole, *The Story of Fabian Socialism* (London, 1961) pp. 3–5.

63. Owen Balmforth, *Huddersfield Past and Present* (Huddersfield, 1894) p. 4.

64. *D.N.B.* (1895) p. 451.

65. J. Ramsay MacDonald, *The Socialist Movement* (London, n.d. [1911]) p.
204.

66. Thomas Frost, *Forty Years' Recollections: Literary and Political* (London,
1880) p. 22.

67. Holyoake, *Life and Last Days of Robert Owen*, p. 22.

68. Joseph Clayton, *Robert Owen: Pioneer of Social Reforms* (London, 1908)
p. 13.

69. John Dewey, *Democracy and Education* (New York, 1966 ed.) pp. 266–76.

70. *Report of the Consultative Committee on the Primary School* (London, 1931)
p. 3. See also *Report of the Consultative Committee on Infant and Nursery Schools*
(London, 1933) pp. 4–5.

# CHAPTER FIVE

# Robert Owen and Radical Culture

EILEEN YEO

> Oh! may this feast increase
> The union of the heart;
> And cordial harmony and peace,
> To every one impart.
>
> As one in heart and mind,
> Joint heirs to all on earth;
> Be each to each humane and kind,
> In all our social mirth.
>
> Social Hymn, No. 74[1]

So sang the Manchester socialists on their Whitsun outing in 1839, after they had folded away their banners and flags ready for an afternoon of picnicking and dancing on the grass. On the local level, Owenite branches provided a large menu of recreational, educational and religious activities as well as a blueprint for the ideal community. These activities can usefully be seen as amounting to a culture, a social world in which members could move during their leisure hours. Neither Owenite branch life as a whole nor Robert Owen's relation to it have received much attention from historians.[2] Yet this evidence of radicals in action is just as important as the theoretical writings of a movement for an understanding of the needs and aspirations not only of the leaders but of the elusive ordinary membership. The interest of this type of study becomes more apparent if the net is spread wider to include other working-class movements between 1830 and 1850, like the Friendly Societies and Chartism. It seems a striking characteristic that they also felt it important to offer not only a programme but, to varying degrees, a way of life.

I

That the Owenite movement consistently supplied the widest range of
branch activities sprang partly from the logic of its basic ideology.
Robert Owen's vision of community held out a social and moral as
well as an economic promise. Here, not only would working families
hold real power and get the whole produce of their labour, but the
highest quality of social relationship could be reached and sustained. All
the living arrangements and social activities of the community would
be patterned to embody the basic ethical precepts of 'love thy neighbour' and 'do unto others'. In the words of Dr William King of
Brighton, the 'hard-headed' tutor of the early co-operative shopkeep-
ers, 'the spirit of Co-operation is the spirit of friendship and brotherly
love'.[3] The Owenite critique of the competitive system was an economic *and* moral attack. Competition did not only lead to poverty in
the midst of plenty, but to savaging of the relationship between man
and man, between classes and between members of the same class.

Local leaders who were captivated by the communitarian vision tried
to create a round of activities which would prepare in the widest way
for community life. Of course the basic and urgent problem was to
raise the funds which would finance a community, but the local
leadership was also attentive to the need for incorporating ethical
values into local action in order to shape the social discipline required
to maintain community life. The Equitable Exchange Bazaars and the
Grand National Consolidated Trades Union (G.N.C.T.U.) may have
attracted producer groups with less enthusiasm for community. But
between 1829 and 1834 many local societies were of a mixed occupational character and dedicated to the William King – William Thompson strategy of running a retail store, then moving into co-operative
production and, when the capital had accumulated sufficiently, using
the funds to buy land and set up a full community. Even though Owen
'looked somewhat coolly on those "Trading Associations"' and declared
'that mere buying and selling formed no part of his grand co-operative
scheme', the local leadership in places like Brighton, Birmingham and
Manchester saw the store as much more than a fund-raising device.
It was to be a new socialising centre, a veritable 'Co-operative Union
Club House', in the words of Hawkes Smith, a founder member
of the First Birmingham Co-operative Society.[4] Weekly meetings to

run the business of the store would educate members in working together, in participation and in democracy, while social conversation and mutual instruction evenings would further deepen the grasp of basic co-operative principles and reinforce the cohesion of the group. Classes for children and social festivals would bind in the whole family, not simply the male member. The solidarity of a close-knit and loving group was clearly in the mind of a local organiser like William King when he wrote: 'friendly feeling, among the members generally, must not be left to chance and accident. It must not only be recommended as an advantage; it must be enforced as an imperative and paramount duty and obligation. When a man enters a Co-operative Society, he enters upon a new relation with his fellow men. . . .'[5]

Even in the movement's early days, the shape of the local branch was a multi-purpose 'Institution', which could be housed in anything from a humble room to an entire building, where a range of economic, educational and convivial activities took place. The most ambitious socialising centre was the Institution for the Association of the Industrious Classes, established first at Gray's Inn Road in London, then moved to the Rotunda and finally to a large building in Charlotte Street. Owen was, of course, the Governor and his constant presence was felt in all aspects of its life. By August 1833 the Institution had developed its heaviest weekly schedule. The National Equitable Labour Exchange operated daily on the premises. Of the evening activities, by far the most popular and numerously attended were the fortnightly social festivals which took place on Mondays and attracted up to a thousand people. The festivals always followed the same ritual pattern, providing a stupendous mix of entertainment and 'improvement'. Doors opened at about five in the evening and the programme began with an orchestral and vocal concert which offered such popular favourites as:

> Overture, Full Band – Italian Song, Rossini – Catch, Would You Know – Song, My Lute – Glee, Aldiborontiphoscophornio – Song, Bonnie Laddie – Introduczione and Air, O Dolce Concerto – A Duetto on the Pianoforte, Mr Stevens and a Young Lady, his pupil with full Band accompaniment – Glee, My Father Land – Song, The Anchor's Weigh'd – Glee, the Chough and Crow – Finale, Organ Concerto, Stevens.[6]

Midway through the festivities, the Governor would give a 'short' address on the co-operative social system and then the dancing would begin – quadrilles, waltzes and country reels – and last until one or two in the morning.

Tuesday evenings at the Institution were reserved for lecture series by prominent speakers on scientific subjects or topics to the labour movement; thus Rowland Detroisier talked in August about 'Knowledge and Union'. Every Thursday evening the trades delegates to the Labour Exchange met. On Friday evenings the Female Employment Association held its meetings.

On Sunday morning at eleven and again in the evening at seven, Owen delivered lectures, or more accurately sermons on ethical and religious themes related to the Social System. These meetings were interspersed with musical performances and were occasionally followed by Owen baptising or 'naming' the children of members.[7] On Sunday afternoon at three, the members of the Social Community took tea together at the Institution. This interesting group attests to the persistence of communitarian efforts during the labour-exchange phase of the movement, when they supposedly disappeared. While supporting the work of the Equitable Labour Exchange, this group offered community enthusiasts the chance to become an 'incipient community' and 'form a family compact to shield and protect their members from the inroads of the irrational system of competition and contest'. The Social Community met during the week in class groups held at coffee-houses and private dwellings spread across London and joined together at the Institution again on Wednesday evenings for discussions on burning issues such as 'Are Republican Principles or those of the Social Community best calculated to promote the happiness and prosperity of a nation?'[8]

It is not quite accurate to say that between 1829 and 1834 Owenism was a militant mass movement absorbing for a brief time the many strands of working-class activity and aspiration, while after 1834 it became an exclusive classless sect building local activity around the rational religion as a preparation for community life. The religion of brotherliness was fully present in the earlier phase too, both in institutional and ideological form. The great difference was that in the pre-1834 phase, first principles about 'each for all' were embodied most widely and even extended to crucial economic activities like production, exchange and consumption. After the collapse of the exchange bazaars and the rout of the G.N.C.T.U., the area to which first principles could be applied in branch life was narrowed to leisure-time activities alone. Along with this retreat, the realisation of some first principles like 'the right to the whole produce of labour' was projected into the future community and not even partly acted upon in the local branches. But the postponement did not mean a disappearance of class consciousness or class-based strategies.[9]

Indeed it is on this very issue that significant differences can be detected between Owen and the localities about the purpose of branch culture both before and after 1834. Owen considered brotherliness and many of the London branch activities as the means of bringing about class conciliation. He continually praised the social festivals at the Institution of the Industrious Classes as multi-class occasions which would defuse class conflict and soften class contempt.[10] Despite his flirtation with the Labour Exchange, he never abandoned the upper classes as necessary agents to bring the new moral world into existence, and he always leaned towards paternal government in branch life. There is truth in Lovett's observation about 'how anti-democratic he was notwithstanding the extreme doctrines he advocated'.[11] By contrast, many of the provincial branches wanted to inculcate brotherhood in a vigorous working-class culture with the accent on collective self-help, on democracy and on participation.

The collapse of the G.N.C.T.U. brought to the surface again and intensified Owen's suspicion of independent working-class action. From then on, he stressed the need for class collaboration and guidance from men 'who have been in the practice of *directing extensive operations in the old society*'.[12] When Owen reorganised the movement into the Association of All Classes of All Nations (A.A.C.A.N.) and designated the London Institution as the headquarters of the parent branch, the structure was markedly patriarchal rather than democratic. Control was to be vested in a president of Father (Owen, of course), an Executive Council of Six, a Senior Council (composed of selected members between the ages of thirty-five and fifty) and a Junior Council (aged twenty-five to thirty-five). Provisionally all the councils were *appointed*, 'consisting of such friends as the Social Father may have been advised as the most harmonious in action one with the other'. Although laws approved by the councils and the Father were to be sent back for consideration by the membership arranged in classes, these decisions could not be vetoed but only 'suspended until their assent shall be obtained through conviction produced by sound argument and mature judgment'.[13] Significantly, working-class 'prejudice' against this undemocratic arrangement was given as the main reason for the slow growth in the London membership, which had reached only 150 by

October 1835:

> This has been owing . . . chiefly to the peculiarity of the Constitution
> of the Association, its government being a Patriarchal one; and its
> mode of electing its officers and conducting its business being differ-
> ent, therefore, to that of other Associations founded on a different
> basis, it requires some time for the people to rightly appreciate its
> claims to their approbation.[14]

Reassuring remarks had to be made that, eventually, the community
would be 'the perfection of democracy'.

By contrast, in many localities – and especially in the Manchester
area, which boasted the strongest and most continuous Owenite
grouping throughout the history of the movement[15] – branch activity
was directed towards creating a participatory and democratic radical
culture. Local personnel, traditions and conflicts must always be
explored to illuminate this kind of difference in intention. In Manchester, the first demands for independent cultural institutions arose in
the battle against the middle-class imposition of education and culture
through Mechanics' Institutes.[16] This struggle in turn can be seen as yet
another episode in a bitter history of ideological and actual class conflict
which flared up at Peterloo in 1819 and again during the agitation for
the 1832 Reform Bill.[17] The local Owenite leadership spearheaded the
struggle over the Mechanics' Institute. Several of the key local activists
had met for the first time as students in the Mechanics' Institute. They
were working men from various occupations who set up the Manchester and Salford Association for the Dissemination of Co-operative
Knowledge in 1831, who gingered into existence the local co-operative
stores and workshops and who were mostly still to be found prominent
later on in the ranks of the Rational Religionists. They shared a deep and
passionate concern for the 'moral and intellectual' dimensions of life and
for the creation of a truly emancipated working-class consciousness.
Once in the Owenite movement, they worked together on a series of
educational experiments which sought to make a relevant education
more available to working families. These included a Scientific Society
which met at night and a Utility Society, attached to the First Salford
Co-operative Society, which provided a Sunday school for the children
as well as evening classes.[18] Their attack on the Mechanics' Institute
culminated in 1829 with the foundation of a breakaway 'New Mechanics' Institution'.

Their critique of the Mechanics' Institute was fundamental and comprehensive. It was aimed partly at the autocratic government of the Institute, which was controlled by a board of directors elected entirely by the honorary members, those upper-class patrons who paid annual or life subscriptions. Democratisation was demanded: elected representatives from the working-class student body to sit on the board.[19] But it was also aimed at the content of the education, at the excessively individualistic and technological orientation of the courses. Instead of equipping students with the scientific knowledge which would enable them to 'get on' in their jobs as rational competitive atoms, attention should be focused on the crucial social and moral questions affecting the whole community. In the words of Rowland Detroisier, president of the New Mechanics' Institution and spokesman for the rebels:

> the great end of Public Institutions established for the purposes of education, ought to be the dissemination of those principles, on the knowledge and practice of which depend the obtaining and securing of '*the greatest happiness to the greatest number*', as well as the enabling of the students to fulfil those particular requirements which are connected with the various trades and professions. We have seen that a knowledge of those sciences which are usually esteemed essential for a trading population, may be obtained by becoming a member of Mechanics' Institutions; but there are two subjects which have hitherto been considered as unnecessary to be attended to in the education of the people at these justly popular seminaries – Moral and Political Philosophy: yet who so hardy as to deny their importance to man?[29]

In the aftermath of the secession, plans were mooted for more ambitious institutions to serve as independent centres for working-class cultural life. A Mechanics' Hall of Science, endorsed by the Owenite leadership and by John Doherty, the leader of the Spinners' Union, was partly funded from the sale of £1 shares but never actually built.[21] Later the Operative Carpenters and Joiners erected their Carpenter's Hall at a cost of £4500. Leased by the Owenites in 1838 and then taken over by the Chartists in 1842, it was used throughout the period for any large meeting in a radical cause.[22]

Given the local confrontation with culture provided *for* the people by the middle class, it is not surprising that the Manchester Owenites should have jealously safeguarded working-class democracy and participation in their local branches, in contrast to and sometimes in polite opposition to Robert Owen in London. By 1833 the local societies engaged in retail trade or manufacture had broken up and the Owenite activists grouped themselves mainly around the social institution and school which had developed out of the First Salford Co-operative Society. The school was run on remarkably democratic lines. All decisions about administration or curriculum were taken by the teachers (working men who gave their services gratuitously) and the most advanced class, while the other classes had a right to petition for any demand. And they had some weight. When the teachers resolved to ask Parliament for a subsidy, the scholars 'petitioned the masters to abandon their resolution, as it might subject the school to some tyrannical restraint. At the suggestion of the scholars, the masters cancelled their resolution.' There was little social distinction between students and their teachers, the whole school taking tea together on Sunday afternoons, the students forming a 'scientific school amongst themselves', to train as teachers and propagandists.[23] Predictably when the Salford group enrolled in the A.A.C.A.N. they politely refused to adopt Robert Owen's patriarchal constitution for local branches. Instead of placing control in the hands of two elders who took orders direct from London, they elected a board of management consisting of a governor, two secretaries and a council of twelve, one-half of whose members would be up for election every three months.[24] It was Manchester, not Owen, which charted the direction that the movement eventually took; as the movement increased its working-class membership, so its structure on the local and national levels become democratised, depending on elected officers and councils.[25]

A curious and almost comic incident highlighted the difference in strategic approach between Owen and his Manchester – Salford followers. Owen's trip to Manchester in September 1836 turned into a bizarre crusade to win the upper classes to his movement. He and Joseph Smith, the master plumber and glazier, made a point of attending a local charity ball in fancy dress. Representing the 'High Priest of the New Moral World', Smith was clad in a flowing white satin surplice, his 'beautiful' beard and mustachios capped with a white satin head-dress, and he carried a white satin banner inscribed in gold lettering with three great truths about the formation of character. Owen, dressed as Diogenes, gave out notices informing the merrymakers, 'you are on the wrong road to happiness', and advising them to consult the priest. Owen was highly pleased with the night's work: 'our object was thus obtained, far beyond our expectation, and the

fifty or sixty thousand pounds expended at this festival, have thus been
unintentionally devoted to laying the foundation among the gay and
wealthy for a grand change in the System of Society'.[26]

On the same trip, Owen made contact with the former millowner
and philanthropist Joseph Brotherton, M.P., and naïvely began to
think that success in Manchester would hinge entirely on his conversion. Owen warned local socialists that he would support their plan
for a community fund only if they made Brotherton and John Fielden,
M.P., their treasurers.[27] Both Owen's antics and his advice were politely
ignored by the local branches.[28]

The branches doggedly pursued the path of collective working-class
self-help as they moved into the Universal Community Society of
Rational Religionists (U.C.S.R.R.) phase of the movement.[29] By 1839
and 1840 when clerical opposition had reached a vicious climax and all
efforts were made to deny the Owenites places to meet, and when the
movement was once more finding it easy to attract working-class
support – it must be remembered that the Chartists were reeling under
the multiple blows of 1839, the rejection of the National Petition, the
Bull Ring riots, the abortive Newport rising and the imprisonment of
many leaders – the socialists turned again to the building of socialising
centres, this time in the form of halls of science, to be financed and
controlled by working men.[30] With the exception of Liverpool, the
standard practice was to issue shares of £1, which could be paid up
in weekly instalments, thus putting them within the reach of working
men.[31] The building was to be managed by elected committees of the
shareholders.

Although intended primarily to provide the local socialists with a
home for their branch activities and a base for district missionary and
propaganda work, the halls of science did in theory and practice have
more oecumenical aims. With little variation, the prospectuses would
open with an observation

> that the working classes in this city cannot be accommodated with
> any commodious place of meeting without it is for such purposes
> as the classes above them approve of; we propose to raise an Institu-
> tion that shall be open to all parties. The want of large public rooms
> wherein the working class might assemble with their wives and
> children, to acquire and communicate useful knowledge, and where-
> in they might have innocent recreation and rational amusement at
> so trifling an expense as to be within the means of the poorest when
> employed, has been long felt and is generally admitted.[32]

Even if the Chartists had their own local rooms, they often used Owen-ite halls for large meetings, lectures and convivial functions.[33] The kind of common culture that the Owenites were after was also to be found in the Hyde Working Man's Institution, which was not owned by the socialists but used for their branch activity. A glowing Owenite report noted how

the trustees of the building engaged the Rev. Mr Hill, editor of the *Northern Star*, to give two lectures on Sunday, the 8th and we got Mr J. Smith, of Salford to lecture in the evening; the three lectures seemed to give general satisfaction to very large audiences, composed of Chartists, Methodists, Socialists, and many of the supporters of the Rev. J. R. Stephens. A tea party was got up on the Monday by the trustees, and about 300 partook of the refreshing beverage, and were afterwards entertained with several speeches recommending peace and goodwill to all, and lauding their champion Stephens. The trustees had also announced a concert for the Tuesday evening, which, at their request, was conducted by the members of our Branch, very much to the satisfaction of an audience of nearly 300, so much so, that at the conclusion it was agreed that the amusements should be repeated on the Wednesday evening, when a still larger number attended, and were so highly satisfied that it was determined that similar festivals should be held monthly. Thus, for the first time, have the working class of Hyde had the opportunity of enjoying rational amusement in large numbers, in their own building, and of bringing together many who have hitherto held aloof from us.[34]

On the local level, the various working-class protest movements were never hermetically sealed off from each other; no matter how the national leadership and some social missionaries might preach against the Chartist strategy, on the local level the ordinary membership of both movements often overlapped.[35] Less frequently, Owenite halls were also used by working-class teetotal groups and even by Non-conformist congregations for functions like Sunday School recitals.[36]

Before examining the content of the Owenite culture available in these institutions, it might be as well to try to fix the social composition of the membership at least in the large urban branches. If we are arguing that the nature of branch activity gives an important clue to the needs of the rank and file, then it is necessary to attempt some analysis of who that rank and file was. This is the hardest job of all. Once out of the labour-exchange and G.N.C.T.U. phases of the movement, there are no convenient lists of goods shipped to the bazaars or lodge affiliations to identify even the occupations of ordinary members. Only by collecting odd references in the *New Moral World* to the names and jobs of shareholders or individual members, and putting these together with the financial constraints imposed by membership and entrance fees, can some sort of picture be built up.

By and large, the fully participating shareholder members would be a mixed occupational group drawn from the best-paid strata of the local working class. The report of a Manchester shareholders' tea party and ball, attended by over 400 people, proudly announced that

> a working man paid down £20 as his instalment on sixty new shares, having already paid up forty, making 100, the earnings of several years of hard and honest industry. . . . It is worthy of remark that the large body of individuals who compose the shareholders of this Hall, are working men, principally foremen and the most skilful operatives in their respective departments of the trades of this locality, such as machinists, engravers, founders, millwrights, smiths, carpenters, dyers, calico-printers, etc.[37]

Besides his weekly instalment on shares, the member would have to pay a subscription to his local branch (the amount left to local discretion) and a penny contribution to the general fund which went to the Central Board; a weekly contribution of at least 7*d.* was required for the community fund (when his total had reached £50, he was eligible for a place at Queenwood). These were steep requirements and sometimes members defaulted on their community payments in order to meet their obligations on shares.[38]

During the earlier period, the entrance fees at Robert Owen's various London Institutions had been fairly high. If a man, his wife and family wished to attend all the Sunday meetings, evening lectures and social festivals, the annual subscription, which was the cheapest way to cover costs, would be £8 a year or over 3*s.* a week.[39] This was, of course, far beyond the means of any of the lower-paid workers in the sweated or dishonourable branches of metropolitan trades like tailoring, shoemaking, carpentry or cabinet-making. In the localities, charges were lower. At the Sheffield Hall of Science, there was no charge for Sunday lectures but teas cost 6*d.*; admission to the Monday dancing class was 3*d.*, while 1*d.* was charged for the Wednesday and Saturday cheap concerts. Weekly evening classes were available at 1*s.* 6*d.* per quarter and a day school for children at 4*d.* or 6*d.* a week depending on age.[40]

The major social festivals, with dancing and refreshments included, were usually priced at 1s. for ladies and 1s. 6d. for gentlemen, 6d. less than in the metropolis. It is clear that many people did not partake of the whole Owenite menu and that the social festivals and lively religious debates were the most popular events, always attracting much larger attendances than the number of paid-up members.[41] Although the odd function was available to any working family, the fully participating members would have to come from the upper artisan bracket. Rather than being less interesting, it is *more* interesting that people doing comparatively well should find their most comfortable social identity in the ranks of a protest movement.

II

Owenite branches claimed to offer an alternative culture. As already indicated, branches often took shape in opposition to Mechanics' Institutes and repudiated the culture imposed by the middle class which stressed individual competitiveness and job productivity and was emphatically male-centred. But equally, branch culture was juxtaposed to another mode of urban working-class leisure activity centred around the pub. Drunkenness, although seen as a misguided escape from social misery, was attacked for being destructive of the gentle display of brotherly love. A Huddersfield socialist, returning home from a Christmas festival,

> could not help contrasting the sobriety and civil manners of those who had participated in our 'feast of reason' with the brutal language and bullying conduct of the unfortunates who were reeling from the public houses; and when I considered that those who were now so sober and courteous might, but for the circumstance of our festival, have been similarly situated to the individuals around me, the good moral results of these kind of institutions, and the general want of them appeared to me clear and self-evident as light amid darkness.[42]

Sobriety was not esteemed in a middle-class way as an instrument of capitalist labour discipline but as a prerequisite for the loving group 'discipline' needed to sustain socialist community life.

Increasingly after 1835, the Owenites saw themselves as an alternative to all denominational religion. It is not necessary to describe the many flanks of the attack on other religions, Owen seeing the churches as the main support for individualism, competitiveness, divisiveness and private property in the old immoral world, provincial Owenites echoing this message. What was to be substituted was a religion in the control of ordinary members, a religion of brotherliness and joy, to be supported by a generous ration of festive entertainments which would banish the gloom-and-doom atmosphere generated by the exponents of original sin. The London A.1 branch boasted that 'we truly look as if we had been in company with the sun of righteousness', while the Methodists next door 'look as if they had been facing a nor'wester, they are so sour and uncomfortable like'.[43]

More positively, Owenite culture was intended to inculcate brotherly communal feeling. All the social festivals were supposed to be pleasant 'classrooms' for the practice of the sedate disciplines of friendliness, politeness and consideration. In this socialising crusade, even the smallest details came under scrutiny, sometimes resulting in what some would regard as a confusion between manners and morals. The Stockport branch boasted that in its Saturday amusement class

> a spirit of neat cleanliness and order is evidently on the increase. Some used formerly to come to these meetings in their greasy jackets and working gowns; and it was not looked on as anything extra-ordinary, even at their festivals, for individuals to run from their seats and jostle each other to obtain what the Old World's teaching made them believe was a preferable place, viz. the head or top of the dance, which could only make them objects of *envy* to others who had been trained equally erroneous with themselves, for a little reflection mixed with social feelings will shew that in order that *all* may enjoy happiness it is necessary each would endeavour to give up as much of their Old World feelings as possible on such occasions.[44]

Since total group solidarity and harmony was the aim, the culture was family-oriented and placed great emphasis on the equality and participation of women. Undoubtedly one element of Owenite attractiveness was the provision of activities for women and children, who were not catered for either by the Mechanics' Institute or by the working-class-generated Friendly Society movement – women especially. In a society where the middle-class wife was little more than a domestic ornament, a decorative piece of personal property, the working-class socialists opened their classes to women, encouraged women to become lecturers in the cause[45] and admitted women on an equal footing to traditionally masculine social rituals like the ceremonial dinner. The militant feminist 'Kate', having attended a dinner at the London John Street Institution, lavished praise on the 'arrangements that were provided for the appearance of both sexes at the dinner table, as equal and rational beings; instead of as is usually the case, excluding the females, or permitting them the high privilege of looking on and watching the proceedings from a seat in the gallery'.[46]

To instil the desired communal discipline, the movement attempted to bring as many leisure pursuits as possible within its orbit, especially where this meant wresting control from the church or the pub. Its manifold activities and ceremonials, at the peak of U.C.S.R.R. popularity, did amount to one collective working-class attempt to establish control over social life and rites of passage. For purposes of analysis, branch activities can be divided into a weekly cycle, an annual cycle and a life cycle.

The weekly cycle was an amplified version of Robert Owen's earlier schedule at the Institution of the Industrious Classes, though of course now excluding the economic activities. As soon as funds would allow, local branches mounted classes in academic subjects for adults and children and put on mid-week evening lectures of scientific or Owenite ideologist interest. But the highlights of the weekly routine were the weekend functions, which in their turn generated the need for supporting weekday activities. Saturday, rather than Monday as had been the London practice, became the night for the main festival, either a musical concert or a concert with dancing. The advantage of adapting to the working man's customary weekly routine was strongly urged by provincial Owenites, both on moral and financial grounds; Isaac Ironside of Sheffield wrote:

> I strongly recommend the Saturday evening concerts to all our branches – on that evening the working man has a little money, and the socialist comes to the room to buy his *New Moral World*, and to chat a little; when he leaves he goes, perhaps, to the public house, and returns to his home certainly no better, perhaps worse, for what he has had there. Open the room, get coffee ready for them at a reasonable price; try the song and glee, etc., let a few *New Moral Worlds* be laid for them to read; and, mark this fact, by this means more will be sold.[47]

Every Sunday, to the indignation of local clergymen, two lecture meetings which were really Owenite religious services were held in the

morning and evening, often interspersed with an afternoon tea party.
These were built around a sermon delivered by a local lecturer or
social missionary and involved frequent audience participation in the
singing of social hymns. Again, local Owenites quite deliberately
adapted what they considered useful elements from the enemy's
armoury; a correspondent from the Salford branch, which compiled
the first slim book of social hymns, wrote:

> Congregational singing cannot be too strongly recommended, its
> influence having been found greatly beneficial, as most individuals
> have, from infancy, been trained under religious tuition, they have
> been accustomed to the pleasing sensation which music generates.
>   To be confined Sunday after Sunday, morning and evening, to
> listen to lectures, however important or philosophical, is, to persons
> of even unlightened minds, dull and monotonous: the want of
> variety, which is the zest of existence is experienced; a fact which
> the religions of almost all sects seem to have discovered, and which
> they have endeavoured to avoid by alternations of prayer, singing
> and preaching. For these reasons, therefore, and the delight which
> the most rational and reflective feel, when the melody of music is
> mixed with the benevolent and philosophical sentiments of the most
> sympathetic and enlightened of our species, congregational singing
> should be encouraged. When our finest affections, mingled with
> softest and sweetest vibrations shall carry man without his narrow
> self, and point out the means by which he may make a perfect
> diapason of all the jarring and conflicting interests of the great family
> of man.[48]

The music for these functions was self-supplied, branches enthusiastically training up their own bands, choirs and 'artistes'. The tremendous popularity of musical events created the need for weekday
training classes and practice sessions which became part of the ordinary
routine. Sheffield, for example, held a dancing class on Monday nights
which was so well attended that the admission price was raised above
3d 'to thin the numbers'.[49] Here was the origin of those proud bands
and choirs so omnipresent in the later nineteenth-century Co-operative
movement, already at this period displaying a great fondness of the
'Grand Hallelujah Chorus' which had to be repeated twice at a Manchester festival by audience demand.[50] Indeed the musical fare was so
greedily devoured that it is quite likely the appeal of Owenite culture
for some attenders was simply its entertainment value; they probably
came along for a good time and had little appetite for the more serious

'theological' and protest items on the menu. Nevertheless the local branch did provide the setting and the incentive for more committed members to develop artistic talents which otherwise might have lain undiscovered; the setting of the movement made it possible for culture of the sociological kind and culture of the artistic sort to be thoroughly interdependent. William Tarr, a Manchester carpenter and joiner and local lecturer, busied himself making musical instruments and arranging 'many sets of quadrilles, Cotillions, Country Dances, and Waltzes, for four, five, six or more performers, correctly written copies of which he would be glad to furnish to any of the branches'. Poetry and hymns were written for the movement; artisans with a flair for the plastic arts contributed paintings, models and stained-glass windows to the local institutions. Even cabinet-maker William Lovett, who later repented his Owenism, was inspired to make 'a model of an industrial village', devoting months of loving work to the project during a period of unemployment.[51]

The annual cycle had two components: the inverted Christian year and the specifically Owenite festivals. Again the traditional ceremonial year was adapted to socialist purposes. 'Major' festivals were held on Christmas Day, New Year's Day, during Lent, on Good Friday, Easter Sunday and during Whitsun. Wherever possible the most solemn of the Christian holy days were turned into occasions for maximum 'hilarity'. Robert Owen's London Institution put on a series of concerts and balls during Lent while, several years later, London Branch 16 was continuing the blasphemous tradition with the added attraction of scientific entertainments:

on Friday last – the Good Friday of the Christian world – we had an excellent social tea party, about 280 persons were present. . . . The philosophical experiments, under the management of Mr Thorne, were of a superior description. Amongst some of the experiments were oxy-hydrogen and Bude lights, the last new invention of Mr Gurney for lighthouses; decomposition of various chemical compounds, as sugar, potass, etc.; and with a good electrical machine we were enabled to electrify nearly all present at one time. Besides other experiments, a model of a Montgolfier balloon ascended in the hall twice during the evening, and at the close was committed *ad nubes*. The nitrous oxide, or laughing gas, exerted its full powers on this occasion, delighting all by its singular effects. Between the leading experiments the lively dance was indulged in, thus at once blending the acme of mental and physical enjoyments.[52]

Attempts were made to invest customary holidays with Owenite commemorative significance, so that several local branches scheduled their annual anniversary festivals for Christmas Day,[53] while Whitsun junketings were turned into celebrations of Robert Owen's birthday.

Internal to the movement, nearly every branch held monthly and quarterly festivals, an anniversary festival and periodic Sunday-school 'recitations'.[54] The laying of a cornerstone for a new hall of science and the opening of the building when completed were highlights of the annual cycle between 1839 and 1841 sometimes occasioning festivals spread over several days.[55] In the ordinary annual calendar the most elaborate festivals were the rural excursions held as a Whitsun-*cum*-Owen-birthday celebration. The following Manchester account could as easily have been given by the London socialists:

Early in the morning our friends were all on the qui-vive, and at six o'clock many were on the ground waiting for our country brethren, who by seven o'clock came in great numbers, after which they proceeded to the boats. One large boat was filled with the children of the school, with their teachers and the officers of the associations; and by eight o'clock three or four boats were loaded with our friends. . . . We had a pleasant passage, and, at our landing, we formed into procession with our flowing banners and flags. After entering the park, our friends distributed themselves in various parts to partake of their refreshments. A broad even spot in front of the mansion was chosen whereon to commence our festivities. The trumpet was sounded, and the friends collected around our standard, which was a splendid green flag, near which were placed the musicians. There could not be less than one thousand persons then assembled. After forming a large circle, we commenced by singing the first festival song, 'O may this feast increase the union of the heart', which was sung with high spirit and delight. A short address was then given and immediately afterwards the dancing began, and hundreds mingled in the mazes of the whirling dance, with such manifestations of innocent joyousness, as might have thawed the heart of the coldest misanthrope. At the termination of the dance, the friends distributed themselves among the sylvan scenes around, and commenced a variety of rural and cheerful games, whilst others threaded their way among the trees, to view the varied beauties of the park. . . . We left the park about four o'clock, and proceeded homeward, where we arrived soon after seven. We then went to the hall, which was prepared for our reception, and here we congregated to upwards of 800 persons. Our friends forgot the previous exertions of the day, they felt fresh vigour, and entered into the various amusements with high spirits and delight. Mr Charles Junius Haslam had prepared a quantity of laughing gas, which was partly used in the park, and the remainder at night, which gave us some exhibitions, to the great pleasure of our young folks. The festivities terminated at twelve o'clock, and our friends returned home well satisfied with their whole day's amusements. The night was beautiful and calm, and the bright shining moon lit the paths of many of our branch friends, who had to return home at the close of our holiday ten or twelve miles, wearied yet delighted, and anticipating the return of similar enjoyments next Whitsuntide.[56]

Besides providing weekly and annual activities to occupy the hours outside work, the branches catered for the life cycle, taking out of the hands of the church the crucial rites of passage: baptism, marriage and death. Owen of course started the practice of baptising or naming infants in London, but by the later 1830s baptisms were being performed by any social missionary or local lecturer, male or female, thus abolishing the mystique as well as the cost of the ceremony. The naming of an infant, the public recognition of his belonging to the socialist group, would be the occasion for a homily on the 'ductility of human nature', or for the expression of a wish that he might grow up to take his place in a community. Children were often given the names of luminaries of the movement; an orphan went for several years without a name until his guardian was able to call him after the deceased 'Julian Hibbert'; a brother and sister was called 'Frances Wright' and 'Owen' Clark.[57]

The most perplexing issue is that of branch behaviour on marriage. Of course it was Owen's teaching about marriage which raised clerical tempers to fever pitch and provoked hysterical outbursts about the base threat to the very foundations of civilised society. In fact, Owen's prescriptions would not jar the modern ear. In the interests of communal harmony, he called for more flexibility in marriage and divorce and more specifically for a cheap marriage ceremony outside clerical jurisdiction, to be followed by a year of probation which would end with a simple divorce by mutual consent if the couple found themselves incompatible, or a further six-month trial period if only one party wished to dissolve the union.[58] How much of this procedure was ever followed in the branches is the tantalising question. The role of the minister was certainly abolished. From the early days, the Owenite press spotlighted any examples of unorthodox marriage practice and were especially favourable to the Lawrence Street chapel, a Southcottian

foundation in Birmingham, where couples simply married themselves.[59] After 1840, local branches, which were already registered as
places of worship to avoid the interruption of Sunday meetings under
the still operative provisions of the Six Acts, also got themselves licensed
'for the solemnization of marriages under the new Marriage Act'.[60]
Marriages were actually performed in the Sheffield and London A.1
branches among others, using the civil ceremony. The expropriation of
the priest did not mean a decrease of ritual; in London, the branch
organist and choir performed several numbers and, after the branch
president had administered the vows, a local lecturer provided an
apposite sermon on the socialist recipe for marital bliss. Then the
company sat down to a wedding breakfast.[61]

But whether the divorce procedure was ever used is a thornier
question. The constant, urgent warnings that this must be reserved
for community, where the children could be taken into proper
care,[62] make one suspect that where there was smoke there may have
been fire. Such admonitions may have been needed not only to placate
clerical critics but to curb individual Owenite enthusiasts. Occasional
problematic pieces of evidence suggest this may have been the case. In
1839, Mary Ann Bennett, dressmaker, applied to the Manchester
magistrates for assistance, claiming that John Joyes (!), a local engineer,
had 'represented himself as a member of Mr Owen's "Social Community", and importuned her to become his "partner" under that
system, assuring her at the same time, that the greatest possible happiness
would be the result'. He abandoned her after the birth of a baby. She
claimed that a 'sort of' marriage ceremony was performed by Owen at
the Carpenter's Hall which included a proviso that 'if either of them
found anybody else who would do them greater good, and with whom
they could be more happy to separate and have them'. Of course the
local Owenites roundly denied this slander, pointing out that her story
was set seven months before the socialists began using the Carpenter's
Hall.[63] But even if her memory for dates was hazy, and even if it is
certain that Owen never performed such a marriage service, it is
possible that he or some other lecturer did talk on the new system of
marriage and that Joyes then put it into practice on his own initiative.

Finally, Owenite branches provided dignified and impressive funerals. In an earlier phase of the movement, the G.N.C.T.U. followed the
practice of trades unions and Friendly Societies in catering for the all-
important event, death. The lavish ritual available even to the simple
working man was considered a trump recruiting card. The funeral of

a Barnsley linen weaver, organised by the Union, boasted a procession of 1500 lodge brothers wearing rosettes. It was led by a band and accompanied by a choir singing hymns and stretched for a full quarter of a mile. Witnessing the spectacle, ' "Yes", some were heard to say, " if this be union, I will be made a member next Saturday night"; and some that had got the name of being black did promise to become white.'[64] With equal solemnity, though on a smaller scale, the U.C.S.R.R. branches buried their comrades. The funeral for Leeds member John Smith, who had remained steadfast in the cause despite the efforts of the 'so-called religious' to 'surround his dying bed', began with a procession to the municipal (not a church) cemetery. Relatives followed the coffin and behind them came the female socialists, followed in turn by the local officials and by 'a numerous and respectable body of male members'. The local missionary Fleming preached a sermon at the graveside and social hymns were sung. Vicious opposition to these funerals from the local clergy simply redoubled the determination of the working-class socialists to take the life cycle into their own hands: 'let the Socialists name their own children, bury their own dead, and celebrate in their own Halls their own marriages, according to the laws of the land'.[65]

III

When the Owenite movement is placed alongside other working-class movements of the time, its cultural provision does not appear unique or 'cranky' but rather as an exceptionally pure current in the mainstream. It seems a striking fact that some working-class movements between 1830 and 1850, and especially protest movements, aggregated to themselves leisure activities along with the ritual of religion and the life cycle even if these did not seem directly relevant to their professed aims and objects. The Friendly Societies, which were allowed to write only their insurance benefits into their rule-books, offered a rich annual calendar of monthly club nights, secretive initiation ceremonies and lavish anniversary feasts, often held on tradition holidays like Christmas, Good Friday and during Whitsun.[66] By providing impressive funerals, even if an ordained minister actually performed the burial service, the Friendly Societies went a long way towards appropriating this crucial right of passage.

Chartism, supposedly a mass action movement dedicated to winning the Six Points from Parliament, developed, with increasing deliberateness, a panoply of local activities resembling the Owenite. These appear to have little relevance to Chartist aims if the aims are defined too narrowly in terms of political pressure. After the multiple catastrophes of 1839, the movement was primarily concerned to build up firm local groupings within a national structure. To leaders supposedly as far apart as O'Connor and Lovett, the priority became to create a dependable and vigorous radical culture at the grass roots which would sustain agitation over the long term and prepare Chartists to make the most socially beneficial use of the Charter once it was won.[67] It is not accurate to say that the increasing development of social activities corresponded neatly with the 'failure' of political tactics. By 1842 when the movement was again gearing itself up for an assault, by petition, upon Parliament, a weekly, annual and life cycle was evident in many local branches and many of the activists were saturated with Chartist religious ceremonial. When mass demonstrations were outlawed in 1839, the Chartists began holding mass weekly camp meetings on the Primitive Methodist pattern but using original democratic hymns and preaching democratic sermons which were often laced with a strong anti-clericalism. The camp meeting became a standard item in the Chartist repertoire and was especially frequent during the years of maximum political agitation, 1839, 1842 and 1848.[68] By 1842, the local branches of the National Charter Association ranged from those holding just the weekly 'class' meeting for a political lecture or discussion to the Leicester Shakespearian Association with its remarkably full menu of evening classes and Sunday meetings punctuated with Chartist hymns which were composed by members of the branch.[69] Increasingly branches laid on evening classes, reading rooms and Sunday schools.[70] And, as local authorities increasing denied them the use of public rooms, the Chartists took to building their own halls which could accommodate political, educational and recreational activities, financing them like the Owenites from £1 shares.

One of the most interesting developments from 1839 onwards was the formation of a Chartist church in several of the branches which not only held Sunday services but performed baptisms, marriages, funerals and even communion.[71] Indeed, to some members like Rev. W. Hill, the editor of the *Northern Star*, who held 'the principles of Chartism to be Religious principles and every Chartist Society to be consequently a Religious Society', it seemed only logical for branches to register as religous bodies like the socialists and get the political protection such registration afforded.[72] Where the Chartist church was not formally present, branches still held funerals and the movement supplied infants with names, one poor tyke having to support the heavy burden of 'Feargus O'Connor, Frost, O'Brien, McDouall, Hunt, Taylor'.[73]

The Chartists held their own Christmas, New Year and Easter celebrations, which followed very much the same pattern as the Owenite with tea drinking, concerts (the music supplied by branch bands and choruses) and dancing. The anti-clerical note was often struck. Harney's address to the Leicester Chartists during the Christmas season was 'peculiarly felicitous in describing the cant of priests: roars of laughter interrupted parts of his lecture wherein the farcical pathos of parsons was depictured'.[74] Even Owen's birthday party had its analogue in Chartist celebrations of Henry Hunt's birthday.[75]

This tendency of working-class movements to cater for social needs in a broad way can be fitted into the scenario of rapid social change in the early nineteenth century, but only if the staging is done with care. Too much use has been made of the 'functional' language of sociology, which talks about the 'adjustments' made by people suffering 'disorientation' at a time of 'economic and social dislocation'; too little about positive and creative efforts to build an alternative society. Harrison uses the sociological concept of a sect to make sense of Owenite branch culture as a whole after 1834. But he falls into the functionalist trap when he says that 'the function of Owenism as a sect in relation to the needs of individuals was not markedly different from similar millenarian groups' and even goes so far as to insist that the Owenite working man who sang his social hymns in the Manchester Hall of Science was striving for much the same goals as his neighbour who sang Wesley's hymns in the Primitive Methodist chapel or listened to the prophet in the Southcottians' meeting place at Ashton'.[76] For Harrison, the sect performs a role of de facto adjustment because it is a response to rapid social change based on 'withdrawal and redemption'. Of course protest movements offered the basis for community and a satisfying social identity for their members. In the cities they may have facilitated new communities, as in the case of Owenite branches drawing members from different neighbourhoods and various trades; though often in villages with a continuous radical tradition, like Samuel Bamford's Middleton, radical allegiance seemed to cement an already existing community.

But it must be remembered that sects are not simply to be defined

by characteristics but also by context; in certain conditions, groups
with sect-like characteristics do not play an adjustive or escapist role.
The protest movements did not aim to be nor were they adjustive. In
the early nineteenth century, although the mould of capitalist industrial
society was setting fast, there was a widespread and heightened feeling
of the plasticity of social institutions; after all, if social change had
taken place so fast in an intolerable direction, why not guide change
along a more beneficial road just as quickly? The Chartists and Owenites did not feel that they were retreating from a capitalist house which
had already been built, locked and shuttered, they felt that they were
creating alternative and competing cultures in a still-molten situation.
Certainly their goals were not other-wordly. Their cultures were not
only ways of life in the here and now but harnessed to aspirations for
real structural change through communities or by means of political
power and necessary to sustain the proper quality of life after these
bigger changes had been achieved. Either the notion of the social
role of sects must be broadened to include constructive attempts to
change society, or the concept of 'sect' ought to be dropped altogether.

At the very least, the Friendly Societies provided a social ritual of
fellowship and conviviality where middle-class culture provided nothing. At most, Owenism and Chartism offered a more total cultural
*alternative* in the areas amenable to their control, that is leisure pursuits
outside working hours. The very comprehensiveness of their social
provision revealed how deep and pervasive was the dissatisfaction with
emerging capitalist industrial society. Not only was there protest
against working conditions but, and even the well-paid Owenite
shareholders could feel this keenly, a revulsion against the very quality
of social life – ranging from personal conduct to community relationships to man's relation with his Maker. The protest movements aimed
to build an alternative culture on a foundation of values – equality,
brotherhood, collective self-help and democratic control – which were
different from those of middle-class culture. We have already seen that
the emphasis on collective self-help and democratic control was the
local Owenite contribution to the movement, not Owen's. The
Friendly Societies, which were not a protest movement, none the less
fought to preserve the utmost democratic control compatible with a
national organisation, even though they had to surrender primitive
democracy as the Affiliated Orders spread across a national map.[77]

Not only did the Chartists aim for a representative democracy, they
practised one within the National Charter Association, although they

had to step gingerly to avoid the traps laid by the Corresponding Societies Act of 1799.[78] The primitive democracy of the Chartist church is extremely interesting. In Glasgow, where the basic precept was that 'all men are equal', there was no minister: rather the congregation took on the offices of chairman and vice-chairman in rotation and conducted services, performed marriages, baptisms and communion.[79] Chartist religion, both as expressed in the formal Chartist church and in the hymns sung at camp meetings and weekly classes, was profoundly democratic and egalitarian. Their God was a God of Justice who had endowed men with social and political rights:

> All men are equal in His sight, –
> The bond, the free, the black, the white; –
> He made them all, – them freedom gave –
> *He* made the man, – *Man made the Slave!*[80]

Their Christ was a working man who had been crucified on the social rack like they; their mission to win back the rights which God had given but which the rich and powerful, the priesthood among them, had taken away:

> Rouse them from their silken slumbers,
> Trouble them amidst their pride:
> Swell your ranks, augment your numbers,
> Spread the Charter far and wide
> Truth is with us,
> God himself is on our side.[81]

The Chartist and Owenite movements gave their members the chance to experience an alternative way of life in their own lifetimes. But they did more; they left a proud legacy to later working-class movements. The idea that the working class, through its own collective efforts, could build a culture which allowed for active participation and control in social as well as economic life persisted through the mid-century in the Co-operative movement. With the later nineteenth-century socialist revival, it flowered vigorously again in the Blatchford Clarion movement and in the local branches of the S.D.F. and I.L.P. It is a proud and peculiarly indigenous tradition that British socialism and radicalism have been concerned not only with structural shifts of economic and political power but with the very quality and excellence of all dimensions of human existence. It is a tradition we should not forget, for the struggle still remains to be won.

## NOTES AND REFERENCES

1. *Social Bible . . . Social Hymns for the Use of the Friends of the Rational System of Society* (Manchester, 1835) p. 56.
2. The early Owenite movement has mainly been studied to the extent that it contributed to the development of the modern trade union and Co-operative movements, with a heavy concentration on the period 1829 to 1834. G. D. H. Cole's work is, of course, central here – *A Short History of the British Working Class Movement*, 1 (London, 1925) and *A Century of Co-operation* (Manchester, 1944). Another well-worked vein has been the Owenite contribution to Marxist ideology, explored in M. Beer, *A History of British Socialism* (London, 1929). More recently, Owenite educational efforts have figured in works like B. Simon, *Studies in the History of Education 1780–1870* (London, 1960). But these tend to rip education out of a more organic cultural matrix and give a distorted and partial idea of Owenite provision and aspirations. E. P. Thompson, in *The Making of the English Working Class* (London, 1963), does focus on the creation of a radical culture during the 1820s but narrows his definition of culture to ideology and literary output, concentrating on the fight for the unstamped press. Only J. F. C. Harrison's *Robert Owen and the Owenites in England and America* (London, 1969), which supersedes much previous work, takes account of Owenite activities in the round, especially during the Universal Community Society of Rational Religionists phase of the movement. Harrison is very keen to use sociological work on sects and sect formation. But in depicting Owenism as a secular millenarian sect, he detaches the Owenite movement too sharply from other social and protest movements of the time and brings in misleading (and, to my mind, distasteful) sociological descriptions about 'adjustment' to times of severe social dislocation through 'withdrawal'. This sort of language trivialises widespread and constructive attempts at culture building which left an important legacy for later working-class movements. Moreover, Harrison gives little sense of the actual content of the culture or the social terrain where it took root and makes too little distinction between Owen, the local leadership and the rank and file.
3. *Brighton Co-operator*, 1 Nov 1828; [W. Pare], *An Address delivered at the Opening of the Birmingham Co-operative Society, November 17, 1828* (Birmingham, n.d.) pp. 20–1.
4. W. Lovett, *The Life and Struggles of William Lovett, in his Pursuit of Bread, Knowledge and Freedom* (London, 1876) p. 43; *Birmingham Journal*, 19 Feb 1831.
5. *Brighton Co-operator*, 1 Nov 1828; Pare, *Address*, p. 24. For specific activities and their intended social function, see the *Brighton Co-operator*, 1 Oct 1828 (the issue cited by many co-operators as their main lesson in how to organise a co-

operative society), 1 June 1829, and *Lancashire and Yorkshire Co-operator*, 1 Oct 1831.

6. *Crisis*, 12 May 1832.

7. Ibid., 18 May, 6 June, 6, 13 July, 19 Oct 1833; 22 Feb, 9 Aug 1834.

8. Started in July, the Social Community claimed sixteen classes and over 300 members by September; ibid., 6 July, 21 Sep, 12 Oct 1833.

9. As suggested by Harrison, *Robert Owen*, p. 224.

10. *Crisis*, 14 Apr, 19 May 1832; *New Moral World*, 21, 28, Feb 1835.

11. Lovett, *Life and Struggles*, p. 48.

12. *New Moral World*, 11 July 1839.

13. Ibid., 23 May 1835, 6 Feb 1836.

14. Ibid., 17 Oct 1835.

15. Harrison, *Robert Owen*, p. 225; A. E. Musson, 'The Ideology of Early Co-operation in Lancashire and Cheshire', *Transactions of the Lancashire and Cheshire Antiquarian Society*, LXVIII (1958) 128-9.

16. Although the subsequent discussion will focus on Manchester, it was common for working-class halls to be conceived in opposition to Mechanics' Institutes. See, e.g., J. Salt, 'The Sheffield Hall of Science', *The Vocational Aspect of Secondary and Further Education*, XII 25 (autumn 1960) 133, 137; for Birmingham, even though the Owenites captured the Mechanics' Institute for a time, see *New Moral World*, 6 June 1840.

17. For discussion of class hostility in Manchester, see A. Briggs, 'The Background of the Parliamentary Reform Movement in Three English Cities', *Cambridge Historical Journal*, X 3 (1952) 302, 307, and D. Read, 'Chartism in Manchester', in A. Briggs (ed.), *Chartist Studies* (London, 1962) pp. 34–41.

18. Among those who had attended the Mechanics' Institute and manned the various Owenite schools were E. T. Craig (1804–84), a fustian cutter by trade, an eyewitness of Peterloo, president of the Manchester Owenian Society, delegate to the early Co-operative Congresses and editor of the *Lancashire Co-operator*. Leaving the area in 1831 to manage the Ralahine community in Ireland, he remained an enthusiast for communitarian socialism through the mid-century, when he worked as a journalist and lecturer on phrenology. E. T. Craig, 'Socialism in England: Historical Reminiscences', *American Socialist* (Oneida, N.Y.) (Aug 1877–Feb 1878). James Rigby (b. 1802) worked as a boy in a spinning mill and was then apprenticed to master plumber and glazier Joseph Smith, also a prominent Owenite. Rigby served as congress delegate, member of the Central Board, social missionary and deputy governor of the Queenwood community, ending up as personal secretary to Owen. He was also active in the Ten Hours Movement. See *Northern Star*, 1 Jan 1842. Abel Heywood (1810–93), starting as a warehouse boy, became a radical publisher and bookseller who was gaoled several times for selling the unstamped press. He was active in all the radical campaigns of the period, including Chartism. Later prosperous and prominent in local politics, he became Mayor of Manchester in 1862.

19. M. Tylecote, *The Mechanics' Institutes of Lancashire and Yorkshire before 1851* (Manchester, 1957) pp. 134–6.

20. R. Detroisier, *An Address Delivered at the New Mechanics' Institution, Pool Street . . . December 30th 1829* (Manchester, 1829) p. 9. Detroisier struggled through a series of jobs – warehouse boy, fustian cutter, clerkships in spinning and mer-

chant firms. An archetype of the working-class autodidact, his interest was in the educational rather than the industrial side of co-operation, although he was a delegate to the 2nd Co-operative Congress. Popular as a lecturer, he toured the London Owenite halls in the early thirties, making his living out of the movement. See G. A. Williams, *Rowland Detroisier: A Working Class Infidel, 1800–1834*, Borthwick Papers, No. 28 (York, 1965).

21. R. Detroisier, *An Address on the Advantages of the Intended Mechanics' Hall of Science . . .* (Manchester, 1831); *Poor Man's Advocate and People's Library*, 25 Feb 1832.

22. *New Moral World*, 1 Dec 1838; *Northern Star*, 16 Apr 1842. A radical tea party to celebrate Henry Hunt's birthday was chaired by Abel Heywood and addressed by Feargus O'Connor. Ibid., 9 Nov 1839.

23. *Crisis*, 19 Oct 1833.

24. *New Moral World*, 17 Sep 1836. G. A. Fleming (d. 1878), the Corresponding Secretary who tactfully informed Owen of this departure from A.A.C.A.N. directives, had a career which followed the same pattern as many of his local colleagues. A journeyman housepainter, he made his first appearance on the radical scene as secretary to the associated trades trying to rescind the sentences of the Dorchester labourers in 1834. He began editing the *New Moral World* in 1838 as the movement began to build up local working-class strength once again, and after the collapse of the Queenwood community, where he lived for a time, he made his living from journalism, even trying in 1851 as editor and proprietor to revive the *Northern Star*. See *Manchester City News*, 25 May 1878.

25. In 1837 the national government of the A.A.C.A.N. was put into the hands of a Central Board elected by the delegates from the branches at annual congress, and local branches were left great autonomy to decide their form of government and finance. The 1839 Congress stipulated that local branches should have an executive committee, three members of which must come up for re-election every quarter. *New Moral World*, 10 June 1837; *The Constitution and Laws of the Universal Community Society of Rational Religionists* (London, 1839) p. 20.

26. *New Moral World*, 1 Oct 1836.

27. Ibid.

28. The community fund was finally created in 1837 when the national movement set up the National Community Friendly Society (N.C.F.S.), registered under Act of Parliament, a working-class self-help foundation without any middle-class patronage. Ibid., 10 June, 17 June 1837.

29. In 1839, Congress amalgamated the A.A.C.A.N. and the N.C.F.S. into the U.C.S.R.R. to gain the benefits of Acts applicable to religious and Friendly Societies. Ibid., 8 June 1839. For the real measure of political protection afforded by religious registration, see below, pp. 102–3.

30. The Birmingham socialists, for example, relied upon support from the Chartists to finance their hall of science. Ibid., 14 Sep 1839.

31. Halls were built in Sheffield, Huddersfield, Glasgow, Radcliffe Bridge, Worcester, Yarmouth, Macclesfield, Manchester, Halifax, Stockport, Bristol and London. Birmingham bought and converted a Southcottian chapel. A. Black, 'Education before Rochdale; the Owenites and the Halls of Science', *Co-operative Review*, XXIX (Feb 1955) 42–4; Harrison, *Robert Owen*, p. 222.

32. From the Worcester prospectus, *New Moral World*, 20 July 1839; see also

the London and Glasgow prospectuses, ibid., 21 Sep 1839, 18 Apr 1840.

33. Among the many instances of the use of Owenite halls by the Chartists were Bronterre O'Brien's lecturers (by socialist request) and Rev. W. V. Jackson's farewell to his radical friends in the Salford Social Institution. O'Connor gave lectures at the Manchester and Birmingham Halls of Science, while the John Street Institution in London was used for a festival and ball to raise money for the Chartist convention. Ibid., 9 June, 17 Aug 1839; *Northern Star*, 21 Mar, 9, 16 Apr 1842.

34. *New Moral World*, 28 Sep 1839.

35. In Leeds several leading Chartists were Owenites, while in Manchester Abel Heywood was a bridging figure. In Leicester some socialists were also Chartists despite social missionary Campbell's set-piece debates against the Chartists. J. F. C. Harrison, 'Chartism in Leeds', in *Chartist Studies*, pp. 68–70; T. Cooper, *The Life of Thomas Cooper* (London, 1872) p. 174. The *New Moral World* is not a good source for tracking down the multiple political allegiances of Owenites because it kept scrupulously to reporting Owenite activity in order to preserve its un-stamped status and hold its selling price down to 2d; otherwise it would have been deemed a newspaper. Indeed the paper was acquitted in several prosecutions as an illegal publication; *New Moral World*, 16 May 1840. Only by chance do items about overlap occur, as in the case of a Stockport socialist, Frederick L. P. Fogg, who reported that he and others had been busy manning a co-operative store, half of whose profits would go to the families of Chartist prisoners in Chester gaol. Later a correction notice said sharply that the store was 'a speculation of the Chartists', not under the official aegis of the Stockport socialist branch. Ibid., 18 Apr, 2, 9 May 1840.

Harrison's picture of the local socialist branch as an exclusive religious sect, quite separate from other working-class protest activity, begins to break down under the weight of evidence like this: *Robert Owen*, pp. 222, 231.

36. Especially the Salford Social Institution. *New Moral World*, 9 Feb, 25 May 1839.

37. Ibid., 4 Apr 1840.

38. *Constitution . . . of the U.C.S.R.R.*, p. 30; *New Moral World*, 16 May 1840.

39. *Crisis*, 25 May 1833.

40. *New Moral World*, 27 Apr 1839; Salt, 'Sheffield Hall of Science', p. 134.

41. At a time when the Salford membership was claimed to be 440, the Carpenter's Hall could hold 800 for a social festival and was often filled; a marathon debate between Lloyd Jones and a Mr Palliaster attracted an estimated, and probably exaggerated, 2000. *New Moral World*, 8 June, 20 July 1839.

42. Ibid., 19 Jan 1839.

43. Ibid., 23 Nov 1839.

44. Ibid., 7 Dec 1839.

45. For ladies' classes in Birmingham, where the Mechanics' Institute had rejected them, and Manchester, see ibid., 6 June 1840, and *Report of a Committee of the Manchester Statistical Society on the State of Education in the Borough of Manchester in 1834* (London, 1835) p. 32. Among the female lecturers who toured nationally were Mrs Chappelsmith, Mrs Martin and Mrs Morison, who even 'named' children. *New Moral World*, 28 Mar 1840, 5 Apr 1845, 17 Nov 1838.

46. Ibid., 25 Apr 1840.

47. Ibid., 27 April 1839.

48. Ibid., 30 July 1836.

49. Ibid., 27 Apr 1839. Earlier in London there had been a number of vocal, instrumental and dancing classes which were meant to service Owen's Institutions, although they met at other London venues. *Crisis*, 30 Mar, 28 Sep 1833.

50. *New Moral World*, 1 Dec 1838.

51. Lovett, *Life and Struggles*, pp. 41–2; *New Moral World*, 11 May 1839, 28 March 1840, for Tarr. Before the 1840 edition of the *Social Hymn Book*, a compendium of work from all over the country, branches had compiled their own hymnals, the Leeds *Social Harmonist* being a collection of 'music from the works of Handel, Haydn, Mozart, Beethoven . . . adapted to the hymns sung by the social friends'; *New Moral World*, 6 July 1839. Huddersfield and Bilston boasted 'splendidly' stained-glass windows; Birmingham and Worcester, paintings; Manchester, a 'beautiful' model full nine feet square. Ibid., 9 Nov, 2 Mar, 30 Nov 1839, 3 Nov 1838; *Crisis*, 2 Feb 1833.

52. *New Moral World*, 13 Apr 1839; *Crisis*, 22 Feb 1834.

53. *New Moral World*, 18 Jan 1840.

54. Indeed, one feels that the branches made every possible occasion the excuse for a festival, the Manchester Owenites even holding one at four in the morning, complete with music, to say goodbye to members setting off for Queenwood; also a festival to mark 'Her Majesty's Nuptials'. Ibid., 30 Nov 1839, 22 Feb 1840.

55. Manchester planned a six-day marathon. Ibid., 23 May 1840.

56. Ibid., 8 June 1839; see also 23 July 1836, 1 June 1839, and *Crisis*, 24 May, 14 June 1834, for similar Whit and summer excursions in London.

57. *Crisis*, 12 Oct 1833, 22 Feb, 8 Aug 1834. Among eminent Manchester members whose children were named were Lloyd Jones and the Heywood brothers. *New Moral World*, 19 Jan 1839, 16 May 1840.

58. *Crisis*, 18 May 1833.

59. Ibid., 24 May, 12 July 1834. Significantly, this chapel became a radical centre, taken over by the Owenites and used by the Chartists. *New Moral World*, 6 Apr, 18 May 1839; R. F. Wearmouth, *Methodism and the Working-Class Movements of England 1800–1850* (London, 1947) p. 120.

60. *New Moral World*, 23 May 1840. The fact that branches were licensed by the bishop of the diocese as a place of religious worship for a 'congregation of Protestants called Rational religionists' has been used to show how the movement was thinking of itself as a religious sect in the later thirties by Harrison, *Robert Owen*, p. 136. While this is true, it should be realised that a necessary measure of political protection was also being sought; this registration was the main case for the defence when an action was taken against the Manchester Hall of Science. *New Moral World*, 20 June 1840.

61. Ibid., 29 Mar 1845.

62. Among many examples, see ibid., 20 Dec 1834.

63. Ibid., 16 Nov 1839.

64. *Crisis*, 29 Mar 1834. After a London funeral with a procession a mile long, an eyewitness wrote effusively: 'the ceremony had an imposing effect. It has already reconciled many of the Operatives to the Union. The sublimity has completely overwhelmed their objections, and accomplished what mere dry reasoning could never effect. There is nothing like ceremony after all. There is a

passion for it in human nature, and it must be gratified, only let the purpose be generous.' Ibid., 5 Apr 1834.

65. *New Moral World*, 11 Apr 1840. For other funerals, see ibid., 30 May 1835, 9 May 1840.

66. The tremendous importance attached to social functions was signified by the frequency with which the Registrar, Tidd Pratt, had to warn societies not to submit rules concerning convivial activities and by the marked failure of societies founded under upper-class patronage which tended to underplay conviviality. P. H. J. H. Gosden, *The Friendly Societies in England 1815-1875* (Manchester, 1961) pp. 20, 128, 137, chap. v *passim*, for the annual calendar.

67. See the constitution of the National Charter Association, which provided for local "class" groups and councils and for a missionary corps to inculcate Chartist consciousness. *Northern Star*, 1 Aug 1840. After his release from Warwick gaol, Lovett again struck up what can be called his signature tune, insisting that 'unless the social and political superstructure were based upon the *intelligence* and *morality* of the people, they would only have exchanged despotism for despotism, and one set of oppressors for another'. The way to 'best aid the holy cause of man's social regeneration and political freedom' was for Chartists to erect public halls offering facilities for meetings, education and recreation. *Life and Struggles*, pp. 245-6, 248. While O'Connor at first opposed 'Church Chartism, Teetotal Chartism and Knowledge Chartism' to the extent that these might become splinter groups, he still maintained that should their adherents act 'inculcating religion, abstinence, and knowledge, as a means to any end they might unitedly produce, without establishing man's adhesion to any of them, as a political test, then I will give them my blessing and my every assistance; and I am sure that each and all will lead to the accomplishment of our civil and religious regeneration'. *Northern Star*, 3 Apr 1841. He vigorously supported the establishment of Chartist schools and halls mentioned below.

68. Wearmouth, *Methodism*, pp. 108ff.

69. Cooper, *Life*, pp. 165, 169-70.

70. For a useful list, see Simon, *Chapters in the History of Education*, pp. 243-53. O'Connor made a point of attending Sunday-school recitations, for it gratified him 'to know that there was a little army coming up, who if the old one was to die before the liberties of the country were gained would take the field and finish the work their fathers had so nobly begun'. *Northern Star*, 20 Apr 1844. A sense of the breadth of the curriculum was given by graduating scholars, who felt that the merit of the course consisted 'not only in giving us the simple rudiments of education, but in also teaching us our duty to each other as members of one great family; and, above all, for the pains you have taken to instil into our young minds the principles of pure democracy, and the rights of man'. Ibid., 24 Aug 1844.

71. Among areas which had Chartist churches were Glasgow, Dundee, Birmingham, Nottingham and Newcastle under Lyme.

72. *Northern Star*, 6 Mar 1841, 26 Aug 1843.

73. Ibid., 9 Apr 1842; *Manchester and Salford Advertiser*, 2 Oct 1841.

74. *Northern Star*, 1 Jan 1842, and 2 Apr 1842, when a huge demonstration, tea party and ball were held on Good Friday in Manchester to lay the cornerstone for a monument to Henry Hunt.

75. Ibid., 9, 16 Nov 1839.

76. Harrison, *Robert Owen*, pp. 137, 231. Seeing Owenism among a proliferation of religious sects, Harrison plays heavily on the theme that social dislocation encourages sect-formation: 'problems of readjustment for individuals and groups, and the fears, insecurity and general upset that accompany the interruption of normal economic and social relations probably account for the proliferation of sects at such times'. Ibid., p. 136.

77. Gosden, *Friendly Societies*, pp. 7, 18; see also pp. 52–3 for the societies under upper-class patronage and control which never attracted a numerous membership.

78. For the legal difficulties, see the *Northern Star* editorial, 18 July 1840, and G. D. H. Cole and A. W. Filson, *British Working Class Movements: Select Documents 1789–1875* (London, 1965) p. 374.

79. *Northern Star*, 23 May 1840.

80. Ibid., 4 Apr 1846. An editorial defending Chartist churches insisted that 'principles' of social benevolence and justice, of civil equality and political right, though recognised by the Bible are denounced by the priesthood and hence their determination to 'erect their own temples and offer their own worship to the God of Justice whom they serve'. Ibid., 3 Apr 1841.

81. As quoted in Cooper, *Life*, p. 167. In Ernest Jones's 'Easter Hymn' the plight of the working man was identified with the crucifixion 'Crucified! crucified every morn,/Beaten, and scourged and crowned with thorn!/Scorned and spat on and drenched with gall;/Brothers! how shall we bear the thrall?' *Red Republican*, 3 Aug 1850.

# CHAPTER SIX

# J. E. Smith and the Owenite Movement, 1833-1834

## JOHN SAVILLE

I

THE trade union phase of Owenism reached its climax in the late spring and summer of 1834 with the collapse of the Grand National Consolidated Trades Union. Its history is recorded in the pages of the *Crisis, Pioneer* and *Poor Man's Guardian.* The editor of the weekly *Crisis,* the main Owenite journal, from the autumn of 1833 until its demise in August 1834 was James Elishama Smith, a remarkable personality whose own career in the Owenite movement was as meteoric as the rise and fall of the G.N.C.T.U. itself.

James Elishama Smith was born on 22 November 1801 in Glasgow.[1] His father, the son of a weaver of Strathaven, was in some sort of business in Glasgow, probably the weaving trade; and the combination of a not very successful business and a large number of children kept the family in relatively poor circumstances. James was reared in a strict Calvinist atmosphere which did not, however, exclude all references to the arts, especially painting and drawing. There was talent in these directions on his mother's side of the family, and James himself showed some ability, even at one time in his career earning his living as an artist and a teacher of art. It was this interesting combination of a narrow theology and a degree at least of artistic imagination that provide some clues to his later emotional and intellectual development.

He entered Glasgow University at an early age to study theology – this was his father's decision – and he graduated in 1818 when he was seventeen years old. He then spent several years as a private tutor and as a 'probationer', the name given to unplaced divinity students who held a licence to preach. From his student days, on the evidence of his correspondence, he was immersed in theological disputations, and he was obviously a young man of restless and inquiring mind. His letters also show a continuing interest in imaginative literature, for there are references to his reading Dante and *Tristram Shandy*. He passed an uneventful few years after his graduation and it was only in the second half of the 1820s that he began to turn to millennial religious views; as with all his changes of ideas, his 'conversion' took place quickly and with a remarkable thoroughness.[2] We cannot be quite certain when he began definitely to be influenced by more extreme sectarian ideas, but there was a contact with a Swedenborgian early in 1827, although there does not appear to have been any immediate response. He was, however, at this time becoming increasingly dissatisfied with the Church of Scotland,[3] and then, in the middle of 1828, he heard Edward Irving preach in Edinburgh. This seems to have been decisive in his acceptance of a millennialist position. In a letter dated 10 June he wrote:

> I have not yet escaped from the city, and will be here for several days yet; but I think it a very fortunate thing for myself that I have been detained so long, for I have heard Mr Irving's lectures – lectures which have fully confirmed me in an opinion which I was beginning to adopt, or rather had already adopted, before his arrival, viz., the personal reign of Christ during the millennium, which, of course, is just at hand.[4]

There are some interesting parallels between the careers of James Smith and Edward Irving.[5] Both came out of a Presbyterian background; both graduated from Glasgow University; both were interested in imaginative literature; and both had to wait some years before they found their audience. Irving, who was nine years older than Smith, had contemplated missionary work abroad before he was offered an assistantship to Thomas Chalmers in 1819. This was followed in 1822 with the charge of the Caledonian Church, in Hatton Garden, London. Both Smith's and Irving's Calvinist upbringing had much to do with their concern with contemporary political and social problems. The doctrine of the 'Two Kingdoms' was deeply embedded in the Scottish Presbyterian tradition, and the Church of Scotland had always claimed the right to interfere in civil affairs.[6] The broader curriculum of the Scottish universities no doubt also played a part in shaping their attitudes in this respect. Irving, so he said himself, was concerned to teach 'imaginative men, and political men, and legal men, and scientific men who bear the world in hand',[7] and it was Hazlitt who remarked that Irving had 'converted the Caledonian Chapel into a Westminster Forum or Debating Society, with the sanctity of religion added to it'.[8] It was appropriately said of Irving that he was 'the mystic in fervent action, not in calm contemplation'.[9] By the time Smith heard Irving in Edinburgh, the latter had been developing his millennialist views for over half a decade, and he made a powerful impact upon the younger man, although Smith, unlike some other members of his family,[10] did not stay long in the Irving camp. But the effect of his conversion among the respectable circles within which he moved was sensational. At the end of December 1828 a correspondent wrote to his brother John:

I am sorry to inform you that your brother James is far from well. He has just been calling for me, and I cannot better explain to you the nature of his complaint than by describing to you something of his conversation. He has learned, he says, from the prophecies that Christ's second coming is just at hand, that He is to come and take up his abode in Edinburgh, that Arthur's seat is the Mount of Olives, etc. A few days ago I chanced to call for him, when he assured me that he had that day discovered a key to the whole of Scripture, and so persuaded was he of its efficacy, and that some great crisis was approaching, that he had determined to go to London to communicate his views to Mr Irving. . . . I am fully persuaded now that it is not a mere fit of enthusiasm with him, but that he is the victim of a real disease which is gradually increasing. . . . He confessed to me tonight, when I was expostulating with him on the folly of allowing his mind to be led away by such strange fancies, that he was aware his mind was in a strange state; but, he added, I cannot help it – some evil spirit has got possession of me. He is averse from talking upon any subject but that of the prophecies, but when he does so he is perfectly sensible, and coherent, and collected. . .[11]

This was the beginning of a rapid shift to more extreme sectarian views. The first mention of Joanna Southcott[12] was in a letter dated 20 March 1829, and within a few months he had left Scotland to visit John Wroe of Bradford, the 'prophet' who had established himself at Ashton under Lyne as the successor to Joanna. Here Smith totally involved himself in the sect, which practised complete obedience to the Mosaic laws as the necessary means of ensuring immortality. He grew a beard – in those days one of the outward signs of the heretic – was circumcised and observed all the Jewish laws regarding food and social habits. The Christian Israelites, as they came to be called, had no ordained ministry, preaching and propaganda was carried on by the lay members, especially in the open air. Smith, as an educated man, had no difficulty in keeping himself by teaching and preaching. At last he had an audience:

> I have got an opportunity of preaching such doctrines as I like, and an audience to hear me. Little did I think, New Year before last, there was a people in the country who were taught by revelation a doctrine so closely allied to my own. I never had heard of them. Yet I discovered, by the grace of God, such doctrines as they hold, and, of course, must have been led and taught by the same Spirit which teaches them, for it was such doctrine as never man taught or heard of before, being hid in the mysterious language of Scripture, and reserved for the latter days to be brought forth to the light. I preach now extempore, and find after all that I go to the pulpit with greater ease than I used to do in Scotland, and preach a half hour's sermon as freely as if I had committed it to memory. All doctrines I preach now – eternal punishment and universal redemption in one and the same discourse.[13]

This period of his life, though it lasted only a short time, seems to have been of considerable importance in the development of his theological ideas. It was his discovery and acceptance of the unity of God and the Devil, of good and evil – the doctrine of universalism – that gave him a tolerance of all religions that he never lost. As he wrote on 15 June 1831, when on the point of leaving the Ashton sect: 'I am not a bigot or fanatic, I assure you, for I believe in all religions', and he held to these ideas to the end of his life. There was in general a liberality about his attitudes, even in his most sectarian days, that helps to account for his continued receptivity to new ideas in later years; although the much discussed relationship between millenarian religious movements and movements of social unrest – a matter of partial but by no means complete coincidence – must also have some bearing on James Smith's particular acceptance of an extreme radical position.[14] The Doctrine of the Woman, for example, was a key principle in the Southcottian scheme of things. Joanna Southcott, who had announced herself as the woman spoken of in the Apocalypse (chap. 12), argued that as it was the woman's hand which had brought the evil fruit to man in the Garden of Eden, so it would be the woman's hand which brought to man the good. Extreme Protestant sects have nearly always, of course, offered sexual equality or a large degree of independence to women, and it was not difficult for James Smith, after he had made contact with Owenite and other radical opinion in his London days, to translate the Doctrine of the Woman into a socially conscious feminism.[15]

There are a number of aspects of Smith's stay at Ashton that remain obscure.[16] John Wroe was expelled from the sect for sexual misconduct with certain of the brethren, and Smith evidently, on his own admission, had some hand in the expulsion. He also hinted in one of his letters that he expected to take Wroe's place, but in this he was apparently frustrated by the arrival of John (Zion) Ward from London.[17] Whether it was for this or other reasons, Smith left Ashton in late June 1831. There were financial irregularities to which he had made reference in his correspondence, but his disillusionment with the sectarian position he had adopted stemmed from growing intellectual and no doubt emotional doubts as much as from adventitious causes. We cannot be sure of this except for the last months of his stay at Ashton, but there are occasional remarks in his correspondence which suggest that he was at least partly conscious of the outside world throughout his stay at Ashton, and still able to make some judgment upon himself. In a letter written to his brother some nine months before he left Ashton, at a time when he declared his full conviction in what he was doing and preaching, he could still ask, in a half-apologetic way:

> No doubt you imagine that I have taken the pet, and that your wise saying is truly verified – that a madman is first of all afraid of his own friends and then of himself; and probably it is true enough, and I don't feel disposed to gainsay it. But it is some consolation to me to think that I am now arrived at the last stage of madness, for in many respects I am afraid of myself.[18]

This is hardly the supreme confidence of the wholly converted; and in the last few months before his departure, he began to express positive criticism of the ways into which he had been led. He now acknowledged that all the prophets he had followed, Joanna Southcott included, had 'mixed up a great deal of trumpery with the truth', although he softened criticism by noting that this had always happened to prophets as far back as the Apostles.[19] By the time he was ready to leave, the bitterness within himself spilled over in a remarkable piece of self-criticism:

> I am very sorry to leave this place, and yet I have a desire to face my old friends and acquaintances to let them see how mad and how foolish I am. . . . I hope this will find you sounder in mind and body than your humble servant, and I sincerely hope that you may never inhale any of the contagious vapour of that palace of the moon which they have erected in your neighbourhood. Take a good large bolus of indifference and thoughtlessness now and then with a glass

of toddy, and there is no fear of you. If I had done so I might have escaped the brand of infamy with which the world has marked me.

The letter was signed 'Yours intolerably'.[20]


II


There was a small sect of Southcottians in Edinburgh, some of whom had remained faithful to James Smith throughout all the recent disputes, but we hear little about his religious activities once he had arrived there in late June 1831. His main concern was to earn a living. He began painting and drawing, staying in Edinburgh for about a year, but then left for London, again assuming that he would have to earn money as an artist and teacher of art. He arrived in London in August 1832 and already in September he was writing to his brother that he had begun lecturing. He mentioned hearing Edward Irving preach in the hall of the Owenite Equitable Labour Exchange in Gray's Inn Road, and through Irving he came into contact with Owenite ideas and possibly with Robert Owen himself. One of his early letters from London, for instance, noted the opening of the Labour Exchange 'on Monday last' (3 September 1832), and he then proceeded to give his brother, to whom he was writing, a short account of the principles on which it worked. 'And this they call the millennium.'[21] Smith took over a chapel towards the end of September 1832 in which he gave regular Sunday evening lectures. Most of his hearers were what he called 'decent tradesmen', but there was a smattering of radical intelligentsia, among them Anna Wheeler, the feminist; and it was she who introduced him to the ideas of Fourier and Saint-Simon as well as to those of Robert Owen, whom she knew personally.[22] The first letter describing his reception in London shows the new confidence and exhilaration that he was now experiencing. It was a year and a few months since the 'Yours intolerably' letter:

I have taken a chapel for lectures, and gave my first last Sunday evening, when I was received with most enthusiastic cheering, and gratified with the hopes – I may say certainty – of success. My doctrines, which have been coolly received by a parcel of blinded fools elsewhere, are here likely to prevail. I have got many friends already, and every day, I believe, will increase them. Providence has just sent me in the nick of time; if I had gone when I first proposed it would not have done. I charge one penny only for admission to my lectures, and I believe I will fill the chapel, which holds 500, and perhaps I may give another during the week; at any rate, I will easily support myself. There are vast numbers of people here ready to receive what I can give them. The church is evidently on its last legs; several of the clergy have lately petitioned the King to call a general convocation to devise some method of saving it. It would have surprised you to have seen the warm greetings, the clapping of hands with which I was received, whilst at the same time they paid the utmost attention to every sentence of my discourse. I never had such an attentive audience. If I succeed in London, I shall get known in other places, and may take a tour through the provinces, and soon you will see plenty following in the same footsteps.[23]

Smith was being ingenuous in suggesting that elsewhere he was badly received but that in London audiences were warmly receptive to his ideas. What he was missing out was the change in his ideas, for he was now preaching his universalist doctrine without the extreme messianic content of his Ashton days. All the evidence points to a quite rapid adaptation of his general approach to the radical atmosphere of the London circles he had settled in, and he quickly won a notable following. He took over the chapel vacated by John Ward, the Shiloh, who was in prison for blasphemy,[24] and no doubt took over at least part of Ward's congregation. Ward was a violent critic of the priesthood and the clerical establishment, and although Smith wrote that he was not preaching Ward's doctrines,[25] it was still a radical Christianity that he was offering every Sunday. His reputation among London radicals must have grown rapidly, for in June 1833, within nine months of coming to London, he had been invited to lecture regularly on Sunday mornings at the Charlotte Street Institution of the Owenites. The invitation was to a Christian who had already given evidence that he was well along the Owenite path.[26]

The key document to the change in his mode of thinking – to the intellectual marriage between his now muted religious millennialism and the radicalism of the Owenite position – was the *Lecture on a Christian Community*, delivered first at the Surrey Institution in the early months of 1833, later repeated at the Rotunda in April and May and then published as a twenty-page pamphlet. The *Lecture* is a remarkable witness to Smith's extraordinary ability in absorbing and digesting

new information and new ideas. His reading in radical literature must
have been both wide and thorough, for the Lecture contains ideas from
a range of previous writers in the radical, socialist and Owenite
tradition. He opened the Lecture by attacking established Christianity
in the accepted way of millennial preachers, but it was now argued
within a framework of explicit social criticism. The Christianity of the
rich was Antichrist, and a true Christian was 'one who turns the old
world upside down';[27] one who recognises that Christianity can only
be realised by the 'establishment of a social community'. Christianity
'had never yet been established in the world', although the early
Apostles had clearly and obviously understood Christianity to be a
community, for all the precepts of Christ pointed to this conclusion:

> If Christ gave moral precepts, surely he never intended that they
> were to be despised and trampled under foot, that they were to be
> evaded by any casuistry or sophistical jargon of the schools; and if
> he gave commandments that were impracticable, as the clergy main-
> tain, what does this imply but a reflection upon his wisdom, and the
> folly of that common cry of the religious world concerning the
> adaptation of Christianity to the present state of human nature.
> When Christ taught his followers to forgive their debtors, he did
> not mean to defend or institute a system of society in which Christians
> should be daily prosecuting one another, before the courts of justice
> – imprisoning, distraining, and vexing one another in an infinite variety
> of ways, worthy of the genius of an inquisition to devise. . . . Or
> when he prayed to his father that his followers might be *one* even as
> he in God, and God in him, he surely did not mean to give counten-
> ance to a form of society in which all his professed disciples were at
> variance, all scrambling and fighting about pounds, shillings, and
> pence; each accumulating in his own coffers as much as fortune cast
> his way, regardless of the tears, and penury, and hunger of widowed
> mothers and fatherless children. . . . But men have perverted all his
> doctrine, for it has fallen into the hands of rich men, the very men
> of whom Christ said that it was easier for a camel to go through
> the eye of a needle, than for them to enter into the kingdom of
> God.[28]

The present system of christianity was a wolf in sheep's clothing;
the metaphor expressed perfectly the present ravenous, wolfish spirit of
unfeeling selfishness that must pervade every society based on unjust
foundations. Christianity must put an end to private property, for as
long as private property remained, so will there exist the desire to

accumulate riches at the expense of everyone else. The competitive instinct was founded upon private ownership, and the only way to put an end to self-seeking ambition and individual selfishness was to do away with private property and to put all things in common. But why, if a community of goods was the obvious form of a christian community and one which came directly out of the teaching of Jesus, was it not established with the early Christian fathers and continued ever since? The answer that Smith gave to his question was based upon his doctrine of the analogy between nature and the moral world, and the unity that existed between good and evil. It was a law of nature, he argued, that men 'reap experience by difficulties'; and since difficulties are met with only in a state of evil, it followed that men acquire experience in evil as a result of which they discover the good. If a real Christian community had been established immediately following the death of Jesus, then men would have been unable to learn the nature of evil, and they would therefore have not been able to discover the good out of their own experience. Moreover, and here his new social awareness led him into a *post hoc, ergo propter hoc* argument, in those far-off days a real and lasting social community was not practicable for scientific reasons, because the level of material existence was still far too primitive. But now,

when the arts are all in blossom, when science is every day pouring forth her discoveries; when the experience of evil is already abundant, and man has learned all the rocks, the shoals, and the whirlpools, by which former generations have suffered – now is the time for reducing his experience to practice with the certainty of success. Christianity is like a tree – it has first grown downwards, to take root in the earth; afterwards it ascends, and spreads forth its branches and its leaves. It is quite natural, therefore, that it should first prove a curse before it prove a blessing; that it should first be Antichrist before it be Christ.[29]

He went on to develop an ingenious parallel between Owen's theory of the non-responsibility of the individual for his actions ('The character of every Human Being is formed for, and not by, the Individual') and the Pauline doctrine of justification by faith. St Paul, Smith wrote, said that man was not justified by his works: 'it is not I that sin, but sin that dwelleth in me', while Owen on his side argued that the wickedness of man was the product of his social environment. St Paul further said that 'faith is not of ourselves, it is the gift of God'; and as all mankind is within the body of Christ, it follows that all men have faith since they are all part of mankind. A true religion cannot be exclusive, and a comprehensive view of Christianity must reconcile all its doctrines with science and philosophy, for Nature is the true word of God, and the Bible is only a type of it, just as Christ himself was only a type of God. The mistake made by sectarian Christianity had been to circumscribe faith and to pay no attention to works; yet it was Jesus who said: 'Ye shall know them by their works.' Faith belonged to the mind and works to the body, and what we now have to do is to bring faith and works together to exist in harmony. Like its founder, Christianity must have a death and a resurrection: 'and this no doubt is the second crucifixion mentioned in the Revelation'. The original crucifixion had already taken place: it was the corrupt and false order of society and its sectarian divisions. The Resurrection which will establish the millennium and the kingdom of God will be the constitution of a social order founded upon the original Christian principle of a community of goods.[30]

By way of conclusion to his *Lecture*, James Smith sketched the outline of the new social order which he was advocating as the expression of Christian morality upon earth. It would emerge, he said in authentic utopian tones, naturally and simply 'as the blossom upon the hawthorn'. His new society was couched in familiar Owenite terms, and there were direct echos in his statement of both William Thompson's *Practical Directions*[31] and certain of Owen's own writings.[32] Smith's style was, however, a good deal livelier than that of Owen, and the picture of the millennium in the concluding sections of the *Lecture* was vividly and attractively presented. There would, for a beginning, be no kings, aristocracy or ranks in society, and everyone would receive a truly liberal education. With the continued advance of science, work would cease to be a burden and would become an offering to society by each individual. No trade would be deemed dishonourable or demeaning, for mental and manual labour would no longer be opposed one to the other. There would be leisure for all to enjoy the many amusements society had to offer. Every kind of encouragement would be given to the fine arts and to works of the imagination. Architecture would hold a special place among the arts, for it provided houses for the people and made beautiful the environment. Building would be as magnificent in the village as in the town; and Smith added to the usual Owenite emphasis upon the village and the small community by accepting the existence of 'large and splendid cities' as a necessary part of the new order of society.

It was impossible, he wrote, to provide anything but a general outline of the new order, 'for experience has yet to reveal many unknown secrets, in the application of the principles of social equality, to the minute details of the system'. Man was always adding experience to his present knowledge, and it would be foolish to lay down a rigid plan of political and social government which, like the laws of the Medes and Persians, would be unchangeable for ever. But some points could be made of a general kind. There would undoubtedly be an astonishing flowering of mental and imaginative vigour. In present-day society 'the greater portion of the mind is lost', through poverty and lack of education at one end of the scale and idleness and dissipation at the other. And there would, without question, be a major change in the relations between the sexes (a subject to which Smith was to return on many occasions and at greater length.[33]). He hinted, on this occasion, at more natural marriage laws when the independence of women was assured. When the new social order was established in Britain, and here he was to echo Robert Owen almost word for word,[34] its adoption would be followed 'instantly' by a similar revolution in every civilised country. Such a change would lead to unrestrained travel and social intercourse between nations: 'no particular community or country would constitute a home; every country would be the home of all; and every country would be the favourite resort of all'.

But how was the change to be brought about? And to this question Smith gave only the most perfunctory and utopian answer. It would happen because it was inevitable. 'The old system cannot stand in this or any other country', for the hearts of men will be weaned away from their present selfish interests. When men learnt what their real self-interests were, they would establish the social system of communities forthwith. Necessity would in the end force mankind to put an end to cupidity and national strife; and when all interests were merged as one, the millennium would be with us.

III

James Smith continued lecturing throughout the winter of 1832–3 and into the spring and summer of 1833. By the early months of 1833 he was becoming well known in radical circles in London, and as already mentioned he was invited from early May to lecture regularly at the Charlotte Street Institution; the *Crisis*, from the issue of 4 May 1833, now always carried a summary of his Sunday morning lecture on the front page. He continued to write as a Christian socialist, and developed in some detail the themes he had already sketched out in the *Lecture on a Christian Community* without going beyond the Christian Owenite categories he had there established. There was a tendency, to be much more pronounced in the next stage in his career, for his writing to become more secular in content and tone, but until the late autumn of 1833 he remained well within the orthodox Owenite tradition. His writing was confident, lively and vigorous and he continued to steep himself in the radical literature of his day. In March 1833 he published a translation of Saint-Simon's *New Christianity*, and his preface to this was an elaboration on some of the ideas he had already set forth in the *Lecture on a Christian Community*.[35] Three months later he published *The Anti-Christ, or, Christianity Reformed*,[36] a volume of 252 pages in which he set out his radical theology at considerable length. He was obviously working extremely hard, and it is probable that he also began to take part in the editorial work of the *Crisis* in the summer of 1833 before he actually assumed the position of editor.

Smith took over the editorship of the *Crisis* from the first issue of the third volume on 7 September 1833. His editorials were written in a straightforward secular style and there was nothing to indicate, for the first few months at any rate, the shift to a more radical position that was to bring him, by the early spring of 1834, into a revision of the ideas of Owenism and into sharp conflict with Robert Owen himself. These six months beginning with his assumption of the editorship of the leading Owenite journal represent almost as large a change in his intellectual premises as the acceptance of Owenism after his millennial period. Against a background of widespread and vigorous trade union activity throughout the country at large, the major influence upon him was James Morrison, the editor of the *Pioneer*, whose own ideas were also evolving rapidly, from a more or less complete acceptance of Owenism to something akin to militant syndicalism.

James Morrison was born in Newcastle of working-class parents in 1802.[37] In his early adult life he worked at his trade of housepainter in Birmingham, and it was this town with its vigorous radical traditions which gave Morrison his first introduction to both unionism and politics. He and his wife had both been influenced by Owenism from at least 1828, and Morrison became on friendly personal terms with William Pare.[38] By 1831-2 he was becoming prominent in his union, at a time when there was much forward movement among the building unions, and he also took an active part in the unstamped agitation.[39] When the *Birmingham Labour Exchange Gazette* was begun in January 1833, Morrison's union was among the trades which promised to back it, and Morrison himself took an active part in the organisation of the Birmingham Labour Exchange.[40]

The Operative Builder's Union, which was to play such an important part in the trade union developments of 1832-4, had been formed by the coming together of seven building trades. Its date of foundation, Cole noted, is uncertain but it was probably late 1831 or early 1832. Although precise details of Morrison's connection with these trade union developments are lacking, there is no doubt that he became involved, for by the summer of 1833 he was preparing to launch a weekly paper as the journal of the Builder's Union. In the struggle inside the union between the 'exclusives' and the 'centralisers'[41] – between those who wanted a loose federation of independent craft unions and those who argued for a single centralised body under a unified executive and conference – Morrison, like all the other Owen-ites involved, was a centraliser, and the *Pioneer* was to be a powerful influence on their side.

Thus far, up to the publication of the first issue of the *Pioneer* on 7 September 1833, Morrison was a whole-hearted and dedicated supporter of Robert Owen. He wrote a charming letter to Owen on 23 July 1833[42] in which he averred that the acceptance of Owen's doctrines had made him 'a better and happier being. Before I knew the great truths which you have developed I was a rough and irritable stickler for vulgar liberty'; and he went on to express his desire that he should become even more imbued with Owen's principles so that charity should enter into all his feelings and calculations. He ended: 'I shall look to you as a Father and try to become a faithful son. May circumstances be auspicious to my Baptism and make me worthy to be Yours truly, James Morrison.' But there was an interesting phrase at the beginning of this letter which offers at least a hint of the later bent of Morrison's thinking. He wrote that he craved 'for a *practical knowledge* of the means whereby to effect a change in the conditions of my fellow workmen and to devote my whole energies to their complete eman-cipation'. It was to be this insistence on the means to the end that led

him into ways of thinking and acting whose class-conscious awareness
and practical militancy were to horrify Owen, and to lead to a major
breach between them. Already by early September he was beginning
to move away from Owen's position, as represented by the Labour
Exchange idea. In a letter dated 2 September 1833,[43] while still addressing Owen as 'the Father of our Great Family' and entreating him to
write an article for the first number of the *Pioneer*, Morrison then
explains, in a half-defensive way, why he has 'retired' from the
Birmingham Labour Exchange in order to 'devote the whole of my
time and energies to the Union', the Union being 'more likely to
accomplish the same great object'. He went on to urge that there
should be no sectarian divisions in this new situation and that co-
operators should themselves form lodges alongside the union lodges.

Exactly when James Smith met Morrison cannot be positively
identified, but it must have been in this summer of 1833. Smith was in
London while Morrison was still in Birmingham, but the *Pioneer* was to
be printed and published in London by B. D. Cousins, who also owned
and published the *Crisis*. The two journals used the same office in 18
Duke Street, Lincoln's Inn, and the two editors must have seen a good
deal of each other. Morrison and his family came to live in Camden
Town. The two men brought to each other complementary strengths.
For Morrison it meant contacts with the advanced radical groups in
London, and for Smith it offered a detailed insight into the trade union
movement, at a time when the confrontations with the employers were
reaching new heights of struggle and intensity. From the time when
they became editors, Smith in the *Crisis* and Morrison in the *Pioneer*
began to develop identical views. This does not mean that their
respective journals became identical. The *Crisis* remained the official
journal of the Owenite movement, and Smith, while achieving a much
livelier paper than it had been under the direction of the Owens,[44]
was careful to maintain its particular character. It still carried a contribution from Robert Owen in most of its issues, and his own Sunday
morning lecture continued to occupy the front page. The *Pioneer*, by
contrast, was from its outset a propagandist paper for the trade union
movement.

The turning-point for Morrison would seem to have been the Derby
lock-out which began in December 1833, for he rightly saw the Derby
affair as of major importance for the whole movement. He published
in full the employer's resolutions[45] and threw the whole weight of his
paper's influence – whose circulation was now rapidly approaching its

peak figure of 30,000[46] – behind the Derby unionists in their struggle against the Document. He visited Derby himself and became the paid secretary of the Committee of United Trades which was established at Birmingham to organise support and to receive subscriptions.[47] This militant attitude on Morrison's part provoked the first open conflict with Owen. The latter sympathised with the Derby unionists and supported their financial appeal, but he became increasingly alarmed at the tone of writing in the *Pioneer*, and at its use of a very direct class analysis of the industrial situation. In a letter addressed to the *Pioneer*, and published in both the *Pioneer* and the *Crisis* on 11 January 1834, Owen wrote:

> Sir – I have been watching your progress with deep interest, and with many of the general sentiments expressed in the various papers in the *Pioneer* I am much pleased; but sometimes you and your correspondents seem for a time to have lost the spirit of peace and charity by which alone the regeneration of mankind can ever be effected. You have drawn a line of opposition of feelings and of interests between the employers and employed in the production of wealth, which, if it were continued, would tend to delay the progress of this great cause, and to injure those noble principles which you are so desirous of seeing carried into practice . . .

and he appended a long 'Address to the Trades Unions' in which he reiterated once again the many familiar arguments: that capital and labour have basic interests in common; that what was needed was a union 'of masters and men, producers of all that is useful and necessary for happiness. They are, in fact, one and the same body, the masters having gradually arisen out of the mass of workmen'; and he ended the Address by recommending the cordial union of both employers and employees, and the cessation of 'this senseless warfare, carried on between masters and operatives solely for the gain and advantage of those who neither produce wealth, knowledge, or anything really useful and beneficial for any portion of mankind. . .'.

We have no direct means of knowing what Smith thought about this particular dispute between Owen and Morrison; but once more there is really no doubt about his attitude, for all the evidence shows clearly that he was in general and particular matters firmly on Morrison's side, and that he was beginning to resent the dictatorial approach of Owen to those who opposed him.[48] By early 1834 Smith, like Morrison, was moving away from what they both now considered to be the static utopianism of Owen; and they were both beginning to accept an approach that stressed the permanent conflict inherent in the structure of property relationships.


IV


The most theoretically integrated of all Smith's writings, and those that represented the most advanced socialist position he was to take up, were published under the pseudonym of Senex in the *Pioneer*. The shift in his thinking towards a syndicalist outlook is not easy to document on a month-to-month basis, although it is quite clear taking the beginning and the end of the six months between September 1833 and March 1834. One can sense the change in his Sunday morning lectures, but no reading of these would prepare one for the much more advanced statement of his ideas in the fourteen Letters on Associated Labour which he began publishing on 15 March 1834. It is assumed here that James Smith was their author, but the matter of authorship is not completely certain, and G. D. H. Cole in his last writing in this field threw out a rather casual query which suggested a doubt on his part.[49] What can be said is that it is *improbable* that anyone else but Smith wrote these articles, and there is a good deal of circumstantial and positive evidence to identify him as their author.[50]

The treatment of the themes he dealt with would have been familiar to anyone in the contemporary movement who had read carefully, and who had thoroughly absorbed, the writings of the social critics and socialist thinkers who had preceded him. In particular these would be Charles Hall, Thomas Hodgkin and William Thompson, in addition, of course, to Robert Owen. What Smith offers in these Letters is a guide to a socialist analysis of contemporary society written in a lively and interesting fashion.[51] He began, rather unusually, by noting the three historical stages of labour: enslaved or compulsory labour, which in Britain had long passed into the second stage of hireling or market-able labour. Morally, this second stage of society, based on hireling labour, was a vast improvement on the slave-labour society which had preceded it, yet at the same time for many thousands it meant depriva-tion to a degree which has exceeded that of the slave period. The hireling labourer was compelled by hunger to sell himself, the purpose of his buyers being to make a profit and thereby accumulate riches. Obviously it was in the interest of the labourers to keep up the price of labour, and the question that immediately presented itself was why the labourers were always beaten down. There were two answers to this question, Smith wrote: the first was the lack of knowledge of their general position in society by the labourers – what later socialist writers would call the problems of consciousness; and the second reason was their utter dependence upon wage labour: 'the absolute necessity of an immediate and constant market for labour'.[52] The labourers had to earn their subsistence at any price, otherwise they and their families starved, and the result was a position of such material degradation that nothing was left for mental improvement. Self-esteem was lost and the labourers sank 'into an abject course of conduct'. This was why unity in the form of trade combinations was the only way the labourer could remedy his position.

He enlarged on some favourite themes of the Owenites, among them the way selfishness in man was implanted by a competitive society based upon private property. God had made all men equal, but in a society of private property there were now two distinct classes, 'the enjoyer and the producer, the grower and the feeder, the wearer and the weaver'. This society of hireling labour had enormously increased the productive capacity of mankind, but the plenty which was produced could not be equally distributed. Moreover, there was a basic contradiction (although Smith does not use the phrase) between plenty and profit. 'Plenty is a terrible foe to profit. Every capitalist hates the plenty of another;' and in a most telling paragraph Smith explained to his working-class readership how irrational present-day society was:

> Can it, I ask, be reconciled to Christianity, by any pretence worthy of the name of common sense, that the pious manufacturer, after having heard the gospel on Sunday, shall tell the wretched hundreds that surround his works and warehouses on the Monday morning, that they have made so much plenty that they must starve? That they have called into existence, by the energy of their minds and the strength of their hands, so much clothing, that nakedness must be their lot? That they have, in fact, created so much wealth, that they must pine in poverty?[53]

Such a system was 'totally at variance with the welfare and improvement of mankind'; and to achieve the just society hireling labour must give way to the third stage of labour, associated labour. And to achieve a society based upon associated labour we must first have all the labourers in combination and then proceed with schemes of co-operation. The self-interest of the labourers was clear, but what of those who failed to appreciate the need for union, and who insisted on remaining outside the trades combinations? Smith then proceeded to argue the case for a closed shop in a quite remarkable statement for a man of middle-class origin whose acquaintance with trade unions was only from the outside, and whose concern with the day-to-day problems of the unions was a matter only of six months' standing.[54]

Running through these letters was a commentary on the crucial debate between those who placed their emphasis upon the role of the unions and those who argued for political solutions. The debate became intense during the early years of the 1830s, with the trade union movement achieving growth and short-term successes on a scale never previously known. On the political side Bronterre O'Brien and Henry Hetherington were vigorous critics first of the orthodox Owenite position and then of the syndicalist standpoint represented by James Morrison and Smith.[55] The latter's view was a mixture of the Owenite approach and an increasing emphasis upon the central role of trade unions, although he never fully integrated his analysis. He began, in the Letters, by stating categorically that it mattered little who directed the affairs of the state, since the Reformed Parliament was 'pretty equally divided' between the capitalists and the landowners; and what was needed was the alternative source of power represented by the over-whelming numerical and moral strength of the people. Working men had little to fear from state power, while 'the selfish, the foolish, the vicious and the illiberal' would urge recourse to coercive measures, it was necessary to remember that England was not France, and the whole political and social structure was different from that over which Louis-Philippe ruled. In France 'the proportion of the manufacturing productive power to other labourers is . . . *as one to two*, while in England it is *two to one*'. Moreover, in England there was a close sympathy between the urban labourers and those in the rural areas, as witness the contemporary protests on behalf of the Dorchester labourers, while in France the peasant masses were estranged from the workers in the towns. Finally, and this presumably was meant to clinch the argument, 'it cannot be proved, by any perversion of our publications or pro-ceedings, that there is the slightest degree of disloyalty in our views or intentions. We have worked with hand and mind. The greatness of the King and the Kingdom is the result of our labour, and all that we ask for, is to secure for ourselves, and our families in the future, a just share of the plenty we produce. No, my brethren, we have little to apprehend from the King or the army'; and the King's ministers were likely to be very reluctant to follow the lamentable example of the present French Government.[56] It was an interesting echo from Robert Owen, but then Smith thought further, admitting that there was much more to be feared from the London police and the London and provincial magistracy; but the people were well aware of the problem and they were always in a state of 'watchful endurance'.[57]

This uncertainty about the role of force in society and the place of coercive power in the direction of affairs continued throughout all the Letters. Without doubt, in these last few months after the arrest and transportation of the Dorchester labourers, he was coming to a much firmer and sharper analysis of class relations, but the argument was still nearly always a qualified one. In both the *Crisis* and the *Pioneer* he was constantly hinting, or being specific, about the realities of power and their political expression, but then he would draw back, into the argument of rational self-interest or Owenite benevolence. Thus he asked bluntly in one of his Sunday morning lecturers: 'How can men love one another when their interests are at variance';[58] and in a discussion of the Dorchester labourers, whose treatment exercised such a profound effect upon the whole radical movement, he vigorously attacked *The Times* which had used the word 'intimidation' to describe the protest meeting of 21 April in London,[59] arguing that the whole weight of the propertied classes in society represented a permanent intimidation of the working people:

And why has the cruel, the unjustifiable sentence of transportation been carried into effect against inoffensive beings [i.e. the Dorchester labourers] so blameless as those victims in equity and even in regular law? The answer is plain: it has been done to *intimidate* us, brethren; and it has been done under the *intimidation* of capitalists, landowners, and other men of property, to whom the ministers and the parliament are compelled to be subservient. The present system of government, and the present order of society, cannot be maintained without *intimidation* on their part. What is their standing army – what is their well-organised police? Are not these instruments of *intimidation*? And how do they *intimidate*? Is it not by threats of worse than brutal force? Is it not by a strictly disciplined – a perfected system of murder? Look at the science that they have enlisted in the cause of *intimidation* – listen to the honourable appellations, and view the splendour of apparel, by which their system of *intimidating violence* is rendered glorious and seductive! When their forces move, blood is shed, and the widow, surrounded by orphans, mourns amid its triumphs. They fill graves, and they boast that they have restored peace.

But Smith continued: 'Ours is a very different movement, brethren.' The working people were not out to destroy but to convince and enlighten, and by paying attention to their own unity, the working class must take every opportunity of exhibiting their strength. When, of course, the working people stand firm in their overwhelming numbers, it will be called intimidation. Such intimidation, however, 'will be good for them. It is our business to prevent them, and their army, and their police, from *intimidating us*.'[60]

Smith returned on a number of occasions to this question of state power and the means by which the working people could achieve victory over their class enemies. His argument remained contradictory and unfinished, but one thing at least was clear to him. In words that were to be echoed years later by Marx, Smith said plainly: 'Do not deceive yourselves, brethren; none but yourselves can be your liberators.'[61] The discussion of means and ends, of course, forced both Smith and Morrison to take up a position on politics, and in his last Letter published in the *Pioneer* Smith elaborated his ideas on the subject. He was emphatically against getting mixed up with the political party games. Revolutions, by which he meant political revolutions, were party concerns and of no interest to working people whose social rights had first to be gained before any political change could benefit them. This is what he and Morrison meant by their advocacy of a Trades Parliament which would replace the existing Parliament and would be truly representative of the working people;[62] but how to achieve such a representation was left obscure. The implication was that the unions would undertake associated labour projects throughout the length and breadth of the land, and that this would create the alternative power to set against the present owners of property. But neither Smith nor Morrison developed this argument to any length.

Despite these confusions and contradictions, and Smith is hardly alone among socialist writers then or later in not making plain the logic of his analysis of the power structure, these last essays by Smith in his socialist period were a powerful statement of the contemporary indictment of society by the radical movement of the 1830s. What is so interesting about Smith is the way he takes up arguments that have remained standard themes in the socialist movement since his day. Thus, in Letter X, 'On the Pretended Ignorance of the Labouring Classes',[63] he answered what was even then the hackneyed argument that the working classes were too ignorant to conduct their own affairs or the affairs of the nation. He agreed that education and more enlightenment were necessary, for it was the whole purpose of 'our task-masters' to keep the working people in a state of mental blindness. But, he went on,

> do not suffer yourselves to be tricked and bamboozled out of your rights under the notion that you must have education before you are fit to have justice. Education is a very good thing; but men and children must live as well as learn; besides, there is such a thing as education without knowledge, and there is also such a thing as knowledge without education; and of these two things the last is much better than the first. Perhaps, after all that can be done in the business of education, the common sense of mankind will remain pretty nearly at the same level. There are many learned men who are very great fools, and there are men who do not know 'a B from a bull's foot', and yet are very sensible and intelligent members of society. All useful knowledge consists in the acquirement of ideas concerning our condition in life; and there are few men of common observation who do not get into their minds, whether they can read and write or not, the ideas that are most serviceable to them. The position of a man in society, with its obligations and interests, forces ideas upon him which all the theory of education would not have impressed upon him as long as he was not called upon practically to make use of them.

The answer, then, for those who were deprived of political rights was clear. Change the situation in which men are living, alter their position in society and there would be no difficulty about their adaptation to new duties and obligations. But the real problem was that the working people had been so long without their rights; they had been so long accustomed to their inferior station in life; that they lacked the consciousness of what society ought to be offering them.

> No, brethren, it is not ignorance, it is not vice, that unfits us for the conduct of our own affairs; it is nothing but a deep sense, a full consciousness that *our own* affairs are really *our own*! We have been so long deprived of *our own*, that we can hardly persuade ourselves that *our own* is actually *our own*. . . . We want no new knowledge, no new powers of mind, no new doctrines of any sort; all that we

want is confidence in ourselves and an exertion of common sense, a resolute determination to look straightforward.


v


James Smith's last Letter on Associated Labour was published in the *Pioneer* of 28 June 1834, and the issue which followed, that of 5 July, was the final number. Morrison had been in open conflict with Robert Owen and the executive of the G.N.C.T.U. for some months ever since his resignation from the executive in late March. His first reason for resigning was on the issue of oaths, but there were other matters of conflict, notably the mishandling of the Derby lock-out and the general passivity and incompetence of the executive.[64] In the weeks which followed, Morrison's criticisms became more pointed and like his contributor Senex he was extending and making sharper his class analysis of the industrial situation. Towards the end of May Owen demanded that Morrison turn over the *Pioneer* to the executive, and on Morrison's refusal, Owen announced that they would be publishing their own *Official Gazette* (the first number of which appeared on 7 June).[65] With the demise of the *Pioneer* in early July, together with the rapid fragmentation of the trade union movement in the country at large, Morrison lost overnight the considerable influence that he had acquired over the previous nine months, and he virtually disappeared from public view. Within just over a year he was dead. He was not quite thirty-four.[66]

In his political and industrial attitudes Smith followed a parallel course to that of Morrison. He had never been as committed to Owen or to Owenism as had Morrison, and in public at any rate he was to be bolder and more forthright than Morrison in his criticisms. The two men by the early spring of 1834 were clearly working closely together. Like Morrison, Smith urged that the oath should go, for it was a 'barbarous practice' which got in the way of the real objects of the union;[67] and on 12 April in the first leader of the *Crisis* he launched a major attack on the executive for its general incompetence and lack of energy which ended with the questions: 'Have the Unions an Executive? How many of its five senses has it lost? We pause for a reply.' And the reply came on the next day, Sunday, when Owen at his evening

lecture in the Charlotte Street Institution provided at great length a
detailed statement of his total incapacity to understand what the
argument was about, or what the increasingly desperate situation
confronting the unions demanded. It was published in full in the following week's *Crisis*.[68] It was the speech of a benevolently-minded doc-
trinaire who showed himself wholly insensitive to the meaning of the
turbulent events that were taking place around him, who was quite
incapable of learning from experience, and who could repeat only the
abstract precepts that had been his stock-in-trade for so many years.
The central contribution of Robert Owen to the development of
socialist ideas in Britain is not in question: the issue here, however, is
the immediate and conservative influence which Owen exercised within
the leadership of the trade union movement at this critical moment in its
history. He had become formally a member of the Consolidated Union
after the arrest of the Dorchester labourers, and from that time (early
April 1834) his influence within the counsels of the executive was
predominant. His analysis was unrealistic, and the advice he offered
irrelevant; and because it was irrelevant in a highly volatile and
difficult situation, it was disastrous. It is highly probable that nothing
could have saved the movement from physical disintegration in the
summer of 1834; it is equally necessary to add that without Owen it is
unlikely that the astonishing response of the early months of the year
could have been evoked. Yet something was lost: a conjuncture,
perhaps, between a working-class ideology and the grass-roots organisations of working people. At best, it was a fragile possibility, and the
historical moment during which the union might have been effected
quickly passed.

The evidence is only partially coherent, reflecting as it probably
does a lack of co-ordination, a looseness of practice. In these months
between March and June 1834 Smith and Morrison were together
evolving the elements of a new strategy and tactics for the trade unions:
urging the coming together in much closer relationship of the Northern
and the Southern unions, insisting upon a firm and vigorous direction
by a closely integrated executive, exploring the possibilities of a general
strike, tentatively working out the thesis of a House of Trades as an
alternative to the strategy of universal suffrage within the existing
framework of society. Individually and together these ideas can be
documented from the files of the *Pioneer* and the *Crisis*,[69] but there was
a general incompleteness about their writing which reflects partly the
step-by-step process by which their ideas evolved, but even more the

growing difficulties of the situation within which they worked. The movement was rapidly disintegrating from May onwards, and a by-product of the decline was the rapid fall in the circulation of the journals. There was considerable hostility towards them because of their criticisms of Owen,[70] who himself was never one to accept criticism passively; and both Smith, in private, and Morrison, in public, made clear references to the hostile forces who were working against them.[71] There was inexperience and incompetence among the trade union leaderships as well as within the executive of the Consolidated. Above all, both men were losing heart: Morrison after the end of the original *Pioneer* in early July[72] and Smith along with him. On 1 August 1834 Smith wrote to his brother that he had resigned from 'Owen's party', and it was the announcement that one more stage in his extraordinary career was coming to an end. The *Crisis* finished publication with the issue of 23 August and Smith began publishing *The Shepherd* a week later. It was printed and published by B. D. Cousins, but this was the only thing that connected *The Shepherd* and the *Crisis*, for no one could possibly guess that the editors of the two papers were the same man. Smith shrugged off his militant socialism without any apparent emotional or intellectual difficulty, and within a few years he was to become a thoroughly respectable and very successful editor of a family religious journal. He had summed up his future in the letter of 1 August already quoted: 'It is probable I am now nearly done with the Infidels. . . . I shall most probably be back to the Believing again.'[73]

NOTES AND REFERENCES

1. The main biographical source for his life is the volume by his nephew, W. Anderson Smith, '*Shepherd*' *Smith, the Universalist: The Story of a Mind* (1892). (All places of publication are London, unless specifically noted.) This is a curious work, with little understanding of the subject, but it has the great merit of printing a considerable number of letters from Smith himself, although these are very badly arranged. Other material includes an inaccurate account in the *D.N.B.*; a short chapter in R. W. Postgate, *Out of the Past* (1922); a typescript MS. by John Sever, 'James Morrison of the Pioneer' (Oxford, 1963), copies of which have been deposited in a number of libraries, including the B.M., the Bodleian and the Co-operative Union Library, Manchester (and upon which I have relied heavily for the part which Morrison played in the year 1833–4); and an excellent sum-

mary of Smith's life and ideas in J. F. C. Harrison, *Robert Owen and the Owenites in Britain and America* (1969) esp. pp. 108–22. Harrison also quotes an unpublished thesis by D. R. Cook, 'Reverend James Elishama Smith: Socialist Prophet of the Millennium' (M.A. thesis, State University of Iowa, 1961) which I have not seen.

2. The literature is growing on revivalism, millennial religious movements and early industrialisation, much stimulated by E. P. Thompson's *The Making of the English Working Class*, 1st ed. (1963; Penguin ed. 1968). For an indispensable introduction, see Norman Cohn, *The Pursuit of the Millennium* (1957; Paladin ed. 1970); and for the relationship between religious millennialism and Owenism, see Harrison, *Robert Owen*, pp. 92ff.

3. Smith, '*Shepherd*' *Smith*, p. 33.

4. Ibid., p. 34.

5. Edward Irving (1792–1834) was a middle-class Scots Presbyterian minister who from the early 1820s became interested in prophecy and millennialism. He attended the interdenominational Albury Conference in 1826 which came to the conclusion that the Second Coming was near. He was expelled from the Scotch Church, Regent Street, London, in April 1832, and he immediately accepted the offer of Robert Owen to use the Owenite Institution, Gray's Inn Road, as a temporary home for his congregation (*Crisis*, 12 May 1832). There is a considerable literature on Irving and the Catholic Apostolic Church which he inspired: Margaret O. W. Oliphant, *Life of Edward Irving*, 2 vols (1862); *Encyclopaedia Britannica*, 9th ed. (1875) *s.v.* Irving, Edward; Thomas Carlyle, *Reminiscences*, 1 (1881); *Encyclopaedia of Religion and Ethics*, VII (1914) *s.v.* Irving and the Catholic Apostolic Church; and two modern works: A. L. Drummond, *Edward Irving and His Circle* (1938); P. E. Shaw, *The Catholic Apostolic Church* (New York, 1946). There is the usual helpful summary in Harrison, *Robert Owen*, pp. 96ff.

6. J. D. Mackie, *A History of Scotland* (Penguin Books, 1964) pp. 162–3.

7. *Encyclopaedia Britannica*, 9th ed. (1875) *s.v.* Irving, Edward.

8. William Hazlitt, *The Spirit of the Age* (Everyman ed., 1910) p. 207.

9. *Encyclopaedia of Religion and Ethics*, VII (1914) *s.v.* Irving and the Catholic Apostolic Church.

10. His father became an Irvingite. Smith, '*Shepherd*' *Smith*, p. 16.

11. Ibid., p. 40.

12. Joanna Southcott died in 1814. The most extended modern study is G. R. Balleine, *Past Finding Out: The Tragic Story of Joanna Southcott and Her Successors* (1956), and for an interpretation, Thompson, *The Making of the Working Class*, pp. 117–19, 382–8.

13. Smith, '*Shepherd*' *Smith*, p. 52. The date of this letter is uncertain: probably about September 1830.

14. See Cohn, *The Pursuit of the Millennium*, *passim*, and Thompson, *The Making of the English Working Class*, esp. chap XI, ii, 'The Chiliasm of Despair'.

15. Smith, '*Shepherd*' *Smith*, chap. VI and XXI.

16. James Smith wrote in 1848 an account of John Wroe and other South-cottians in a novel which was in part autobiographical. It was published posthumously in two volumes in 1873 under the title *The Coming Man*.

17. Harrison, *Robert Owen and the Owenites*, p. 112.

18. Smith, '*Shepherd*' *Smith*, pp. 50–1.

19. Ibid., p. 74.

20. Ibid., p. 56.

21. Ibid., p. 81.

22. Richard K. P. Pankhurst, 'Anna Wheeler: A Pioneer Socialist and Feminist', *Political Quarterly*, XXV 2 (1954) 132–43. See also the same author's *William Thompson* (1954) and *The Saint-Simonians, Mill and Carlyle* (1957). Smith's own account is in Smith, '*Shepherd*' *Smith*, p. 90 and chap. XXI.

23. 26 Sep 1832: Smith '*Shepherd*' *Smith*, pp. 86–7.

24. It is not certain whether Smith used Ward's chapel as soon as he began lecturing in London, or whether he started elsewhere and then moved. But the difference in time could not have been more than a few months at the most.

25. Smith, '*Shepherd*' *Smith*, p. 91.

26. The invitation was for quite different reasons from those that prompted Robert Owen to offer hospitality to Edward Irving when the latter had been expelled from his church. With Irving it was Owen exhibiting his theory of toleration in practice, although the fact that Irving was quite a vigorous social critic was not irrelevant to the decision to invite him. But Irving was never a political radical or an Owenite, nor was he ever likely to become either. Owen's very interesting statement of the reasons which prompted him to invite Edward Irving are in the *Crisis*, 12 May 1832.

27. *Lecture on a Christian Community, delivered by the Rev. J. E. Smith, M.A. at the Surrey Institution* (London, John Brooks, 421 Oxford Street, MDCCCXXXIII) 20 pp., p. 3.

28. Ibid., p. 4. It is worth remarking that the use of capitals in the *Lecture* is as in the text above, and that capital letters were not used for 'he', 'him' and 'his father', when referring to Jesus.

29. Ibid., pp. 12–13.

30. It would be an interesting exercise for historians of nineteenth-century religion to relate Smith's eschatology to later developments of Christian doctrine.

31. *Practical Directions for the Speedy and Economical Establishment of Communities, on the Principles of Mutual Co-operation, United Possessions and Equality of Exertions and of the Means of Enjoyments* (Cork, 1830). The *Practical Directions* was widely read and commented on in the years immediately following its publication, and it is just the kind of writing that Smith would have met with in Owenite circles. There is a summary of Thompson's arguments, and of the discussions of his thesis in the Owenite movement, in Pankhurst, *William Thompson*, chaps XV and XVI.

32. An example would be the pamphlet Owen published just before Smith made contact with the Owenites: *Robert Owen's Reply to the Question 'What Would you Do, If You Were Prime Minister of England?'*, 2nd ed. (Stockport, 1832).

33. When the summary of a repeat of this *Lecture* was published in the *Crisis*, 4 May 1833, the discussion on women and their relationships with men was considerably expanded over the pamphlet version.

34. In the 1832 pamphlet noted above (see note 32).

35. There is a summary of Saint-Simon's main ideas in the *New Christianity* in Pankhurst, *The Saint-Simonians*, chap. IX. The major influence upon James Smith to undertake the translation was almost certainly Anna Wheeler, who had been a leading member of a Saint-Simonian circle at Caen as early as 1818.

36. The full title will indicate its content: *The Anti-Christ, or Christianity Re-*

*formed. In which is demonstrated from the Scriptures, in opposition to the prevailing opinion of the whole religious world, that Evil and Good are from one Source: Devil and God are one Spirit, and that the one is merely manifested to make perfect the other.*

37. John Sever, 'James Morrison of the Pioneer' (MS., Oxford, 1963). I am greatly indebted to this account for the details of Morrison's career in the paragraphs which follow.

38. William Pare (1805-73): a first-generation Owenite who founded the earliest Birmingham Co-operative Society in November 1828, and thereafter took an active part in the Owenite movement and later the Co-operative movement, remaining committed to the ideals of co-operation until the end of his life. R. G. Garnett, *The Ideology of the Early Co-operative Movement* (University of Kent, 1966) 18 pp.; Harrison, *Robert Owen and the Owenites, passim.*

39. According to John Sever, the first dated reference to Morrison by name was 9 August 1831 when a Birmingham meeting protested against both the Taxes on Knowledge and the recent imprisonment of a number of publishers of the unstamped press, Morrison being made secretary of a committee to raise subscriptions (pp. 17ff.).

40. *Crisis*, 27 Apr 1833, for a letter from Morrison to Robert Owen, read by the latter at one of his regular lectures at the Surrey Institution on 21 April 1833.

41. G. D. H. Cole, *Attempts at General Union* (1953) pp. 105-6, uses the term 'universals' for those who were arguing for centralised control of the union.

42. No. 649 in the Owen Collection, Co-operative Union Library, Manchester.

43. Ibid., no. 659.

44. The *Crisis* was edited by Robert Owen from no. 1, 12 Apr 1832, until 27 Oct 1832, after which it was jointly edited by Robert Owen and Robert Dale Owen, his son. The journal became noticeably duller and less interesting during this period of joint editorship, especially when Dale Owen began writing the editorials. An announcement in the issue of 27 Apr 1833 said that Dale Owen had returned to America, and that new editorial arrangements had not yet been completed. B. D. Cousins took over the journal from this date, and the following issue of 4 May 1833 had a new masthead on the title page: 'Under the Patronage of Robert Owen'. See the final number of the *Crisis*, 23 Aug 1834, for an editorial statement by Smith explaining the editorial and business changes in 1833.

45. Reprinted in Cole, *Attempts at General Union*, pp. 115-17.

46. Smith gives this figure on at least two occasions: the first time in a letter written in the early months of 1834 (Smith, *'Shepherd' Smith*, p. 98) and then in the obituary notice of Morrison, first published in the *London Free Press* and reprinted in the *Birmingham Journal*, 19 Sep 1835, and again reproduced in full in Sever, 'James Morrison', pp. 60-3.

47. The Committee also hoped to be able to organise co-operative workshops for those trade unionists who were locked out. Sever, 'James Morrison', pp. 35-6.

48. See especially letters dated 15 May 1834, Smith, *'Shepherd' Smith*, pp. 99-100, and 30 May 1834, ibid., pp. 103-4.

49. G. D. H. Cole, *A History of Socialist Thought*, 1 (1962) 125, n.1.

50. The evidence that Smith wrote for the *Pioneer* is quite specific: 'I have always one and sometimes two articles in the *Pioneer*, but I have no share in the paper. I get £1 per week for what I write' (letter of James Smith to his brother John, 28 Mar 1834: Smith, *'Shepherd' Smith*, p. 98).

51. Smith, however, lacks the sweep of Bronterre O'Brien's writing in the *Poor Man's Guardian* in these years, who was developing the same kind of socialist analysis, although they differed sharply on the tactical problems of working-class struggle.

52. *Pioneer*, 10 May 1834.

53. Ibid., 12 Apr 1834.

54. The occasion of Smith's defence of the closed shop was a *Times* attack on the trade unions for their 'tyranny' over their fellow workmen who refused to join (*Pioneer*, 10 May 1834).

55. For Bronterre O'Brien, see the summary of his ideas in T. Rothstein, *From Chartism to Labourism* (1929) pp. 100ff.; and for James Morrison's polemic with Hetherington's articles in the *Poor Man's Guardian*, *Pioneer*, 31 May and 7 June 1834.

56. Smith was here referring to the suppression of the uprising in Lyons in February–March 1834.

57. *Pioneer*, 26 Apr 1834.

58. *Crisis*, 22 Mar 1834.

59. This was the great meeting in Copenhagen Fields which Robert Owen led to present the Petition to Lord Melbourne. There are reports in both the *Crisis* and the *Pioneer*, 26 Apr 1834.

60. *Pioneer*, 3 May 1834.

61. Ibid., 28 June 1834.

62. Ibid., 7 Feb, 17 May, 14 June 1834.

63. Ibid., 31 May 1834.

64. Ibid., 29 Mar 1834; Cole, *Attempts at General Union*, pp. 133–4.

65. Cole, *Attempts at General Union*, chap. XVIII; Sever, 'James Morrison', pp. 45ff.

66. Sever, 'James Morrison', p. 48, provides all the available evidence for Morrison's career after the last issue of the *Pioneer* on 5 July. Morrison began publishing the *Weekly Chronicle and Pioneer* on 12 July, and although no copies are extant, it is known to have continued throughout July and August. One copy exists in the British Museum of *The Pioneer and Official Gazette of the Associated Trade Unions* for 20 Sep 1834, and Sever suggests that this was an amalgamation of *The Pioneer and Weekly Chronicle* with the *Official Gazette of the G.N.C.T.U.* There is internal evidence that Morrison was continuing to edit his section of the amalgamated journal. It continued to be advertised until the end of October. Between October 1834 and August 1835 there is no information available about Morrison's life. He died on 21 August 1835 in Manchester Infirmary.

67. *Crisis*, 29 Mar 1834.

68. Ibid., 19 April 1834. Given the background of events against which it was delivered, it really was a most extraordinary and revealing document. Owen listed six objects of the G.N.C.T.U.: the need for union among themselves, the elimination of drunkenness, the provision of productive employment and the good life for all, education of the children and adults, and proper relations with the Government. He ended his summary of these objects: 'And that measures be adopted to negotiate with the government that it shall carry the views of the United Consolidated Union into execution in the shortest possible time, for the benefit of the whole population; but that if government is not yet prepared for

national employment and national education, that the Consolidated Union should adopt measures to insure employment and education to all members of the Union.'

69. The issues of the two journals have to be read as a whole for these summer months of 1834, but see especially *Pioneer*, 7 Feb, 15 Mar, 25 May, 31 May and 7 June; and the *Crisis*, 12 and 19 Apr, 12 and 26 July, 9 and 23 Aug.

70. One matter of conflict between Owen and the two editors which is always remarked upon and has not been discussed here is the criticism that both Morrison and Smith made of Owen's atheism and the effect this had upon the trade unions. There are two pieces of evidence for the allegation that the infidel character of Owen's thought was either being used to discredit the unions or that Owen himself was using his position inside the unions to propagate his anti-religious views: letter of James Smith to his brother dated 30 May 1834 (Smith, 'Shepherd Smith', pp. 103–4), and the *Pioneer*, 7 June, when Morrison was commenting on the attempt by Owen to take over the paper for the executive of the G.N.C.T.U. While there is no doubt about the 'odium' attaching to Owen's name for his free-thought views, it is difficult to believe that this question of religion was a major factor in the conflict between him and the other two, not least because all the other issues of conflict had been brought out into the open weeks before this religious question was mentioned.

71. Smith, '*Shepherd*' *Smith*, pp. 99–100 (letter dated 15 May 1834); and *Pioneer*, 17 May 1834.

72. Sever, 'James Morrison', pp. 46ff.

73. Smith, '*Shepherd*' *Smith*, p. 112. *The Shepherd* was published in three volumes: vol. I, 30 Aug 1834–22 Aug 1835; vol. II, 1 Jan 1837–31 Mar 1837; vol. III, 1 July 1837–31 Mar 1838. It is difficult to substantiate J. F. C. Harrison's claim that Smith in *The Shepherd* 'elaborated most completely the combination of religious millennialism and social radicalism which he termed universalism' (*Robert Owen and the Owenites in Britain and America*, p. 114). *The Shepherd* was an early version of his later *Family Herald* but with a larger admixture of Smith's ideas of the unity of Nature and examples of his science of analogy. It is true that Smith remained aware of social problems, but his awareness, and his discussion of these problems, is qualitatively different from his writings in the *Crisis* and the *Pioneer*; and in this context there is an illuminating letter from Smith to Owen (Owen Collection, Manchester: letter no. 761 dated 28 Dec 1835) in which the element of millennialism is obviously growing again in Smith's thinking. In 1840 he confirmed this by publishing *The Little Book; or Momentous Crisis of 1840; in which the Bishop of Exeter and Robert Owen, are weighed in the Two Scales of One Balance, and a New Revelation of Demonstrated Truth is Announced to the World*. The purpose of the book is a juggling with mystical numbers in order to determine the precise date of the Second Coming, something which had fascinated him in his earlier millennial period (Smith, '*Shepherd*' *Smith*, p. 63). For a short time in the early 1840s he became enthusiastic for Fourier's ideas and he wrote for Hugh Doherty's Fourierist *The Phalanx*, but it was a phase that passed quickly, a flirtation compared with his deep commitment in the *Crisis* period. And then in 1842 he began *The Family Herald: A Domestic Magazine of Useful Information and Amusement*, his most successful journalistic venture which gave him both respectability and an income – the search for which, if his letters reflect the man, he had always been interested in. In the late 1840s he began to be attracted to

occult studies and spiritualism: he continued throughout his life his fascinating long-distance relationships with women, which included for some of them their financial support of Smith's work and activities; and he published in 1854 what he himself regarded as his major work, *The Divine Drama of History and Civilisation*. He died in 1857.

# CHAPTER SEVEN

# Robert Owen, Cotton Spinner: New Lanark, 1800-1825

## A. J. ROBERTSON

ROBERT OWEN is, of course, best known as a social philosopher and leader of early British socialism. But he was also, at least until 1827, a practical man of business, closely involved in the direction of some of the largest and most advanced industrial undertakings of his time. Owen the industrialist has, however, tended to be overshadowed by Owen the social reformer. Nevertheless, he enjoys in some quarters a considerable reputation as a pioneer of modern large-scale industrial management, particularly as a result of his humane and enlightened treatment of a large labour force in the days before the first effective factory legislation. Thus, for example, Messrs Urwick and Brech describe Owen as 'The Pioneer of Personnel Management' and argue that 'Generations ahead of his time, he preached and practised a conception of industrial relations which is, even now, accepted in only a few of the most progressive undertakings'.[1] More recently, Professor Checkland remarked that 'Robert Owen's principles of management were a revelation. Many of the larger men took up Owen's mode of factory management just as they had adopted Arkwright's plan of construction. . . .'[2]

Others, however, do not rate him so highly. Dr Fitton and Mr Wadsworth, for instance, observed that 'The idealized community which Robert Owen thought he had invented at New Lanark was not much different from those at Cromford and Belper that had preceded it'.[3] More generally, Professor Pollard has stated that 'the notion of his great ability as a businessman is a myth, as his later career surely adequately shows'.[4] And it seems true that after his final break with New Lanark, Owen behaved in a remarkably unbusinesslike fashion and incurred serious financial losses in his community-building at New Harmony and other activities.

There is, in fact, one view of Owen which regards him not only as a man of great conventional business ability but also as an important innovator, especially in the field of labour management. Others, meanwhile, see him in a less heroic light, as a man of mixed abilities whose role in the development of modern management was something less than unique. This essay will, it is hoped, help to establish which of the two points of view is likely to be the more accurate, first by trying to ascertain the degree of business success Owen achieved, and secondly by attempting a critical assessment of those aspects of his business career, especially at New Lanark, which appear to have a particular bearing on his reputation.

I

An earlier study of Owen's business career pointed out that his capabilities as a businessman are difficult to assess, but concluded that 'Certainly he was financially very successful'.[5] Many of his contemporaries would have been content to have their abilities assessed on this basis alone, but Owen's outlook was not so narrow, and indeed his interest in financial success may well have declined as his career in business developed. On the other hand, he claimed that the techniques of management he employed were not only new and based on assumptions different from those employed by other managers, but also that they paid off in the tangible form of handsome profits. Thus, in 1816, he wrote: 'it will soon appear, that the time and money so expended in the manufactory at New Lanark, even while such improvements are in progress only, and but half of their beneficial effects attained, are now producing a return exceeding fifty per cent, and will shortly create profits equal to cent per cent on the original capital invested in them'.[6] On his own terms, therefore, an assessment of Owen's capabilities based at least partly on his purely financial achievements seems valid enough.

New Lanark under Owen appears definitely to have been profitable. Mr Gorb cited the various refinancings through which the concertn passed as evidence of this, though it could be argued that they were rather evidence of Owen's inability to remain for long on good terms with his partners.[7] Owen himself provided more concrete evidence; he calculated that in the thirty years (1799–1829) when he was associated with New Lanark, he and his various partners received interest payments of 5 per cent on the capital they had invested and in addition shared out a total of £300,000 in profits. His first partnership (1799–1809) produced, as well as the annual 5 per cent, a total profit of £60,000, including £24,000 from the sale of the mills in 1809 and £7000 paid out in wages during a prolonged stoppage in 1806. The short-lived second partnership (1809–13) returned a vast £160,000 profit over and above the annual 5 per cent interest, but again including the £30,000 profit from the sale of the mills when the partnership broke up.[8] The profitability of Owen's third and last New Lanark partnership is difficult to establish. Using Owen's own figures, a surplus of £80,000 can be calculated for the sixteen-year period during which he was connected with it.[9] If this figure is accurate, it seems likely that New Lanark must have suffered occasional years of very low profits, if not actual losses. The disposable surplus available after the annual accounts were made up for 1817 was £9000, while the comparable figure for 1819 was £15,500, and for 1825 about £20,000.[10] If profits on such a scale had been normal, the total disposable surplus available for the years 1813 to 1829 would have been at least twice as much as the £80,000 that Owen's figures suggest. But the fifteen years after the end of the Napoleonic Wars were not the most prosperous in the cotton industry's history, and many mills, even well-managed ones, returned occasional losses.[11] There is no reason to suppose that New Lanark was insulated from general commercial trends.[12]

On the whole, though, there seems little doubt that New Lanark under Owen's management was a profitable concern. When it comes to measuring Owen's achievements in this respect against those of the management of other similar undertakings, however, the lack of information both about New Lanark and other mills presents serious difficulties, rendering a valid comparison virtually impossible. The only undertakings in any way comparable with New Lanark for which an adequate body of financial data appears to be available are, first, the Manchester spinning firm of McConnel and Kennedy, and secondly, William Marshall's Water Lane flax-spinning mill in Leeds.[13] Unfortunately, no adequate information is available for New Lanark in the period 1803–10, when the profitability of McConnel and Kennedy is known, and only in two isolated years, 1818 and 1825, is material available at present on which to compare the profitability of New Lanark with that of Marshall's mill.

The American educationist John Griscom estimated that in 1818 Owen and his partners enjoyed a rate of return of $12\frac{1}{2}$ per cent on capital, while another estimate for 1825 recorded a rate of return of

10 per cent on a capital of £200,000.[14] The corresponding figures for the Marshall concern can be calculated at 21 per cent and 12 per cent respectively. No valid conclusion about Owen's performance can be reached on the basis of such a limited comparison, but taking it together with Podmore's statement (apparently accepted by Professor Pollard) that this was 'an age when capital had an extraordinary monopoly value, and when enterprising manufacturers were making with ease 20 per cent and more on their capital',[15] there seem to be sufficient grounds for concluding that New Lanark under Owen was not exceptionally profitable.

II

Owen's financial success may not have been spectacular, but it was real enough. In accounting for it, Mr Gorb stressed Owen's 'understanding of the administrative processes of factory management which must have been very largely unique at the time'. Messrs Urwick and Brech take a similar view, and remark on his 'intuitive grasp of the principles of sound management and of the methods of applying them effectively'.[16] Professor Pollard's view is that 'his competitive advantage could not have come either from a harsh bargaining ability or from particularly effective marketing arrangements, but arose out of his ability to win the co-operation of his workers while paying them no more than competitive wages, as well as out of the 'orderly arrangement' of the works, an alert policy of technical up-to-dateness, and a careful selection and training of under-managers', but that Owen's possession of 'a monopolistic position at the fine end of the spinning industry' created an advantage so overwhelming that 'any policy would have produced large profits'.[17] Owen's humanity towards his workers, and his understanding of their needs, are stressed by all commentators as important factors in his effectiveness as a manager, of course, and in these respects he enjoys a popular reputation for uniqueness: he alone among the large-scale employers of labour during the Industrial Revolution is widely supposed to have avoided exploiting and degrading the new industrial proletariat.

As well as the factors which contributed to Owen's business success, there are others which detracted from his effectiveness as a manager and partner, and placed limitations both on the length of his active business career and the extent of his success. It is time to scrutinise both sets of factors in more detail.

III

Owen's labour-management policy, the cornerstone of his reputation as a businessman, provides an obvious starting-point for any appraisal of his career. His concern with what he once described as 'improvements of the living machinery' manifested itself at New Lanark after 1800 in an attempt to provide a total environment, involving the entire New Lanark community, that was conducive to the physical and moral welfare of his employees. In practice, this meant careful control of the physical conditions and moral climate both in the mills themselves and in the village they supported, this control being exercised, of course, by Owen himself, in a spirit of paternal benevolence.

Leaving aside any philosophical considerations, it is worth considering what, in practice, Owen's policy meant for the workers at New Lanark. In the factory, it meant a prohibition on corporal punishment (a ruling which, however, may not always have been enforced[18]), freedom from summary dismissal except for persistent drunkenness, a working day which was eventually reduced to $10\frac{1}{2}$ hours,[19] and – what was most novel, and perhaps most important – the right of appeal to Owen himself by workers who were not satisfied with the decisions of supervisors over performance-ratings. In New Lanark village, Owen provided more and better houses, instituted a system of inspection over housing and sanitation to ensure high standards, supplied good-quality food and drink through the company-controlled shop, and provided facilities for social activities in the Institution for the Formation of Character. The community's religious activities were subsidised by the firm, education on rather advanced lines was provided for the community's children, a contributory sickness-benefit scheme was instituted and a savings bank set up. Not all of the money needed for these amenities came from the management: the workers made a substantial direct contribution, and an even greater indirect one perhaps. The schools, of course, were partly financed from the proceeds of liquor sales to operatives in the village shop, while one-sixtieth of each worker's wages was deducted to finance the sick-fund. And then again, it seems possible that wages at New Lanark were not only 'no more than competitive' (as Professor Pollard puts it) but actually lower than in other comparable establishments, and substantially lower than in mills in towns like Paisley and Glasgow, whose owners did not need to provide housing and the like to attract and maintain a labour force as did the owners of country mills like New Lanark.[20]

It would be wrong to regard New Lanark under Owen, however, as anything but a sternly paternalistic foundation. The whole aim was to promote the 'religious, educational and moral improvement of the workers' *as defined by Owen himself* (and to a lesser extent by the other partners), and the means by which this was to be achieved were, it appears, imposed on the workers without consultation. For the most part they accepted the situation, not least because they derived real benefit from it, but there are indications that they occasionally found it irksome. Thus, for instance, a group of workers complained to the other partners in November 1823 about Owen's management of the sick-fund. They wished to know 'whether a friendly invitation or a determined compulsion shall hereafter constitute the society . . . we view it as a grievance of considerable magnitude to be compelled by Mr Owen to adopt what measures soever he may be pleased to suggest on matters that entirely belong to us. Such a course of procedure is most repugnant to our minds as men, and degrading to our characters as free-born sons of highly favoured Britain.'[21]

The 'social welfare' aspect of Owen's labour-management policy does not, in practice, appear to have differed a great deal from the practices adopted by the owners and managers of some other establishments in the cotton industry – men who have not been given credit for their enlightenment and humanity to the same extent as has Owen. Even in the factory villages of industrialists who were in the forefront of the fight against early factory legislation, the quality of life for the operatives compared not at all unfavourably with that of New Lanark. For example, although the Strutts of Milford and Belper vehemently opposed the 1819 Act, their works were 'a model, spoken of in praise by such severe critics as Owen, Faucher and Gaskell'.[22] The mills of James Finlay and Company were favourably noticed by, among others, the Factory Commissioners of 1833, yet the firm's principal partner, Kirkman Finlay, was among the most outspoken opponents of the 1833 Factory Bill.[23] Men like Strutt and Finlay opposed factory reform on practical and philosophical grounds, albeit misguidedly, and not because they feared exposure. Finlay's Deanston mill had its model village, built at a cost of £20,000, to house its workers: a company shop supplied good merchandise at low cost; positive incentives were instituted (in the form of prize competitions) to encourage cleanliness; a model farm was run by the mill manager, James Smith, and supplied the village with produce. Deanston, too, had its sick-fund and its school.[24] Altogether, the lives of Finlay's workers at Deanston seem to have been no less pleasant than those of Owen's at New Lanark. The late Miss Frances Collier's study of Samuel Greg's Quarry-bank mill at Styal prompts a similar conclusion with regard to that community as compared with New Lanark, while Professor Pollard's general study of early factory villages seems to indicate that a number of other establishments, in the cotton industry and other sectors, must have measured up pretty well to the standards of New Lanark.[25] Nor can it be said that the owners and managers of these concerns were merely copying Owen: many had advanced far along the path before Owen even went to New Lanark, like the Strutts and Samuel Greg who had begun their work in the last two decades of the eighteenth century. It should not be forgotten that Owen's father-in-law, David Dale, enjoyed in his own day the reputation of an enlightened and benevolent employer, and that Owen at New Lanark was to a certain extent building on foundations that Dale had already laid. There are grounds for supposing that Owen's account of New Lanark in 1800 is more than a little ungenerous to Dale.[26]

On the other hand, Professor Checkland's view that 'Many of the larger men took up Owen's mode of factory management . . . the more rapidly as a painful soreness of conscience and a vulnerability to social criticism was nagging many of them' seems a trifle over-generous to Owen.[27] Not all enlightened employers were following his example: several, as we have seen, had anticipated him in many respects. Nor is it fair to ascribe the actions of those others who treated their operatives decently to feelings of guilt (to which, in any case, men of such force of character as Arkwright and Finlay were not notably susceptible). Their motives and principles were not Owen's, admittedly, but the Strutts, David Dale and Samuel Greg, for example, appear to have had sufficiently well-developed social consciences to care quite genuinely for their employees' welfare. To a certain extent, their motives were self-interested, and their policies made good commercial sense. This would be especially true of the owners and managers of water-powered factories like Deanston, or for that matter New Lanark, located in areas remote from adequate resources of labour. To such places, labour had to be attracted and retained: good housing, good working conditions, amenities like medical care, education and so on were among the methods used to achieve these aims, to counterbalance the attractions of higher wages which the town mills in Glasgow and Manchester could afford to offer. Even Owen could hardly afford to reject such considerations entirely, however much he and his admirers chose to cloak them in philanthropic rationalisations *post facto*.

That Owen, too, was concerned to build up an efficient, stable and trustworthy labour force is clearly shown by his contribution to what Professor Pollard has described as the assault on working-class morals. This meant instilling in the labour force a discipline which was not among its native characteristics (but which was necessary for the regular and efficient functioning of the factory) and a new set of values which brought the interests of employer and employee closer together and so secured for the employer a greater willingness to co-operate in the efficient running of the factory on the part of the employee. Owen attacked the problem on two fronts, in the factory itself and in the wider context of the village community of New Lanark. On the wider front – that of the village – he mounted campaigns against drunkenness, immorality and theft, partly by attacking these symptoms themselves and partly by directing his attention to their fundamental causes, ignorance, improvidence and squalor. His weapons included punishment (fines levied on the parents of illegitimate children and in cases of drunkenness, for which habitual offenders were liable to dismissal), exhortation (as in the case of the two boys he caught cutting shinties in Braxfield Wood), 'police' systems like the patrols that were instituted to keep a check on drunkenness and household cleanliness, and education. Owen's actions in this respect put him in good company: similar campaigns with similar weapons were being mounted, or had already been mounted, in other factory villages, for example Finlay's at Deanston, Catrine and Ballindalloch and Monteith's at Blantyre. Indeed, Owen was only doing, perhaps more successfully, what David Dale had been trying to do at New Lanark since its foundation in 1783.[28]

Inside the factory itself, Owen relied on a system of close supervision and publicity to secure the discipline and co-operation he needed for regular and efficient production to good standards of quality. He preferred not to have recourse to such negative methods as fines, dismissals and corporal punishment, a preference he appears to have shared with only a small number of employers in the cotton industry at the time. The cornerstone of the system was, of course, the silent monitor, a system whereby each worker's performance was indicated by a colour-coded block of wood, prominently displayed over each machine. The operative's rating was decided by the departmental overseer, who was in turn himself rated by the under-manager who directed his work. But the final say rested with Owen himself, to whom anyone who disagreed with his or her rating could appeal before the rating was recorded. In principle, the system was by no means novel: broadly similar methods had been used by other managers as far back as about 1740.[29] But the right of appeal which Owen instituted may well have been an innovation in labour management, and one that contributed more than a little to the workers' willingness to co-operate with him.[30] Owen also claimed to have devised a way of dealing with the problem of theft in the factory. He gave no details of it, but, like the silent monitor, its effectiveness depended largely on the maintenance of detailed stock records, which made the detection of thefts easier and more certain.[31]

The educational provisions that Owen set up at New Lanark are often regarded as the most remarkable feature of his management system. Mr Gorb, for example, has said that 'In his educational experiment, Owen was anticipating a concept which only in recent times has been accepted by the businessman as part of his approach to administration'.[32] But New Lanark was a Scottish factory, and Scotland in the early nineteenth century possessed a tradition of popular elementary education which England did not share. As Professor Pollard has pointed out, 'even the less enlightened owners of flax-mills around Aberdeen and Dundee, and of cotton mills round Glasgow and Paisley, provided at least schoolrooms and often the teaching also'.[33] Therefore, as far as Scotland was concerned, the fact that Owen provided for the education of his factory children was in no way remarkable, though it is probably true that the type of education available at New Lanark was superior to what was offered elsewhere.

IV

The management of a concern the size of New Lanark, even at a fairly modest level of success, obviously required a good grasp of the necessary administrative techniques and procedures on the part of management, to run even quite simple systems of stock and quality control, cost accounting and the like. Owen, however, must have been quite well equipped for the task, since by the time he arrived to take up the management of New Lanark in 1800 he had served a twenty-year apprenticeship which provided him with a wide knowledge of the administrative, technical and commercial facets of the cotton trade.

Between 1780 and 1789, in the employment successively of the Misses Tilsley in Newtown, McGuffog in Stamford, Flint and Palmer in London and Satterfield in Manchester, Owen formed a first-hand acquaintance with most aspects of the wholesale and retail textile business, and had, in Professor Cole's words, 'completed a valuable career as a junior. He had acquired a sound knowledge of textiles and their qualities, a good business training, including a grasp of stock records and book-keeping, and personal experience of arduous work in not over-pleasant conditions.'[34]

The years between 1789 and 1792 equipped Owen with experience of the technical and production aspects of the cotton trade, and provided him with his first taste of management on a small scale, to add to the knowledge he had already acquired. In the little machine-making business in which he partnered Jones at Dolefield, Manchester, he dealt with 'book-keeping, finance, the superintendence of men' and maintained 'order and regularity throughout the establishment', while Jones contributed only his mechanical knowledge and skill.[35] It seems unlikely that a man of Owen's calibre and in his position would long remain ignorant of the working of the relatively simple machines which were then in use and which his firm produced, though he protested his ignorance of these matters. At Dolefield also, he first became involved in the production of cotton yarn: as a side-line, he and Jones produced rovings for sale to the spinning trade.[36] His next venture, cotton spinning with three employees at Ancoats Lane, increased his experience of cotton production in a managerial capacity, and also led him to establish his first connections with Scotland, as the fine yarn he produced was sold to 'an agent for some mercantile manufacturing houses in Glasgow'.[37] As well as adding to Owen's technical knowledge and management experience, therefore, the little Ancoats Lane concern provided him with the basis for his marketing policy when, in 1792, he became responsible for fine-yarn production on a very large scale as manager of Peter Drinkwater's Piccadilly Mill.[38]

Owen gave the impression that he was not really fitted for the job he undertook in Drinkwater's mill, but there seems little reason to take his protestations too seriously.[39] On his own admission, he mastered the new job in six weeks, and he admitted the relevance of his previous experience with the statement that 'My previous habits had prepared me for great nicety and exactness of action, and for a degree of perfection in operations to which parties then employed in cotton spinning were little accustomed'.[40] Indeed, the only important difference between Drinkwater's mill and the little Dolefield and Ancoats Lane concerns appears to have been one of scale: where previously he had dealt with forty employees at Dolefield and three at Ancoats Lane, he now had to handle five hundred.

From 1792 to 1800, Owen, as a manager and later as a managing partner, consolidated his knowledge and experience of large-scale fine cotton spinning in Manchester before emerging at the peak of his business career as managing partner of New Lanark, then perhaps the largest establishment of its kind in Britain (or, for that matter, the world). Far from being intuitive, the grasp of the principles and methods of sound management he brought to bear on his work at New Lanark was the result of a prolonged and comprehensive training in almost every aspect of the manufacture and sale of cotton textiles. His training was perhaps less systematic than that of, say, Alexander Buchanan of Deanston, who had served a formal apprenticeship under the great Arkwright at Cromford, but it must have been as thorough and practical as any man who aspired to a high position in cotton-factory management at the time could have desired. To argue, however, that Owen's grasp of factory administration was very largely unique, as Mr Gorb has done, seems to exaggerate the position. In fact, Owen's rise to the position of managing partner of New Lanark seems to have followed quite a well-trodden path. The late Professor Unwin noted, for example, similarities in the training of Owen, Samuel Oldknow and David Dale, while the career of George Augustus Lee – Owen's immediate predecessor as Drinkwater's manager – followed a course remarkably similar to Owen's, as apparently did the careers of a number of other men in the cotton industry and in other sectors.[41] Altogether, Owen's training for high management positions seems to have been quite conventional, and in no way calculated to endow him with a greater administrative competence than men of roughly equal intelligence and capacity to assimilate information such as Buchanan or Lee.

V

Unlike several other managers of large-scale cotton mills in Scotland, Owen never achieved any great reputation as a technical innovator. Though he may have made original improvements in detail to the machinery installed at New Lanark to suit his own purposes, it is very doubtful indeed if he can be placed on the same plane in this respect as, for example, James Smith of Deanston and Archibald Buchanan of Catrine (both of whom produced important modifications to roving-frames, mules and power-looms), or Henry Houldsworth of Anderston, whose contribution lay in the field of coarse-spinning frames.[42] Nor does there seem to be any basis for assuming that Owen developed any substantial innovation as regards factory layout. On the whole, the physical configuration of New Lanark mills suggests that he, like most others, followed pretty closely the pattern set by Arkwright, who had addressed himself to the problem of securing an efficient layout of machinery and floor-space in the 1770s and had demonstrated the important contribution that layout could make to efficient production.[43] So, although Owen pursued policies of 'technical up-to-dateness' and 'orderly arrangement', as Professor Pollard has suggested, in neither respect does it seem possible to regard him as outstanding. In following such policies, he was probably doing no more than most managers of similar large establishments in the cotton industry, especially at a time when innovation followed innovation with remarkable rapidity and machines quickly became obsolescent.

Owen may have exaggerated the extent to which he improved the layout and technical efficiency of both Drinkwater's mill and New Lanark. He claimed to have perceived defects in the various processes at Drinkwater's, and to have put them right, soon improving the quality of the product.[44] And yet he admits that Lee, his predecessor, was considered a man of great technical ability, and that the factory as Lee left it was regarded as 'almost one of the wonders of the mechanical and manufacturing world'.[45] If Lee and his work were as good as they were reputed to be, it seems unlikely that many significant improvements remained to be made by Owen. His accusations of technical backwardness and bad organisation at New Lanark in 1800 are, however, more serious, but their accuracy is perhaps also more open to

question. For the man Owen replaced at New Lanark was William
Kelly, who is credited with the development of the water-powered
mule in 1790 and of the first workable self-acting mule in 1792.
Admittedly, Kelly's self-actors were not a commercial success, but he
had no hesitation in scrapping them when this became apparent.[46]
Kelly, therefore, does not seem like a man who would put up with
unsatisfactory or obsolete machinery in his mills, so perhaps Owen's
account of the situation should not be taken completely at its face
value, especially since he indicated that a certain antipathy lay between
himself and Kelly in any case.


VI


Had Owen enjoyed a quasi-monopolistic position at the fine end of the
spinning trade, it would undoubtedly have created for him profits that
were higher than the average for spinners. For spinners' margins
increased sharply in proportion to the count of yarn (i.e. the number of
840-yard hanks per pound weight) they spun, the although fine-
spinners' overheads were higher than those of coarse-spinners, the
difference in production costs was probably not proportional to the
difference in margins. And although spinners' margins fell steadily
from about 1802, fine-spinners were not as adversely affected as
coarse-spinners.[47]

But it is doubtful if Owen can be numbered among the spinners of
fine yarn after 1800. Most of the large Scottish country mills specialised
in spinning medium-to-coarse counts (no. 80 and below), and New
Lanark seems to have conformed to this pattern. From figures drawn
up on Owen's instructions in 1821, it appears that the average count of
yarn spun at New Lanark between 1814 and 1821 was in the range
24 – 30, a far cry from the counts of 250 and 300 he claimed to have
been producing in Manchester in 1792.[48]

It is unlikely, then, that Professor Pollard's observation that such
was the nature of Owen's product that he could hardly help making
high profits has much validity as far as New Lanark was concerned.
In fact, the apparently mediocre profits of the concern in the 1820s can
probably be ascribed largely to the low counts of yarn spun.

VII

As a businessman, Owen seems to have suffered from at least two serious deficiencies. One was his apparent inability to maintain harmonious relations for long with any of his partners, a failing that not only affected his business career but also bedevilled his subsequent activities.[49] His second major weakness lay in what Podmore described as a 'carelessness in money matters', which was such that 'on more than one occasion he was accused – and not, it would seem, without some superficial justification – of actual dishonesty in his dealings'.[50]

It is clear from his autobiography that Owen's inability to agree with his partners in matters of social and educational policy contributed in some measure to the breakdown of all three New Lanark partnerships in which he was involved. Thus, in 1809, his original partners, with the possible exception of John Atkinson, objected to his educational plans on the grounds that expenditure on educational facilities on the scale Owen intended would seriously deplete the profits of the concern.[51] The parting, when it came later in the year, seems to have been quite amicable, which is more than can be said of the dissolution of the second partnership in 1813.

The new partnership made a good start, but once again Owen's social and educational plans began to create dissension within its ranks, with Owen this time standing alone against Atkinson and the other partners, Robert Dennistoun and Alexander and Colin Campbell, all Glasgow merchants.[52] But social and educational factors were not the only ones involved in the dissolution of the partnership in July 1813. Owen's financial 'carelessness' had laid him open to charges of dishonesty, and had brought him to the verge of bankruptcy. Owen, in his autobiography, dismissed the matter quite lightly,[53] but it seems to have been a great deal more serious that he was prepared to admit, and to have given some substance to the doubts that were expressed from time to time, as Podmore says, about his financial integrity.

The facts of the matter, in so far as they can be accurately established at all, appear to be these.[54] Archibald Campbell of Jura – a Scottish landowner associated with David Dale and the father-in-law of Robert Dennistoun and Alexander Campbell – had entrusted £20,000 of his money, on the advice of Dale before the latter's death in 1806, to

Owen's care. In 1810, when Owen's new partnership had been formed, Owen requested that the money be left with him, a request which Jura claimed he granted only on condition that the money be placed, not with Owen personally, but with the new firm, which offered more adequate security.[55] Jura subsequently discovered, perhaps through one of his sons-in-law who may have wished to embarrass Owen because of a difference of opinion on social matters, that Owen had not complied with his conditions,[56] and that the money still had no more security than Owen personally could guarantee, and which Jura had reason to consider inadequate.[57] By the time Jura made this discovery, accrued interest had raised the sum in contention to over £26,000, of which Owen paid £6000 in July 1812 and granted a promissory note payable on 11 November 1812 to cover the remainder. On the due date, however, he was unable to redeem his note, repaying only a further £1100 and offering the excuse that, in the circumstances then prevailing, it was difficult to furnish large sums of money at short notice.[58] At the same time, Owen gave a statement of his affairs which 'if . . . near the truth' indicated his impending bankruptcy.[59]

Jura, therefore, instituted legal proceedings to have Owen declared bankrupt and to have his own son, John Campbell, W.S., appointed trustee of Owen's assets on behalf of his creditors as the best way of safeguarding the Jura interests. The 'trust disposition' (the first step towards an admission of bankruptcy) had already been drafted and apparently approved by Owen, when David Dale's unmarried daughters (Owen's sisters-in-law) intervened to save him by assigning their entire estates to Jura as security for his money.[60] Terms of settlement were drawn up, which Owen managed to honour, and the whole matter was finally cleared up on 11 November 1822, when the final instalment of the debt was paid.[61] But it was a close call for Owen, reflecting adversely on his integrity as well as his ability, which provided his partners with their ostensible reason for winding up the partnership.[62]

Owen's third and last set of partners at New Lanark were men with whom his relationship might be expected to be good. Unlike his previous partners, they were at least as interested in the place as a base for social experiment and development as in its profit-making potential. Owen certainly remained connected with the firm longer than with any previous partnership – sixteen years altogether, twelve of them as the active partner. But even with Bentham, Walker, Foster, Allen, Fox and Gibbs he was incapable of working in complete harmony. His view of religion, and the educational practices based on it, eventually brought him into conflict with Allen, who was supported by Foster and Gibbs, and in 1824 Owen was forced to make changes in the New Lanark educational system to make it more acceptable to the other three.[63] From this point on, Owen's interest in New Lanark seems to have declined rapidly: he remained manager, in name at least, until 1825, but between 1824 and 1829 he spent most of his time, not in Britain, but in America, and he finally sold off his interests at New Lanark in 1828. It would be wrong to put the final break entirely, or even mainly, down to his conflict with Allen, Foster and Gibbs. The New Harmony settlement in Indiana took up most of his attention by that time and it seems likely that he simply lost interest in New Lanark, the potential of which for applying Owen's views on social organisation was much more limited than that of New Harmony and elsewhere.

It has been remarked that many of Owen's differences with his partners 'were attributable to Owen's own ruggedness of character, his unwillingness to give way or compromise, and his inability to see that, while he had social experiment as his primary aim, they had sunk their money in an enterprise for the purpose of earning a profit. Their concept of business was entirely different from his own.'[64] As a summary of Owen's character, the view seems remarkably acute. He appears to have completely lacked the tempering qualities of tact and diplomacy so important in dealings with those who put up the money for a business venture. As a result, he was forced on two occasions to seek new backers, and on one such occasion, in 1813, in circumstances which were hardly likely to inspire confidence in potential partners.

VIII

Robert Owen was undoubtedly a remarkable man. In his business career he displayed all the characteristics of the model Smilesian self-made man, building a substantial fortune from very small beginnings in the space of forty years or so, as well as leaving his mark on the politics and society of his time. But he operated in what might be described as the Golden Age of the self-made man, and it it important to remember this context. As far as his business achievements were concerned, Owen was something less than unique: there were other men around whose training and grasp of management techniques were at least as thorough as his, whose methods of management were arguably as humane and enlightened in practice as his were (though they perhaps lacked the philosophical backing that Owen's had), and whose contributions to the technological development of their industries were probably greater than his. This is not, however, an attempt to belittle Owen, but simply to put his achievements in some sort of perspective. He was not unique, perhaps, but he was undoubtedly among the leaders in his field of activity. Perhaps his greatest contribution to the development of industrial management (certainly to its history) was to set his methods, aims and experiences in Manchester and New Lanark in print, in what Professor Pollard has called 'one of the few isolated examples of conscious thought on management and the attempts to systematize it'.[65] This, by itself, was no mean achievement, but there has been a tendency on the part of students of Owen's career to accept, perhaps too readily, his own estimation of his eminence in the development of management. Owen, like many prominent businessmen, appears to have had 'a guid conceit of himself', and in his writings he, perhaps unconsciously, seems to have exaggerated his own importance. The fact that his contemporaries left few records of their activities, on the basis of which a comparison with Owen might be attempted, has contributed to the continued exaggeration of Owen's importance. What is needed, therefore, as well as further scrutiny of Owen himself, is more study of other managers of large-scale industrial concerns in the early nineteenth century, to supplement the excellent work already done in this field by Professor Pollard and others, and against whose achievements Owen's can be more accurately measured.

NOTES AND REFERENCES

1. L. Urwick and E. F. L. Brech, *The Making of Scientific Management* (1949) II 40.
2. S. G. Checkland, *The Rise of Industrial Society in England, 1815–1885* (1964) pp. 116–17.
3. R. S. Fitton and A. P. Wadsworth, *The Strutts and the Arkwrights, 1758–1830* (1958) p. 98.
4. S. Pollard, *The Genesis of Modern Management* (1968) p. 286.

5. P. Gorb, 'Robert Owen as a Businessman', *Bulletin of the Business Historical Society*, xxv (1951) p. 145.

6. 'Preface to the Third Essay on the Formation of Character, 1816', reprinted in R. Owen, *The Life of Robert Owen, written by himself* (1857) I 261. It is hard to see how Owen arrived at these figures: he almost certainly did not know at any time the extent to which the social and occupational improvements he instituted at New Lanark affected the concern's profits, and possibly he did not much care. In 1816 he was probably more interested in the effect his statement had on other managers rather than in its accuracy.

7. Gorb, op. cit., p. 145; but see also below, pp. 158–60.

8. Owen, *Life*, I 87, 98.

9. According to the deed of co-partnery of 1813, this surplus was not to be shared out by the partners but applied instead to the 'religious, educational and moral welfare of the workers, and of the community at large' (quoted in G. D. H. Cole, *The Life of Robert Owen* (1965) p. 206). The third partnership was also unusual in that its shares were transferable, a feature that marked it as an un-incorporated joint-stock company rather than strictly a partnership. Such organisations were apparently less rare in Scotland than in England, thanks to the less restrictive features of Scots commercial law, but were still uncommon. See S. Shapiro, *Capital and the Cotton Industry in the Industrial Revolution* (1967) pp. 157, 161–2; also British Museum, Add. MSS. 33545, fol. 641, Robert Owen to Jeremy Bentham, 31 Dec 1823, asking that two of Owen's shares be transferred, one to R. D. Owen, one to Wm. Owen.

10. For the 1817 surplus, see B.M. Add. MSS. 33545, fol. 260, R. Owen to J. Bentham, 8 Feb 1818. For 1819, see fol. 392, Owen to Bentham, 21 Feb 1820. For 1825, see below, p. 148.

11. See, e.g., the evidence of Kirkman Finlay and other cotton manufacturers before the *Select Committee on Manufactures, Commerce and Shipping, 1833* (S.P. 1833, VI).

12. For instance, towards the end of 1818 Owen was caught out by 'a considerable fall in the price of cotton', which, by affecting the value of stocks on hand at New Lanark, posed a threat to its profits. Then, at the end of 1819, 'one of the large mills and attendant buildings' were destroyed by fire, which probably also resulted in a reduction in profits for that year. See B.M. Add. MSS., 33545, fol. 338 (Owen to Bentham, 25 Dec 1818) and fol. 372 (Owen to Bentham, 1 Dec 1819).

13. For McConnel and Kennedy, see Shapiro, *Capital and the Cotton Industry*, App. 12, p. 252. For Marshall's, see W. G. Rimmer, *Marshalls of Leeds, Flax-spinners, 1788–1886* (1960), table 12, 319.

14. J. F. C. Harrison, *Robert Owen and the Owenites in Britain and America* (1969) p. 155. The accuracy of these estimates is, of course, open to doubt.

15. F. Podmore, *Robert Owen* (1906) II 642; Pollard, *The Genesis of Modern Management*, p. 286.

16. Gorb, op. cit., pp. 134–5; Urwick and Brech, *The Making of Scientific Management*, II 55.

17. Pollard, *The Genesis of Modern Management*, pp. 293, 286.

18. See *Factory Commission, 1833, First Report* (1833 (450) XX), A1, p. 74: 'Duncan McKinlay . . . depones . . . that he has known instances of ill-treatment

at Lanark Cotton Mills about thirty years ago, when the works were under the superintendence of Mr Robert Owen and Mr Humphrey . . . a constant system of beating took place, not a day without someone suffering . . . that Mr Owen was, at this period, going about the works.'

19. By 1819, but in the period 1800–13 the working day was of 14 hours: Podmore, *Robert Owen*, I 162.

20. On wages, see ibid., I 165–6. The summary of conditions, etc., at New Lanark is based on the accounts of Podmore, Owen himself and G. D. H. Cole. The system was not established overnight, and was not fully operational until 1816 at the earliest. Opposition from partners was an important delaying factor.

21. Quoted in ibid., I 169. As Podmore remarks, 'The benevolence of the most benevolent of despots will not always reconcile his subjects to the loss of freedom'.

22. Fitton and Wadsworth, *The Strutts and the Arkwrights*, pp. 169, 189, See also Harrison, *Robert Owen and the Owenites*, p. 156.

23. See, e.g., *Factory Commission, 1833, First Report*, pp. 16–18. The Finlay factory villages of Deanston and Catrine, like New Lanark, survive virtually unchanged from their early nineteenth-century form. The physical resemblances between the three are striking. Deanston mill closed in 1966, but Catrine is still partly in operation.

24. On Deanston, see *James Finlay and Company Limited, 1750–1950* (1951) pp. 67–74; *New Statistical Account of Scotland* (1845) X 1233f. The manager, James Smith, was a remarkable man whose activities extended over the fields of factory management and design, mechanical inventions, agricultural innovation (for which he is perhaps best known) and public health.

25. F. Collier, *The Family Economy of the Working Classes in the Cotton Industry, 1784–1833* (1965) pp. 38–46; Pollard, *The Genesis of Modern Management*, pp. 231–42 (see also *English Historical Review*, LXXIX (1964) ).

26. Owen, *Life*, I 79, 83–4. This should be compared with Sir John Sinclair (ed.), *Statistical Account of Scotland* (1791–9) XV 34–42. See also Podmore, *Robert Owen*, I 82. Owen sometimes tends to elevate himself by decrying others: for other examples, see W. H. Chaloner, 'Robert Owen, Peter Drinkwater and the Early Factory System in Manchester, 1788–1800', *Bulletin of the John Rylands Library*, XXXVII (1954–5) 87–92. See also below, pp. 156–7.

27. Checkland, *The Rise of Industrial Society*, pp. 116–17.

28. For an account of the 'assault on working-class morals', see Pollard, *The Genesis of Modern Management*, pp. 226–31. For Owen's contribution to it, see especially ibid., pp. 227–8, and Podmore, *Robert Owen*, I 166–9.

29. The system is described in Owen, *Life*, I 80–1. Other examples of similar systems are mentioned in Pollard, *The Genesis of Modern Management*, p. 225; Fitton and Wadsworth, *The Strutts and the Arkwrights*, p. 100; and A. P. Wadsworth and J. de L. Mann. *The Cotton Industry and Industrial Lancashire, 1600–1780* (1965) p. 439.

30. See Urwick and Brech, *The Making of Scientific Management*, II 51.

31. Owen, *Life*, I 80.

32. Gorb, op. cit., p. 144.

33. Pollard, *The Genesis of Modern Management*, p. 236.

34. Cole, *Life of Robert Owen*, pp. 53–4. See also Owen, *Life*, I 13–20, and Urwick and Brech, *The Making of Scientific Management*, II 42–3.

36. Owen, *Life*, I 23.

36. Ibid., I 23; Chaloner, op. cit., p. 80.

37. Owen, *Life*, I 25.

38. Ibid., I 33.

39. 'I had no idea of the task which I had to perform, in many respects entirely new to me, or I should never have made the attempt to perform it': ibid., I 28.

40. Ibid., I 29.

41. G. Unwin, *Samuel Oldknow and the Arkwrights* (1924) pp. 4, 118; Pollard, *The Genesis of Modern Management*, p. 180.

42. See E. Baines, *History of the Cotton Manufacture of Great Britain* (1835) pp. 205–9, 230–1, 241; C. Singer *et al.*, *History of Technology* (1958) IV 283, 286–8; *New Statistical Account*, VI 142–5, 152–3.

43. Smith of Deanston can, however, be said to have made a contribution in this field too. His new mill at Deanston was a model adopted by, e.g., John Marshall of Leeds: see M. J. Flinn (ed.), *Report on the Sanitary Condition of the Labouring Population of Great Britain, 1842* (1964) p. 307.

44. Owen, *Life*, I 28–9.

45. Ibid., I 31.

46. Baines, *History of the Cotton Manufacture*, pp. 205–9.

47. The margin being defined as the difference between the cost per lb. of raw cotton and the selling-price per lb. of twist. Owen described how, in 1792, he sold a batch of no. 250 yarn for £9 18s 6d per lb., having paid 5s per lb. for the raw cotton, giving a margin of £9 13s 6d (Owen, *Life*, I 35). In 1833, the margin on no. 30 yarn (medium-coarse) was 4d; on no. 100 (medium-fine), 2s 10d; on no. 170 (fine), 6s 5d (G. R. Porter, *Progress of the Nation* (1851) p. 182). Kirkman Finlay, in 1833, reckoned 1802 the most prosperous year he had seen in the spinning trade in his forty-five years' experience of it: *Select Committee on Manufactures, Commerce and Shipping, 1833* (S.P. 1833, VI, Q. 648–50, p. 37).

48. Reproduced in Podmore, *Robert Owen*, I 164.

49. See, for example, the account of the disputes between Owen and James Morrison and T. G. Smith, which contributed to the failure of the Grand National Consolidated Trades Union, in Cole, *Life of Robert Owen*, pp. 286 f.

50. Podmore, *Robert Owen*, II 644.

51. Owen, *Life*, I 85–6.

52. Ibid., I 87.

53. Loc. cit. He certainly gave no impression of having been on the verge of bankruptcy.

54. A detailed account of the whole affair is in A. J. Robertson, 'Robert Owen and the Campbell Debt, 1810–1822', *Business History*, XI (1969). I am obliged to the editors of *Business History* for permission to use material therein.

55. Scottish Record Office, Campbell of Jura Muniments, G.D. 64 I 247 (hereafter cited as Jura Muniments), Owen to Jura, 17 Oct 1810. Jura's side is stated in Jura Muniments, Memorial and Queries for Archibald Campbell of Jura, 8 Mar 1813.

56. Owen claimed that he had complied (Owen, *Life*, I 86). But if he had, Jura would have had no grounds for the legal proceedings he instituted against Owen.

57. A statement of Owen's affairs obtained by Jura (Jura Muniments, 15 June

1813) showed liabilities of over £31,000 and 'realised' assets of over £38,000, with 'unrealised' assets of a further £17,000. So Owen's security was, in fact, adequate, if only just. The statement, however, does not appear to take into account Owen's share of the profits of New Lanark since 25 Dec 1812.

58. Jura Muniments, Owen to John Campbell, W.S., 8 Oct 1812.

59. Jura Muniments, John Campbell, W.S., to Colin Campbell, 11 Nov 1812. These two Campbells were Jura's sons, who, with Andrew Clason, W.S., handled negotiations with Owen on Jura's behalf. They should not be confused with Owen's Campbell partners.

60. Jura Muniments, Draft Trust Disposition by Robert Owen, Esq., 19 Mar 1813, and Bond between R. Owen, the Misses Dale and A. Campbell of Jura (copy), 15 July 1813.

61. In May 1818 Owen gave notice of 'an extraordinary meeting of the partners' of Robert Owen and Co. 'to consider the propriety of empowering me as manager to use the name of the House in accepting five bills of four thousand pounds each at one, two, three, four and five years date from Martinmas next to be placed to the debit of my account as they shall severally be paid' (B.M. Add. MSS. 33545, fol. 286, Owen to Bentham, 15 May 1818). The amount and dating of these bills conform to the settlement arrangements agreed with Jura.

62. See Jura Muniments, Alexander Campbell to John Campbell, W.S., 5 July 1813, in which it was stated that the partnership had been wound up 'in consequence of Mr Owen's refusal . . . to contribute his proportion of the necessary funds for the company's business. . . .'

63. Cole, *Life of Robert Owen*, pp. 210–13.

64. Urwick and Brech, *The Making of Scientific Management*, II 49.

65. Pollard, *The Genesis of Modern Management*, pp. 292–3.

# CHAPTER EIGHT

# Owen in 1817: The Millennialist Moment

## W. H. OLIVER

In religion, Robert Owen was both a deist and a millennialist, a child of the Enlightenment and an example of enthusiasm. Conventional views of eighteenth- and early nineteenth-century religion and irreligion do not easily accommodate these antitheses. We are used to a pattern which contrasts cool rationalist deists with unstable enthusiasts, locating millennialists at the extreme of instability and irrationality. To suggest that a man such as Owen straddles the division is like suggesting that Joanna Southcott and Lord Melbourne are close kin. Clearly, they are not: if Joanna (or any other of the weak-minded fanatics who populated the religious underworld of the period) is a typical millennialist, then the conventional view may stand. But her reputation is a continuing source of delusion. Millennialism specifically and prophetic attitudes generally are, over the period of Owen's life, far more diverse, more widespread, and (in most of their manifestations) more 'normal' than any but a handful of subsequent accounts would encourage us to suppose.[1] Owen and with him a numerous company of millennialists occupy, without strain, a position near the cool end of a spectrum which extends from, say, Joseph Priestley to Richard Brothers. In his rejection of orthodox religious beliefs Owen reveals himself as a late eighteenth-century rationalist who had absorbed (probably at Manchester) the positions of Voltaire and the *philosophes*, although he was never to acknowledge this influence. This essay does not attempt to deny this inheritance, but rather to demonstrate the significance of another inheritance and to suggest that the two might readily co-exist.

That Owen was not a Christian – except in so far as he would agree with the residue of all religions once what he considered to be nonsense has been knocked out of them – is a further obstacle. Can a non-Christian be a millennialist? Clearly he cannot be a millennialist of the kind which accepts the biblical prophecies in a Christological sense and sets about dating and describing the returned Christ's personal reign. But not all millennialists did this, even though most of them did. Two collateral developments within millennialism help to locate Owen within the tradition. In the first place, and precisely among those most influenced by the rationalist, utilitarian temper of the later eighteenth century, there was a persistent tendency to allegorise the biblical images (of Antichrist, Armageddon and the millennium) into social and intellectual manifestations of decline, crisis and recovery. Second, there was the illuminist habit of transforming the Christ-figure (whether of the First or the Second Coming or of both) into the life of the illuminatus in question, of becoming oneself the Christ-figure, not necessarily in a miraculous way, but sometimes as simply a liberation-figure. This habit of mind thus intersects with allegorisation, and here is almost the point at which Owen is to be found.

Almost, for one needs to add his own piece of originality: the transfer of the total argument to an extra-Christian dimension. But there are others who come fairly close to this position. It was a dissenter commonplace to subsume all ecclesiastical establishments under the image of Antichrist, and to argue historically that this had been brought about by a process through which the original deposit of pure Christianity had been overlaid and perverted by the falsities of anti-Christian establishments. Owen simply extends these two arguments further: from established churches to all churches of all religions, and from the original purity of Christianity to the original purity of human nature. It was a quite considerable step, but the ground on which he stood had been well prepared.

These transitions, from a situation within to one outside Christianity, mean that Owen's millennialism is recognisably Christian while being post-Christian: the content alters – but the form, the style, the vocabulary and the general tone of his utterances remain recognisably Christian-Millennialist and even distinctly biblicist. This paper will try to show the truth of these general statements by examining some of Owen's writings: those produced in and around 1817, and those in which he reflects upon the events of 1817 some forty years later.

Owen was sharply distinguished from the great majority of contemporary millennialists by the role he assigned to himself. Most others were prophetic commentators, identifying the signs of the times and predicting the course of events. He was, in his own estimation, the most eminent of the signs of the times, and himself the occasion of the critical events. They looked forward to the return of the Messiah, either in an allegorical or a literal way; he saw himself as the redeemer, in a way which is both allegorical and literal. As he held no brief for the

First Coming, he had no reason to see himself as the Christ of the Second Coming – though he did occasionally apply this image to his message. In a general way he regarded himself and his ideas as providentially sent; in many specific ways he applied to himself the biblical characteristics of the Messiah; in a very emphatic way he represented his utterances of 1817 in London as the announcement of a universal gospel. Owen, then, did not write as a millennialist expositor; he acted as the person millennialism was about.

Though Owen regarded his addresses and letters of August and September 1817 as the climatic revelation, all the themes are present, though muted, in his first publications – the four essays in *A New View of Society* (1813) and *An Address to the Inhabitants of New Lanark* (1816). The first of the four essays has the form of a sermon: it is built around the contrast between the misery that exists and the felicity that shall exist. He moves from his description of misery to his prediction of felicity by advancing a double argument: first that misery is approaching a crisis point, and second that the truth which will resolve the crisis into a happy outcome is now announced. This pattern is the stock-in-trade of the exhortatory preacher – the appeal is addressed to the heart of the sinner, to acknowledge his sinfulness and the possibility of an escape from it, and to move from death to life by a double recognition, of his helplessness as he is, and of his desperate need for the saving truth now offered. Specifically, Owen looks, in the company of a host of contemporary preachers, to the 'extraordinary events of the present times' for confirmation, and in particular to Napoleon's role in preparing the way for change 'by shaking to its foundation that mass of superstition and bigotry, which on the continent of Europe had been accumulating for ages, until it had so overpowered and depressed the human intellect, that to attempt improvement without its removal would have been most unavailing.'[2] This bears a close relationship to the role ascribed to Napoleon by such Christian expositors of prophecy an James Bicheno, George Stanley Faber and James Hatley Frere. Further, Owen (in this essay and in everything he wrote) shares with the preachers the certainty that the onset of the crisis and its resolution do not depend on human effort: 'the time is now arrived when the public mind of this country, and the general state of the world, call imperatively for the introduction of this all-pervading principle. . . . Nor can any human power now impede its rapid progress. . . . The commencement of the work will, in fact, ensure its accomplishment. . . .'[3] For the Christian preachers, God dominated the picture;

for Owen, his principles which 'require only to be known in order to establish themselves. . . . They direct that the governing powers of all countries should establish rational plans for the education and general formation of the characters of their subjects.'⁴ The role of men is to follow and co-operate with the 'principles' which are an autonomous external agency. This brief introductory essay provides the framework into which the lengthy and detailed exposition of the bulk of the *New View* fits. The keynotes of misery and felicity, enslavement and deliverance, the inevitability of change through sudden crisis, recur throughout the succeeding essays. Owen's diagnosis and prognosis are of social ills and social goods, but his style and his cast of mind derive from millennialist exhortation. He is not, *au fond*, arguing a case; he is making a prophecy.

In opening the Institution for the Formation of Character at New Lanark in 1816, Owen was doing far more than taking a stage further an important educational experiment; he was demonstrating that the future really worked, that the new age had begun. The purpose of the Institution was to *'give happiness to every human being through all succeeding generations'*.⁵ Hence his address upon its opening is more a millennial proclamation than a scientific argument. His was 'the only path to knowledge'; error had (like original sin) passed 'from one generation to another', so that 'none was in the right path – no, not one'; 'the minds of all men must be born again'.⁶ All men will be so impressed by the 'principles' and the 'system' that they will confess that they have previously been in error; they will greet the system of the Institution 'as the harbinger of that period when our swords shall be turned into ploughshares, and our spears into pruning hooks; when universal love and benevolence shall prevail; when there shall be but one language and one nation; and when fear of want or of any evil among men shall be known no more'.⁷

Though Owen was primarily interested in total social reconstruction – and hence his constant appeals to the great ones, ministers, emperors and presidents – he was also, like a good preacher, concerned with the regeneration of the individual. The recognition of the truth about the formation of character – than an individual is in no way responsible either for his original 'faculties and propensities' or for the circumstances in which he is placed – will lead all men to the new world, and (in the meantime) lead individuals to a better relationship with their neighbours. The final piece of exhortation to his New Lanark listeners is in fact a piece of advice on how those who have been introduced to the truth should in the future deal with the recurrence of 'injurious dispositions'.[8] Owen, true revivalist, had a proper concern for the sins of the regenerate. The shadow of Calvinism lies, in fact, heavily over the whole exposition. The individual is called upon to reject wholly his old life – 'Yes! they will reject with horror even those notions which hitherto they have from infancy been taught to value beyond price.'[9] And behind conversion lies predestination: 'every infant has received all its faculties and qualities, bodily and mental, from a power and a cause, over which the infant had not the shadow of control'.[10] But election and reprobation, as individual destinies, do not follow. There is no capricious God in Owen's theology; men in general, previously, have known 'every conceivable evil'; all humanity, from now on, will follow 'the true and only road which can lead to happiness'.[11] Hell and heaven have been socialised, and – though Owen's later spiritualism implies another meaning for the word – he knew that the proper and time-hallowed term for a socialised heaven is the Millennium.[12] Ignorance, the cause of all misery, is again a piece of socialised theology; the devil retains his terrifying aspect while being translated into a social force. Ignorance is 'the evil spirit which had dominion over the world . . . which has grossly deceived mankind'.[13] It is 'the roaring lion going about seeking whom he may devour'.[14]

His doctrine of circumstances gives Owen an especially thorny problem in explaining his own immunity from inherited error. In the event, he has not much alternative but to 'deify' himself, or, at the least, to make himself the first new man of the new creation. In fact, in all his self-reflections (which are numerous) he oscillates between the role of redeemer and that of innovator. The former role inevitably makes him assume a messianic character. But even the latter requires some pretty special explanation. Just as Christians have had to go to great lengths to detach Jesus from the chain of original sin, so Owen, simply as innovator, had to work hard to show how he got sufficiently clear of 'circumstances' to enable him to innovate. The logic of his own system required him to slide across from innovator to redeemer.

This *Address* makes some significant approaches to self-messianisation. His message will arouse the scorn of the conventionally learned and wise, for their real ignorance is especially great. Here Owen does not use biblical imagery, but his argument is close to that of the Magnificat, to the parable of the stone which the builders rejected, and to St Paul's well-known strictures upon the foolishness of the Greeks.[15] The chief function of this description of the folly of the wise is to focus attention

on the problem of Owen's immunity from the blindness of all humanity. The answer, guardedly given in this *Address*, is a secular approxi-
mation to a special choosing, a sort of immaculate upbringing. 'Causes,
over which I could have no control, removed in my early days the
bandage which covered my mental sight.' Having been thus enabled to
see the truth, Owen goes on, could he refrain from pointing out to all
men the true path to happiness? No! The causes which fashioned me
in the womb, – the circumstances by which I was surrounded from
my birth, and over which I had no influence whatever, formed me with
far other faculties, habits, and sentiments. These gave me a mind that
could not rest satisfied without trying every possible expedient to
relieve my fellow-men from their wretched situation, and formed it
of such a texture that obstacles of the most formidable nature served
but to increase my ardour, and to fix within me a settled determination, either to overcome them, or to die in the attempt.' Difficulties,
initially appalling and apparently insurmountable, have disappeared
'like the fleeting clouds of morning'. The path forward is now clear;
he need no longer work silently and alone. 'The period is arrived when
I may call numbers to my aid, and the call will not be in vain.'[16] The
language is still that of faculties, propensities and circumstances, and
is as unmystical as it could be. But the problem of Owen's special role
is simply met with bald assertion that, in his case, the faculties, propensities and circumstances were wholly different, and that the cause of
the difference is wholly external to him. Providence is not excluded,
but dressed in new clothes. The notion that he was specially selected,
that he was the beginning of a new creation, grew upon Owen in
later life, till it reached a climax in the account of his childhood set
down in his autobiography. Owen, to repeat, was not essentially a
millennialist, but rather the occasion of the millennium; this, as well as
the special problems posed by his doctrine of circumstances, faced him
with the need to give such an account. Here, for once, the example of
Joanna Southcott is to the point. A society which contained a number of
solid and reputable men ready to heed her claim to divine motherhood
in 1814 would be likely to contain many more ready to go along with
Owen's essentially mild and cool messiahship.

But the coolness – including the reiterated assertion that the change
must be carefully managed to prevent any abrupt dislocation, that his
listeners must not try to move precipitately from the old to the new –
cannot disguise the highly personal excitement which underlies this
studiously restrained *Address*. 'Old things shall pass away, and all shall

become new'; 'in one generation' the rulers of the world will be able to make the change. The charge that he is insane is rehearsed and rejected; he will astonish theologians as well as politicians; he knows society as well as if it was set out on a map; he knows the thoughts of his listeners. With regular echoes from St Paul's discourse on charity he offers men his version of true religion and true Christianity.[17]

In the essays of *A New View* and in this *Address*, Owen elaborated the principles which, with varying internal emphasis, he was to reiterate for the rest of his life. Here by argument and at New Lanark by demonstration they had been shown to be true. The rest was proclamation. During a hectic few weeks, in London late in 1817, Owen proclaimed his gospel, and called numbers to his aid. This was the millennial moment; not the time of the second stage in revelation history, as it was for Christian millennialists, but the time of the revelation itself. In old age, after nearly four decades of effort, Owen could apply to himself the words of the psalm he must have regularly heard as a child at Matins: 'it will in six months be just *forty years* that I may say "I have been grieved with this generation", while it has been passing through the wilderness of ignorance and gross superstitions'.[18] Specifically, in later life, Owen identifies a precise instant as that of revelation: his delivery of the sentences announcing the error of all religions in his Address at the London Tavern on 21 August. This was the moment at which the new world began – and this was Owen's opinion at the time as well as in long retrospect.

Of course, Owen's manifest purpose in his 1817 propaganda was to persuade the influential to adopt his scheme for poor relief. If this scheme was to be simply ameliorative, then there is an immense and inexplicable distance between the object sought and the means employed to urge it. But the scheme, because it was an application of the 'principles', was seen as salvific, not reformist, the beginning of a new, not just of a better world. The gap, from this vantage point, narrows and disappears: no rhetoric can be too extreme for the millennium. At the London Tavern, on 21 August 1817, Owen inaugurated the millennium. The exact context of this millennial moment is the contrast between 'the Cottage system' of relief and 'the plan now advocated'.[19] The comparison shifts from a matter-of-fact discussion of food supplies to an eloquent discourse on the problem of death – a transition which will appear less abrupt if Owen is considered in the role, not of political economist or reformer, but of preacher and prophet. In the old order, death brings grief and despair; there is no communal comfort for 'All are individualised, cold, and forbidding'. But under 'the proposed system' all is to be otherwise. 'The intelligent resigned sufferer waits the result with cheerful patience, and thus most effectually parries every assault of disease, when unaccompanied by his fell companion, death; and, when death attacks him, he submits to a conqueror who he knew from childhood was irresistible, and whom for a moment he never feared!' The bereaved feel only natural grief, and no more, for 'around them on all sides . . . thousands on thousands, in strict, intimate and close union, are ready and willing to offer them aid and consolation'. Fitly enough, the passage ends 'O death, where is thy sting? O Grave, where is thy victory?'[20] Orthodox preachers offered a fearful generation one set of consolations; Owen a rather different set. But both were very concerned with death, and thus with religion.

Why, Owen goes on, have 'the new arrangements', which would bring all these advantages, not been introduced long ago? Because, simply, the ignorance perpetuated by all religions has not been destroyed; because no one has been prepared to sacrifice his life by bringing salvation through the destruction of the religions; because, in a word, Owen had not been brought to his millennial moment.

The announcement of the falsity of religions is thus the point of time at which the new world begins. Here Owen, as an old man remembering, may provide his own commentary upon the occasion.[21] He described how he went to 'this meeting, ever-to-be remembered in the annals of history', determined 'at a particular place of my address, to denounce and reject all the religions of the world'. He believed 'the public mind' to be 'highly excited', that even the phlegmatic Lord Liverpool had been relieved of great anxiety by an interview with Owen, and indeed that the Government were so bewildered that 'they felt they were at my mercy'. He had copies of the address prepared for the reporters, but the copiers were instructed to leave the crucial passage blank for Owen himself to fill in before the meeting. He believed himself to be 'by far the most popular individual in the civilised world, and possessed the most influence with a majority of the leading members of the British cabinet and government'. He 'went to the meeting with the determination by one sentence to destroy that popularity, but by its destruction to lay the axe to the root of all false religions, and thus to prepare the population of the world for the reign of charity in accordance with the natural laws of humanity. . .'. And as other phrases (both at the time and in retrospect) make clear, it was not simply popularity, but life, that he was prepared to lay down, and even expected to lay down, that all men might live.

At this point, Owen may take up his own tale.

I commenced my address, and continued amidst much applause and cheering from the friends of the cause which I advocated, until I approached that part in which I denounced all the religions of the world as now taught; when by my manner I prepared the audience for some extraordinary proceeding. And when in a firm voice I said – 'A more important question has never been put to the sons of men – Who can answer it? Who dares answer it? but with his life in his hand – a ready and willing victim to truth, and to the emancipation of the world from its long bondage of error, crime, and misery? Behold that victim! On this day! in this hour! even now! shall those bonds be burst asunder, never more to re-unite while the world lasts! What the consequences of this daring deed shall be to myself I am as indifferent about, as whether it shall rain or be fair tomorrow! Whatever may be the consequences, I will now perform my duty to you and to the world. And should it be the last act of my life, I shall be well content, and shall know that I have lived for an important purpose. Then, my friends! I tell you, that hitherto you have been prevented from knowing what happiness really is, solely in consequence of the errors – gross errors.' The meeting here became excited to the highest pitch of expectation as to what was to follow; and a breathless silence prevailed, so that not the slightest sound could be heard. I made a slight pause, and, as my friends afterwards told me, added a great increase of strength of feeling and dignity to my manner, of which at the time I was wholly unconscious, and in that state of mind I finished the sentence . . . and I then again paused for some seconds, to observe the effects of this unexpected and unheard of declaration and denouncement of all existing religions, in one of the most numerous public meetings of all classes ever held in the British metropolis under cover and at mid-day.

My own expectations were, that such a daring denouncement in opposition to the deepest prejudices of every creed, would call down upon me the vengeance of the bigoted and superstitious, and that I should be torn to pieces in the meeting. But great was my astonishment at what followed. A pause ensued, of the most profound silence, but of noiseless agitation in the minds of all, – none apparently knowing what to do or how to express themselves. All seemed thunderstruck and confounded. My friends were taken by surprise, and were shocked at my temerity, and feared for the result. Those who came with the strongest determination to oppose me, had, as

they afterwards stated to me, their minds changed as it were by some
electric shock, and the utmost mental confusion seemed to pervade
the meeting, none venturing to express their feelings; and had I not
purposely paused and waited some demonstration from the audience,
I might have continued my address in the astonished silence which
I had produced. But when I did not proceed, and while I evidently
wanted for some expression of the feeling of the audience, after the
long pause in silence, about half-a-dozen clergymen, who had
attentively listened to all I had said, deemed it incumbent upon them
on account of their profession to attempt to lead the meeting by a
few low hisses. But these, to my great astonishment, were instantly
rebutted by the most heartfelt applause from the whole of the meeting, with the exception stated, that I ever witnessed, before or since,
as a public demonstration of feeling.

I then said to the friends near me – 'the victory is gained. Truth
openly stated is omnipotent'.[22]


It is not claimed here that Owen is a reliable reporter of the scene in
the London Tavern, but only of his own motivation, expectation and
general state of mind. Nor is this simply the product of forty years'
hindsight. The account written in the 1850s is obviously full of an
expectation of martyrdom in the cause of truth; of dying to bring
life. It goes on to point up the vital significance of this day, 'the day on
which bigotry, superstition, and all false religions, received their death
blow'. 'The deed was done. Truth had escaped, as it were by a miracle.
. . .' There is, in this old man's account, more than a hint of divine
guidance and protection: 'when I went to the meeting I felt uncertain
whether I should return alive. . . . I never felt more strongly than at this
period, that none of the power which carried me through these
measures with the success which attended them was of my own
creating. . . . On calmly recurring to these three addresses, it is now
evident to me, through the experience which time has given, that the
knowledge of the good and superior Spirit which directed and controlled all my public proceedings, was . . . far in advance of the age. . . .'
The later account is certainly shaped to some extent by the novel
convictions of Owen's last years – especially by his more habitual
recourse to a deity as an explanation and his belief in spiritualistic
communication with the dead. But – spiritualism apart – the retrospect
does not in any way contradict Owen's view of his role as it may be
deduced from the letters and addresses written in 1817. The most
eloquent testimony comes from the *Letter* which appeared in the news-

papers on 10 September, but the other documents of the period also point in the same direction.

The *Address* of 21 August itself is full of millennialist and apocalyptic language, quite apart from the lengthy passage quoted. He speaks of the wrong principles which in all religions have been 'fast entwined with all their fundamental notions'[23] – a phrase which recalls the belief, commonplace among Protestant exegetes of biblical prophecy, that an original 'pure' Christianity had been overlaid and perverted by the centuries of papal and political error which constituted the reign of Antichrist. He tells his hearers that they 'must be attired in proper garments' before they can enjoy the new world – a direct reference to the wedding garment imagery which was commonly employed to describe the messianic feast.[24]

In the *Letter* published on 10 September, Owen proclaims that the applause which greeted his announcement of freedom of opinion (which here and elsewhere he presents as a natural right, but, within the terms of his own doctrine, would be more properly regarded as a consequence of the equality of errors) showed him 'that the world was delivered from mental slavery – that the shackles of ignorance, superstition, and hypocrisy, were burst asunder for ever. . .'.[25] Even in the brief period since he began his teaching, it had become clear that 'in the minds of all, the existing order of things has no secure spot on which to rest. . .'.[26] The bulk of this lengthy letter is taken up with the details of community organisation, a rather quaint exercise which leads to a full and sustained flight of millennial eloquence.

He explains, temperately enough to begin with, that his denunciation of existing religious and political systems was a necessary piece of preliminary demolition; that it was necessary that he 'for a time offend all mankind'; and that men will in due time be given 'a new understanding, a new heart, and a new mind': 'Ere long there shall be but one action, one language, and one people.' As it is, the time has almost arrived 'when swords shall be turned into ploughshares, and spears into pruning hooks – when every man shall sit under his own vine and his own fig-tree, and none shall make him afraid'. Yet more marvellous, the time is close when men will love those who differ from them more than they now love those who agree with them.[27] Then follow three paragraphs of great significance:

> Yes, my friends, in the day and hour when I disclaimed all connexion with the errors and prejudices of the old system – a day to be remembered with joy and gladness henceforward throughout all

future ages – the Dominion of FAITH ceased; its reign of terror, of disunion, of separation, and of irrationality was broken to pieces like a potter's vessel. The folly and madness of its votaries became instantly conspicuous to the world. When the benighted intellects of humanity were opened, and it was clearly perceived that *any* faith, however horrible and absurd, could be given to all of the sons of men, – it was in the same hour made known, that, therefore, Faith could be of no practical value whatever; but that its longer Dominion on earth must be productive of error and misery; and, if permitted to remain, that its continuance among the children of light would produce only evil continually.

Now from henceforth CHARITY presides over the destinies of the world. Its reign, deep rooted in principles of DEMONSTRABLE TRUTH, is permanently founded; and against it hell and destruction shall not prevail.

Yes, on this day, the most glorious the world has seen, the RELIGION OF CHARITY, UNCONNECTED WITH FAITH, is established for ever. *Mental liberty for man is secured; and hereafter he will become a reasonable, and consequently a superior being.*[28]

This rejected Age of Faith is simply a post- and extra-Christian extension of the prophetically conventional reign of Antichrist. Owen nowhere uses this latter term; it is hard to see how, writing from a vantage-point beyond Christianity, he could. For Christian millennialists, especially Protestants, Antichrist's reign was a period occurring between the First Coming and the Second: for many it was almost the whole period; for others is stretched from Constantine to Luther; for others, especially for the least anti-papal, it was to be a short period of total and triumphant error immediately preceding the return of the Messiah. For Owen, talk of a First and a Second Coming could only be nonsense: Christianity was just another wrong religion.[29] Still, his Age of Faith is quite close to the Reign of Antichrist of a dissenter like Bicheno, for whom the term referred to that combination of religious error and church–state oppression which had in the early centuries overcome Christianity and was still dominant, in Great Britain as well as on the Continent. Owen's Age of Faith is Bicheno's Reign of Antichrist extended backwards and sideways to include all history and all religions. Nor is such a concept an entire novelty: some mystics in seventeenth-century England had seen themselves as the inaugurators of the Age of the Spirit which should supersede the previous dispensations, those of the Father and the Son; and though Owen does not do anything with this venerable triad, there is a good deal of this kind of mystic in him. Earlier mystics, still committed to the triadic-trinitarian framework, were not thoroughly post-Christian; Owen, concerned with a simpler transition from error to truth, and wholly untouched by ideas of progress, left all Christian apparatus, except the simply millennial, behind him. Antichrist becomes all error and so becomes all that has gone before, the Age of Faith. The whole past will dissolve before the onset of the Religion of Charity. Owen is not a commentator showing how all this will come to pass as a fulfilment of a change that began earlier; he is the Messiah bringing about the total change. But the Christian vocabulary was less easy to escape from than Christian theology. The concluding passages of the letter make this abundantly clear.

First, this 'new religion' is defined by means of a paraphrase on 2 Corinthians 13, Owen inserting his rather awkward glosses upon St Paul's words from time to time: charity 'believeth all things (WHEN DEMONSTRATED BY FACTS, – BUT NOTHING THAT IS DISTINCTLY OPPOSED TO THE EVIDENCE OF OUR SENSES.)'.[30] Abruptly, this exordium is concluded by the question 'What are the signs of the last days of misery on earth?' This is answered by an adaptation of the central apocalyptic passage from the Gospel of St Luke (21:25–33):

> 'And there shall be signs in the sun, and in the moon, and in the stars; and upon earth, distress of nations, with perplexity. . . .' 'And then shall they see the son of man' (or TRUTH) 'coming in a cloud with power and glory. And when these things begin to come to pass, then look up and lift up your heads, for your redemption' (FROM CRIME AND MISERY) 'draweth nigh.' 'THIS GENERATION SHALL NOT PASS AWAY UNTIL ALL SHALL BE FULFILLED.'

Abruptly again, the argument swings from the horrors of the last days to the joys of the new era, and again a central millennialist passage from the Bible is pressed into service: 'Then shall the wolf dwell with the lamb . . . and a little child shall lead them. They shall not hurt nor destroy in all my holy mountain; for the earth shall be full of the knowledge of the Lord, as the waters cover the sea.'[31]

Owen then proceeds to speak of the change in the past tense:

> What overwhelming power has done this? Where is the arm that has crushed the mighty ones of the earth, and made them afraid? Who has said, Let there be light, and there was light, and all men saw it?

This marvellous change, which all the armies of the earth could not effect through all the ages that have passed, has been accomplished, (without an evil thought or desire toward a being with life or sensation), by the invincible and irresistible power of TRUTH alone; and for the deed done, *no human being can claim a particle of merit or consideration*. That hitherto Undefined, Incomprehensible Power, which directs the atom and controls the aggregate of nature, has in this area of creation made the world to wonder at itself.

Carefully, Owen de-personalises his messiahship – and throughout his long life he was to insist that there was no special merit in him, that his disciples were followers of the truth, not followers of Owen. Nevertheless, this habit of self-deprecation needs to be set alongside the over-riding assertion that his teaching had destroyed error and established truth. Owen was not laying claim to any personal charisma (though he was to exert it later); he was simply a chosen vessel, a means of communication between that 'hitherto Undefined, Incomprehensible Power' and man; he was the available agent of the 'marvellous change'. The Messiah is not cast in the role of miracle-man, but of teacher; he is not constructing a sect, he is instructing mankind. In the New Lanark address, and later in old age, Owen found it less easy to by-pass the problems raised by his individual significance.

He goes on to preserve this impersonality by a brief world-view of history as a struggle between ignorance, assisted by superstition, faith and hypocrisy, and nature, aided by experience, knowledge and truth. This is a cosmic battle; a secularised version of the everlasting struggle between good and evil, light and darkness, God and Satan.

Ignorance then called in Superstition and Hypocrisy to its aid; and together they invented all the faiths or creeds in the world; – a horrid crew, armed with every torture both for body and mind. . . . War was then openly declared against Ignorance, Superstition, Faith, Hypocrisy, and all their dire associates. The latter instantly sounded the alarm, collected their forces, and began to prepare for battle. . . . To their utter dismay, however, Charity . . . escaped their toils, and declared she would henceforward unite herself solely with Nature, Experience, Real Knowledge, and Demonstrable Truth. . . .

At this point the forces of ignorance were disheartened, were offered terms (by Charity) and accepted them – that is, to live on with their possessions intact in the territory conquered by Nature and her allies. 'And Charity, assisted by Demonstrable Truth and Sincerity, was to preside as the active agent over the whole dominions of the New State of Society.'

Here the apocalyptic-millennial style is explicit. Christians, in a long tradition, had seen the world as a battleground, had foreseen the victory of the Messiah, had lovingly depicted the social and political arrangements in the new world of the millennium. Owen modulates the *dramatis personae* into a secular cosmogeny, demonology and angelology, a secular Messiah and a secular millennium. The modulation is of great importance, but it occurs within an inherited Christian myth, which it does not so much replace as restructure.

When Owen came, in the 1850s, to write his autobiography, he reflected at length upon his career and message, and in particular upon the 1817 flashpoint. There is no inconsistency between the early and the late statements; the chief difference is that later the theological aspect has become more explicit and that theological terms are much more common. Thus the introductory dialogues[32] use phrases like 'the Great Creating Power of the Universe', 'the origin of evil', 'the good, wise, and unchanging laws of God and Nature', 'after death through a life immortal' and 'the Millennium' itself, far more regularly and casually than in the earlier essays. There is also a heightened sense of crisis, entirely appropriate to the tense atmosphere of the mid-1850s[33] – a situation referred to at one point as 'this awful suspense between such conflicting parties and principles'. Again, there is a fairly lengthy account of his youthful religious opinions, which will be taken into account later with other autobiographical fragments of this kind. The preface, further, contains a significant assertion of a 'double creation' doctrine, which amounts to a secularised version of the idea of baptism and original sin. Man is created twice: before birth by 'a mysterious and divine organisation of wonderful powers, yet more wondrously combined'; and by ' a secondary or new creation, super-added, to bring the first to its earthly maturity'. It is supremely important that 'this secondary creation should be in accordance with the first'; if it is not, 'man will be mis-formed, and will not attain the happiness for which he is evidently intended by the perfection of his first or divine creation'. The parallel with everyday Christian teaching is exact: man was created by God for perfection; this purpose is frustrated by original and actual sin; it may be restored by a new birth through baptism and the operation of grace. In Christian teaching the return to the original divine purpose is affected by a Messiah; in Owen's teaching he is that Messiah.

The following pages contain the history, step by step, of the progress
of the mission to prepare the population of the world for this great
and glorious change, which, when accomplished, will yet more demonstrate the knowledge, wisdom, and goodness of the Eternal
Creating Power of the Universe. . . . In other words, and to simplify
the subject, the mission of my life appears to be, to prepare the
population of the world to understand the vast importance of the
second creation of humanity. . . . In taking a calm retrospect of my
life from the earliest remembered period of it to the present hour,
there appears to me to have been a succession of extraordinary or
out-of-the-usual-way events, forming connected links of a chain, to
compel me to proceed onward to complete a mission, of which I
have been an impelled agent, without merit or demerit of any kind
on my part . . . man may now be made a terrestrial angel of goodness
and wisdom, and to inhabit a terrestrial paradise . . . the earth will
gradually be made a fit abode for superior men and women, under
a New Dispensation, which will make the earth a paradise and its
inhabitants angels.[34]

The straight narrative of the *Life* contains a good deal about the evolution of his religious opinions: Owen seems to feel obliged first to show
that his acquaintance with normal Christianity and religion in general
is deep and wide, and second to consider the problem of his own
immunity from past error. In the dialogue cited earlier he stresses his
early religiosity, the Methodist overlay (applied by two evangelical
ladies) to his Church of England parentage, his wide reading in religious
tracts and books, and the seed of doubt planted by his reading of so
many opposed controversial works. His general reading increased his
store of conflicting notions; history and the accounts of discoverers
'exhibited to me in strong colours the endless variety of character'. The
problem of variety, and of truth in variety, was resolved in ways which
led directly to the doctrine of circumstances. His religious evolution is
carried further by the account of his time spent with the McGuffog
family, during which he 'began seriously to study the foundation of
all [religions]. . . . Before my investigations were concluded, I was
satisfied that one and all had emanated from the . . . same false imagina-
tions of our early ancestors. . . .'[35] He recounts at some length the story
of how, while yet a Christian, he wrote to Mr Pitt expressing the hope
that the Government would enforce Sabbath observance, and how, to
his gratification, the Government issued a proclamation to that effect
within a few days. The possibility of the letter causing the proclama-

tion is not seriously entertained – but still the story is told with loving detail.

In Manchester, in the 1790s, Owen came into contact with the Unitarian Manchester College, where he had discussions upon 'religion, morals, and other similar subjects, as well as upon the late discoveries in chemistry and other sciences. . .'.[36] It is possible, though no more, that here Owen became acquainted with the progressive millennialism of the Unitarian Joseph Priestley; it is, in fact, not likely that continued discussions of religion in the 1790s could have for long avoided prophetic commentary: the Revolution and the French war provoked a major surge of such writings in this decade. For that matter, anyone inquiring into religion in the 1790s could hardly have avoided the spate of these publications; yet earlier, the two Methodist ladies may well have pressed tracts of this kind upon him.

This speculation becomes a little more substantial in the case of another acquaintance, James Haldane Stewart.[37] Stewart, who married Owen's wife's sister, Mary, published a notable prophetic work in 1825, *A Practical View of the Redeemer's Advent.* The relations between the families (including the household of another sister, Jane, who married another evangelical Anglican clergyman) were close, though the difference of opinions eventually brought the intimacy to an end. But, Owen adds, 'Each knew the other's conscientious convictions', and he goes on to recount how Mary, in a series of letters, constantly urged him to be converted. It is very likely that through the Stewarts, and especially Mary's letters, Owen was brought into touch with current millennial doctrines. All these possible influences would have operated well before the inauguration of his mission in 1817. The ground is uncertain, but it leads (at least) to the conclusion that Owen had had, by that year, many opportunities to become acquainted with millennial thought. It is certain, from the text of his statements alone, that he set out his message and depicted his role in a manner which owed a good deal to the millennial tradition. It remains to identify the ways in which he is related to contemporary varieties of millennialism.

The first point to re-emphasise is that millennialism is a way of looking at the world, not a set of conclusions; the conclusions which may be reached through this way of looking are extremely diverse, and though their family relationship is apparent, it is a relationship of style, concept, vocabulary and mood, dependent ultimately upon reference back to a common set of biblical tests and symbols. Millennialism is a mood of expectation, not a doctrine. The symbol of the statue made of four metals shattered by a stone[38] is common to Joseph Priestley, Edward Irving and J. E. Smith, but in little else do these three agree. Millennialism is a cluster of attitudes united by a common core of images; the images may be explicitly explored, as is the case with professional biblical exegetes; they may be casually employed, either as figures of speech or as conveniently recognisable reference points, by writers and preachers adopting and adapting a means of communication. There is, then, a double range of variables, the first of the nature of the opinions and conclusions being urged within the millennial framework, the second of the way in which the symbols and texts are employed, extending from explicit exegesis to implicit reference. Further, because throughout its history millennialism has tended to spill over into personal messianism, there is another range extending from personal messiahship to a total absence of such an identification.

In the fifty-year period which followed the French Revolution, the millennial style was employed as a vehicle for a wide range of arguments. For some it provided evidence of the truth of Christianity as they identified recent events which had been, arguably, predicted long ago by biblical writers. For others, it was a way of giving a cosmic significance to Great Britain's role in the international conflict, either that of the elect or that of the apostate nation. For evangelical preachers the picture of pending doom for the world leading to joy for some and grief for others was a normal way of calling individual sinners to repentance and a sinful nation to, for instance, stricter Sabbath observance. For a host of writers in missionary journals it was a way of enlisting effort in a process which should itself, under divine guidance, bring about a millennium which was in essence a perfected *status quo*. For the despairing 'students of prophecy' who gathered around Henry Drummond and Edward Irving, it was a way of condemning an apostate church and nation which had, among other iniquities, conceded that Catholics could be citizens. For at least a handful of political radicals, among whom Richard Carlile may be ambiguously and 'Zion' Ward palpably reckoned, it was a way of urging a libertarian programme. For a handful of trade union advocates in the mid-thirties, it was a vehicle for a producer-based socialism. For the Mormon colonisers, it was a recruiting argument to draw men across the Atlantic to the American frontier. For a few deluded souls, it was a way of staking out a claim to personal near or actual deification.

Owen clearly fits neatly into none of these categories, but he is related to most of them. Obviously he was not at all interested in

finding 'Christian evidences'. Nor was he anxious to settle whether
Great Britain was on the side of Christ or Antichrist. Nevertheless, he
shares with those who took that sort of question seriously a general
excitement about the international situation. Again, he effortlessly
assumes a view which was strenuously argued for by the 'elect nation'
and pro-missionary commentators, that the millennium would begin
in Great Britain and thence spread to the rest of the world. To continue
down the categories, Owen could be at times (though he was not all
the time) as anxious as any evangelical preacher to convert individuals
by a finely balanced picture of opposed misery and felicity. Sometimes
he is as progressivist as any Christian optimist finding evidence of
divine activity in a variety of recent achievements, from (in their
writings) improved navigation and efficient production to apostolic
preaching and moral behaviour. His progressivist appearance is
superficial – he is more on the side of crisis than continuity – but he does
dwell upon the multiplying power of production and the spread of
correct ideas in a way that has obvious similarities with the view that
the millennium is a perfected *status quo*, its advent merely hastened by a
recent acceleration of progressive tendencies: the spread of the gospel
for some, the increase in production for Owen. It is not until the 1850s
that his similarity to the Irvingites is evident: in his later writings
(though it is to be detected in the earlier) there is the same urgent stress
upon the imminent parting of the ways, the option open now but not
open for long between disaster and deliverance. Further, there are the
'spiritual communications' of the later years – usually written off as the
imaginings of an old man going soft in the head. Perhaps they were,
but Owen accorded to these intimations the same function which
Irving accorded to the more spectacular voices speaking in his churches.
They were a manifestation of the ruling power of the universe, and
'the good and superior Spirits' responsible for the communications
were 'actively engaged in their new spheres of existence to turn the
threatening evil to good'.[39] His resemblance to the radical and unionist
millennialists hardly needs emphasis; he and they are closely comparable examples of the use of a millennial style for socially reformist ends
– and the unionists, in any case, were considerably under his influence.
Again, there are clear similarities between Owen's recruiting for
communities and the Mormon colonising campaign; both were calling
men to come out of iniquity, to enter as much as could be had of the
new world immediately, and there to await its early total arrival. He
and they each used a glowing description of millennial bliss to attract

recruits.

If Owen is related at most points to the millennial family of ideas, he is more closely related at some than at others. His unquenchable optimism (he no more believes that, at the crisis, men would take the wrong turning than the Irvingites believed thay would take the right one) links him in temper closely to the progressives. Like them, too, he allegorises millennial symbols into everyday if still striking phenomena of amelioration; and, still like them, he does not think of this movement to better and best as autonomous, but as the consequences of the initiative taken by some external agency. But he is quite unlike them on two major points. For them the movement towards their cozy millennium began from a situation which could be called good. For Owen, the departure point was distinctly more bad than good; crime, vice and misery are its leading characteristics. Set against this total darkness, very recent discoveries are not examples of progress but heralds of sudden and total change. Owen's favourite words were perhaps 'new' and 'crisis', and he took them both entirely seriously.

He had to, in an almost occupational way, for he was personally involved in the millennial process far more than the normal millennialist progressive. They were speaking on behalf of an acknowledged Messiah who had come once and would (in whatever form) come again; he was speaking on behalf of himself, and his life was the first coming of the saving truth. So he is far more millennialist, though less Christian, than they. They speak for the known dispensation rapidly progressing towards its millennial climax; he for a totally new dispensation only now revealed, his own – 'his' in the sense of agency, not of personal responsibility. He, accordingly, thinks of a sharp break; they of progress. Here Owen is closer to the 'students of prophecy', with the difference that he is confident of the irresistible onset of peaceful change, while they despairingly anticipate disaster as the needed purifying prelude to perfection. But for both, the old world shall utterly pass away.

In sum, then, Owen is closely related to contemporary millennial attitudes at three points – to the optimism of the progressives, to the crisis-expectation of the anti-progressives, and to the personal identification of the self-proclaimed Messiahs. He is, to revert to the three scales of classification suggested earlier, close to the progressive pole in terms of conclusions, to the implicit pole in terms of biblicism, and to the messianic pole in terms of self-identification. He reflects the whole millennialist tradition, and cannot be understood except against the background of the complex patterns in which this tradition is expressed in his lifetime.

NOTES AND REFERENCES

1. See, in particular, two books by E. L. Tuveson, *Millennium and Utopia* (1949) and *Redeemer Nation* (1968). The former is centred upon seventeenth- and eighteenth-century England, the latter upon nineteenth-century America; in each, by concentrating upon the progressive and optimistic elements only, the author fails to illustrate the scope of millennialist thought. J. F. C. Harrison, in *Robert Owen and the Owenites in Britain and America* (1969), devotes nearly fifty pages to millennialism, but gives undue weight to the eccentrics and fails to locate Owen meaningfully in a context which requires a more systematic analysis than he gives it.

2. G. D. H. Cole (ed.), *A New View of Society and Other Writings*, Everyman ed. (1949) p. 18.

3. Ibid., p. 17.

4. Ibid., pp. 19–20.

5. Ibid., p. 95.

6. Ibid., pp. 93–4.

7. Ibid., p. 97.

8. Ibid., p. 119.

9. Ibid., p. 102.

10. Ibid., p. 103.

11. Ibid., p. 104.

12. See his careful introduction of this term in this Address (ibid., pp. 104, 106), where the phrasing suggests that Owen knew that he was inviting a new content into an old concept.

13. Ibid., p. 103.

14. Ibid., p. 105.

15. Ibid., p. 107. But in later life Owen does apply to himself the image of the stone which 'the builders up of society' rejected (*Life*, I 203).

16. Cole (ed.), *A New View of Society*, pp. 108–9.

17. Ibid., pp. 111, 114, 115, 116, 117, 118.

18. *Life*, I 207. See Psalm 95 in which Jehovah is represented as reproving Israel for its iniquities while passing through the wilderness to the promised land.

19. *Life*, Ia 113.

20. Ibid., p. 114.

21. *Life*, I 158–65. The quotations which follow are from this passage.

22. The quoted passage corresponds almost exactly to the text of the *Address* given in *Life*, Ia 115, except that the punctuation has been revised to make it more exclamatory.

23. Ibid., p. 115.

24. Ibid., p. 116.

25. Ibid., p. 120.

26. Ibid., p. 121.

27. Ibid., pp. 132–3. The biblical reference is to Micah, 4: 3–4.

28. Ibid., p. 133.

29. Though, temporarily in 1834, he does toy with the Second Coming image to describe his ideas.

30. *Life*, Ia 133. For the quotations which follow, see ibid., pp. 133–7.

31. Isaiah 11. Later, in a rare biblical citation, Owen refers his readers to Isaiah 58, 59 and 65 for more on the calamities of ignorance, the omnipotence of truth, and the changes to take place.

32. *Life*, Ia iv–v, xviii–xxi, xxx–xxxiii, for the quotations which follow.

33. It is significant that this part of the introduction is dated December 1856; the restoration of the Napoleonic Empire and the Crimean War had stimulated a flurry of millennial-apocalyptic publishing and re-publishing in the United Kingdom in the 1850s.

34. *Life*, Ia xlii–xliii.

35. *Life*, I 16.

36. Ibid., p. 36.

37. Ibid., pp. 100–1.

38. Daniel 2. This symbol is the basis of the ancient habit of periodising history into four world monarchies followed by a fifth, or messianic reign.

39. *Life*, Ia xxxvi.

CHAPTER NINE

# Owen's Mind and Methods*

## MARGARET COLE

LET us begin with some quotations:

1. My treatment of all with whom I came into communication was so natural that it generally gained their confidence, and drew forth only their good qualities to me; and I was often much surprised to discover how much more easily I accomplished my objects than others whose educated acquirements were much superior to mine. . . .

In consequence of this to me unconscious power over others I had produced such effects over the workpeople in the factory in the first six months of my management that I had the most complete influence over them, and their order and discipline exceeded that of any other in or near Manchester; and for regularity and sobriety they were an example which none could then imitate.

> Robert Owen, *Autobiography*.
> The reference is to the year 1790.

2. My intention was not to be a mere manager of cotton mills, as such mills were at the time generally managed; but to introduce principles in the conduct of the people, which I had successfully commenced with the workpeople in Mr Drinkwater's factory. . . . I had now, by a course of events not under my control, the groundwork on which to try an experiment long wished for, but little expected ever to be in my power to carry into execution.

> Owen, *Autobiography*.
> The reference is to 1 January 1800.

---

* This chapter was already written when Professor J. F. C. Harrison published his study of *Robert Owen and the Owenites in Britain and America* (Routledge, 1969), in which he advances the view that 'millennialism' was a fairly common phenomenon of the age. This is certainly correct; but I am concerned not so much with Owen's leanings towards millennialism as with his apparent loss of all sense of the practical and abandonment of all his earlier caution.

3. Thou needest to be very right; for thou art very positive.

> David Dale to his son-in-law Robert Owen.
> No date known, but some time after 1800.

4. Why, you love these children better than your own!

> Caroline Owen on the children of the New Lanark schools.
> Quoted in Owen, *Autobiography*.

5. I pray to God that He will turn your dear father from the error of his ways, and make him pious like your grandfather.

> Caroline Owen to her son Robert. Quoted in R. D. Owen, *Threading My Way*. Date about 1812. Young Robert obediently tried to convert his father, but with singular ill-success.

6. He persists in asserting that his plan is the wisest, best, and most admirable scheme that ever entered into any human comprehension. It is – because it is. 'See what a pretty plan I have drawn out *on paper.* . . . There you will put the men, there the women, and there the children. . . . All the bad passions will be eradicated, and I should like to live there myself. Nobody that *understands* it can for a moment object to it. . . .' Such is the reasoning Mr Owen condescends to use; and if he had to make the beings who are to inhabit his paradises, as well as to make the laws which should regulate them, there can be no doubt that he would manage everything extremely well.

> *The Black Dwarf*, 20 August 1817.

7. We view it as a grievance of considerable magnitude to be compelled by Mr Owen to adopt what measures soever he may be pleased to suggest on matters that entirely belong to us. Such a course of procedure is most repugnant to our minds as men, and degrading to our characters as freeborn sons of highly favoured Britain.

> Extract from a memorial of some members of the New Lanark Sick Fund to Owen's partners, quoted in the Rev. John Aikin's *A Refutation of Mr Owen's System*, a hostile pamphlet published in 1824, the year in which Owen severed connection with New Lanark.

8. Before I knew the great truth which you have developed, I was a rough irritable stickler for vulgar liberty – since my personal

acquaintance with you I have become better – but I do not feel satisfied. I have not the charity.

From a letter of James Morrison
of the Builders' Union to Owen, 1838.

9. Always a gentle bore in regard to his dogmas and his expectations; always palpably right in his descriptions of human misery; always thinking he had proved a thesis when he had only asserted it in the force of his own conviction, and always really meaning something more rational than he had actually expressed.

[Of Owen and the Bible]: Robert Owen is not the man to think differently of a book for having read it.

Harriet Martineau,
*Autobiography* and *Biographical Sketches* (1877).

10. All of this [his record in manufacture, at New Lanark, and as a public lecturer and pamphleteer] must have been well known to the parties calling this extraordinary Educational Conference in the present year; and yet I was not called to assist, nor was my name once mentioned in the whole proceedings of the three days, until I made an attempt to speak on the last day. . . . But no doubt for an ulterior purpose, the parties present were insanely determined that I should not be heard.

Peroration to Owen's *Autobiography*, September 1857.

I

The quotations printed at the head of this chapter have been chosen to illustrate the difficulties which any biographer or critic finds in either making sense of Robert Owen's attitude to human organisation or in fitting him in to any picture of the development of socialist thought. On the one hand we find an astonishingly practical business organiser, making money without trouble in quantity sufficient to finance equally practical experiments in the organisation of human beings – up to the time when, almost as though by intention, it would seem, he lost together both financial and organisational sense; we find a man of human sympathy, courtesy and self-restraint, loved by all children (including his own, which is for reformers often the stiffest test), looked

up to by the workers in his factories, respected and listened to by the
respected among contemporary employers and politicians, and throw-
ing out, as 'side-lines' to the main lines of the theory of society which
he was gradually building up, proposals of such obvious good sense
that it took more than a hundred years to put some of them into
practice. This chapter is not the place in which to list them all in detail;
but one may mention town-planning and Green Belts, the 'economy
of high wages' and the economic dangers of under-consumption, the
need for destitution to be relieved out of national resources and for
industry to bear its share of providing help for its employees in sickness
and unemployment, as major contributions to what are now common-
places of political thought; to which may be added such 'throw-aways'
as space-heating; bulk purchase of foodstuffs; and a full census of
production and employment.

All these suggestions, as well as some less practical, belong to the
formative years in which the essays which he called *A New View of
Society*, and 'Mr Owen's Plan' for beginning with the reformation of
the poor law were gradually taking shape. At the same time, while the
'civilised' world was crowding to gape at the visible success of New
Lanark, the political radicals, the men with names like Cobbett, Hunt
and Wooler, whom historians of the working class generally accept as
part of the tradition of 'the Left', were pouring scorn, sometimes very
scurrilous scorn, upon Owen himself, his policy and his ideas – 'a
*beastly* writer', Cobbett called him in later years. Nevertheless, and
more confusingly, when Owen returned from America with his fortune gone and his organisational gifts of 'looking very wisely at the
men in the different departments' apparently vanished beyond recall,
it was just the ideals to which those radicals had taken most exception
which made him the most adored – *personally* adored – leader of the
unenfranchised working classes, the people for whom the *Political
Register* was mainly written. It was these ideals also which eventually
gave Owenism its permanent position in the philosophy of nineteenth-
century working-class organisations, long after the disastrous leader had
left his own creation like a discarded umbrella and lost himself in millennial and eventually spiritualist speculations – and when others who
had once listened with deep interest found him no more than an ultra-
bore with charming manners. Small wonder that historians of labour
as different as the Webbs and Mr E. P. Thompson have failed to fit
Owen in anywhere; that Leslie Stephen in the *Dictionary of National
Biography* could find nothing more helpful to say than that 'Owen

was one of the bores who are the salt of the earth' – which really tells us nothing whatever; that the authors of the latest book on the history of progressive education[1] seem less interested in Owen than in sundry minor characters; and that even G. D. H. Cole, his most sympathetic of non-contemporary biographers, can only conclude that he was 'a little mad'.

So, of course, he was, though only in specific directions, and at first only intermittently. The impression left on me after much reading of and about Owen is rather that of a motor-car with a fine construction, but a flaw in the transmission which every so often sets the engine racing wildly so that the car makes a very great noise but fails to move at all. This result may have had different causes: one such, I am convinced, was the brutal disappointment over Peel's Factory Bill of 1816 and the almost simultaneous (and shocking) treatment of Owen himself by Sturges Bourne's House of Commons Committee on the Reform of the Poor Laws – which were followed in 1817 by the wronged one's extraordinary apocalyptic outbursts at the City of London Tavern, and the newspaper propaganda campaign which caused the London mail coaches to be delayed for twenty minutes taking Mr Owen's printed packets on board. A reaction such as this passes. To pursue the metaphor, the car resumes its journey as though nothing much had happened; in the 1817 case, the effect of Owen's anti-religious harangue seems by all the evidence to have been much less than he himself believed – though Brougham did take him by the arm and ask him why he had made such an idiot of himself. But it recurs, and eventually it does bring the observers, however reluctantly, to the conclusion that, beautiful and impressive though the outward appearance of the car may be, it cannot be relied upon to get you to any journey's end. The astonishing thing is that the appearance did remain so beautiful – otherwise, how account for the decision, *in 1841*, to put Owen in sole control of the Queenwood experiment, for which, as a contemporary put it, he would have bought up the whole of Hampshire if the funds had been there?

I cannot, of course, offer proof of this metaphor; one can only arrive at some conclusions by looking at the development of Owen's own mind and ideas, and of his relationships with others, and it is unfortunate that there is very little documentation with which to illustrate. Owen's own autobiography, published within a year of his death, is remarkably vivid for most of its length, though the engine still races from time to time, when bits of *Robert Owen's Millennial Gazette* or

some other of the many journals he managed to edit make appearances
in the text. But it is, after all, the chronicle of what seemed most
important and memorable to one man in his eighties; it has some
detectable inaccuracies and misleading statements – though singularly
few – and of course it stops short. Owen's own correspondence is not
illuminating, and the journalistic matter, after the *Book of the New
Moral World* had been completed, is both tedious and trivial; our debt
to R. D. Owen for writing *Threading My Way* is all the greater. For
the rest, it is very much a matter of poking around, of collecting and
weighing odd bits and pieces, sentences even, from here and there, in
reminiscences of contemporaries, for example. But a good deal must
remain guesswork, or, as Owen might have put it, 'rational speculation'; in death, as in life, Robert Owen remains a self-made man.

II

It is logical, when it is Robert Owen who is being studied, to give
first attention to his early years, since the early years form the basis of
his own philosophy – and also provide the clearest proof of his inconsistency. His own view of the influence of men's circumstances upon
their characters he expressed over and over again in speech and writing.
The words used varied slightly, though only slightly, on different
occasions; it is simplest here to quote the best known, the rubric which
prefaces the first, Wilberforce-dedicated, essay of the four which
together make up the *New View of Society*.

> *Any general character, from the best to the worst, from the most ignorant to
> the most enlightened, may be given to any community, even to the world at
> large, by the application of proper means: which means are to a great extent
> at the command and under the control of those who have influence in the
> affairs of men.*

Sometimes he put his point more drastically, asserting dogmatically
that the character not only of the community but of every single individual within it is developed with equal fatalism, that 'it is *impossible*
[my italics] that any human being could or can form his own qualities
or character'; sometimes he is more human and allows himself to
express straightforward dislike of 'the money-making and money-

seeking aristocracy of modern times' without thinking it necessary to assure his reader that the cotton lords could not help being such unpleasant characters. But nowhere that I can find does he face the obvious fact that whoever his generalisation applied to, it certainly did not apply to Robert Owen. Though in the 1816 *Address to the Inhabitants of New Lanark* and in various others of his later writings, he does refer to 'causes over which I had no control, which removed in my early days the bandage which covered my mental sight', he is alluding only to the claims of revealed religion, the removal of which can hardly have been the concern either of Mr Thickness's village school or of the 'community' of Newtown. The little society in which he was born and grew to the ten-year-old maturity in which he set out to seek his fortune in London does not seem to have the slightest bearing on his character or his opinions. What is very clear – and the more significant in that he never noticed it himself – is the early emergence of certain marked characteristics which had a strong bearing on his relations with other people.

The first is his extraordinary kindness and sympathy. This is not just the 'unfailing courtesy' which right up to the end of his life so many, like Harriet Martineau and that 'very bustling' partner of his, William Allen the Quaker, found so disconcerting – courtesy not being too common a trait among radical thinkers. It goes deeper – it is an instinctive distress at the sight of pain, physical *or* mental, inflicted upon anyone. '*You must never strike anyone*', he told his angry son Robert in his boyhood; and there is no reason to doubt the passages in his own autobiography in which he condemns competition among school-children and says how he disliked 'coming out top' because of the misery of those who had to remain below. This is more than kindliness, more than righteous anger at the sufferings of children in other men's factories; it comes out over and over again, as in casual demands that a new society should show 'especial consideration for those poor miserable creatures whom the errors of past time have denominated the bad, the worthless, and the wicked'.[2]

'Why should we *ever* irritate?', he asks, a little plaintively, in the second essay in the *New View of Society*. Cynics may observe that he did in fact quite often irritate characters like Francis Place and even the more amenable William Lovett – but mainly because he could not be induced to stop patiently explaining and *go away*; and may, if they choose, derive this from the sermons he tells us he used to write as a very little boy, and the letters he sent to Pitt, when an apprentice shopman, directing his attention to the non-observance of the Sabbath in Stamford. More serious is the criticism that he seems not to have applied his remarks about the evils of competition to his own rise to affluence. This is partly due, no doubt, to the unique economic conditions in the cotton trade during the period when he was making his fortune, and when, as he seems to have thought, anyone with a head on his shoulders who was prepared to work reasonably hard could have done likewise. This may have been true enough, and he may have well deserved all he got without making any effort to grab even what he was legally entitled to; but though he must have known that there was a good deal of chance contributing to his success, even in Lancashire of the Industrial Revolution, and that there were many who fell by the way, he does not show any sign of feeling sympathy for his unsuccessful fellows, going only so far as to observe that he bore them no ill-will.

The other important characteristic is, of course, his complete, if narrow, rationalism, his belief that he had arrived at his own convictions by the pure use of reason, without any emotion, and that anyone who would similarly exercise his own reasoning powers – or, which might be more easy, would listen for a sufficient time to Mr Owen's exposition – could not fail to come to the same conclusions, unless he was prevented by deficiencies in his own education or social conditions. Here we have the great contradiction in his life – the simple inconsistency between the theory that all men believed what education and society had moulded them to believe, whereas he, and he almost alone, *knew*, untaught, what was the truth and needed only to tell it to others – a self-made man, a Samuel Smiles hero in the world of ideas as well as of practical business.

It is manifestly impossible that this should be true, however often and however fervently he asserted it. He was not a hermit; he mixed with other people, even sharing rooms with men like Robert Fulton the engineer, and though shy at first, and 'subject painfully to blushing', he was friendly and popular, and welcomed at discussions such as those held by the Manchester Lit. and Phil.; he took the chair for Joseph Lancaster's meetings on the Lancasterian system of mass elementary education. And at some time he must have read voraciously; it is unfortunate that long before he came to write his autobiography he had apparently forgotten about his early reading except the massive investigations (undertaken, it would seem, some time in his early teens) through which he convinced himself of the essential falsity of the tenets of all organised religions. By the time that Robert Dale Owen came to take notice of the library at Braxfield House, he observed that though it contained many books, his father seemed to confine his reading to official papers and statistical studies like those of Patrick Colquhoun. There is some indication that at one time or other he had read Godwin's *Political Justice*, but no account of what he made of it; and though he finally dismissed the views of Bentham and the Utilitarians, which anyone might well have expected him to endorse,[3] as 'all based on a fundamental error', one can find no specific reference to his having read any of Bentham's own writings. The passage referring to Bentham, in fact, castigates the philosopher mildly as having 'little knowledge of the world except through books and a few deemed liberal-minded men and women who were admitted to his friendship'.

Owen himself certainly had a good deal of discussion, in his early manhood and right up to the time of New Lanark's greatest success, with the like-minded and with others, and it is exasperating that we know so little about the content or the manner of these discussions, and cannot discover for how long Owen continued to listen to what anyone else had to say. The circle which he, with John Dalton and others, formed at the Manchester College in the early 1790s must surely have been run on a system of give-and-take; and though one may discount to some extent Owen's recollection of the young Coleridge being repeatedly worsted in argument by him, his high-sounding sentences being countered by 'my few words, directly to the point' – a remarkable contrast, if correct, to all Owen's later writings and speeches – to the extent that Coleridge, twenty years later, was constrained to apologise in person for his earlier brashness, there is no reason to dismiss it altogether. There was also the occasion, recalled with manifest satisfaction, when Owen crushed the unfortunate Dr Ferrier, the Vice-President of the Lit. and Phil., who had finished reading a 'very learned' paper proving the possibility of any one of determination and industry making himself into a genius, with a couple of devastating sentences which apparently put a stop to any discussion. Dr Ferrier, Owen adds, 'was never afterwards so cordial and friendly as he had been previously' – and no wonder. The occasion is remarkable as almost the only one on which Owen can be convicted on his own showing of discourtesy in public – unless calling the vocal opposition at the City of London meetings 'ill-trained and uninformed persons', whose opinions he did not wish to solicit, be so reckoned.

III

Admittedly, these conclusions are based principally upon Owen's own statements, since until the success of New Lanark and the publication, in the *New View of Society*, of the principles on which his experiment there had been based, Owen was not a public figure interesting enough to find place in newspaper reports or the reminiscences of great men. In his Manchester days, he was known principally as the young man who, scarcely twenty years old, had been taken on by Mr Drinkwater at a relatively enormous salary as manager of his mills and had immediately proceeded to show his value by taking up and selling the famous Sea Island cotton; who was so competent and companionable that he was rapidly co-opted to the organising committee of the Lit. and Phil; who was already beginning to make comparison between the assiduous attention which his fellow manufacturers gave to the condition of their inanimate machinery and the contempt in which they held the human material which operated it – and who had, at that time, 'a high opinion of the attainments of the wealthy educated classes and of all above them'. It is inconceivable that Owen should not have discussed the views which he was beginning to evolve about the proper running of industry – and those of society at large; in fact, we know that he did so, with one or two friends. Unfortunately, what we do not know at all is what any of the friends made of them; we do know that he did not at that time thrust them down everybody's throat.

About his own attitude to the human material – the working class – we know a little more. We know that from the first he aimed at, and succeeded in, making Mr Drinkwater's factory into a model place of employment for his day; and that he did this by a combination of bluff and patience, by staring in silence at the manufacturing processes until he felt that he had fully absorbed them all, and not until then making any alterations on his own responsibility – though he was, it must be remembered, entirely in charge from the very first day of his appointment. After this, he succeeded in improving the machinery, human and material, to such an extent as to earn all the desired profit for his employer – and for himself to reach the unexpressed conclusion that profit was so easy to make that it was unnecessary for a manufacturer of competence and humanity to worry himself about it.

For eight years he watched and planned, increasing his personal wealth and importance with each change in his business connections, until in 1799 he began the management of the New Lanark estate, which was to become his glory, even though in later years he was to write ungratefully that 'its foundation is an error; and its superstructure could be amended only by an entire re-creation of new conditions'. 'Let it be kept in everlasting remembrance', he wrote in impatience with those who kept on thinking of him as 'Mr Owen of New Lanark', 'that that which I effected at New Lanark was only the best I could accomplish under the circumstances of an ill-arranged manufactory and village, which existed before I undertook the government of the establishment.'

It seems probable that, apart from whatever were the personal attractions of David Dale and his daughter Caroline, the main reasons for Owen's decision to acquire what he later called 'the very wretched society' of New Lanark were the existence of the boarding-home for child apprentices, which the falling-off in the supply of pauper children had made redundant; the partial, though not complete, separation of the 'new' factory village from the Royal Borough of Lanark; and the possibility which this opened of experimentation freer than that obtainable in the crowded districts further south. At the least, this separation, and the knowledge that he was not in sole ownership of the concern but must continue to satisfy those who were from time to time his partners with a healthy meal of profit (and the fact that he was now a married man with a steadily growing family for whom, Caroline Owen's comment notwithstanding, he felt great affection), both slowed down his experimentation and caused him to take more interest in the views and individualities of the members of his own working force than he had been accustomed to do in Lancashire. For eight or nine years at least, until after David Dale's death, the need to satisfy his partners' requirements, much as he came gradually to resent them, out of the exertions of the human material he had on hand and not of a hypothetical population brought up and educated on Owenite principles, forced him to proceed gradually. He had to persuade a pretty reluctant and prejudiced population – prejudiced against him both because he was not a Scot and because they suspected, quite correctly, that he intended to change the establishment into something very different from the free-for-all place which it had been in the days of the kindly, philanthropic, but ageing and largely absentee David Dale.

He probably exaggerated in retrospect the sins of the 'very wretched society'; but that is no reason to suppose that it did not share to the full the usual faults of factory labour, particularly Scottish factory labour, of drunkenness, dirt, dishonesty, and sexual habits which shocked the ministers. These faults in his human machinery he had to correct, and without doing violence to his own non-coercive principles.

This he did, in effect, by 'looking very wisely' at the human machinery during those years. We may perhaps be moved to smile at the enthusiastic detail with which he described the devices of his introduction – the 'silent monitor' of coloured wood hanging over the worker's machine, and the sensible checking system which eliminated pilfering; though we ought not to forget that more than a century later the masters of the Russian Revolution were not too proud to make use of the first, or that, *after another fifty years*, the scandal of the *Queen Elizabeth II* showed that so old and lordly an industry as Clyde shipbuilding had signally failed to establish the second. But it must be clear that neither the 'silent monitors' nor any other of the sensible changes which it is unnecessary to list here could have been put into effect without the co-operation and understanding of those who would be principally affected by them; and Owen at first set about securing this by what would seem to us today perfectly normal and sensible methods. 'I sought out', he tells us, 'the individuals who had the most influence among them from their natural powers or position, and to these I took pains to explain what were my intentions for the changes I wished to make. I explained that they were to procure greater permanent advantages for themselves and their children, and requested that they would aid me in instructing the people, and in preparing them for the new arrangements which I had in contemplation.' There is some indication that, at this stage, Owen did at least listen with a fairly open mind to criticism coming from below: 'I never knew in a single instance', says the writer of the defensive pamphlet *Robert Owen of New Lanark*, 'Mr Owen ever dismiss a worker for having manfully and conscientiously objected to his measures'; and R. D. Owen, in the pleasant story of the 'Committee of Bughunters', has preserved for us what may not have stood alone as an attempt to induce the village community to embark upon a little real 'self-government' and responsibility.

In this instance, it will be remembered, Owen had found himself for once at a loss to bring the private dwellings of the villagers to the standard of cleanliness which he had prescribed and performed for the roads and lanes, and had suggested to a general meeting of villagers that they should themselves choose a committee of their own to visit and report upon the interior conditions of the individual houses and to award prizes for the best-kept – with the amusing if not altogether unexpected result that the die-hards of privacy who had at first flatly refused to open their doors to the prying noses of the committee decided before very long that they had heard quite enough of the public commendation of Mrs Campbell and Mrs MacDougal for the spotless condition of their houses, and opened their own to the investigators.

Owen's autobiography does not mention the bughunters' committee, possibly because he had forgotten all about it; more likely because, even at that date, he was not much interested, except as immediately necessary, in methods of securing the active participation of adults; he shows rather more realisation of the impression made by his gesture of continuing to pay the full wage-bill of the factory when the American cotton embargo had forced it temporarily to discontinue production. He could see that willingness to lay out £7000 on the pure 'maintenance' of the human machinery was a more potent engine of conviction than any of the argumentative discourses which he had given to the leading spirits in the factory; unfortunately he never fully understood how exceptional, for making such a gesture, was the position of a highly successful manufacturer in the cotton trade in the first decade of the nineteenth century.

In comparison, then, with the wealth of reports and information about the schools of New Lanark, we know all too little about what Owen did with the adult population or what was the answer of the factory 'leaders' to the propositions he put before them – whether they felt like his business partners of 1809 who, after they had visited New Lanark and exposed themselves to Owen's persuasive tongue, presented him with a large silver salver, and the somewhat discouraging reply to his proposals for expansion: '*Each of your propositions is true individually, but as they lead to conclusions contrary to our education, habits, and practices, they must in the aggregate be erroneous, and we cannot proceed on such new principles for governing and extending this already very large establishment*' (Owen's own summary of their conclusions).

The later Owen, unhampered by having to pay attention to the views of commercial men who were 'merely trained to buy cheap and to sell dear', would have brushed any remarks of this kind aside. The earlier one, still without hurrying, set more seriously about winning

support, though it was three more years before the first part of the
*New View of Society* was printed and circulated for comment and study
by those to whom the pamphlet was sent, and as it turned out for the
further purpose of getting himself the solid support of men like John
Walker of Arnos Grove, of substance sufficient to allow them to
finance experiment without thought of immediate gain. The response
to the first two essays, from persons as 'respectable' as the Archbishop
of Canterbury, astonished and delighted Owen, who had not until
then, or so he tells us, met with anyone who was willing to be converted to his ideas; and it should be noted that these two essays are
brief, comparatively sober, and lay stress on a prophecy, very comfort-
ing to politicians, that it will only be necessary to take the smallest of
steps at any one time. Even in the subsequent and much longer pair of
essays which contain the detailed history of the New Lanark experiment as well as a much more specific account of what he thinks might
be done in the near future in the country as a whole in order to make a
start with a new society, Owen still does not envisage any precipitate
transformation. His plans are to be submitted 'to the dispassionate and
patient investigation and decisions of those in every rank and class and
denomination of society who have been in some degree conscious of
the errors in which they exist, who have felt the thick mental darkness
in which they are surrounded, who are ardently desirous of discovering
and following truth wherever it may lead,' and who can perceive the
inseparable connection which exists between 'individual and general,
between private and public good' – which, allowing for differences in
style, reads very like one of H. G. Wells's pleas for the Open Conspiracy more than a hundred years later. Only at the very end of the
fourth essay (originally dedicated to the Prince Regent, of all people),
did the writer, admitting that his analysis might not be 'forthwith
palatable to the world at large', threaten his audience that if the small
dose of 'unpalatable restorative' which he is now administering to them
turns out to be of insufficient strength, he is intending to follow it up
with larger and stronger medicament until 'some health to the public
mind be firmly and permanently established'. They had been warned.

But for the moment the effect was all that could be desired. The
great, the interested, the philanthropic, and the worried, all began reading the *New View*, and making the journey to the wilds of Scotland
to see for themselves that all that had been said of New Lanark was
perfectly true; Owen secured for himself the new partners who really
understood up to a point what he was trying to do. There followed

the joyful story of how the last (and in some ways the worst chosen) of all his commercial partners laid a great trap for him, fell into it themselves, and had to be congratulated, at their own public dinner, on having not only got rid of that incompetent fellow Owen, but having actually sold for £114,000 a property which they themselves had publicly declared not to be worth half the £84,000 they had originally paid for it; and the final triumphal journey, when the other part of Owen's supporters, the working people of Old and New Lanark, turned out in their thousands to unship the horses and drag the carriage containing him and the alarmed Quakers in his entourage up and down the steep hills of the Royal Borough, up and down again to the falls of Clyde, through all the streets of New Lanark and back again through the grounds of his house at Braxfield. 'It interested me deeply', wrote Owen with remarkable restraint, 'and, if possible, increased my determination to do them and their children all the good in my power.' Two years later, at the opening of the Institute for the Formation of Character – the project which had stuck in the throat of his partners of 1809 – he took his people thoroughly into his confidence and told them what he proposed to do for them, and the world, and why. In the meantime, he had been absorbing the whole-hearted interest and enthusiasm shown both by the visitors to New Lanark, and by those public characters who had read the *Essays*.

IV

The *Address to the Inhabitants of New Lanark* (New Year's Day, 1816) marks the apex of Robert Owen's career, before he became involved in serious and continuing relations with practising politicians; it is therefore worth looking rather closely at its nature and content. The first reaction of today's reader may well be that it was very lengthy; though it should be remembered that his audience was probably well inured to sermonising by the Kirk, and that Owen tempered the wind – and imparted a certain effect of mystery – by arranging that 'soft music from a hidden source' should be played, possibly during some sort of interval. (Owen was given, upon occasion, to pieces of rather elephantine mystification and by-play – witness his attempt on his honeymoon journey to make his bride and her maid believe that a very poor sort of house was to be her future home, his popping in and out of a dance carrying a lantern and pretending to be Diogenes looking for a just man, and his challenge to the Eglinton Tourney.)

Lengthy though it is, though, the *Address* is quite calmly written. It sets out briefly what were Owen's ideas when he came to New Lanark, says what he has done since he arrived and invites the members of the audience either publicly or privately to tell him whether there is any single one of his measures that was not clearly and decisively intended to benefit the whole population. Having (presumably) paused for a reply and got none, he goes on to describe what he thinks the Institute should be and do in the future, of which the third item is:

> By showing to the master manufacturers an example in practice, on a scale sufficiently extensive, of the mode by which the characters and situation of the working manufacturers whom they employ may be very materially improved, not only without injury to the masters, but so as to create to them also great and substantial advantages;
> And by inducing, through this example, the British legislative to enact such laws as will secure similar benefits to every part of the population – this to be achieved, not through any party, but by 'withdrawing the germ' of party, sect and even nationality from society as a whole, and establishing new principles.

These new principles, expounded in terms whose eloquence still falls far short of messianism, may have elicited slightly over-enthusiastic response from those who remained attentive. For with a palpable drawing-in of horns he ends the speech by adjuring his hearers to take no sudden and positive action nor to desert the house in which they live at present, however imperfect, until the new one is ready to receive them; but to 'continue to obey the laws under which you live, and although many of them are founded on principles of the grossest ignorance and folly yet obey them – until the government of the country (*which I have reason to believe is in the hands of men well disposed to adopt a system of general improvement*) shall find it practicable to withdraw those laws which are productive of evil and introduce others of an opposite tendency' (italics mine). This was persuasively said, and showed restrained optimism. One can scarcely doubt that Owen, at the beginning of 1816, believed what he said about the future; and at that gathering of his supporters and beneficiaries, he obviously was not having to face any criticisms or interruptions. But within a year and a half all had changed. For the first time in his life, Owen was faced with public and outspoken opposition to his propositions by persons who thought themselves as good as he; and he reacted, to put it bluntly, like a baby. In the two packed meetings of August 1817 in the City of London Tavern, and in the columns of verbiage with which he crammed the newspapers and the stage-coaches, he showed himself as ignorant of the barest elements of persuasion as anybody could be, and responded to those who criticised him with the remark that he regarded them 'with exactly the same feelings with which I should have noticed as many individuals in a very ill-conducted lunatic asylum'.

This is not exactly what one would expect from the man who in his Manchester days, according to himself, had learned *illimitable charity* for all his fellow creatures' thoughts and actions. The apostle of sweet reason had clearly lost his temper; and though he had the elementary sense to withdraw the long list of prepared resolutions which he had brought with him when he saw that they were certain to be heavily amended, if not defeated outright – they included one for the appointment of a 'Committee of Noblemen and Gentlemen' to work out the details of Mr Owen's Plan, which Mr Owen now decided could be no more than a hindrance to him – he was in a state of such incoherent indignation that at the second of the meetings, when the huge mass of newspapers bought by himself and sent all over the country had failed to produce any effect, he burst out into his famous and feverish declaration of atheism, and followed it by an exposition, in fullest detail, of what the new Villages of Co-operation would be like, and a peroration, set out in all variations of roman and italic type, of small and large capitals, which can only be described as slightly demented. What had happened during the eighteen months to produce this result – even if Owen himself, in the intervals of anticipating martyrdom, professed to find it 'satisfactory'?

There really seems little doubt. Owen had come face to face with the men of the world of politics and industry outside his private garden, and had found out what they really made of his proposals, not in amicable and prolonged discussion in their studies and over their breakfast-tables, but in hard fact.

Immediately, as he had told his Institution, the prospects might have been reckoned good. The Essays – whose publication was in due course followed by the *Address to New Lanark*, printed and circulated – had certainly combined with Owen's persuasive and confident manners to suggest to some of those in high places that here was a successful and *civilised* manufacturer who might really be able to make a contribution to the problem of civilising, or at least of making more tolerable, the conditions of life in the new factory systems which were seriously perturbing members of the Government whose incomes did not depend upon Lancashire – and also of the Poor Law, which was already a burden and was about to become so much heavier a burden when the war ended and 'the great customer of the producers' died – and this, as he seemed to say, without any of the horrors of rioting and revolution which gave such nightmares to those enlightened persons. So, indeed, he had; but he was never allowed to make any contribution at all. This was no fault whatever of Owen's. Peel's Factory Bill, which he had been asked to draft, came in the end to nothing worth having; and he could not really have been expected to have foreseen the instant reaction of his fellow manufacturers to its contents or to his exposition of it when he remarked, almost casually, that if British employers found that they could not afford the simple and obvious reform of reducing factory hours to twelve a day, and restricting child labour (for six hours a day) to children of ten and over who had received a proper elementary education, and still induce their customers to pay a price for the goods sufficient to maintain their expected rate of profit, the British Government would hardly put the chance of 'the trivial pecuniary gain of a few' in competition with the welfare of so many human beings.[4] They were horrified: no less so when Owen calmly observed that 'the main pillar and prop of the political greatness of this country is a manufacture, which, as it is now carried on, is destructive of the health, morals and social comforts of the mass of the people engaged in it'. When he added that if the cotton trade could not reform itself, it had better perish, this was rank blasphemy. He could not understand this attitude at all, especially as he himself was firmly convinced that it *could* be reformed, and still make profit; he was staggered to hear the arguments, so painfully familiar to later reformers, of 'experts' explaining the social and medical benefits of the existing system; and when, in an expedient not wholly tactful, he formed himself into a one-man team of inspection of other people's factories, he was astounded by the amount of scurrilous abuse which he brought upon himself. Even though Sidmouth as Home Secretary sent the most flagrant of the scandal-mongers away with a flea in their ears, the course of the Bill 'opened my eyes', said Owen, 'to the conduct of public men and to the ignorant and vulgar self-interest, regardless of means to accomplish their object, of trading and mercantile men, even of high standing, in the commercial world'.

His eyes were only partially opened: the process was carried rather

further by the proceedings over the Poor Law. It was quite sensible
and reasonable to call on Owen to give his advice on what could be
done about that; and when Owen rose to the occasion so promptly
and fired at the Archbishop's Committee his full Plan for the establishment of communities, it was not unreasonable for that rather startled
collection of eminences to avoid immediate discussion of it by handing
the baby to Sturges Bourne's House of Commons Committee, which
was already in session; it is not necessary to conclude, as Owen did, that
that Committee had been deliberately set up in order to frustrate his
own efforts. One cannot help regretting that outside 'authorities' such
as Colquhoun, Mills and Ricardo denied themselves, or were denied,
the chance of an examination, in the atmosphere of a comparatively
small group rather than a large public meeting, of the statistics and
economics of Mr Owen's Plan; but one can see how it happened,
knowing the eternally tender *amour propre* of Members of Parliament.
Owen, in March of 1817, had as yet no great grievances over the Poor
Law.

But it was a real and calculated insult for Sturges Bourne to keep
this distinguished industrialist and philanthropist kicking his heels in a
back room for two whole days and then to dismiss him unheard.
Brougham, when he came to deliver the ungracious message, might
well have expected an angry explosion rather than the calm assurance
that Owen had 'other means' of bringing his views before the country
at large – by the use of his private fortune, as a matter of fact. But
before he had had time to appeal from Philip greedy and selfish to
Philip enlightened and rational, he received a further shock from an
unexpected quarter. His Plan, which he had been denied the opportunity of explaining, was now circulating among the political radicals,
and writers and orators like Hunt, Cobbett and Wooler were rising
in fury to denounce the 'parallelograms of paupers'. This attack hurt
Owen sharply. The radicals took no account whatever of the proven
fact that the conditions of the New Lanark workers had been greatly
improved, and that they were enthusiastic for Owen; these 'democratic'
leaders of the organised working classes – the very people in whose
interests he was working most strenuously (though he admitted he had
never met them publicly in the flesh) – were engaged in telling their
followers that Robert Owen was their enemy, a fraud, a supporter of
their oppressors, and that he 'desired to make slaves of them in these
villages of unity and mutual co-operation'. It really was unendurable,
this combination of ignorant opposition from so many different

quarters; and it is not really surprising that Owen exploded. One may even guess – though he himself would have certainly denied it – that he was not altogether unaffected by the feverish state of government and public opinion in the first years of peace. He certainly did explode in a burst of hysteria, in which, he says, he expected to be torn limb from limb, and was probably slightly disappointed to meet with nothing worse than some 'low hissing' from representatives of the Established Church, some radical cat-calls, and Brougham, after all was over, inquiring chaffingly why he had made such a goose of himself. The apocalyptic storm passed, though it left him committed in print to the statement, scarcely calculated to conciliate the radicals, that nobody in his senses could conceive of extending voting rights to persons as ignorant and stupid as the attenders at the City of London Tavern had shown themselves.

He recovered from the shock pretty quickly – or rather grew a protective skin over the wound. He had not, indeed, done himself much public harm by his outburst. He was not the first nor the last man of strong convictions to make a bungle of an appearance on a public platform; and though he gradually lost the support of *The Times* and the organised Church, he had done a fair job of self-advertisement. Though one would take with a grain of salt his own assertion that he was 'the most popular man of the day', he remained a sight worth seeing. The Owen of the years before would, perhaps, have withdrawn for a while, gone back to New Lanark to think things over, to devise fresh approaches and secure new supporters as he had once secured more amenable partners. But the Owen of 1817 was not going to do any such thing. He had a message now, not merely for New Lanark, but for the whole country – and indeed for the world at large – which had barely been challenged, much less refuted, and he must get on with spreading it.

By this time, indeed, there is some suggestion that he was getting a little bored with New Lanark itself – even with the schools. It is understandable; he had got as far as he could, or thought he had, with experiment in the limiting conditions. He had not the kind of mind which goes on experimenting, in education or anything else, for experimentation's sake; and he had trained up subordinates who could be trusted to keep the institution running on correct lines without its author's eye being constantly trained upon it. Of course he would continue to act as guide and showman; he would look proudly at the lengthening list of remarkable names in his visitors' book, and would make courteous concessions to persons like his partner William Allen, who fussed about the possibility of irreligion growing in the schools and little boys jumping about in kilts without underpants. But he became more and more of an absentee, travelling around the Europe which he had never seen, being received with respect by crowned heads and their most important servants, marvelling a little at all this lionising but putting it down entirely to the fact that enlightenment had come to him so decisively in his early days. Proudly he wrote in his last years: 'in all my intercourse with the Ministers of despotic powers I uniformly found them in principle favourably disposed to the introduction in practice of the new system of society, and that they gave me all the facilities and aid which their position would admit'. He had no breath of suspicion, as Harriet Martineau subsequently pointed out, that Metternich, for example, might not be moved exclusively by desire to improve the health and social conditions of the working classes. Only when Gentz, the secretary to the Aix Congress, having sat next to Owen at dinner and having been obviously bored to death by his harangues impatiently interrupted, 'Yes, we know that very well; but we do not want the masses to become wealthy and independent of us. How could we govern them if they were?' – only then, Owen says, were his eyes opened, but to nothing more than 'the incompatibility of the European systems of government' with his own ideas. But it did not worry him long; he reflected on the story which had reached him that Napoleon in exile had thought that if he had his time again. . . .

He returned to produce, temperately and without excitement, the *Report to the County of Lanark*, which gives the clearest picture, before he went to America, of what he had in mind for the future (which in his thinking was becoming more and more the *immediate* future) of the social system. 'Your Reporter', as he calls himself, is now ready, as soon as a modicum of capital has been found, to start the first operation 'with those who are now a burthen to the country for want of employment'. As the transition proceeds, 'much care and circumspection will be requisite in bringing each part into action at the proper time, and with the guards and checks which a change from one set of habits to another renders necessary. . . . Yet, a man of fair ordinary capacity would superintend such arrangements with more ease than most large commercial or manufacturing establishments are now conducted.' After 'looking very wisely' at the men in the different departments? As it is all so simple, however, it is perhaps not surprising that the future government of the communities is simple also – based upon 'principles that will *prevent* divisions, opposition of interests, jealousies, or any of the common or garden abuses which a contention for power is certain to generate. Their affairs should be conducted by a committee composed of all the members of the association between certain ages – for instance, of those between thirty-five and forty-five, or between forty and fifty.'

The casualness of these suggestions is almost beyond belief, particularly when it is remembered that according to Dr Grey McNab, the Duke of Kent's physician who visited New Lanark in 1819, Owen was still the unquestioned autocrat there – 'he has as little direct intercourse with the inhabitants of his colony as a general has with his soldiers'. Though in the *Report* there is a hint or two of the possibility that some committees may in the first instance be elected, no importance is attached to this, or to any means for *gradual* elimination of the desire for power; its disappearance is assumed. The engine is still racing, though quietly. And so it continued, Owen waiting for the *Report* to be put into effect – until displeasing activity by his New Lanark partners coincided with the news of a settlement for sale on the banks of the Wabash. And so to New Harmony.

v

And so we come to America, and to New Harmony – to which there is no need for this chapter to devote much space, since this subject is being covered by others. All that is necessary is to point out that the haste with which the property of the Rappite Community was purchased by Owen, the rapturous hero-worship with which the purchaser was welcomed, late in 1824, in New York, Philadephia and Washington, and the breathless off-handedness with which he inaugurated his own community, its constitution, its membership, and the regulations under which it was to live – all these combine to show that vision had now well eclipsed practicality in his mind. There was, of course, much excuse for this. The respectful attention which he had received from European rulers and administrators was far outshone by the extravagant admiration poured upon his head by eminent Americans from the President and President-elect downwards; and Mr A. E. Bestor in

*Backwoods Utopias* and Professor Harrison in his recent thorough-going study[5] have done well to remind us of the wide prevalence, particularly in the United States, of 'millennialism' among members of the first generations to experience the potentialities and the horrors of the Industrial Revolution. But it is Owen's attitude to the human material for his own revolution that we are looking at; and ponder upon it how you may, the *volte-face* from his earlier principles and practice remains amazing. The man who could arrive in New Harmony bearing with him the detailed draft of the Constitution of a Preliminary Society; who could replace it within nine months by a Community of Equality whose Assembly a few weeks later, in despair at trying to govern themselves, requested 'the aid of Mr Owen in conducting the concerns of the community in accordance with the principles of the constitution'; who could dictate a complete reorganisation of his community half-a-dozen times within just over two years before he finally gave it up as a bad job; and who could write in his final address that it was evident 'that families trained in the individual system, founded as it is upon superstition, have not acquired those moral qualities of forbearance and charity for each other which are necessary to promote full confidence and harmony among all the members' – he could hardly be called realistic in the art of administration of any kind. And the agonised letters of his son William, even more than R. D. Owen's autobiography, demonstrate clearly enough how disastrous were his personal adventures in the field.

But of course he was nowise deterred or shaken in his convictions; he had ceased to listen to other voices. The ink was hardly dry upon the agreements for the sale of the property of New Harmony when he was off to Mexico with a proposition that he should be given a free hand to reorganise the whole society of the then Mexican territory of Texas in accordance with the principles of a free and prosperous Owenite society; when this handsome offer was finally rejected, he returned to find himself the unexpected hero and prophet of the 'industrious working classes', whose trade unions had so recently been emancipated from the bondage of the Combination Acts, and who, in the decade of hope begun after Peterloo and the open scandal of the Queen Caroline case, were feeling that oppression might indeed be coming to an end. They – or the more literate among them – had read Owen's writings, and found in 'Owenism' the faith and the blueprints for a new world – a world of justice and happiness. Now, to enable them to achieve it, there returned the Teacher, the Leader, the Priest; and after a certain period of hesitation not surprising in one whose attention was invited to descend from the prospect of administering the millions of acres of Texas to the coral-insect affairs of obscure co-operatives in English townships – 'he looked somewhat coolly', William Lovett tells us, 'on these Trading Associations and very candidly declared that their mere buying and selling formed no part of his grand co-operative scheme' – he was moved by their patent enthusiasm for Mr Owen's Plan and Mr Owen's ideals to assume the proffered leadership.

So, from 1831 to the autumn of 1834 he led, or attempted to lead, the great swelling movement of discontent, through the Co-operative Congresses, the National Equitable Labour Exchange, the Builders' Union and the Guild of Builders, to the Grand National Consolidated Trades Union which crashed almost before it was formed – and the rump of whose delegates meekly, *after sixteen days' deliberation*, agreed at Owen's dictation to rename themselves the British and Foreign Consolidated Association of Industry, Humanity and Knowledge, and to set about reconciling 'the masters and operatives throughout the Kingdom'. This is the too well-known story of disaster, with Owen shaking himself free of institution after institution (and from colleague after colleague) with no more apparent feeling than if he had divested himself of a shoe that did not fit. Of course, the cause of the successive disasters was not wholly or even mainly Robert Owen's; the down-trodden were defeated by the conditions of the time and the ability of the governing classes eventually to make the necessary concessions – and would have been defeated no matter who had led them. But it is clear enough that Robert Owen was as bad a leader as could have been found.

It is not only that the aims of himself and his followers in the short run essentially differed: the co-operators were hoping to build communities out of small savings whereas Owen wanted large communities to be started here and now; the builders and the other unions were engaged in a fierce class-war while Owen was adjuring them to bring the masters into their guilds. These differences might well have been composed, at any rate for the time being, by discussion and compromise, as actually happened on one occasion on Owen's own initiative. This occasion was the London Co-operative Conference of 1832 when, after Owen had excited the fury of Joseph Hume and other radicals by declaring that as far as the co-operative movement was concerned it did not matter whether governments were despotic or not, he yielded to the extent of proposing and carrying a resolution which read: 'it is unanimously resolved that co-operators *as such* are not identified with any religious, irreligious, or political tenets whatever; neither those of Mr Owen nor of any other individual'.

This sounds more like the Owen of New Lanark; but it stands alone. More typical, unfortunately, is the incident described by Lovett when Owen inserted into a Congress manifesto passages of his own which the Congress drafters had refused to accept, and when pressed to account for this 'despotic' conduct answered off-handedly that 'it evidently was despotic; but as we, as well as the committee that sent us, were all ignorant of his plans, and of the objects he had in view, we must consent to be ruled by despots until we had acquired sufficient knowledge to govern ourselves'.

In the same temper he dismissed his two faithful supporters, the editors of the *Pioneer* and the *Crisis*, for being insufficiently polite to the employers.

No democrat, in the accepted sense, certainly – no head-counter. But, Lovett's scandalised account notwithstanding, there was scarcely anything of the arrogant contempt of, say, Bernard Shaw in Owen's repudiation of the 'voice of the majority'. He was autocratic because he was *right*; but he was right because, as he had explained thirty years earlier, he had been fortunate enough to have the scales of error removed from his eyes at a very early age. He never used his wealth, or any other sign of class distinction, to bolster up his assumption of authority – 'You came amongst us', said Ebenezer Elliott the anti-Corn Law poet, 'and did not call us a rabble. There was no sneer on your lip, no covert scorn in your tone' – and he was as near to egalitarianism (which must be the fundament of any effective democracy) in his aspirations as anyone of middle-class habits could be expected to be. To this should be added his fine manners, the total incapacity to bully or shout down anyone which distinguished him from the great majority of those convinced preachers who have enjoyed personal authority as great as his; and it is then easy to understand why those who differed from him most strongly, in tactics and in some of his assumptions, found it so difficult to quarrel with him face to face. A somewhat rueful acknowledgment of this is to be found in the resolution passed by the British and Foreign Consolidated Association only a few months after he himself had founded it, to the effect that 'This meeting respectfully declines holding any conference with or receiving any communication from Mr Owen, and that the Secretary *be requested to communicate this resolution by letter*' (my italics).

What he himself really believed about the business of government appears to be a kind of inversion of Pope's maxim – that some form of administration, national as well as local, would have to exist, but that in a real community of equals or near-equals, such as he envisaged, where all were brought up and educated rationally, so that bitter emulation had ceased to exist, techniques of government would cease to matter greatly; from time to time he threw out differing suggestions on how leadership and consent might be secured, without seeming fervently wedded to any of them. It was the purposes and principles of his New View of Society that made him the inspirer of so many organisations and their leaders during the last half of his life and for generations after his death. That is why this volume of essays has been written today.

## NOTES AND REFERENCES

1. W. A. C. Stewart and W. P. McCann, *The Educational Innovators* (1967).

2. *Address to New Lanark,* (1816).

3. Cf., for example, 'the end of government is to make the governed and the governors happy. That government, then, is the best which in practice produces the greatest happiness to the greatest number, including those who govern and those who obey' (*New View of Society,* essay iv).

4. Owen, *On the Effects of the Manufacturing System* (1815).

5. J. F. C. Harrison, *Robert Owen and the Owenites in Britain and America* (1969).

# CHAPTER TEN

# Owen and America

## W. H. G. ARMYTAGE

I

> New Harmony, the future name of this place, is the best half-way
> house I could procure for those who are going to travel this extra-
> ordinary journey with me; and although it is not intended to be our
> permanent residence, I hope it will be found not a bad traveller's
> tavern, in which we shall remain only until we can change our own
> garments, and fully prepare ourselves for the new state of existence
> into which we hope to enter.[1]

LISTENING to him in their hundreds at New Harmony, Indiana, on
25 April 1825, few indeed of Owen's fellow-travellers realised that the
first ergonomist to hit America was speaking, one to whom humans
were 'vital machines' with 'curious mechanism' and 'self-adjusting
powers' needing 'a proper main-spring' to be applied to move them
in any direction desired. Owen held that the wrong people were
moving them in the wrong directions.[2]

Nor did they realise the significance of his idea that in order to start
the scheme it would be necessary to import some men of science from
outside who would have to be given accommodation and food at a
level above that of the ordinary workers. That several of these scientists
were Frenchmen is even more significant.[3] For though they might not
have heard of Saint-Simon, they certainly believed in the emancipating
power of science. This was especially true of the scientists like C. A.
Lesueur[4] and the cohort of Pestalozzians led by Joseph Neef,[5] Madame
Fretageot[6] and Phiquepal d'Arusmont.[7] This indeed was their
Ménilmontant.

Before Saint-Simon began to issue his technocratic blueprints, Owen
was working or (as his son would have said) threading his way in
Manchester where he earned from friends like John Dalton, and the
steamboat pioneer Robert Fulton, the nickname of the 'reasoning
machine'.[8] The structure of atoms and the potential of inanimate power

were grist to an enlightened mill manager in the prosperous war-order economy of late eighteenth-century Manchester, and were no doubt confirmed in his paper *Thoughts on the Connection between Universal Happiness and Practical Mechanics* given by him to the Manchester Literary and Philosophical Society on 13 March 1795. Mill machinery (which Owen had had to master when it was installed in the Chorlton Twist Company the year before) demands workmen who can get the best out of it, and Owen was later to develop an ingenious if modest mechanical device to maximise production. This confronted each worker with one coloured face of an elongated pyramidal block to stimulate him from sloth (black), idleness (blue) or to raise more industry (yellow), to excellent (white). One of these four classes literally faced every workman at New Lanark for six days a week as long as he worked there. Moreover, the classes (black = 4, blue = 3, yellow = 2 and white = 1) were entered into a register by the superintendent.[9] These 'silent monitors' (as he called them), applied at New Lanark as 'a check upon inferior conducts', were but a prelude to other experiments. Confident in his power to convert New Lanark into a 'model' example of how the environment could be organised to form the very character of the workpeople (thereby checking 'the ruin of the Empire'), he secured in 1813 new partners in the Quakers. For another eight years, until 21 January 1824, he worked not so much with, as steadily away from them, till circumstances forced him on 21 January 1824 to seek an ally more sympathetic to his science of social organisation. This ally was an American. When an opportunity of buying a settlement in America coincided, Owen took the step. And, attracted by Owen's 'immense mecanizm',[10] this American ally took the step too.

II

His ally was a true scientist, William Maclure. A friend for seven years, they had travelled in 1818 to the environmental experiments at Yverdun and Hofwyl. Maclure for his part found himself 'in a state of agreeable feelings approaching to extacey' at the 'vast improvement' in society affected by Robert Owen, whom he considered to be 'the only man in Europe who has a proper idea of mankind and the use he ought to make of his faculties is going to join the finest and most rational Society on the Globe.'[11]

Now sixty-three – some eight years older than Owen – Maclure had attracted to Philadephia a veritable corps of dedicated veterans of Yverdun like F. J. N. Neef, Alexander Lesueur, William Phiquepal d'Arusmont and Madame Fretageot. The last named was Maclure's particular confidante. He had helped her to emigrate to Philadephia in 1821, where she had established a Pestalozzian school and, two years later, was participating in the scheme for an Owenite community with members of the Philadelphia Academy of Natural Sciences.

Maclure was not Owen's only American friend, for since 1815 he had known George Rapp and in 1820 had asked him for operating details of his religious community of Harmonie and of an older settlement in Pennsylvania. When the Rappites decided to move back eastwards to this older settlement and sell Harmonie, Owen seized the opportunity and bought it, hoping that his ideas could be more rapidly put into practice on some 20,000 acres on the Wabash river – most of it cleared and on which some 180 buildings of various kinds had been run up by the Harmonie Society.

The mediator between Owen and Rapp was an English immigrant, Richard Flower, who in 1817 had settled with his son George and Morris Birkbeck on the other side of the Wabash at Albion, Illinois,[12] which by 1822 had become the county town of Edwards County, Illinois, weathering the criticisms of Cobbett and the wiles of eastern land speculators. It was probably to avoid being caught up with the latter that the Harmonists commissioned Richard Flower in 1824 to sell their land. Visiting New Lanark on 14 August 1824, Flower found Owen so enthusiastic that seven weeks later, on 2 October 1824, Owen sailed for the United States to conclude the purchase.

And in so doing, he provided a refuge for an odd mixture of socialists whose micro-groups had already been activated by his writings.[13]

Thus, when he arrived on 4 November 1824, they were vibratingly responsive to what he had to say. Disciples were propagating his doctrines, among them writers like Langton Byllesby, Thomas Skidmore and Paul Brown, and projectors like Dr Cornelius C. Blatchley and Edward P. Page. As organisers of the New York Society for Promoting Communities (in 1820), and advocates of a 'Scientific Commonwealth', Blatchley and Page were the first to greet him. Scientists too, like the chemist John Griscom, and patrons of science like General Stephen van Rensselaer, entertained him. So did the merchants.

But it was at Philadelphia that he struck the most responsive chords, for here a community was being discussed by Maclure's associates in Natural Sciences, in which the moving spirits were Dr Gerard Troost and John Speakman.

III

With his most mechanically-minded son, William, and a former engineer officer, Captain Donald MacDonald,[14] he sailed for the United States on 2 October 1824. On landing on 4 November 1824, he met former visitors to New Lanark like John Griscom of Columbia. He was fêted by academic, business, political and, curiously enough, by real-estate men, before going on to meet Maclure's French imports, Thomas Say and Marie Fertageot, at Philadelphia. Not for two months, until 16 December 1824, did he reach Harmonie to be met by Rapp's adopted son. Here he inspected the property and visited Richard Flower at Albion. On the same day – 3 January 1825 – he bought the property and returned to the east – alone.

Left behind at New Harmony in charge of some 20,000 acres of land on which there was accommodation for 700 persons, William Owen did not see his father (with the exception of a brief visit from 13 April to 5 June, when he delivered the speech with which this paper begins) for nearly a year. Already in June William's difficulties were multiplied by having to deal with eight or nine hundred persons 'indiscriminately admitted by his father', whilst having to remember the other promise given by his father to the New Harmonists on 25 April 1825 that the 'men of science' whom it would be necessary to import to get the colony under way would have to be given specialist accommodation, since they 'would not be satisfied with the plain fare and simple accommodation which would be the lot of the ordinary workers'.[15]

Owen's 'immense mecanizm' led him to recruit so many mechanics that poor William confessed himself 'surprised' that he 'should advertise for so many', adding 'we have received a good many valuable mechanics since you left us, and all the brick and frame houses are filled except one, which we reserved for those you might bring with you'.[16]

IV

When Owen did finally return to America for a second time on 6
November 1825 it was with a six-foot model and an architect, Stedman
Whitwell. But instead of hastening to New Harmony, he spent a long
time lecturing at New York, Philadephia and Washington. In Washington the model was placed in an ante-room at the White House
where Whitwell, assisted by Captain Donald MacDonald, dilated upon
its advantages till the end of the year. His son William began to fear
that the model might actually take shape. Outraged, he complained to
his father on 16 December 1825 that there was 'no lime, no rocks (ready
blasted), no brick, no timber, no boards, no shingles, nothing requisite for
buildings, and as to getting them from others, they are not to be had in
the whole country'.[17]

But Owen was intent on capturing his scientist ally and his friends
in Philadelphia, whither he bent his way in November 1825. Having
in Professor Bestor's words brought 'the smoldering embers of communitarian enthusiasm in Philadelphia into a flame of enthusiasm that
eventually lighted the way to New Harmony',[18] the forty boarded
the boat. In addition to the Yverdun veterans mentioned earlier, the
group included Thomas Say,[19] an entomologist of distinction, and
Gerard Troost, a veteran geologist and chemist.[20]

Posting ahead of the party, Owen arrived at Harmonie on 12
January 1826 and treated the colonists to a euphoric account of forty
savants who were on their way. These forty had to adapt themselves
to a group which had not accommodated itself literally or psychologically to its own Rappite inheritance. The Rappite huts were inadequate to house the recruits that had poured in, with little or no
selection. The Rappite industries – spinning, fulling, dressing and dye-
ing – lacked craftsmen and managerial skills. Services in the bakehouse,
the tailor's shop, the smithy and the brewhouse were also needed.
True, there was also a school and a newspaper, but they did not feed
the inhabitants. Now with 'the proprietor' in residence the time had
come to form the body of nearly a thousand persons into a community. For decisions, suspended during Robert Owen's absence in
Europe, now had to be made, notably on Owen's own role vis-à-vis
the committee. This committee he had appointed before his departure,

but to the original four had been added a further three elected by the assembly of the community. This assembly had also acquired a corporate sense, having flexed its agelic muscles in regular Wednesday sessions.

To sort out and draft a constitution for the community, the assembly met within a fortnight of his arrival and elected three new arrivals (Owen, his eldest son Robert Dale Owen, and Captain MacDonald), together with William Owen and three other members of the original committee. These seven all had different ideas, ranging from Robert Dale Owen's chain of deliberative assemblies to Captain MacDonald's broad anarchism. Failure to hammer out an administrative and economic plan led the community on 4 March 1826 to make Owen the 'sole director' for the rest of the year, with full responsibility for all the profit and the loss which the community might make.

That March was mad for one described as 'a great smooth meditative hare'.[21] For in his role of sole director he helped three suckers to root themselves from the New Harmony stock. To a group of some eighty American backwoodsmen he gave some 1200 or so acres of land for some $5000 to build a new community, Macluria, and in doing so precipitated a second community of some forty or so English farmers on another 1400 acres at Feiba Peveli.[22] A third, activated by his sons William and Robert Dale and a Universalist minister, was for a work-based community in New Harmony itself.

The latter Owen could neither afford nor tolerate. Only $55,000 had been paid to Rapp, and to ensure that the rest was paid, he offered to turn over part of New Harmony to the remaining settlers at an agreed price, to be paid over twelve years at 5 per cent interest. That price was announced on 18 March as $126,520, since it had been augmented by his stores and the efforts of the previous year. To ensure the acceptance of this price, he nominated his own committee of twenty-four to govern the community on these terms, and organise its work on Owenite lines by close monitoring.

April brought no remission from calendarial aptness, for on the day after April fool's day a fanatical egalitarian anarchist arrived: Paul Brown. Already known as a writer, he was soon at loggerheads with Owen over the question as to whether Owen had any moral right at all to demand repayment or indeed to retain any property at all. His strident voice demanding 'a true commonwealth on earth'[23] may well have brought William Maclure back into the picture.

## V

MACLURE preferred functionally to align the community on corporative rather than co-operative lines, such corporative groups, educational, agricultural and manufacturing, being united by a community of interest rather than of principle. After some discussion Owen saw that his principles would be satisfied if the communities adopted currency based on labour notes and were united by a Board of Union.

As adopted on 28 May, the corporative constitution established three societies based respectively on Agriculture, Manufacture and the School. This merely intensified Brown's conviction that autocracy, and private property, were clouding his vision of a true commonwealth. He attacked Maclure through his favourite child, the School Society, where some three or four hundred children were receiving a scientific and cultural education, reinforced by ever-increasing imports of books, apparatus and specimens.

For, shrewdly as it turned out, Maclure was making the School Society his own by paying Owen first $25,000 in early June and another $14,000 by the end of the year.[24] For this he received 900 acres of New Harmony, and several of its public buildings on a 10,000-year lease. By so doing he was able, apart from some $10,000, guaranteed at the beginning, to pursue his educational experiments on children alone whilst Owen continued them on adults. This separatism probably explains why the Agricultural and Mechanical Societies jettisoned their links with the School in August.

Deprived of the School Society, Owen now launched his own and on 6, 13 and 20 August spelt out a new plan of educating adults and children together in the evenings, three times a week, on the trades and occupations of social life. He had a day school for children too, but not enough staff. When Maclure left New Harmony three months later, Owen tried to get some of his School Society's land. He also asked Maclure's brother for money.

## VI

In Maclure's absence Owen tried first occupational and then territorial devolution. In January 1827 occupations were listed in groups, each self-governing group paying a weekly contribution to the town. But not all could be employed in such occupations, so Owen thought of subsidising them to form communities outside the town. He seems to have envisaged seven such communities, the first, based on a grant of 1500 acres, being announced in January 1827.[25] The other six remained aloft in Owen's imagination.

Owen might be excused for thinking that such communities could be established, since the diasporic principle seemed to activate others far from New Harmony. After several visits to New Harmony in 1825, William Hall returned to the English settlement in Illinois to organise a Co-operative Association at Wanborough.[26]

A second, at Blue Springs near Bloomington, Indiana, took more visible shape in January 1826 and seems to have lasted till 1827.[27]

A third, led by Paul Brown and a contingent of eighty New Harmonists, was attempted in March 1827 at Neville in Clermont County, Ohio.[28]

A fourth, in which Robert L. Jennings (the Universalist minister who, with Owen's two sons, projected a community in March 1826) played a part with another English associate of Owen's, George Houston, took shape in New York State at Haverstraw, Rockland County. Based, as might be expected from its name Franklin, on rationalist principles, it soon collapsed.[29]

A fifth, in which another rationalist and visitor to New Harmony, William Ludlow, was active, was up the Wabash at Lebanon in Warren County. Having left it to join New Harmony, he rejoined it in October 1826 only to return again to New Harmony in January 1830.[30]

A sixth at Yellow Springs, Ohio, was founded by Daniel Roe, who returned from a visit to New Harmony to his native city of Cincinnati to establish a community, on the site of which Antioch College is now built. This was subsequently visited both by Robert Owen and William Maclure in 1826 and by the fanatic Paul Brown, but it broke up in 1827.[31]

A seventh was essayed near Philadelphia, by an uncle by marriage, Benjamin Bakewell, of another New Harmony settler, Thomas Pears.[32]

VII

Owen's imaginative forays were brought to earth when William Maclure returned on 20 April 1827. He was followed by Owen's debtor Frederick Rapp, anxious to collect some $20,000 for the 1827 instalment and a discount offer for the 1828 instalment. Maclure settled both instalments and seized the opportunity to oust Owen by paying him a further $5000 for derestricting the 490 acres belonging to the Education Society, and on 14 May 1827 he was able to undertake what he had long been anxious to do – the education of orphans.[33] Using the *New Harmony Gazette* as his platform, he spelled out from 20 June to 5 December of that year a philosophy of education that was further amplified on 16 January 1828 by another journal, *The Disseminator of Useful Knowledge.*

But before Maclure began wielding his pen Owen had left – on 1 June 1827.

Behind him remained two of the scientific luminaries who came down with Maclure: Say and Lesueur. Six feet tall, slender, with a lisp, Thomas Say stayed on in New Harmony to complete the third volume of his *American Entomology.* The six volumes of his *American Conchology* were published there also. With him remained Lesueur, who taught in the community school for another ten years, engraving plates for Say and for his own *American Ichthyology.* With Say and often alone, he made expeditions to draw and map the area of St Louis, Nashville and New Orleans. Say died in 1834, however, and Neef returned the same year.

Troost had already left in 1827, taking his beloved collection of birds and minerals across to Nashville, Tennessee, where they became the nucleus of the most notable museum west of the Appalachians. As professor of geology, mineralogy, chemistry and natural philosophy at the university and later (1831–50) as state geologist, he mapped both the geological and archaeological treasure of the state.

## VIII

One remaining experiment, the outlines of which had been published in the *New Harmony Gazette* of 1 October 1825, was essayed by a woman who had been both to New Harmony and Albion. Her scheme owed something to both Robert Owen for the idea of co-operation and to George Flower for the idea of Negro emancipation.[34]

Briefly, she proposed to introduce Negroes to the principle of co-operative labour so that they could, by labour, repay the cost of their purchase from slave-owners in five years, after sickness, accident, the expenses of colonisation and misconduct were taken into account. To replace them on the slave-owner's plantations, Fanny Wright envisaged a flow of white labour.

She proposed to start with a hundred slaves, and a capital of $41,000, and, while enabling the Negroes to work for their purchase price and freedom, to afford them a comprehensive system of education for their children based on the Lancasterian system. The original site for this experiment in emancipation was to be either in Texas or in California – away from the slave-owners – but in her travels with George Flower she settled upon the recently acquired lands on the Wolf river, not far from Memphis in western Tennessee. These were inspected on 8 October, and christened Nashoba, from the old Chicksaw name for 'wolf'. George Flower returned to Illinois to arrange for the transportation of his family to Nashoba and Fanny remained to superintend the erection of two double cabins on the 300-acre plot she had bought – a plot she subsequently increased to 2000 acres. She decided to invest $10,000 of her own money, George Flower adding livestock and food to the value of $2000.

Her hopes ran high. She got a present of linen, shoes, blankets and other necessary items of clothing, and by February 1827 the experiment was under way, George Flower having arrived with his family and her sister Camilla. The slaves arrived, one family from South Carolina, and five males and three females being purchased in Nashville. Whites and Blacks settled down in Nashoba, the Whites in one cabin, the Blacks in another. They were soon joined by a fellow countryman of Fanny's, a Scot called James Richardson, and a Quaker called Richeson Whitby, a quondam disciple of Robert Owen. These two, with George Flower, constituted the executive quorum of three. Two other trustees, Robert Jennings and Camilla Wright, were also resident in Nashoba, but the real power seems to have lain with the first three. Nashoba's laws became more strict. There was something monastic in the new code:

This community is founded on the principle of community of property and labour; presenting every advantage to those desirous, not of accumulating money, but of enjoying life and rendering services to their fellow creatures; these fellow creatures, that is, the blacks here admitted, requiting these services, by services equal or greater by filling occupations, which their habits render easy, and which to their guides and assistants might be difficult, or unpleasing.

No life of idleness, however, is proposed to the whites. Those who
cannot work must be given an equivalent in property. Gardening
or other cultivation of the soil; useful trades practised in the society,
or taught in the school; the teaching of every branch of knowledge;
tending the children; and nursing the sick – will present a choice of
employments sufficiently extensive.

This new orientation of the community owed much to the influence
of Robert Owen, whose name, together with that of his son Robert
Dale Owen, was on the list of trustees.

When the community experiment at New Harmony came to an
end in 1827, Robert Dale Owen migrated to Nashoba, hoping to find
there 'more cultivated and congenial associates than those among
whom, for eighteen months past, I have been living'.[35]

But by far the most congenial person whom he found there was
Fanny Wright herself. Though she was ten years older than he was,
her 'tall commanding figure' and masculine face seemed to awe him,
while her volatile and ranging intellect made him her disciple. By May
1827 he had accompanied her to New Orleans en route for Europe,
where they hoped to find not only health for Fanny Wright, but
further support.

Back in England, Fanny Wright seems to have redoubled her efforts
to gain further adherents to her side. Owen seems to have interested
Leigh Hunt and Mary Shelley, while Fanny persuaded Mrs Trollope to
abandon the security of England and come over to Nashoba with her
three children. Poor Mrs Trollope. She was so affected by the tall,
imperious Fanny Wright, 'unlike anything I had ever seen before, or
ever expect to see again', that she came out on 4 November of that very
year only to be 'dismayed at the savage aspect of the scene'. Appalled
by the fact that 'they had not as yet collected round them any of those
minor comforts which ordinary minds class among the necessaries of
life', she stayed at Nashoba for only ten days before departing to
Cincinnati. The irony of that bitter disillusionment undoubtedly contributed in great measure to the tone of her later observations on *The
Domestic Manners of the Americans*.


IX


Mrs Trollope was at hand to record both visually and literally Robert
Owen's next impact on the United States – a teach-in. This arose out

of Owen's public challenge in January 1828 to the clergy of the United States to debate the five propositions that all religions were based on ignorance, that they were opposed to the laws of nature, that they were the cause of 'vice dissension and misery of every description', that they were the only real bar to the formation of a society of virtue, and that they could no longer be maintained.

But the Rev. Alexander Campbell was determined to do so, and at Cincinnati for eight days, from 13 to 21 April 1829, in the presence of a thousand people, he (according to Mrs Trollope) 'brought forward the most elaborate theological authorities in evidence of the truth of revealed religion', whilst Owen 'disarmed zeal' to produce 'a degree of tolerance that those who did not hear him would hardly believe possible'.[36] This tolerance is scarcely credible in view of his own explanation for the initial collapse of what might, had it got off the ground, been his most ambitious project on the North American continent: the settlement of a coast-to-coast strip, 150 miles broad, in Texas. For according to him the project was dependent on the Mexican Government granting freedom of religious belief. This they refused to do.

Certainly he was 'perfectly confident of the practicability of his proposal and of its adaptation' (according to David G. Burnett, who called on him twice).[37] So perhaps the embers of his enthusiasm stirred the French socialist, Étienne Cabet, to buy in 1848, on his advice, a million acres of land in Texas and send an advance guard five months later. Cabet found the challenge impossible, and opted, like Owen had done in New Harmony, for buying a ready-made settlement from a religious group, the Mormons, at Nauvoo, Illinois,[38] which he renamed Icaria. This in turn was to inspire Bristol-born William Lane to lead 220 colonists to Paraguay.

If Icaria provided the inspiration for Lane, another Owen provided the model. This was Albert Kinsey Owen, who began in 1876 to negotiate with the Mexican Government for a site on a Mexican inlet on the east coast of the Gulf of California, known as Topolobampo. By 1886 a prospectus was issued and stockholders enlisted to support four hundred settlers labouring to build canals, a railway and a settlement. Lane got in touch with him in 1889 just as the idea of founding a 'New Australia' in Paraguay was taking shape. Perhaps too the presence at Topolobampo of Evacustes Phipson, founder of a colony in South Australia, also helped. Certainly Lane continued to seek information from Topolobampo and enlarge upon it in his newspaper

*New Australia.* And ironically enough, just before he and his colonists left Australia for Paraguay on 16 July 1893, A. K. Owen left Topolobampo in May 1893 because of a split between his followers, the communists and the 'kickers' – as the believers in private ownership were called.

X

We now return to New Harmony, which after Owen's departure was virtually an enlarged family town. Four of his sons and his daughter lived there, together with their wives and families, in a large mansion. William became a merchant and bank director, Robert Dale managed the estate, David Dale was a geologist, Richard a farmer and Mrs Fauntleroy the wife of an American officer.[39]

Two of them, Robert Dale and David Dale, earned a place in the *Dictionary of American Biography*. Robert Dale Owen, after clashing with the radical Thomas Skidmore for the control of 'the Association for the Protection of Industry and for the Promotion of National Education',[40] followed his father to England where he helped co-edit the *Crisis* in 1832. On returning to the United States, Robert Dale Owen went to Indiana, serving as a Congressman, in which capacity he was a moving spirit in the establishment of the Smithsonian Institute: a growth-bed of scientific knowledge. He remembered New Harmony only as a 'heterogeneous collection of radicals, enthusiastic devotees of principle, honest latitudinarians and lazy theorists, with a sprinkling of unprincipled sharpers thrown in'.[41]

Owen's third son, David Dale Owen, who only arrived at New Harmony as a young man of twenty when his father left New Harmony for England, stayed on there for three more years with Maclure. Imbued by him with a love for science, he returned with Henry Darwin Rogers to England for a course of lectures in London, and later graduated in medicine at Cincinnati. From 1837–8, as state geologist of Indiana, he established a laboratory at New Harmony and in the same year married Neef's daughter Caroline. Two years later he was commissioned to engage and employ a team of 139 to survey some 11,000 square miles in Wisconsin and Iowa. This, the first chart of the rich pantries of those states, showed that lead and zinc ores were not limited to the magnesium limestone of Iowa and Wisconsin.[42]

It was one of these reports, dangled before the eyes of discontented potters in England by the Owenite journalist William Evans, that led to the establishment of yet another co-operative settlement in Wisconsin.[43]

XI

When Owen returned to New Harmony in 1844, at the age of seventy-four, his enthusiasm for it seemed to have diminished, for we find him telling readers of his English paper, the *New Moral World*:

> If the climate of this place was equal to our climate – which I believe to be the most favourable for physical and mental vigour in the world – it would be now a most desirable site and neighbourhood to commence new world proceedings, but as it is not, I could not recommend any with British formed constitutions to run the risk of a change of climate.

Indeed he found 'more mental slavery' in the United States than in England.

So with 'preliminary aid from the leading Fourierites in New York and in other parts of the Union', Owen hoped to convince the States that they possessed 'the means to place inhabitants, now and for centuries to come, including all the immigrants that may come from Europe, in a condition of high permanent independence'.[44] He found that the Fourierites had 'already battered the old system in many parts most effectually, by the writings of several of their very talented members'. Far from being jealous of their progress, he wrote back to readers of the *New Moral World* that 'they are yet wedded to their groups and series, and mysticisms about some religion and it is well that many of them are so conscientious; for those who cannot yet give up the notion of private property, and who have some notions of some religion and individual recipes for capital, skill, labour, will join them, when, from their early prejudices they would not listen to us'. Or, as he put it more succinctly, 'the step from the extreme of irrationality in principle and practice to full rationality in both, is too long a stride for the present race of men to make at once, and the intermediate step is laying beautifully and I trust effectually by Fourier's disciples'.[45]

So began his courtship of the Fourierists, a group which earlier that year had bracketed his ideas with those of the Shakers as a 'mere scheme'.[46]

Ever since their first convention on 4 April 1844 at Clinton Hall in New York City, the Fourierists, with their theories of Association, seemed themselves to take over leadership of the working-class movement. At that convention, which empowered its newly elected executive committee to edit the *Phalanx*, and 'to arrange a system of concerted action with Associationists throughout the United States, for the thorough and systematic diffusion of social science', two Owenites – grandiloquently called 'a Delegation of English socialists' – claimed seats and were asked if they would unite. This the Owenites refused to do, objecting to the Fourierites' belief in property and religion.[47]

Meanwhile, fearing that they were 'fast approximating towards the disagreeable, servile and degrading state of the English labourer', the mechanics of Fall River called in June 1844 for a general convention of the mechanics of New England. When this duly assembled in October 1844 it discussed the freedom of public lands, a ten-hour day and a general organisation of labourers throughout the Union.[48] One of the vocal advocates of a ten-hour day at this convention was Lewis Ryckman of Brook Farm,[49] who went on to secure the support of another convention at Lowell in April of the following year for an Industrial Congress 'analogous to that which fostered the liberties of the American Republic'. This was to 'direct the legal political action of the working men'.[50]

When on 28 May 1845 Ryckman took the chair at the first meeting of the New England Workingmen's Association, Robert Owen was present. He spoke twice, once following Brisbane's call for a convention to draft a 'Reformative constitution for the United States' and to meet in October at New York; and the second time following a forceful speech from John A. Collins of New York in favour of working men establishing societies throughout the country with teachers to propagate their views. Owen's first address was retrospective, the second expressed his earnest hope that 'much good might be accomplished'.[51] Three days later, on 1 June 1845, Owen left for Europe again.

On his return three months later, Ryckman and Collins helped him organise an Owenite–Fourierist convention (rather grandiloquently called a 'World's Convention' by Owen) to emancipate the human race from 'ignorance, poverty, division, sin and misery'. The order is important, for Owen wanted to consider what measures of a practical character could be adopted to educate for, employ in and expedite the creation of 'the superior state of society', latent in the new technology. Among the twelve immediate measures he advocated on landing in September 1844 were that 'mechanism and chemistry . . . be substituted for laborious, disagreeable and unhealthy manual labour' and that 'scientific arrangements . . . be made . . . to produce . . . the greatest amount of the most valuable wealth in the shortest time, with the least waste of capital, and most pleasure to be produced . . . and . . . distributed in the best manner for the consumers'.[52]

So on 1 October 1845 the curtain rose on Owen's last attempt to enlist the Fourierists under a common banner. Some 300 persons (among them were '25 or 30 very well-dressed and very well-looking women') assembled in the Clinton Hall Lecture Room in New York. The *Daily Tribune* noted that 'many of the men had a meagre and melancholy countenance, a sort of 'let's be unhappy together' style of face, but the majority had a highly intelligent and intellectual expression'.[53]

They might well look melancholy. Fourier's leading American disciple, Albert Brisbane, refused to serve under Owen as a vice-president alongside Ryckman and Collins. Ryckman said he wouldn't serve unless this was a World's Convention with Christians and temperance advocates included, while Collins refused to act unless unity of purpose was the aim. The scruples of the last two were overcome, but Brisbane, adamant to the last, opted out.

For eight days they wrestled till at the end the Fourierists withdrew, leaving the remainder of the conference in Owen's camp, resolved to secure the formation of joint-stock companies to carry out his ideas, and to reconvene annually.


XII


They never did. Owen left for England in October 1845, mandated by his son, Robert Dale Owen, a Congressman, to assure the British Government that the Americans were determined to stick on the 49th parallel between the Rocky Mountains and the Pacific as the boundary between Oregon and Canada. This time his 'authorised interference' (as Sir Robert Peel described it) was rebuffed with the phrase that 'no public advantage would arise' from it.[54]

New Harmony receded into a golden haze of what might have been. As he told the newly formed National Association for the Promotion of Social Science in a paper entitled 'The Human Race Governed without Punishment',

> I have governed a population, originally very inferior, of between 2000 and 3000 for upwards of a quarter of a century without punishment; and they were by public consent allowed to be for that period the best and the happiest working population ever known to exist in any country. And all the children of this population were so trained, educated, and placed, from one year old, that vice, crime or evil passions, or unkind conduct to each other were unknown, and the strongest affection between them and their teachers was strikingly manifest at all times to all who witnessed their proceedings.[55]

His epigraph of New Lanark, were it true, could be a prologue to *Walden Two*.

XIII

But 'social science' in England had derived its stimulus from New Harmony some thirty years earlier. For when Rowland Hill heard what Owen was doing there, he wrote to his brother and partner:

> Here is a specimen of the advantages of the system. The naturalists having made the children acquainted with their wants, the little creatures swarm over the woods, and bring in such an abundance of specimens that they are forming several immense collections, some of which they will present to new communities, and others will be exchanged for collections in other quarters of the world. W— says by these means vast numbers of insects have been discovered, of the existence of which the world was previously in ignorance. What think you of selling Bruce Castle again, and going off?[56]

Hill also confided to his nephew and biographer George Birkbeck Hill that 'Owen's plan was more or less approved of by Brougham and others'. So he wrote a paper for Lord Brougham on the ways in which 'home colonies' might extinguish and diminish crime. In doing so he hoped that by writing it he would be appointed to examine the Home Colonies of Holland with a view to reforming the Poor Law.

He even drafted plans for an experiment of his own based on 'the economy of having men of various professions united, as a medical man, a lawyer, architect, schoolmaster; housewarmer; telegraph for own use and for hired use'. The advantages of so doing he listed as

Release from many unpleasant restrictions as to the free expression of opinion, to dress, to absurd customs.

Economy in houses, clothes, food, fire, artificial light, and matters of appearance generally.

Superior education for our children.

Superior opportunities of obtaining knowledge ourselves by observations, experiments, etc.

Release from perplexing and harassing responsibilities.

Release from the necessity of compelling the observance, on the part of others, of matters often really opposed to wisdom and sound morality, and very frequently of merely conventional value.

Society. Enjoyment of that of most of the members of our own family, and that of persons of similar views, who might be willing to join in the plan.

Probable power of appearing before the world advantageously by means of discoveries mechanical, scientific, agricultural, or otherwise.

Increased security from infectious disorders, anarchy, injury by change in the national prosperity; also the security which arises from the cultivation of economical habits.

Mitigation of the evils consequent upon the employment of servants.

Improvement of habits by the influence of numbers upon the individual character of members of the Community.

Great advantages of the close union of a variety of talent by the collection of a number of persons, and their intimate organization and knowledge of each other.

Facility for bringing the whole strength of the Community to bear upon one point when needful.

Increased opportunities of producing extensive good.

(Improvements in machinery, farming, etc., may be introduced without producing even temporary distress, if the Community can execute its own labour.)[57]

The first meeting took place at Rowland Hill's house.[58] Augmented by his brother Edwin and later by Charles Wheatstone (then experimenting with a telegraph in the vaults of King's College, London, where he was professor of experimental physics), Dr Arnott (inventor of a smokeless stove who practised medicine at 38 Bedford Square),[59]

Dr Lyon Playfair[60] (then a laboratory assistant at University College, London), Henry Cole, a young clerk in the public records (already a member of the Circle that met bi-weekly at Charles Grote's house in Threadneedle Street)[61] and Charles Dilke (the editor of the *Athenaeum*), the most interesting member was of course Edwin Chadwick,[62] the great sanitary pioneer, together with his friend Dr Southwood Smith.

This group in their various ways turned to practical millenarianism, what Professor Finer has called 'a kind of apocalypticism . . . an almost frenzied hatred of bungling and patchwork, a volcanic desire for utter, sweeping change'.[63] Chadwick, for instance, became a moving spirit for the appointment of the Health of Towns Commission in 1843, on which Arnott and Playfair served with a pupil of Lesueur, Professor Richard Owen, who said he 'would rather achieve the effectual trapping of the sewer-vents of London than resuscitate graphically in Natural History records the strangest of old monsters which it has pleased God to blot out of his Creation'.

XIV

The strangest of old monsters lives in the mind, evolving rapidly under paranoidal stress. Such a monster is 'communism', originally the adjective used by Owen's American admirers. As Noyes said, 'his main idea was communism and that he got from the Rappites. His persistent assertion that man's character was formed for him by circumstances was his nearest approach to original doctrine.' Another description of Owenism, also by Noyes, is 'Rational Communism' as opposed to the 'half-way schemes of joint stock and guaranteeism' of the Fourierists.[64]

Owen's own Boswell as far as America was concerned was the Scotsman A. J. Macdonald. Coming to New Harmony in 1842, he remained to roam America for the next fourteen years, salvaging at first hand the histories of some sixty-nine American communities. He heard Robert Owen lecture in New York in March 1845 and again on 26 October. He heard him address the Convention on the New Constitution of the State of New York in June of the following year, and after lunching with him accompanied him to a photographer's. Macdonald's ubiquitous presence led to him seeming 'a little sad', as if 'the scenes he had encountered while looking after the stories of so

many short-lived communities, had given him a tinge of melancholy'.
He was indeed the 'Old Mortality of Socialism'.[65] The writer was
John Henry Noyes, himself the founder of a successful community at
Oneida, who gathered these papers together after Macdonald's death,
paged and indexed them, published them in the official journal of
Oneida – *The Circular* – and then in December 1869 as a book.

He saw embers of Owenism 'in the heart of the nation to this day'.[66]
The 'modulating chord'[67] from the Owenite to the Fourierist Harmony
was, to him, provided by Josiah Warren, aptly enough the former
conductor of the New Harmony Orchestra. For Josiah Warren left
New Harmony to experiment with a labour currency in his Equity or
Time Store in Cincinnati, only to return after a time. The real revolution was effected by his speed press, which made enough money to
enable him to open a similar store at New Harmony and found
another Equity village. By 1846 he established a second, named Utopia,
and in 1850 a third called Modern Times on Long Island.

Today, the hippie communes, Marcuse and Fromm have made
participatory democracy a contemporary agitant idea. Whatever New
Harmony was, we might recall Macdonald's opinion that 'it is possible
yet that man will endeavour to cure his social diseases by some such
means' as communism or Association. He wrote this two years after
he had parted with Robert Owen ('perhaps forever!') at a photographic
gallery. Certainly one needs no photograph to appreciate what
Macdonald called the 'indomitable perseverance' that led Owen to
cross the Atlantic six times after he was fifty and twice after he was
seventy 'in the service of Communism'. That 'indomitable perseverance' was transmitted, as Macdonald acknowledged, 'to a large breed
of American socialists' whose character, hopes and fears he had, in a
modest modern sociological manner, tried to gauge in a 21-item
questionnaire supplemented by personal visits. Of the sixty-nine
associative experiments he found up to 1854, and the 130 found by
Professor Bestor up to 1858,[68] there must have been few indeed whose
existence was not profoundly affected, either by Owen, the ideas he
espoused or the disciples he attracted. We catch sight of him, at the
age of seventy-five, when he visited one of them, the Christian community at Hopedale, Massachusetts, in November 1845, in a verbal
portrait by its founder Adin Ballou:

> in knowledge and experience superabundant; in benevolence of heart
> transcendental; in honesty without disguise; in philanthropy un-
> limited; in religion a sceptic; in theology a Pantheist; in metaphysics

a necessitarian circumstantialist; in morals a universal excursionist; in general conduct a philosophic non-resistant; in socialism a Communist; in hope a terrestrial elysianist; in practical business a methodist; in deportment an unequivocal gentleman.[69]

Terrestrial elysianism involves a picture of the future, and Owen decided to invoke such visions by taking a leaf out of Adin Ballou's table. Through an American medium in England he talked with statesmen like Franklin and the Duke of Wellington on his New Social System, consulting them on this or that tract. Nor should we scoff at this. Today the invocation of the future is a respectable and important communal activity in America, and Owen's consultation of American mediums like Mrs Hayden and P. B. Randolph can be interpreted as an attempt to descry the contours of tomorrow.[70] His present-day counterparts take to computers instead.

NOTES AND REFERENCES

1. Frank Podmore, *Life of Robert Owen* (London: Allen & Unwin, 1923) p. 292.

2. L. F. Urwick and E. F. L. Brech, *The Making of Scientific Management* (London: Pitman, 1957) II 40–59.

3. Was Owenism, however unconsciously, an 'Englishification' of Saint-Simonism, as claimed in Edward Hancock, *Robert Owen's Community System and the Horrid Doings of the Saint-Simonians* (London, 1837) p. 35? Not until after New Harmony were Owen's friends reported by J. S. Mill as translating Saint-Simon's works. That was in 1831, the same year as a Dr C. reported that Owen would be willing to 'host' a Saint-Simonian mission. See Richard K. P. Pankhurst, *The Saint-Simonians, Mill and Carlyle* (London: Sidgwick & Jackson, 1957) pp. 26–7, 36. Owen's embryo technocracy seems to stem naturally from his industrial experience, especially in Manchester, as described by W. H. Chaloner, 'Robert Owen, Peter Drinkwater and the Early Factory System in Manchester 1788–1800', *Bulletin of the John Rylands Library*, XXXVII (1954–5), and his relations with local scientists and savants as described by Miss E. M. Fraser in 'Robert Owen in Manchester, 1787–1800', *Memoirs and Proceedings of the Manchester Literary and Philosophical Society*, LXXXII (1937–8). A characteristic splutter of speculation as to the possible influence of Coleridge's pantisocratic scheme can be traced in J. H. Nodal, Hyde Clarke, John E. Bailey and J. W. W. in 'Coleridge and Robert Owen in Manchester', *Notes and Queries*, VII (1877) 161, 217, 311, 376.

4. C. A. Lesueur had been a French officer. Participating with a French scientific mission from 1800 to 1804 in Australia, he and a friend were credited with discovering more new species (2500) than any other modern naturalist. He met

Maclure in Paris in 1815 and became his travelling companion. Together they toured the interior of America with Maclure geologising and Lesueur sketching. From 1817 to 1825 he was curator of the Philadelphia Academy and helped map the north-east boundary of Canada and the United States. He was the first to study the fishes of the Great Lakes of North America.

5. Fifty-five when he moved to New Harmony, Joseph (as he called himself) Neef had been a 'failed priest' and an army officer, before teaching under Pestalozzi who recommended him to Maclure in 1805. A year later he accepted Maclure's invitation to Philadelphia where in 1808 he published the first English-language pedagogical work in America: *Sketch of a Plan and Method of Education, Founded on an Analysis of the Human Faculties and Natural Reason, Suitable for the Offspring of a Free People and for all Rational Beings* (1808). His was the first Pestalozzian school in the United States, and was based on the idea that books were 'the last fountainhead from which we shall endeavour to draw our knowledge'. He was elected to the Philadelphia Academy of Sciences in 1812. For twelve years before going to New Harmony he taught at Louisville, Kentucky. Will S. Monroe, *History of the Pestalozzian Movement in the United States* (Syracuse: C. W. Bardeen, 1902).

6. Madame Fretageot was the principal of a Pestalozzian school in Paris before Maclure persuaded her to go to America.

7. Guillaume Phiquepal d'Arusmont had also been the principal of a Pestalozzian school in Paris whom Maclure persuaded to go to America.

8. Podmore, *Life of Robert Owen*, p. 56.

9. Ibid., pp. 90–1.

10. A. E. Bestor, Jr, *Backwoods Utopias: The Sectarian and Owenite Phases of Communitarian Socialism in America, 1663–1829* (Philadelphia: University of Pennsylvania Press, 1950) p. 153.

11. W. H. G. Armytage, 'William Maclure 1763–1840: A British Interpretation', *Indiana Magazine of History*, XLVII (1951).

12. A. E. Bestor, Jr (ed.), *Education and Reform at New Harmony: Correspondence of William Maclure and Marie Duclos Fretageot 1820–1833*, Indiana Historical Society Publications, XV 3 (Indianapolis, 1948) 309.

13. David Harris, *Socialist Origins in the United States: American Forerunners of Marx 1817–1832* (The Netherlands: Assen, 1966).

14. Both men have left diaries which have been published by the Indiana Historical Society from Indianapolis. That kept by William Owen from 10 November 1824 to 20 April 1825 was published in 1906 (ed. Joel W. Heathfield, in *Publications*, IV 1), and that kept by Donald MacDonald from 1824 to 1826 was published in 1942 (ed. C. D. Snedeker, *Publications*, XIV 2). Other participants' accounts published by the Society are those of Thomas and Sara Pears (ed. T. C. Pears, Jr, as *New Harmony, An Adventure in Happiness*, in *Publications*, XI 1 (1933)). The best Owenite bibliography is on pp. 263–369 of J. F. C. Harrison, *Robert Owen and the Owenites in Britain and America: The Quest for the New Moral World* (London: Routledge & Kegan Paul, 1969).

15. Podmore, *Life of Robert Owen*, p. 293.

16. Ibid., pp. 295–6.

17. Bestor, *Backwoods Utopias*, p. 130.

18. Ibid., p. 100.

19. The father of descriptive entomology in America was Thomas Say, a great-nephew of William Bartram and son of one of the richest men in Philadelphia. He was so keen a member of the Philadelphia Academy of Natural Sciences that he even slept there. In addition to excursions with Maclure, he went on two expeditions to the Rockies and to the sources of the Minnesota river. He was curator of the American Philosophical Society (from 1821 to 1827) and Professor of Natural History at the University of Pennsylvania (from 1822 to 1829). He pressed ahead and issued two volumes of his description of the insects of North America before going to New Harmony.

20. Another founder of the Philadelphia Academy of Sciences was Gerard Troost, a French geologist and doctor who had also studied under Haüy, the crystallographer. Captured whilst on a scientific mission to Holland in 1809, he decided to emigrate to Philadelphia in 1815 where he established the first alum factory in the United States. When this failed he taught mineralogy and chemistry at the Philadelphia Museum and the College of Pharmacy.

21. Edmund Wilson, *To the Finland Station* (New York: Doubleday, 1940) p. 87.

22. So named by its architect, Stedman Whitwell, to indicate its latitude (38° 11′N.) and longitude (87° 53′W.). Bestor, *Backwoods Utopias*, p. 177.

23. Apart from contributions to the *New Harmony Gazette* published before his arrival, he had written *A Disquisition on Faith* (1822) and *An Enquiry Concerning the Nature, End and Practicability of a Course of Philosophical Education* (1822). Bestor considers that the 'unnamed questioner' who used this phrase was voicing a doctrine that was 'unmistakably Brown's' (*Backwoods Utopias*, p. 188, n. 98).

24. For an estimate of the various sums, see Bestor's discussion in *Maclure–Fretageot Correspondence*, pp. 334–5.

25. Bestor, *Backwoods Utopias*, p. 195, remarks that 'its projector, William G. Owen of Ohio, proved to be a sharper, from whose toils Owen extricated himself only with heavy losses and after protracted litigation'.

26. J. Monaghan, 'From England to Illinois in 1821: the Journal of William Hall', *Illinois State Historical Society Journal*, XXXIX (Mar, June 1946). Walter B. Hendrickson, 'An Owenite Society in Illinois', *Indiana Magazine of History*, XLV (June 1949) 175–82.

27. Richard Simons, 'A Utopian Failure', *Indiana History Bulletin*, XVIII (1941) 98–114.

28. Paul Brown, see n 23 *supra* and op. cit., p. 89.

29. John Humphrey Noyes, *A History of American Socialisms* (1870; new ed., Constable, London, 1966, with introduction by Mark Holloway) pp. 74–7.

30. Bestor, *Backwoods Utopias*, p. 208.

31. Noyes, *History of American Socialisms*, pp. 59–65.

32. Bestor, *Backwoods Utopias*, pp. 213–14.

33. 'I have so far lost the little confidence I had in adults or parents that I believe no system of education can have a fair trial but with orphans'. *Maclure–Fretageot Correspondence*, 11 Aug 1826, p. 351. See also ibid., p. 301.

34. A. J. G. Perkins and Theresa Wolfson, *Frances Wright: Free Inquirer* (New York: Harper, 1939).

35. Fanny Wright's collaboration with Owen's eldest son is interesting when the *New Harmony Gazette* ceased publication as such on 22 October 1828, and

became *The New Harmony and Nashoba or The Free Inquirer* in the following week. By 26 January 1829 Francis Wright began republishing these issues, retitled *The Free Inquirer*, bi-weekly on 28 January 1829, and on 4 March the two journals merged as *The Free Inquirer*. The new name indicated their passionate concern for exposing organised religion, liberalising the divorce laws, redistributing wealth and polytechnising education.

36. Mrs Trollope, *Domestic Manners of the Americans*, with an introduction by Michael Sadleir (London: Routledge, 1927) pp. 121–6.

37. Podmore, *Life of Robert Owen*, p. 340. Wilbert H. Timmons, 'Robert Owen's Texas Project', *Southwestern Historical Quarterly*, LII (1949) 286–93.

38. Gavin Souter, *A Peculiar People: The Australians in Paraguay* (London: Angus & Robertson, 1968) pp. 16, 21, 58. He cites one of the early colonists (also a journalist) as writing in 1894 that Lane ' "cribbed" the idea of "New Australia" from "Icaria" '!

39. Noyes, *History of American Socialisms*.

40. Thomas Skidmore (1790–1832), schoolmaster, journalist, chemist, taught from 1803 to 1815 after which he took up the manufacture of gunpowder, wire-drawing and paper. He argued in his *Moral Physiology Exposed and Refuted* (1831) p. 73, that 'there was no actual experiment made of the community-system at New Harmony – everything being in the proprietorship and under the dictation of a few Aristocratic speculating theorists. Of what use can [it] be', he asked, 'when it is only to be established, not on the *rights* of those for whose benefit it is expressly intended, but on the *permission* of those to whom, according to his plans, it is necessary to apply, before any one of his communities can be allowed to have an existence?' As a teacher and scientist himself, Skidmore argued that even the Owenite–Maclurian educational thesis was wrong, for 'until every relation in life is equalized; till there be equal food, equal clothing, equal instruction, *equal parentage, equal necessity to labour*, etc. Till *all* these and more are at hand . . . an equal *choice* of the pursuits of life will never prevail; and *they* hug a treacherous deception to their bosoms as we believe, who think there ever can or will.' Harris, *Socialist Origins in the United States*, p. 125.

41. Robert Dale Owen, *Threading my Way*, p. 286. See also R. W. Leopold, *Robert Dale Owen* (Cambridge, Mass.: Harvard University Press, 1940).

42. A. H. Estabrook, 'The Family History of Robert Owen', *Indiana Magazine of History* (1923).

43. Grant Foreman, 'The Settlement of English Potters in Wisconsin', *Wisconsin Magazine of History*, XXI (1938) 375–96.

44. John R. Commons, Ulrich B. Phillips, Eugene A. Gilmore, Helen L. Sumner and John B. Andrews, *A Documentary History of American Industrial Society* (New York: Russell & Russell, 1958) VII 166–9.

45. *Phalanx*, 9 Dec 1844, cited in Commons *et al*, VII 225.

46. Ibid., VII 245.

47. Ibid., VII 201.

48. Ibid., VII 88.

49. Ibid., VIII 94.

50. Ibid., VIII 105.

51. Ibid., VIII 111.

52. Ibid., VII 160–3.

53. Ibid., VII 181–2.

54. Podmore, *Life of Robert Owen*, p. 590.

55. *Transactions of the National Association for the Promotion of Social Science, 1857* (London: John W. Porter & Son, 1858) p. 286.

56. G. B. Hill, *The Life of Sir Rowland Hill and the History of Penny Postage* (London: Thos. de la Rue, 1880) I 207.

57. Ibid., pp. 208–9.

58. The date, though not given, would seem to be 1837 or 1838, since Playfair did not come to London until 1838.

59. It is worth noting that both Wheatstone and Arnott were two of the earliest English apostles of Comte. W. M. Simon, *European Positivism in the Nineteenth Century* (Ithaca, N.Y.: Cornell University Press, 1963) p. 173.

60. No evidence of this can be found in the papers of Lyon Playfair. The only two letters from Hill to Playfair are in 1851 and 1875. Wemyss Reid, *Memoirs and Correspondence of Lyon Playfair* (London: Cassell, 1899) p. 47.

61. Sir Henry Cole, K.C.B., *Fifty Years of Public Work* (London: Bell, 1884) 134–5.

62. S. E. Finer, *The Life and Times of Sir Edwin Chadwick* (London: Methuen, 1952). R. A. Lewis, *Edwin Chadwick and the Public Health Movement 1832–1854* (London: Longmans, Green, 1952) p. 85.

63. Finer, *Sir Edwin Chadwick*, p. 14.

64. Noyes, *History of American Socialisms*, pp. 85, 91.

65. Ibid., pp. 1–2.

66. Ibid., p. 23.

67. Ibid., p. 93.

68. Bestor's list is given on pp. 235–42 of his *Backwoods Utopias*.

69. Noyes, *History of American Socialisms*, p. 88. See also Ralph Milliband, in 'The Politics of Robert Owen', *Journal of the History of Ideas*, XV (1954) 233–45, who describes Owen as a 'technological optimist'.

70. Owen's biographer, Frank Podmore, was himself a spiritualist. See his *Mediums of the Nineteenth Century* (New Hyde Park, N.Y.: University Books, 1963). For the general story of 'futureology' in the U.S.A. see W. H. G. Armytage, *Yesterday's Tomorrows: A Historical Survey of Future Societies* (London: Routledge & Kegan Paul, 1968).

# CHAPTER ELEVEN

# Images and Echoes of Owenism in Nineteenth-Century France

## H. DESROCHE

THE fullest reappraisal of Owenism as a social movement is undoubtedly the recent book by J. F. C. Harrison.[1] We in France, who are without direct access to the texts and records, had long been hoping for the appearance of some such perspective.

In comparison with research already carried out or under way on our great French utopians – Saint-Simon, Fourier and Cabet – we realise that our observations can be concerned only with the very general aspects of the emergence of a wider social thought.[2]

We are aware, of course, that none of these three utopian currents failed to cross the Channel and that, having crossed it, each collided with the Owenite current. Saint-Simon was translated by that remarkable Owenite, J. E. Smith,[3] and the Saint-Simonian missions came into contact with the operations of the Owenites.[4] In spite of the Master's denunciation of the 'snares and charlatantry of the Owen cult' (1831), Fourierism was known of in Owenite circles. Through Hugh Doherty it had an English posterity.[5] If the third French utopian, Étienne Cabet, thought seriously in 1851 of 'Icarianising' in England, it was probably because during his exile in London (1834–9) and again in France (1846–7) he was a sincere Owenite in personal contact with Robert Owen.[6]

Already, then, it would seem that here is one dimension of research into the mutual contacts or influences between the English Owenites and the French utopians – through the *excursions* of the latter into the territory of the former. There is plainly a second: that of the *incursions* of the former – this secular Owenism – upon the territory of the latter; that is, into the Continent and, more particularly, into the French hexagon.

Professor Harrison, however, in his meticulous study of the export of the Owenite message to America, has little to say about a corresponding export to the Continent. In the 106 pages of his admirable

bibliography (pp. 263-369) one finds barely half a dozen titles with a
bearing on this French dimension of Owenism (or, subsequently, on
the study of Owen),[7] and in the light of this slightness we cannot help
but ask: If such is the case, is there any real point in looking for a
French dimension to the Owenite legacy? In considering Owenism's
Anglo-American descendants, Harrison shows that the Owenite
phenomenon – Owenite writings encouraging and being encouraged
by practical Owenism – may have lived on in three forms: as legacy,
legend and relic.[8] Can it be said that in France it has been none of the
three? Has it been, and is it, nothing more than a phantom, some
distant foreign spirit raised two or three times a century by a few
devotees, rather as a spirit might be raised at a séance? This, at least,
is a question we would wish to ask in this contribution.

Harrison makes the melancholy remark: 'No one library has anything like a complete collection of Owen's works, still less of Owenites.'[9] He points out that 'Owenite literature lay forgotten in the little
libraries of the co-operative societies, secular halls and Working Men's
Institutes'.[10] Indeed yes! And this is precisely what happened in our
case in respect of our three great utopians: thousands of manuscript
pages of Saint-Simon still lie unpublished in dusty archives, whilst the
documents of the Saint-Simonians are scattered to the four winds.[11]
Fourierist records are now shared by the Archives Nationales in Paris[12]
and the Feltrinelli Institute in Milan: in practice the study of Fourierism
entails peregrinations about North-eastern and Western Europe and
North and South America.[13] In respect of Cabet, not only are the
records dispersed, but some collections are incomplete and the missing
parts undiscoverable. Again, as with Owen, there is the impossibility
of gathering within a single library whatever might be found or brought
to completion.[14]

Given the limitations of this essay and the unfinished – even summary
– character of the documentary research undertaken, the catalogue
which follows must be considered as being only very approximate.
Yet it represents a first step between the half-dozen bridgeheads
established by Harrison and the *Livre Blanc* we hope to publish shortly,
when all the texts have been assembled with the welcome help of our
English colleagues.

In what follows there are four major sections:

1. From 1817 to 1830, i.e. from the first mention of Owen in
   France and his first visit to Paris up to the July Revolution. It

has been suggested that the latter event may have brought Owen to France a second time, or at least tempted him to consider a visit.

2. From 1830 to 1837, i.e. up to his second stay in Paris, duly prepared by the French group of Owenites.

3. From 1837 to 1848, i.e. from the second to the third visit, a phase marked by the final closeness of Owen's relations with Étienne Cabet.

4. From 1848 to the end of the century – Owenite 'fireworks' in Paris in 1848, followed by a slow and irreversible collapse, until an echo of Owenite themes is heard again in the contacts between the English and French Co-operative systems in the last quarter of the century.

## FROM 1817 TO 1830

In this phase Owenism was implanted in France. Owen visited Paris; translations of his works were published and reviewed. The first French Owenites appeared. A network of those attracted by Owen's ideas began to take shape, in spite of the Fourierists, who, having been aroused to take up their positions, wanted to keep their distance, and the Saint-Simonians, who would have preferred rather to export Saint-Simon to England. But these distinctions were neither glaringly obvious nor clear-cut; many people were pondering the problems of agreement or fusion and became message-bearers from one coterie to the other.

### 1817

In 1817 there was what M. Gans suggests might be 'the first mention of Owen in France'.[15] This was a letter from London, dated 23 August, which gave an ironical report of a meeting organised by Robert Owen in which he claimed that there were 'vulgar errors in the fundamental notions of every religion hitherto taught unto men . . .'. The letter was published in the first issue (27 August) of the *Journal des Débats*.

*1818*

Owen was himself in Paris in July 1818. He was on his way to Aix-la-Chapelle, where he was to place his projects before the Congress of the Holy Alliance. On 20 July he presented two of his works to the Académie des Sciences. Again, on 26 October 1818, his travelling companion and translator, Marc Auguste Pictet of Geneva, gave a report on the 'New View of Society' to the same society. At this time, we are told, 'Owen tried to make himself known in government circles and to those close to the Duc d'Orléans, the friend of his patrons, the Dukes of Sussex and Kent'.[16]

It is from this year too that there dates what is thought to be 'the first Memorial of Owen in French'. This was *The Memorial of Mr Robert Owen of New Lanark, in Scotland, Addressed in the Interests of the Working Classes to the Allied Sovereigns Assembled at Aix-la-Chapelle* (Frankfurt, 1818).[17]

1818 was also memorable as the year in which Joseph Rey founded a secret society in Grenoble, 'l'Union', with the aim of spreading liberal ideas. Between 1821 and 1826 Rey was exiled in England. Here he came to know Owenism, which, as we shall see, he began to spread in France on his return.

*1819*

The following year saw the translation into French of two of Owen's works. These were the work of the Comte de Lasteyrie and both were published in Paris. They were *Address to the Sovereigns at Aix-la-Chapelle and to the Governments of Europe* and *Institution for the Betterment of the Moral Character of the People*.

*1820*

At this point there appeared evidence of contact between French and British utopians. A manuscript note from Charles Fourier, addressed to the Académie de Belley and dated 25 May 1820, congratulated Owen on having 'foreseen' the theory of Association and having 'exercised his mind upon so useful a question'. Fourier was, in fact, acquainted with Owen's thought well before he heard tell of the Saint-Simonians.[18] The note antedated by two years the publication of the *Traité de l'Association* in which Owen was to be frequently mentioned.

*1821*

While Fourier's *Traité de l'Association* was being finished, Laffon de Ladébat's translation (Paris and London, 1821) of Henry Grey Macnab's *Impartial Examination of the New Views of Mr Robert Owen and his Establishment at New Lanark in Scotland for the Relief and Most Useful Employment of the Working Classes and the Poor, and for the Education of their Children* appeared. H. Bourgin considers that it is 'not impossible' that, in spite of the short interval of time between the appearance of the two publications, 'certain pages of the one may have inspired several lines of development in the other'.[19] Certainly Fourier was acquainted with a recast by Huard of the translation, a version of which he made much use of in his own work. This was 'An Impartial Examination of the New Views of Mr Robert Owen by Henry Grey Macnab. Translated from the English by M. Laffon de Ladébat', *Memorial Universel de l'Industrie Française des Sciences et des Arts*, tome 5 (1821) 241–55. This, as Fourier commented, contained 'a description of Mr Owen's establishment at New Lanark'.[20] Another recension of Macnab's translation appeared in the *Revue Encyclopédique*, tome 10 (May 1821) 321–6.

If he had earlier knowledge of English Owenism, it was through Huard's note that Fourier came to know of the existence in Paris of 'some supporters of Association' inspired by Owen, and we note that he did not spare his criticism of New Lanark: 'No arrangement can be found in it to satisfy the first condition of the social bond. . . . In the glimpses given in this article I can pick out thirty faults occasioned by the passions. . . .' Fourier added, however, 'I prefer to praise what is worthy of praise', and he bestowed praise, in fact, on three items:

> It is none the less a most worthy establishment in that it is conducive to some of the material advances of Association. . . .
> Mr Owen is the first to have done *practical* research and trials regarding Association. . . .
> I note with pleasure that the English are rallying to the fundamental principle of domestic economy, to work by means of numerous discussions. . . .[21]

To Fourier, at this stage, Owenism was *une demi-issue de civilisation*, 'a half-way stage in the move upwards'.[22] But later Fourier was to regret that he had shown himself well disposed towards Owen:

> It was only at a very late stage that I came to know of Owen's doctrine and, *when I praised the author's intentions in* 1822, I was far from supposing that *in point of fact* he was working to ridicule the whole idea of Association and to make every government suspicious of it. . . . In 1822 I believed that they [the sect] had a few good intentions . . . but the stubborn philosophism of the Owenites I have seen since has convinced me that nothing is to be expected from them in the way of an attempt at *real* Association.[23]

Reference has earlier been made to the *Revue Encyclopédique*. This was founded by Jullien de Paris, probably a disciple of Babeuf, who visited New Lanark in 1822.

## 1823

In 1823 he published 'A Review of the Industrial Colony of New Lanark in Scotland, founded by Mr Robert Owen'. (*Revue Encyclopédique*, tome 18 (April 1823) 1–25) which dealt especially with the educational aspects of the experiment. His 1823 article commented:

> It is fitting that our *Revue Encyclopédique*, in its desire to establish a kind of common meeting-ground for every view on the public good and for every useful work, should proclaim the endeavours – already crowned with great success – by which one of those rare men whose life is a series of good actions has blazed a trail along which it is to be hoped that many other philanthropists might care to follow him. (p. 14)

The conclusion was an appeal for collaboration: 'All right – thinking men must give strong support to Mr Owen in the execution of his views. . . . His government, *and foreigners who are united by a feeling of attachment to the interests of mankind*, must help him in the noble task he has undertaken . . .' (p. 37).[24]

He himself set the example: 'He continued to take an interest in Owen's activities and, in all, no fewer than thirteen articles on this subject appeared in the *Revue*.'[25] It is likely that he published in other reviews (*American Review*, *Mémorial Catholique*, later mentioned in the major text). 'It was he, moreover, who brought the work by Joseph

Rey (the leading French Owenite) to a young man who, disenchanted with both Saint-Simonism and Fourierism, was desirous, because of Fourier's attacks on Owen, to learn more about the latter. This young man of 24, Jules Gay, was to become, together with Jullien de Paris, Rey and Radiguel, the most faithful of Owen's French supporters.'[26]

Bourgin suggests the hypothesis that Fourier may have found the exposition of Owen's educational theory in Jullien's review.[27] This is, in fact, the fullest part of his observations. In the slim volume in which the whole is reproduced (pp. 11–37), it is bound with a *Sketch of the System of Education followed in the Schools of New Lanark* (pp. 49–130), followed by an appendix (pp. 131–65) which reproduces 'summaries' which were 'made for the schools of New Lanark' and 'which might be termed *An Introduction to the Arts and Sciences*'.

*1824*

There followed an interesting correspondence between Owen and Fourier.[28] At this period Owen was becoming preoccupied with the Motherwell experiment.[29] Fourier was informed and offered his services. A letter to J. Muiron, dated 8 April 1824, stated: 'I have sent Mr Owen two copies of the *Traité de l'Association* . . . advising him of the impending publication of the summary, and telling him that if he is willing to found a company with a view to trying out Association, I am willing to serve him as the lowliest clerk in his establishment.' But this offer was declined, the more particularly since, by the time it was made, the Motherwell project was already put aside. Skene, Owen's secretary, in his reply to the original letter, took the opportunity to clear up what he thought were misunderstandings and to attempt a reconciliation. In another letter to Muiron, however, Fourier suggested that he had not given up hope. 'I have had a long letter from Mr Owen's secretary. He praises my *Traité* very highly and tells me that Mr Owen is to found a new settlement. . . . If I were invited there, I might be setting off next spring. . . .'

In a second letter to Owen, Fourier, not without some *hauteur*, repeated the offer of his services, guaranteeing 'a brilliant success for all of you'.

Four criticisms were made of the project, however, all reiterating the same basic complaint: the powers of attractiveness were underestimated.

Your desire in these settlements is to change men, to modify their characters; yet what is *really* needed is to find the machinery by which their vices may be put to good use. I have read in the *Revue Encyclopédique* the maxims that Mr Owen gives his pupils: they are fine and civilised morality, urging the love of virtue for virtue's own sake. But when this is achieved, the charm of virtue will seem but insipid and will cease to attract. In order to attract, the charm must be composed of virtue, a system that will assure for virtue the pleasures of the senses, and advantages: in that case it will attract, it will be loved and practised uninvited.

*1825*

Among the articles appearing in the *Revue Encyclopédique* in 1825 was a review of a translation by M. Desfontaines of Dale Owen's *A Sketch of the System of Education Followed in the Schools of New Lanark* (Paris, 1825). Review and text were bound together in the same volume (tome 26 (June 1825) 831–2). In the same year, too, the same journal published two other articles: 'The United States: An Agricultural and Philanthropic Settlement' (April, p. 270) and 'London: A Society for Mutual Co-operation' (April, pp. 274–7).

*1826*

At this point another man who was to become one of Owen's leading disciples in France appeared in print. This was Radiguet, who was also to become the Paris correspondent of the London Co-operative Society. In his 'Co-operative Society founded by Mr Owen at New Harmony in America', *Journal des Connaissances Utiles*, tome 4, no. 21 (1826), he presented the New Harmony project (pp. 120–2) and also its constitution 'which was designed to bring about world happiness' (pp. 122–7).

At the same time a determined effort was being made by Mrs Anna Wheeler to bring together Owenites, Saint-Simonians and Fourierists.[30] Work begun in Paris was to be continued in England, and it was this lady who initiated into Owenism, Saint-Simonism and Fourierism the chief editor of the *Crisis*, J. E. Smith.

In this year, too, the Owenite retort to the Saint-Simonians was published in the shape of Joseph Rey's 'Letters to the Editor of *Le*

*Producteur* on the System of Mutual Co-operation and Community of Goods according to the Plan of Mr Owen' (*Le Producteur*, tome 4 (1826) 525–44; tome 5, pp. 129–60). It is interesting to note that at this time Rey was attempting to create in Paris a co-operative society modelled on the one in London.[31]

## *1827*

Among the relevant texts dating from this period must be listed 'Extract from a Letter from the State of Ohio, North of Cincinnati, on the Settlement founded by Mr Owen at New Harmony', *American Review* (May 1827) pp. 339–44, and 'Declaration of Mental Independence', *Mémorial Catholique*, tome 7 (February 1827) 148–59. The year 1827 was, however, chiefly remarkable for an attempt to form an Owenite–Fourierist front.[32] Adolphe Radiguel (or, possibly, Radiguet), the secretary or kingpin of the Paris Co-operative Society set up by Rey in the previous year, wrote to Fourier in April 1827 as follows:[33]

> I have not the honour of your acquaintance, but knowing that you have published a work whose principles are largely in accord with those of the co-operative system established by Mr Owen, and in the certainty that you are aware of all that is happening in America and England with the aim of putting this system into practice, I venture to write to you in my own name as in the names of Messrs de Lasteyrie, de Montgary, etc., to ask your opinion as to what you believe to be the best ways of propagating this system in France.

Fourier's reply, dated 3 July 1827, has not been found, but its contents must have been negative, for the reply of Radiguet (or Radiguel) to Fourier's letter, dated 6 July, declares: 'Above all, let me assure you how sensible I am to the interest which inspired your letter of 3 July. I owe it to you, moreover, to undeceive you regarding the error into which your English correspondent has led you in connection with Mr Owen and his establishments.'

There the matter rested. Fourier's resentment grew, bursting forth two years later in his 'Refutation of the Owenites' in *The New Industrial and Societarian World* (Paris, 1829), in which he attacked Owen's 'ambiguity', 'philanthropic platitudes' and 'moral nonsense': 'he is playing the same role as did the alchemists before the birth of experimental chemistry, or the magicians before the birth of medicine'. In

1831, as we shall see, the attack was to be renewed. Yet the resentment was not reciprocated. Owen never attacked Fourier and in his journals even published some quite favourable appreciations. A few months later, in fact (in 1828), the London Co-operative Society published a translation of one of Fourier's texts, *Political Economy Made Easy*, and Pankhurst (q.v.) claims that the Society's statutes were permeated to some extent with Fourierist thought.

## *1828*

In 1828 Joseph Rey published a work that 'long remained the most complete French exposition of the Owenist system'. This was *Letters on the System of Mutual Co-operation and the Community of All Wealth* (Paris, 1828).[34] In the same year, as something of a counterweight to Fourier's hostility, there appeared P. Buonarotti's *Conspiracy for Equality*, said to be by Babeuf (Brussels, 1828), which warmly saluted Owen: 'What the democrats [conspirators] of Year IV could not carry out in France, a noble-hearted man has lately, and by other means, sought to put into practice in the British Isles and America.'[35] A comparison of the 1828 and 1845 editions shows that Buonarotti in the second statement weakened or suppressed his praise of Owen.[36]

## *1829-30*

Fourier's 'Refutation of the Owenists', mentioned above, represented a violent attack on 'these sycophants of the Owen sect', but continued activity by Joseph Rey resulted in a discussion (recorded in *La Fraternité*, 1st year (December 1841) pp 13–15) at the Society for Christian Morality. A report, presented by Joseph Rey and supported by de Lasteyrie and Montalivet, led to an investigation by three members of the Society – Benjamin Constant, Benjamin Laroche and Guizot. This saw the report approved by two votes to one (Guizot) and fuller information was requested from England.[37]

The end of the decade also saw the reaching of a new phase in the relations between Saint-Simonism and Owenism in France. This was represented by the publication in March 1830 in *Le Globe* (a periodical whose Saint-Simonian leanings were equal to those of *Le Producteur*) of 'A Study of the English Co-operatives'. Here it was largely a question of exporting Saint-Simonism into England; and the moving spirit was Gustave d'Eichthal, a young man who had visited England several times and was on terms of friendship with John Stuart Mill in particular.[38] His letters to Mill, from 1829, witness a growing passion for Saint-Simonism. Beginning in that year, more fruitful contacts were established with Thomas Carlyle, whose article, 'Signs of the Times', was translated and published in the Saint-Simonian periodical *L'Organisateur* (21 March and 18 April 1830). In the exchange that followed, Carlyle made an English version of the *New Christianity*, but, greatly to his annoyance, was unable to find a publisher for it. It was whilst these complex negotiations were taking place that *Le Globe* published the study referred to above. Here lies the origin of the planning and realisation of the first Saint-Simonian mission to England, to which some people promised the support of the Owenite organisations.

## FROM 1830 TO 1837

Is it possible that Owen planned a second journey to France in 1830, and that it misfired? In any case, the French Owenites were becoming organised in spite of Fourier's *non possumus* of 1831. The Saint-Simonian missions to England were preparing the ground for links between England and France. The Owenite team of the first phase – Joseph Rey, Jullien de Paris and Radiguet – was strengthened by the addition of the young, headstrong Jules Gay and the woman who was to become his helpmeet, Désirée Véret. Even though the confrontations between Owenism and Fourierism or Owenism and Saint-Simonism were coming to an inconclusive end, the little team in France worked hard at putting their case and preparing for a second visit by Owen. It was hoped that such a visit might crystallise the group's organisation and see the launching of its own publication. Owen came, indeed, in 1837. He would see the visit as a triumph. But after his departure the French Owenite effort would weaken and disintegrate. Yet during these same years the exiled Cabet met Owen in London. And it has been claimed that the message he brought with him on his return to France was merely Owenism Frenchified.

## 1830

Cabet tells us that the advent of the July monarchy and the ambiguous personality of Louis-Philippe aroused certain hopes. They may have been shared by Robert Owen, who had already met Louis-Philippe while on his first visit in 1817. M. Gans, following Holyoake, suggests: 'When Louis-Philippe came to the throne, Owen may perhaps have been tempted to renew the acquaintance and to propound his doctrine to the new King. If one is to believe Holyoake, the historian of the English Co-operative movement, . . . Owen tried his luck in 1830, only to be turned promptly away from France. There is no confirmation of this attempt.'[39]

At any rate complex relationships were being maintained, as a letter from Buonarotti to Joseph Rey, dated December 1830, suggests. It would seem from this letter, discovered by F. Rude in the archives at Grenoble, that Frances Wright wished to meet Joseph Rey, who had made mention of her and her work in his *Lettres*. Buonarotti passed on to his correspondent both good and bad news of the Owenite experiments in America.[40]

## 1831

On the other hand, the rupture between Fourierism and Owenism was made manifest by the publication by Charles Fourier of a pamphlet entitled *The Snares and Charlatanism of the Saint-Simon and Owen Sects, which Promise Association and Progress. A Means of Organising within the Space of Three Months, Real Progress and True Association, or the Combining of Agricultural and Domestic Labour to Give Four Times the Produce and to Raise to 25 Milliards the Revenue of France, which Today is Restricted to 6⅓ Milliards* (Paris, 1831).

This rupture was clearly the product of contacts discussed earlier in this essay. It may be noted, too, that this breach between the two 'sects' occurred precisely when, at the instigation of Eugène d'Eichthal, a union of the two seemed to be getting under way. But Fourier's invective failed to discourage certain of his followers from their later attempts to rally the Owenites to the banner of Fourierism. To the question of whether Fourier himself consented to meet Owen in Paris in 1837 we shall return in due course.

Meanwhile preparations went on for the first Saint-Simonian mission to England – that of d'Eichthal and Duveyrier. In preparation for this mission, articles were published on English 'Co-operatism' in the Saint-Simonian journal *L'Organisateur* (February–March 1831). On the other hand, while pointing out the common platform of Owenism and Saint-Simonism, the organ deplored the excessive egalitarianism and materialism of the English Owenites.[41]

## 1832

The first Saint-Simonian mission to England, beginning in January 1832, was accompanied by great optimism. 'The efforts of the *Owenites*, the Benthamites, the Unitarians and the founders of the Political Union have prepared the ground', wrote the two leaders to Enfantin in their very first letter. And again, Duveyrier wrote to Enfantin in February 1832: 'I am convinced that we shall not leave England without having forged a powerful link of co-patriotism with the French working class, and even closer links of co-religion with our dear manufacturers.'[42]

Armed with letters of introduction from Mrs Wheeler, the two missionaries hoped to 'go straight to Manchester, in the centre of the manufacturing populations of England, there to open a chapel and call a meeting which we hope will draw some 10,000 men'. Before it ceased publication *Le Globe* published letters and reports 'from the missionaries'. There were numerous meetings with 'co-operators' and then a meeting with Owen himself.[43] D'Eichthal was to state that Owenism constituted the most important group in Britain and also that it was the most ripe to be 'Saint-Simonised'. Against this, however, Père Enfantin set a more dialectical opinion: 'The British are not a simple race; in their diversity they reproduce the Trinity of Saint-Simonian humanism: the Englishman is the man of industry, the Scot is the man of learning, the Irishman is the man of religion. . . .' D'Eichthal wanted a coming together of the French and English: 'Though France has had to provide the first priests of the new faith, as she has most sociability, it is England that must provide the first people for the new order.'[44] But in England even friends or disciples remained sceptical. William Cullen wondered 'whether common action could be envisaged between groups whose ideas and principles differ so greatly'.[45]

*1833*

In France, however, the Owenite team was now to be strengthened
by the inclusion of Jules Gay, the self-taught son of a bookseller, who,
like many others, passed from Saint-Simonism to Fourierism and then,
after reading Joseph Rey, fixed upon Owenism. In February and
September 1833 he wrote two letters urging Owen to come (or return)
to France. Désirée Véret, through her marriage to Jules Gay, was to
become Désirée Gay. At this period, however, Mlle Véret, herself a
feminist and Fourierist, was acting as an intermediary between Anna
Wheeler and Charles Fourier. According to M. Gans, Mlle Véret
'wrote several letters to her master from England, some of them
accompanying letters to him from Mrs Wheeler'.[46]

Désirée Véret was delighted with the success of two Italian Saint-
Simonians, Fontana and Prati, who represented the second mission:

> There is an Italian Saint-Simonian here named Fontana, with whom
> all the Owenite ladies are infatuated. Mr Owen pulls faces, but is
> not at all pleased to see his amiable converts seduced from him. I
> have sent many ladies to hear his preaching and all of them are
> Saint-Simonians to all intents and purposes . . . is it love of the
> doctrine or love of the preacher? I do not know, but I think that
> Englishwomen prefer a fine form to a fine idea.[47]

Continuity between the first and second missions had been ensured
by other Saint-Simonians (especially the Spaniard, Étienne Desprat),
though it was jeopardised by the discontinuance of *Le Globe* in April
1832, which had at this time announced the publication by J. S. Mill
of eight articles comparing trends in England and France. The following year, with the blessing of Enfantin, Fontana was to become 'head'
of the English mission, and Prati his principal assistant in the preaching.
The content of this preaching is given in their pamphlet *Saint-Simonism
in Britain*.[48] The most important recruit made by this mission was
undoubtedly J. E. Smith, the editor of the Owenite journal, *Crisis*.

Indeed two important articles which were written by smith[49] for the
*Crisis* of 16 November and 28 December 1833 derived directly from
his contact with their mission, and in his desire for unity Smith mini-
mised the differences between Owenism and Saint-Simonism: 'They
have the same love of co-operation, though with them it has taken on
a monarchical or hierarchical form, with us a republican form; that

is the only difference.'

Perhaps Smith's point is a reflection of the dominant religious con-
fessions of the two countries, the one Catholic, the other Protestant.
Yet it must be stressed that the unity conceived by him was more of
a movement from Saint-Simonism towards socialism: 'As long as the
Saint-Simonians call themselves Saint-Simonians they will remain a
small sect. . . .'[50]

## 1834

Crisis is also valuable as a source of information about a confrontation
between Owenism and Saint-Simonism in the Burton Rooms in
London. The meeting was held on 17 January 1834, the account being
published in Crisis of 26 January of the same year. According to the
report,

> Dr Prati and Mr Owen each expounded his own particular views,
> but we were somewhat disappointed with the result, for neither the
> similarities nor the difference were clearly displayed to the public:
> let a document be produced setting forth their respective views con-
> cerning religion, the formation of character, education, government,
> production, distribution etc. . . . Up to the present, a great deal of
> nonsense has been spoken about both movements; some say they are
> exactly alike; others say they are diametrically opposed. One group
> claims that the Saint-Simonians are fanatical Christians, others that
> they are atheists in disguise.[51]

M. Gans nevertheless holds the theory that Saint-Simonism influenced Owenism in certain ways. He writes:

> There is one aspect of Saint-Simonism, however, which appears to
> have had a certain influence on Owenism: the mystical slant and
> religious organisation of Enfantin's movement. Certain Owenites
> complained that their doctrine was perhaps too severe, that it did not
> appeal sufficiently to the heart, that it did nothing to satisfy certain
> aspirations of the human soul. This tendency may explain all the
> religious paraphernalia gradually acquired by Owen's movement
> after its reorganisation at the end of 1834, as well as the title of
> 'social father' assumed by Owen, which seems clearly to echo the
> title of 'père' used by Enfantin. No doubt it is impossible to state
> confidently that this is a Saint-Simonian influence, yet it is note-

worthy that these reforms had a certain Saint-Simonian character, the absence of which some Owenites had been regretting.[52]

1834 was, in fact, a particularly interesting year. Among its other items *Crisis* published (January, p. 171, and March, p. 258) two notes by Jules Gay. On 8 June 1834 it issued a reply by Robert Owen to the *Address by the Workers of Nantes to the Workers of England* (May 1834). This year, too, saw a letter from Berbrugger to Fourier on the possible break-up of Owenism.[53] The following passage has been transcribed from it:

> As for the Owenites, the moment when they will fuse with us to form the *great socialist party* [author's italics] composed of all those adhering to your discoveries, however they may call themselves, is a moment which, to me, still seems very distant. The Owenites will heed what has just happened to the Saint-Simonians, some obvious disaster. At the moment they are quite puffed up with the influence they have over the Unionists [Syndicalists] and believe that they alone are called to reorganise the society of the future. But they, too, are bound to meet with a signal defeat. I hope it will make them more humble, and less exclusive.

In 1834, too, Étienne Cabet, preferring exile to imprisonment, arrived in London after a brief stop in Belgium 'in the first days of May 1834'.[54] Did he meet Owen? Pierre Leroux claims that he did: 'When Cabet arrived in London, he found Robert Owen back from the United States after the failure of his communistic experiment at New Harmony.'[55] J. Prudhommeaux, on the other hand, challenges Leroux on the trustworthiness of Cabet's declarations in the *Voyage en Icarie*, when he plays down his contacts with Owen:

> Thus, New Lanark, a brilliant but timid venture of employers' philanthropy; New Harmony, a formless and short-lived outline of one of those partial communities of which Cabet, intoxicated by his grandiose dream, had long been proclaiming the inadequacy; and the yet more rudimentary experiments of Titherly and Orbiston, would have the privilege of giving birth to the *Voyage en Icarie*. How was it possible to admit that such poor realities could inspire so ambitious a description of the future city?[56]

The fact is, however, that his contacts with Owen during his stay in London were kept dark by Cabet himself. And, after insisting on the evasive or limited character of the intercourse between Owenism on the one hand and Saint-Simonism or Fourierism on the other, M. Gans is able to suggest: 'There is another [aspect of French socialism] where Owen's influence made itself felt . . . the socialism of Cabet. . . . Cabet . . . whatever he might say . . . is a disciple of Owen.'[57] Perhaps 'disciple' is too strong a word, although the assertion is corroborated in a note by V. Considérant.[58]

The point is that Cabet would not really come to Owen until fifteen years later, when their ability to work together would prove itself in the Texas project. It is probable that Owenism and Cabetism described analogous trajectories, but with unsynchronised rhythms, and this structural analogy and diachronism explain – as much as they may be explained by – the nature of their encounters between 1834 and 1848, including that of 1834, if it ever took place. Whatever the nature of the later meetings, Cabet had in any case studied Owenism at second hand, according to M. Prudhommeaux, who has made abstracts of his reading notes.[59]

## 1835

A demand was now growing for Owen to visit Paris. Jules Gay visited London and secured a promise. A letter from Gay, dated 18 May 1835, declares: 'When I was in London, Mr Owen promised me he would come to Paris . . . he renewed that promise to Mlle d'Espagne and myself in two letters for May or June. . . .'[60]

An interesting 'echo' in this period was Edward Hancock's *Robert Owen's Community System, etc. . . . and the Horrid Doings of the Saint-Simonians* (1835), in which the Owenite co-perative system was said to be a simple 'Englishification of Saint-Simonism'.

## 1836

If Owen's relations with Cabet at this period are open to discussion, Fourier's attitudes were less equivocal. In yet another work the French master was to go on to the attack. This was *False Industry, Unco-ordinated, Repugnant and Mendacious; and the Antidote: Natural Industry, Co-ordinated, Attractive and Veracious . . .*, etc. (Paris, tome 1, 1825; tome 2, 1836), in *Complete Works*, vols VIII and IX. In this work Owen's proposals were attacked as a denial of Christianity. Fourier's proposals, it was argued, represented Christianity transcending itself and achieving fulfilment:

> It behoves us, therefore, to do for the cause of Jesus Christ at least one-tenth of what the atheists have done against Him in this new century; they have helped Robert Owen to found some ten experimental colonies of a kind tending to overthrow religion, property and marriage; let us support at least one trial of the C[harles] F[ourier] method, which is the stay of religion, of property, and of regularised and formalised marriage.

The French Owenites, however, were displaying a continuing vitality. In 1836 Joseph Rey published *On the Bases of the Social Order* (Angers: Lesourd & Paris) 2 vols, 369 and 562 pp. Here was lasting acceptance of Owenism: 'From this point to the end of the chapter I shall have occasion to borrow several passages from the *Letters on the Co-operative System* of Mr Owen which I published in 1828' (II 409). 'Since that time my convictions have only been confirmed by comparing the ideas of Mr Owen with those of all the most enlightened men of the century, and I have thought it necessary to look again at the general result as I then conceived it.'

Jules Gay was similarly active. On 1 October 1836 he again invited Owen to come to Paris, announcing his intention to set up a 'Maison Harmonienne' in the French capital in the spring of 1837 and begging Owen to come 'before that time' so that he would 'ensure the enterprise the greatest possible success'.[61]


*1837*


Again, as the *New Moral World* of 6 February 1837 showed, Gay renewed his invitation to Owen, and in a reply Owen promised to visit Paris in the spring. But the English socialist put off his visit until the publication in French of his *Book of the New Moral World*. In the preface to this translation of Gay's, Radiguel supported the publication with 'the wish of a few of Robert Owen's friends in France, persuaded like himself that the system of mutual co-operation with the community of wealth was the right one to bring about a perfect social order. . . . Their aim is also to link to a common centre of instruction and practice the numerous minds already nourished by these ideas. . . .' This was an allusion to the plan for the 'Maison Harmonienne', which would have been a Parisian replica of the Owenite Halls of Science. 1837 thus saw the publication of a translation by Jules Gay of *The Fundamental Propositions of the Social System of Community of Wealth, Based on the Laws of Human Nature* (Paris).

In May and June 1837, preparations were made for Owen's visit to Paris. The exchanges may be summarised as follows:[62]

| | |
|---|---|
| 6 May | The *New Moral World* announces the intention of Owen to leave for Paris after his return to Manchester on 10 June. Much is made of the importance of the Parisian disciples. |
| 18 May | Another letter from Gay, growing rather impatient. On the organising committee responsible for the invitation there are, as well as Gay, Joseph Rey, the pioneer of 1826, Radiguel, Dr Evrat, provisionally responsible for the Saint-Simonian missions in England, Jullien de Paris, who had placed his *Revue Encyclopédique* at the service of the cause, de Lasteyrie, the translator, and a few others. It is hoped, but not certain, that Owen will arrive on 15 June. |
| 9 June | A letter from Gay to Owen. Hope is expressed for a common front of Owenites, Fourierists and Saint-Simonians: 'The three systems, through tolerance and the universality of our principles, will be but one.' |
| 12 June 14 June 19 June | Further letters from Gay. The date of arrival has yet to be confirmed. A request to bring what is necessary to complete the Owenite Library in Paris. |
| 27 June | Owen announces he will leave next day. |
| 29 June | Gay fixes a date limit for 2 or 3 July. |
| 28 June | Letter from London: an advance party of Owenites has set off that morning. |
| 30 June | Letter from London: Owen leaving within the next two days. |
| 1 July | Letter from London: Owen to depart on 2 July. |

In fact Owen did not arrive in Paris until 7 July: Gay still had time in his last letter to state that he was expected on the 3rd or 4th of the month.

Knowledge of Owen's activities in Paris during July and August 1837 is to be gleaned from reports in the *New Moral World* (up to 28 October 1837) which are, of course, propagandist, and the rather sceptical accounts in the French newspaper *Le National*. The sarcastic conclusion of the newspaper *Le Temps* is to be noted: 'Yet Owenism must be

given its place in that vast register of truth and error which we call
the history of the human mind.' By contrast there is an enthusiastic
French echo in an article published by Jullien de Paris in the *Mémorial
Encyclopédique*. Louis Reyband's *Les Réformateurs Sociaux*, 2 vols (1st
ed., 1840; 2nd ed., 1841; 3rd ed., 1844; 7th ed., 1864), has a chapter
on Owen which even in the seventh edition (pp. 203-60) is indicated
as having been written in 1838.

Again it is possible to summarise:

16 July    Request for an audience with the King.
17 July    Political banquet attended by between two and three hundred
           guests and presided over by Jullien de Paris, assisted by Dr
           Evrat, Owen's translator.
           The setting-up of a French branch of the Association of All
           Classes of All Nationas.
25 July    Meeting at the Société Française de Statistique in the Hôtel
           de Ville, Paris. Owen awarded a gold medal 'for his statistical
           investigations on moral education and the first infants'
           schools founded by him in England and Scotland'.
           Speech by Jullien de Paris in honour of 'the renowned and
           venerable philanthropist who had founded industrial and
           agricultural colonies on a vast and skilfully conceived plan'.

There were receptions at the Institut Historique de l'Académie de
l'Industrie Agricole, Manufacturière et Commerciale and at the Société
de Statistique Universelle. On 2, 4 and 6 August 1837 there were
Owenite meetings at the Athénée. At this period a meeting with
Considérant is attested: one with Buonarotti was to come later.
Whether Owen and Fourier met is doubtful.[63]

FROM 1837 TO 1848

It seems that the journey bore no fruit. The 'Maison Harmonienne'
was not founded. The projected review, *Communauté*, was not launched.
Even Jules Gay gave up and placed his hopes on an alliance with the
Neo-Babouvists. The Fourierists continued to sulk. Cabet himself, the
rising star of the Party of the Community in France, was anxious to

keep his distance. But this did not hinder him from creating the only great popular movement to divide the capital and the provinces into areas, each with its activist cell. At one time he hoped to transform France into a 'large-scale community'. But gradually he came to dread his unpreparedness and to be apprehensive of being provoked. To him the coming revolution was a revolution that would fail before it started. There was indeed only one way out: actually to create 'the large-scale community'. Of course, always – but elsewhere. Where, then? This was the moment when he moved half-way towards Owen. The latter went the other half of the way by suggesting Texas, with its virgin territories, for the foundation of the first communitarian republic. For Cabet, this republic would form the synthesis between 'propaganda' and 'realisation'. The Britisher and the Frenchman drew together again – or found each other for the first time. Cabet was not far from declaring that Icarianism was the French version of Owenism.

## 1837

In the short term there was a positive follow-up of Owen's visit: the Parisian Owenites organised. In November 1837 Jules Gay wrote to Robert Owen:

I greatly regret that you are unable to attend the meetings due to take place in ten days or so, concerning your projects. . . . We are at least forty in number and are about to form an association to undertake several things in their turn. Our first act will be to publish a weekly review on subjects of general concern: politics, philosophy, letters, science, etc. It will be suitable for all classes of society and will make known our sound moral doctrines to public opinion in its entirety. For the review I am getting into communication with every country, in an attempt to procure the collaboration of every person with some particular distinction. . . .

I can already count on the help of a large number of people. I myself shall be Editor-in-charge and shall write the political articles. I have secured the help, as associate editor, of M. l'Herminier, the eminent professor of philosophy, who is devoted to the idea of brotherhood and community; he will deal with philosophy, helped by M. Rey of Grenoble. M. Albitis, the distinguished writer, will be responsible for literature; Dr Evrat for science; M. Blanqui, the professor of political economy, for production; M. Alex Wattemare, the celebrated artist, for the fine arts. All these persons share the

opinions of Mr Owen. In addition to these, all other help necessary
with regard to foreign languages has been secured. Over two hundred people of the same mind will make up the editorial committee.

The other undertaking cannot begin before the beginning of the
year because of the host of preparations which are necessary. In the
first instance, we must set up an establishment for general education
and vocational training: (1) for the younger children to be run by
Dr Evrat; (2) for the older ones, by M. Froussard and Mlle de Gutte,
both of whom will be in charge of the schools; (3) for vocational
training, by M. Blanqui, professor of political economy and Principal
of the École de Commerce; (4) for physical education by Colonel
Amoros, etc. . . .[64]

The Fourierist retort was already under way. In September and
November 1837, Baudet Dulary wrote for *La Phalange* a series of
articles criticising the Owenite societies. Their conclusion: 'To sum up,
we have nothing to look to England for in the field of social ideas.'
V. Considérant, who had attended the lectures at the Athénée in August
1837, remained icy:

> Mr Owen seems unaware that the expression of the synthesis of a
> complete science comprises an explanation of all the phenomena
> within its field. At one of the Athénée meetings he was asked to
> give the synthesis of his science; he did not do so; he did not even
> seem to understand the nature of the request, though his interpreter
> explained it to him most clearly; a person belonging to the Society
> replied on his behalf that Mr Owen's synthesis was universal brother-
> hood, which was doubtless the expression of an eminently religious
> and philanthropic desire, but in no wise a scientific formula.[65]

Anna Wheeler had promised Owen that Fourier's supporters would
be the first to come over to him. She was given the lie.


*1838*


The Fourierist counter-offensive was continued by Dr Amédée Paget
in the *Introduction to the Study of Social Science, Containing a Summary
of Societarian Theory Preceded by a General Glance at the State of Social
Science and the Saint-Simonian School* (Paris, 1838; 2nd ed., 1841) 236
pp. In this criticism it is stressed that the Owenite system 'does not
fulfil the object which Social Science sets for itself. . . . The Community, . . . by setting aside individual inequalities, has not made the

social problem any easier to solve: it has merely avoided the trouble of solving it' (p. xxii). 'Of all the schemes it is possible to imagine, it is the most absurd, the most detestable, the most thoroughly opposed to the satisfaction of the real needs of humanity' (p. xxiv). 'It is, in truth, no more than an arbitrary system, and not a scientific conception approaching the solution of the problem' (p. xxv).

Other critics were kinder, however. Louis Reybaud's *Studies of the Modern Reformers or Socialists*, already mentioned in this essay, included a critique of the 'contradictions' of Robert Owen, 'human community and irresponsibility'. Yet it ended on a note of praise:

> Rather than carry this criticism to its furthest conclusion, it is better to look at the salient feature of Mr Owen's life and to pay a final tribute to the great qualities of his heart.
>
> No man hitherto has demonstrated in a nobler fashion than he the divine gift of influencing character through reason and goodwill united; none has displayed more persistent and generous purpose in the prosecution and accomplishment of good works; none has scrutinised the facts with greater patience, nor governed men with greater moral integrity. (p. 259)

*1839*

In 1839 Théodore Dezamy referred to Owen and Buonarotti as two great men in his *Question Put to the Académie des Sciences Morales et Politiques: the Nations Advance Further in Knowledge and Understanding than in Practical Morality. What is the Cause of this Disparity, and What Remedies May be Indicated?*

Several items from 1839 suggested that the scheme for a French Owenite journal was taking shape. There was a circular (13 January) concerning its publication, a letter from Jules Gay to Joseph Rey in the Grenoble Archives, and another from Gay published in the *New Moral World* of 20 April 1839.

It seems likely that an unsuccessful attempt was made to form a coalition with the Babouvist organ *L'Intelligence*, but it was found necessary to fall back on an autonomous scheme for a monthly, *Communauté: Bulletin de la Science Sociale*, to be distributed in Paris and London. Gay was to have been editor. Rey and Radiguet were members of the founding committee. But the promotion did not go beyond the planning stage.[66]

*1840*

In January 1840 there appeared the first edition of E. Cabet's *Travels in Icaria*. In the previous year a limited edition had been issued pseudonymously and with a different title. After five years in exile in London, Cabet intended this as a manifesto for his return to Paris. Robert Owen, it should be noted, was given honourable mention among the gallery of Cabet's forerunners (pp. 518–19), as was his disciple, Miss Wright. But there were strict reservations:

> It is a pity he [Owen] placed too much reliance on the bounty of kings and the nobility; that he has discouraged the people by assigning too short a period for the realisation of hopes that are not yet realised, and that, in his attempts to establish communities which are incomplete and too small, he has employed a capital which, though considerable, has been insufficient to meet all the needs of a model community, but which, had it been employed solely in the preaching of a doctrine, might have produced an incalculable effect upon public opinion.

There is no point in seeing in this any dissimulation on Cabet's part, even though he had in fact met Owen on divers occasions in England. He himself had gone as far as to plan a 'large-scale community', to be achieved by means of 'propaganda'. He believed that Owen was still only at the stage of the 'small-scale community (the incomplete community), eager for its "realisation". Not until seven years had passed would he exchange the first strategy for the second, and only then would he be actually on the same wave-length as Owen.

But Pierre Leroux and V. Considérant saw it differently:[67]

> Owenism was . . . almost unknown in France, since it had not, to my knowledge, been expounded and argued there except in a little pamphlet well and honestly written by M. Rey of Grenoble; Cabet saw it as a lucky find and soon brought it to the Continent, where he carefully plagiarised it (I do not believe that he has once, spontaneously, mentioned the name of Owen) and duly launched it thus Cabetised, hammered out and inflated, on a sea of words, digressions and banalities that he himself sincerely believed, and made his hearers believe, to be arguments and ideas. . . . Frenchified by a sufficient dose of political verbiage and greatly popularised, this communism became a very easy vulgarisation for the poorer social classes.

In the early 1840s a number of publications illustrating our theme appeared and might be set out as follows:

1. Godwyn Barmby's publication in the *New Moral World*, 1 (1840). Although this is not a French text, the author's narrative of his journey to France is none the less very interesting on the relations between the two countries. A meeting with Mme J. Gay is mentioned (p. 74); there is a list of the French translations of Owen's works and notes on the relationship between Fourierism and Owenism.

2. *A Message from the 'French Socialists' to the English Socialist Congress.* This message was brought on 18 May 1840 by an Irish Owenite resident in France. Among the signatories, Gay and Lasteyrie represented the Owenite group, whose plans for a journal had fallen through the year before. At this time Jules Gay, who was probably the principal French militant, began forming ties with the Babouvists, founding the newspaper *L'Humanitaire* with Théodore Dezamy. Later, in 1849, he would attempt to found *Le Communiste*, which would appear but once.[68] On the other hand, his wife Désirée Gay (*née* Désirée Véret) would write for Cabet's *Le Populaire*.

## 1841

3. Blanqui, *A History of Political Economy in Europe from the Ancients to the Present Day.* The second edition of this work appeared in 1842. Chapter xliv, from p. 339, and the bibliography are relevant to our study. There is mentioned a series of noteworthy articles on Owen in the *Journal de la Science Sociale*, the articles written prior to 1842.

4. Théodore Dezamy, *The Code of the Community* (Paris 1842). According to F. Rude, Joseph Rey had subscribed to this work. Dezamy was Jules Gay's partner in founding *L'Humanitaire*.[69] The same Dezamy wrote *Jesuitism Conquered and Annihilated by Socialism* (Paris, 1845).

## 1841–2

5. Articles by Désirée Gay (wife of Jules Gay) in *Le Populaire*, 1841–2. These are mentioned above.

*1843*

   6. Étienne Cabet, *The State of the Social Question in England, Scotland and Ireland* (Paris, 1843). According to J. Prudhommeaux, this was the first time Cabet 'had made a moderately detailed study of the work of the English reformer'; but even so the pamphlet is 'summary, too frequently inaccurate, obviously written from second-hand documents'.[70]

*1847*

   The year before the Paris revolution of 1848 saw the appearance of two major Owenite texts and a number of memorials which throw light on relations between Owen and Cabet. T. W. Thornton produced an abridged translation of *The Book of the New Moral World, Containing the Rational System Based on the Laws of Human Nature*. This was the same Thornton, a follower of Owen, resident in France, who established, or rather re-established, communication between Cabet and Owen – witness the first sentence of a letter to Owen, dated 25 January 1847: 'Monsieur Cabet who was in touch with you in England a few years ago. . . .'[71]

   In the same year Joseph Rey's 'The Socialists Rallying Cry' in *La Démocratie Pacifique* of 27 June 1847 was published in pamphlet form, with a restatement by V. Considérant entitled *Rey and Considérant, An Appeal for the Rallying of the Socialists. A Letter from M. Rey of Grenoble. The Two Communisms: Observations on M. Rey's Letter by P. V. Considérant* (Paris, 1847).

   Having addressed himself in 1826 to the Saint-Simonian journal, the impenitent Rey appealed here, some twenty-one years later, to that of the Fourierists. But the École Sociétaire, through the pen of Considérant, accompanied his rallying-cry with a restatement – a polemic against Cabet's type of communism which was collaborating at that time, if not with Owenism, at least with Owen himself. On p. 17 Considérant gave Rey his due: 'M. Rey is the oldest and most revered representative in France of the idea of *Community*. In 1826 he published a little book about the views of Owen, which remains to this day a simple, clear statement of everything fundamental and judicious that has been said about the doctrine of Community and its social organisation." But he attacked Cabet, who was busy renewing his contacts with Owen in preparation for his Texas expedition. Rey, on the other hand, would have liked to have brought the two schools – Fourierists and communists (Cabetists) – together, for he could see the latter collaborating with Owenism.

To the Owenite Thornton's mediation in France (discussed above) was now added the mediation of the Cabetist Charles Sully in England. On 14 August 1847 he wrote to Owen:

> If I have understood you, you have a goal from which you will not allow yourself to be diverted.
>
> This goal is the founding of townships, governed by a code of laws which you have prepared for this purpose.
>
> You are striving to persuade the British Government to apply this plan in Ireland, and if you do not succeed, *you will put it into practice in Texas* [author's italics].
>
> You are unable to swerve from the straight path you have planned, since it alone will lead you to success.
>
> M. Cabet can adopt no plan that does not agree with the views and principles expressed in the *Voyage en Icarie* and the *Populaire*, since his followers have accepted these principles and based their faith on them.
>
> This is why the relative positions of yourselves and M. Cabet must be preserved. Nature and circumstance have given each of you the ability to lead one of the two great communistic operations indicated in our Constitution and its appeal to the disciples to follow into Icarie. A complete fusion between the two would lose to communism many of the advantages to be gained by a concerted plan of operations, for the plans of both of you are two great truths leading along parallel lines to the same goal, but they will never meet until the goal is reached.[72]

The difference that Sully claimed to see in the positions would prevent neither him nor Cabet, however, from borrowing Owen's Texas plan, for this is what Owen would allow them to do by putting them in touch with the Peters Company's agent.

On 15 August 1847, Cabet wrote to Owen:

> Dear and revered Brother in Humanity,
>
> I have learned with great pleasure of your arrival in London, as I immediately conceived the hope of seeing you there.
>
> I like to think that you will not have forgotten *our frequent interviews, either at your house or mine (Cirencester Place) during my political exile in England* [author's italics].

For myself, it was there that I learned to know, admire and love your nobility of character, your kindly philosophy, your patient and indulgent benevolence, and your untiring devotion to the cause of the people and of mankind. I admired you so much the more, since your opinions are mine and all my efforts are directed towards the same goal. When you come to a fuller acquaintance with my system and doctrine, you will see that my principles are exactly the same as yours. So that you may know my writings better, I am sending you all those which are still in print. Be kind enough to accept them as a token of my attachment and respect. I trust that you may soon inquire into them.

Mr Thornton and Mr Sully have written telling me that you approve of my great project to emigrate to America, there to found a great community: this gives me great pleasure. I hope that you will help us with your experience, your zeal, and your powerful influence. You have already been good enough to give these gentlemen some important documents for me: I thank you for it.

Let me know when you intend leaving England again for America. I shall come to London for a few days' discussion with you. I set great store by that meeting. In the meantime, please send me, if possible, your ideas, your opinions, your advice, and any information you may have.

Be pleased to accept the assurance that I am to be counted among your most sincere, affectionate and devoted admirers.[73]

The above letter is in the Owen Archives, Manchester, and is quoted by M. Gans. The frequency of the meetings is confirmed by a letter from Owen to Louis Blanc in 1856 (see below). Yet it must not be considered as evidence of Owen's influence over Cabet – and for a very simple reason: if they conversed, it could only be through an interpreter. After the event, they were to overestimate the importance of such meetings: Cabet when, as here, he is asking favours; Owen when he was strutting in the fullness of his glory in 1856.

At this period Cabet's newspaper, *Le Populaire*, published several particularly eulogistic articles and notices concerning Robert Owen. These were immediately reprinted in *La Réalisation d'Icarie*, bk iv, pp. 150ff., 161, 175 (August 1847). In one of them (see *Le Populaire*, 15 August 1847) Cabet answered:

Robert Owen, the great English and American socialist, has just arrived in England from America. Our friends will be pleased to learn that he is in favour of our emigration project and will use all his influence in its support. He has already sent us most valuable information. Before he returns to America we shall have talks together in Paris or London, the results of which will undoubtedly be of great service.

At this time, too, it seems that Cabet discovered or rediscovered Joseph Rey. 'We shall also make known the little book published in 1826 by Joseph Rey of Grenoble, on the doctrines of the founder of communism in England' (*La Réalisation d'Icarie*, bk iv, p. 154). After commenting on Thornton's book, mentioned above, Cabet went as far as to declare: 'These first principles of English communism are practically the same, it is evident, as those of our French communism, and it will be seen from the articles to be published in our next few issues that the entire system of the venerable Robert Owen is full of analogies with our own.'

On 9 September 1847, Cabet and Owen met in conference in London. Despite the strains of this journey and the obstructive wrangling of the Society of Communists (German) in London, the central point of the journey was the conference with Owen. In a manuscript in the possession of J. Prudhommeaux, Owen spoke warmly of the insistence with which Cabet expressed his gratitude for the courtesy of the 'venerable patriarch of communism'. In the report published in *Le Populaire* of 19 September 1847, Cabet bore this out:

We have had great pleasure in meeting once more that venerable patriarch of English communism who has made eleven journeys from England to America in order to teach his doctrines there. . . . In the course of several discussions, Robert Owen has already given us documents, advice and support which will greatly facilitate a rapid settlement, and we are convinced that his readiness to oblige will win the gratitude of Icarians, as his gentle philanthropy and numerous services have long since won our esteem and veneration. . . .

In a similar vein the *Réalisation de la Communauté d'Icarie* (pt 4, October 1847) commented: 'Our investigations are complete; we have inquired in Paris, London and America, of many people, in letters, in books, *in discussion with Robert Owen*, which have helped us greatly, and we believe we know enough. . . .' The date of departure for Texas had already been decided, though the choice of Texas would not be made public until two months later, in December 1847.[74]

## FROM 1848 TO THE END OF THE CENTURY

A few days before the departure of the first advanced party for Texas, the revolution of February 1848 broke out in Paris. Cabet and his company could not but be involved. Owen, who had probably missed the 1830 revolution, did not intend to miss this one. He stayed in the French capital from February to August, expending his energies in dialogues, addresses, proclamations and expositions. The alliance with Cabet was sealed in a memorable meeting at the Société Fraternelle Centrale. But it was already April; the revolution subsided, and Cabet set his Texas emigration project in motion once more. Owen went home to his English destiny. 'That poor Cabet', he sighed in 1856.

Thereafter, the English Owenite heritage came back to France only through the contacts and collusion between certain members of the English and French Co-operative movements in their alliance formed to challenge – or resist – the way in which the Wholesale seemed to be turning into a great commercial company. The former Owenite, Holyoake, now united with certain Christian Socialists, was one of the regular visitors of the French co-operators of the Nîmes school, one of whose members, Auguste Fabre, had Owenite sympathies. This collaboration was finally to produce the short-lived Manifesto of 1892.

From the end of the century, Owenism in France gave way to an Owenology which has reached the stage of awaiting its own revival.

### (a) Robert Owen's Third Visit to Paris (February to August 1848)

*1848*

Before he left for Paris on 27 February 1848, Owen drafted an *Address to the Men and Women of France*, This was published in *Le Populaire* (23 March 1848) and *La Voix des Femmes* (25 March 1848). Speaking to the French people, since 'the opportunity you have wisely taken is glorious, greater than all that has been done', Owen proposed that they should establish a new government based solely upon truth – a government that might serve as an example to the world, that might become 'a boon to humanity'. The address listed the thirteen results that might be expected from such a government.

In discussing this, M. Rubel particularises the influences which acted upon Owen to decide him to make this gesture: 'From the onset this revolution in France will put the question which has occupied our minds for so long under your guidance. The events of one short week alone have set enough work for us in Europe, without bothering about America.'[75]

In late March, Owen's *Address to the French Nation* was published. It appeared in several newspapers as soon as Owen arrived in Paris. The text was short – about fifty lines – and was both an appeal to the nation and an offer of Owen's services 'to the provisional government':

> Next month I shall be 77 years of age; for sixty years I have fought this great cause despite calumnies of every kind. I have created children's homes and a system of education with no punishments. I have improved the conditions of workers in factories. I have revealed the science by which we may bestow on the human race a superior character, produce an abundance of wealth and procure its just and equitable distribution. I have provided the means by which an education may gradually be achieved – an education equal for all, and greatly superior to that which the most affluent have hitherto been able to procure.
>
> I have come to France, bringing these insights and experience acquired in many countries, to consolidate the victory newly won over a false and oppressive system that could never have lasted.

M. Rubel, who gives the text in full, lists several newspapers which published and/or criticised it: *Démocratie Pacifique* (3 April 1848); *La Presse* (4 April); *Journal des Débats* (4 April); *La Réprésantant du Peuple* (4 April); *Le Salut Public* (11 April); *La Liberté* (9–10 April).[76]

Whilst in Paris, Owen attended a reception at the Société Fraternelle Centrale, founded by Cabet. The speeches were reported in a pamphlet, *Société Fraternelle Centrale, Speeches 7 and 8. Reception and Speech of Robert Owen* (Paris, 1848) 14 pp. At the reception Owen is reported to have said, among other things:

> Your glorious victory in February having brought unexpected opportunities for the application of my ideas, I have expressly hastened to France to offer my assistance to your estimable president, M. Cabet, and to the provisional government. It is my intention to propose to France a system of Association as much unlike the former system as railways are unlike the former means of communication.

In reply Cabet is said to have declared:

Robert Owen's system of socialism is so close to our own that it might be said that they merge. His fundamental principle, as ours, is Fraternity. He has no wish, any more than we have, to rob or oppress any man; like us he has but one desire, to extend and to even up, so to speak, the happiness of all.

The 'reception' was likewise reported in *La Voix des Femmes* of 6 April 1848:

He [Cabet] first introduced Robert Owen to his deeply-moved audience. This old man has for fifty years had as his sole aim the happiness of the workers, and has now, at the age of seventy, come to Paris – this enlivening focus of action – to share in the emotion. . . . As he was unable to express himself in the French tongue, Robert Owen has promised a written reply to the meeting's enthusiastic welcome. . . .

According to M. Dolléans, this written reply was the opuscule which appeared in the following year as *The Revolution in the Mind and Practice of the Human Race*.[77]

April 1848 saw the appearance of Owen's *Dialogue between France, the World and Robert Owen on the Necessity for a Total Change in Our Systems of Education and Government* (Paris) 36 pp. In that month, too, appeared 'Robert Owen and his System' in *Démocratie Pacifique*, 24–5 April 1848. These were reflections, both sympathetic and critical, on the publication by 'the famous English socialist' of a 'French translation of the summary of his social and philosophical system'. It was found to contain 'excellent sentiments and a not unoriginal turn of mind'. The public was encouraged, moreover, to 'meditate upon all socialist labours' and were even given the address from which the document might be obtained: 'Hotel des Bains de Tivoli, rue Saint-Lazare.' Nevertheless, 'the System of Robert Owen is essentially different from our own Social theory', his electoral system deserving special criticism.

There were other contributions from Owen in this period: *Dialogue between the Members of the Executive Committee, the Ambassadors of England, Russia, Austria, Prussia and the United States and Robert Owen. Second Dialogue on the Social System of Robert Owen* (Paris, 1848); *Address to the French Assembly, by Robert Owen, Founder of the Rational Social System* (Paris, May 1848); *Proclamation to the French People* – a poster, 1 June 1848; and Robert Owen, 'Letter in Reply to M. Thiers',

*Journal des Débats*, 9 July 1848.

In the last-named work Owen took up the challenge of Thiers, who alleged it was impossible to guarantee the right to work by full employment: 'It is an honest avowal. I accept its terms and I claim that it is impossible to guarantee constant and useful employment to all workers. . . . I am asking to be permitted to treat this question thoroughly before the entire National Assembly.' This 'thorough treatment' was proposed in Owen's *Short Exposition of a Rational System, followed by Three Replies to the Journals Le Corsaire, Le Constitutionnel and Le Journal des Débats* (Paris, July 1848).[78] On the question of the right to work by means of full employment, Owen credited his system with this power in answer to Thiers's original challenge. Owen had, in fact, no doubt that his system had proved itself in New Lanark 'over a period of thirty years, in a settlement of 2500 people', in Ireland, with an 'association of 43 unfortunates who had neither faith nor law' (an allusion to Ralahine), and even in America with 'a colony of 500 Wurtemburgers' (*sic*). This was the Rappite colony, and Owen prided himself somewhat groundlessly on having 'counselled the same system'.

## (b) From Owenism to Owenology

In France, as in Britain, Owen remained important enough for his system to receive sporadic evaluation and criticism.

In 1848, V. Considérant discussed 'The Co-operative System of Owen' in his *Socialism before the Old World, or the Living before the Dead* (Paris) pp. 32–3. In this work Owen is credited with having 'conceived the idea of co-operation and its immeasurable economic and productive virtues'. On the other hand,

it is the Utopia of the great communist . . . the virtuous Thomas More, revived in an industrial age by a manufacturer filled with gentleness, benevolence and love of humankind, but who places far too much reliance on the moulding influence of education, and far too little on the passions, which cannot be forced into a mould.

As a concept, it takes a more sentimental than scientific view of the principle of co-operation and collectivism. As a system, it shows the errors of a mind lacking invention, depth and genius, led on by a heart of gold and deceived by an extreme goodwill, even though that mind be furnished with a great practical knowledge of modern industry.

In 1848, too, Alfred Sudre published his *History of Communism, or a Historical Refutation of Socialist Utopias* (Paris). This was 'a work which won, in 1849, the Grand Prix Montyon, awarded by the Académie Française'. There were several editions, including the third of 1850. Chapter xv deals with 'Owen, Saint-Simon, Charles Fourier'. Owen is dealt with on pp. 308–9:

> The Co-operative Societies of the founder of New Harmony are merely the reproduction of the communistic cities of which More, Campanella, Morelly and Mably drew up plans. . . . The dogma of the necessity of human actions and of irresponsibility . . . is fundamentally the same doctrine as that preached by the Anabaptists under the name of Impeccability. . . . The economic arrangements of his rational system are precisely those which Babeuf and his followers had recently been trying to bring to fulfilment. Barely sixteen years separate the attempt of *Les Égaux* from the moment when Mr Owen raised to the status of a social system the happy exception of New Lanark. On the one side and on the other the aim was the same; only the means differed.

### 1851

Three years later came Proudhon's *General Idea of Revolution in the XIX Century* (1851; new ed., Paris, 1868). In this work Robert Owen's 'system' incurred the same all-embracing reprobation that Proudhon gave to any associationist 'dogma':

> What is Association? A dogma.
> Association, in the eyes of those who propose it as a revolutionary device, is so much of a *dogma*, something fixed, perfected, absolute and immutable, that everyone who has stumbled into this Utopia has ended up without exception in a *system*. . . .
> In this way, the Saint-Simonian school, going beyond the date of its founder, has produced a system; Fourier, a system; *Owen, a system* [author's italics], and all these mutually exclusive systems are equally exclusive of progress. Let mankind perish rather than the principle. Such is the slogan of the Utopians, as it is of fanatics in every century. . . .
> Socialism, thus interpreted, has become a religion which might have passed, five or six hundred years ago, for an improvement on Catholicism, but now in the nineteenth century there is nothing less revolutionary.[79]

*1852*

Meanwhile the direct link between Owen and Cabet was maintained. The latter made a speech at a celebration of Owen's eighty-third birthday (May 1852?). According to P. Leroux, 'Cabet speaks and speaks well. Those who think that Cabet wrote very badly would never believe how well he spoke. The subject was a splendid one, of course.'[80]

*1856*

On 31 December 1856, Owen wrote to Louis Blanc, who was requesting financial assistance for Madame Cabet: 'Poor Cabet; I used to know him during his exile in England. He was a follower of mine and frequently visited me. Of his sincerity and ardent desire to better the condition of men to the best of his particular understanding, none who has known him as well as I can doubt.'[81]

Cabet, on the other hand, claimed that Owen did not discover French 'communautairisme' until 1847, and that he had asked to read his biography, receive his publications and widen his understanding (*Réalisation de la Communauté d'Icarie*, bk iv, p. 155).

*1863–4*

In the second part of the nineteenth century there are miscellaneous references to Owen in a wide variety of French publications. Pierre Leroux's *La Grève de Samarez* (Paris, 1863–4) devotes long passages to Owen and Cabet. He states, for instance, that Cabet's *Voyage en Icarie* is 'basically nothing but an imitation of the practical trials of Robert Owen, magnified and exaggerated as far as the supposed future progress of mechanics can make it'. So Cabetism is nothing more than a barely transposed form of Owenism; and, what is worse, disguising its true source the more it 'perverts' it. 'There is the proof: Cabet is one of Owen's conquests. . . . Of course, Owen's thought is not revived in its entirety in the doctrines of Cabet. . . . Icarian communism is Owenism, but it is Owenism stripped of its philosophy, reduced in its material aspect to its simplest expression, i.e. man served by machines . . .' (p. 360).

All this is, of course, disputed territory. J. P. Prudhommeaux has, I feel, underestimated Owen's influence on Cabet; J. Gans, adopting Leroux's point of view, tends to overestimate it.[82] C. H. Johnson refers the matter to a thesis concerning 'Cabet's Thought and Specifically his Debt to Owen'.[83]

### 1868, 1873

There are mentions of Owen in a Fourierist journal, *La Science Sociale*, October and 16 November 1868. See also Martin Nadaud's *Les Sociétés Ouvrières* (Paris, 1873) pp. 15ff., and the same author's *History of the Working Classes in England*. It is equally advisable to consult the recollections of other French exiles such as Louis Blanc, Ledru-Rollin, Esquiros, etc. The French image of Owen came, however, largely from an image of Rochdale, which in its turn was embellished by Holyoake, who assiduously attended the Co-operative Congresses from 1885 to the end of the century.

### 1881

In 1881 Francesco Vigano translated G. J. Holyoake's *History of the Equitable Pioneers of Rochdale*. Holyoake's book (1857) in fact tempted several French translators during the nineteenth century. See, for instance, A Talandrier in the *Progrès de Lyon*, 6, 13, 21 October; 3, 17 November; 1, 15 December 1862; March–April 1863. Madame Godin-Moret, the wife of the Fourierist manufacturer, T. G. A. Godin, made a pamphlet of it (2nd ed., 1890). Later O. Cambier produced *Self-Help by the People: a History of the Rochdale Co-operative*, by G. J. Holyoake (Paris, 1888).

### 1883–4

An interesting résumé translated from the documents of Messrs Lloyd Jones and J. Humphrey Noyes', entitled 'The Life, Times and Works of Robert Owen', was published in *Le Devoir* (Journal du Familistère de Guise). The details are 1883: 423–6, 439–41, 456–8, 472–4, 488–90, 505–8, 522–4, 536–8, 553–5, 585–8, 596–9, 613–16,

629–32, 648–51, 661–4, 678–80, 714–16, 729–31, 748–50, 763–5, 778–81, 792–5, 812–15, 824–6; 1884: 8–10, 27–30, 43–4, 59–60.


## 1894

The same journal later published articles containing two pamphlets by Auguste Fabre. These were entitled *Two Episodes in the Life of Robert Owen* (Nîmes, 1894) 16 pp. The first dealt with New Lanark, the second with New Harmony (with an enumeration of its seven constitutions). 'The success of one and the failure of the other', the author opined, 'was readily explicable: the experimental conditions were not the same.' There is mention of the last moments of Owen's life. Replying to the admonitions of a clergyman, he is reported to have said: 'No, sir, my life has not been spent uselessly. I have proclaimed important truths to the world, and they have not been accepted. The world has not understood them. How should I blame the world? I am in advance of my times . . .' (p. 4).


## 1895

A year later H. Denis published an article in the *Annales de l'Institut des Sciences Sociales* (1895) in which, according to Dolléans, [84] he criticised Owen's plan:

> Owen wished to ensure the independence of the workers relative to the holders of the purchasing power which all wealth has, by giving the products of labour that purchasing power before any exchange took place. He tried expressly to isolate the purchasing power of work, independent of any exchange and anticipatory of any change; while Proudhon attributed unlimited purchasing power only to those values constituted by exchange effected between individuals.


## 1896

In 1896 M. de Wyzeva in *Petit Temps* published the 'Mémoires' of Mme Smirnoff. The issue of 19 November 1896 contained details of the conversation between Robert Owen and the Grand Duke Nicholas (later Emperor), who had planned to set up a New Lanark in Russia.

In the same year Auguste Fabre published *A Practical Socialist: Robert Owen* (Nîmes, 1896) 136 pp. Charles Gide, whilst admitting his preference for Fourierist beliefs and tendencies, in his preface to the work pays Owen a respect which is guarded, chauvinistic, professorial, undoubtedly ill-informed, yet at the same time bursting with enthusiasm:

> Owen did not have the brilliant ideas of a Fourier or a Saint-Simon. He was no scholar; he never wrote a long, sustained work, but rather an infinite number of pamphlets, those short treatises which correspond so well to English taste and genius (*sic*), and which he broadcast with a prodigality that seems rather ridiculous to us, yet which is more effective than one might think. . . . For eighty years he led the least contemplative and most active life that could be imagined. No other socialist has done more than he: others are greatly superior to him in eloquence, boldness, profundity of thought, and critical power; others have demolished more and in that way have made a bigger name for themselves in the world. Yet no one, I repeat, has exercised a more powerful influence, nor brought into being more positive social reforms. It might even be said that we are indebted to him for the only two great socialist experiments to succeed in this century.

> The first is the Co-operative movement – directly and incontestably descended from Owen.

> The second is industrial legislation: 'We are rather disposed to believe that Owen considered legislative reform as the preliminary condition of the development of co-operative associations. And this is altogether our opinion . . .' (pp. x–xiii).

As Charles Gide tells us in his *Memoirs* (l'École de Nimes, pp. 19ff.), Auguste Fabre was more of a Fourierist fellow-traveller, but his practical socialism, sustained by his visits to the Familistère de Godin, inclined him to approve the socialist – himself *practical* – that he believed he discerned in Owen. With Gide and de Boyve, he may be considered as the co-founder of that Nîmes school which, from 1885, was the pattern of the consumers' co-operative movement in France.[85]

## 1897

Fabre's work was followed by Albert Metin's *Socialism in England* (Paris, 1897). Chapter ii deals with 'The First English Socialism: Robert Owen and the Chartists' (pp. 63–8). On p. 47 we are told that 'Socialism, a doctrine distinct from the old radicalism, grew up in England around 1825 and found a champion in Owen. It was he who gave it the name it still retains.' This chapter is one of the least bad of French summaries of Owen's life and work.

### 1907

With Édouard Dolléans's *Robert Owen, 1771–1858* (1st ed., Paris, 1905; revised and augmented ed., 1907) appeared the first and, to date, the last scientifically planned general study, in French, devoted to Owen's life and work. More than anything else, in fact, it is a French translation of English documents, and especially of Owen's autobiography, which is extensively used. Dolléans, who was to become the great historian of Labour and Chartism, here gave Owen's influence its fullest due and suggested a very tempting hypothesis:

> Owen's influence has not been limited to its own age; it continues in the co-operative institutions, and in the laws relating to the protection of labour, which it initiated. His thought, amended by disciples with more modest and realistic ambitions, is the inspiration of the modern Co-operative movement. Finally, the ideas of Owen, which today are set up, under the name of utopian socialism, against so-called scientific socialism, remain the weft at which contemporary socialists busy themselves at the work of Penelope. (p. 58)

French versions of two texts are appended: *The Catechism of the New Moral World* (pp. 337–51) and *Robert Owen's Address to the Men and Women of France* (February 1848) which has been discussed above.

### 1905–63

The twentieth century has seen a number of studies, the data of which have been reclassified and incorporated in this present study. They are placed in this chronological series as a reminder.

Hubert Bourgin, *Fourier: A Contribution to the Study of French Socialism* (Paris, 1905) 620 pp. See especially pp. 106ff.

J. Prudhommeaux, *Icarie and its Founder, Joseph Cabet* (Paris, 1907).

F. Rude, 'A Forgotten Utopian Socialist: Joseph Rey, 1773–1855',

*Annales des Lettres de l'Université de Grenoble*, xx (1944), off-printed (Grenoble, 1944) 32 pp.

R. Pankhurst, *The Saint-Simonians, Mill and Carlyle* (London, 1957).

M. Rubel, 'Robert Owen in Paris, February and August 1848', *Archives Internationales de Sociologie de la Coopération*, vi (1959) 18–28.

M. Rubel, 'Robert Owen's Visit to Paris in 1848', *Actualité de l'Histoire* (Jan–Mar 1960) no. 30.

J. Gans, 'Robert Owen in Paris in 1837: A Glance at the Owenist Group in Paris', *Le Mouvement Social* (Oct–Dec 1962) no. 41, pp. 35–45.

A. L. Morton, *Robert Owen: Selected Texts with Introduction and Notes* (Paris, 1963, trans. Paul). Though written by an Englishman, this text, in its French translation, demands attention as being effectively the only anthology of Owen's writings readily available to the French reader. The introduction criticises 'the great mistake made by Dolléans in his book on Owen', which was 'to concentrate almost exclusively on the backward agrarian aspects of Owen's socialism'.

J. Gans, 'The Relations between English and French Socialists at the Beginning of the Nineteenth Century', *Le Mouvement Social* (Jan–Mar 1964) no. 46, pp. 105–18.

CONCLUSION

Dolléans's book can be seen as marking the transition in France between literature written by convinced Owenites, Owen's supporters or propagandists, and the scientific study of Owen and his doctrines. The latter is still rather small – witness the last half-dozen studies which have provided the bridgehead for the exploration of these hundred or so texts. Again, this exploration is not exhaustive. Even within its limits it remains summary, as can be seen from the shortcomings or gaps in certain items. We hope to amplify or complete it for this *Livre Blanc* of Owenism in France by which our French team would like, as far as it is able, to take part in the present commemoration.

Two impressions stand out for me:

The first is that this list does not bring into its orbit the great reciprocal influences which, in the second half of the nineteenth century, marked the contacts between, on the one hand, the English co-operators, among them the Christian Socialists, and on the other the

French co-operators, including the Christian Socialists of the Nîmes school, and which ended in their coming together on the platform of the Manifesto of 1892. Former Fourierists, like Godin, and former supporters of Owen, like G. J. Holyoake, stood together to defend, against the single dimension of the consumers' co-operatives, a multi-dimensionalism which seems to imply some nostalgia for Owenism. And here is perhaps the only point upon which I must take up Harrison on what he has to say about Holyoake and the latter's attachment to consumers' co-operatives. In fact, it was this same Holyoake who, in 1895, at the Congress which saw the formation of the I.C.A., became the unashamed advocate of the 'participationism' of the producers against the 'co-operatism' of the consumers. This is still an open question, and one cannot exclude the possibility that the Co-operative movement may see a return to Owenist thought.

The second impression is concerned with the effects of English Owenism and the French utopians upon each other. Their paths indeed crossed and re-crossed, yet the discernible influences remain slight, just as the successive projects for a common front were to come to little. On the contrary, despite the divergences made evident by the controversies between them, everything happened as though there were a structure – even a path – which was analagous, if not homologous; as though, in other words, the same *structural* constant had begun to *function* at the heart of all, with many genetic variations, *without, however, the direct intervention of one variation on the other proving decisive.* Is the structural analogy explicable in terms of the genetic analogy or vice versa? Another open question!

NOTES AND REFERENCES

1. J. F. C. Harrison, *Robert Owen and the Owenites in England and America* (London, 1969).
2. We realise that our observations would not fit comfortably in a history of social ideas, nor in a study of socialist heretics or saints, not in a chapter of philosophy, nor even in a museum of the Science of Man. Each of the references in the major text is a stem bearing a heavy cluster of lively events and dynamic paradoxes, of organisations and institutions by the dozen, of dissident or unorthodox offspring, of clandestine or open infiltration – in short, of the emergence of social attitudes.

3. Saint-Simon, *New Christianity*, translated, with notes and a preface, by J. E. Smith (London, 1834). A few years earlier Thomas Carlyle had himself completed a translation of this work, but failed to find a publisher. See R. Pankhurst, *The Saint-Simonians, Mill and Carlyle* (London, 1957) p. 32.

4. The contact is discussed later in the essay.

5. Harrison, *Robert Owen and the Owenites*, p. 244, n. 5, notes that the London Co-operative Society published a translation of Fourier in 1828. See also R. K. Pankhurst, "Fourierism in Britain", *International Review of Social History*, 1 3 (1956) 398–432. Hancock, the polemicist, went on to suggest that Owen's system was a pure and simple 'Englishification' of Saint-Simon. See E. Hancock, *Robert Owen's Community System, etc. . . . and the Horrid Doings of the Saint-Simonians* (1835).

6. An authority mentions one of Cabet's manuscripts, dating from this time: 'A Plan for a Community in England, by Cabet, Founder of the Icarian Colony in America'. In it Cabet declares: 'I can see in England so much inclination to carry out experiments in the interests of the people that, if I could stay a few more months, I might perhaps make the attempt.' See J. Prudhommeaux, *Icarie and its Founder, Joseph Cabet* (Paris, 1907) p. 273, n. 2.

7. These are:
For 1828: the apologia of Joseph Rey.
For 1831: the pamphlet of Charles Fourier.
For 1838: the 'Studies' of Reybaud.
For 1848: the anti-Utopia of Sudre.
For 1905: the sole essay, unfortunately, by Dolléans on Owen.
For 1927–8: the allusive historical sketch by Charles Gide.

8. 'At this point Owenism ceased to be a *legacy* and became a *legend*' Harrison, *Robert Owen and the Owenites*, p. 254). 'It had come to be regarded not as a *legacy* but as a *relic*' (ibid., p. 260).

9. Ibid., p. 254, n. 1.

10. Ibid., p. 260.

11. In spite of the attempt at compilation represented by J. Walch, *Bibliographie du Saint-Simonisme* (Paris, 1967).

12. See E. Poulat, *A Reasoned Inventory of the Manuscript Notebooks of Charles Fourier* (Paris, 1957).

13. H. Desroche, 'Fourierism in Theory and Practice', in Poulat, *Reasoned Inventory*, pp. 5–36.

14. There is, moreover, a paradox here: in the last two decades the abstract, theoretical study of Utopia has seemed ready to blossom or to blossom anew, whereas the last two years seem to have seen the concrete political nostalgia for Utopia obliged to express itself in behaviour and convulsions of the most immediate urgency; this generality or this ferment seem to remain allergic to the empirical documentary analysis of the great records of the nineteenth century. As Saint-Simon wrote, 'Our children will think they have imagination; they will have only vague recollections'. Or as Marx objected to W. Weitling, a utopian already fairly subject to convulsions, 'Ignorance has never been of use to anybody'. At least we, in our hexagon, are to be numbered among those who take a profound and eager interest in this commemoration of Robert Owen, and bring to it our modest contribution.

15. J. Gans, 'The Relations between English and French Socialists at the Beginning of the Nineteenth Century', *Le Mouvement Social* (Jan–Mar 1964) no. 46, pp. 105–18. This text will be referred to subsequently as *Gans 46*. Messrs Gans and Rubel, apart from their writings, have also given us the benefit of their conversation and advice. Our gratitude must likewise be expressed to M. Abensour of C.N.R.S., a specialist on Dezamy, whose references have verified or completed the notes.

16. Ibid., p. 105.

17. H. Bourgin, *Fourier: A Contribution to the Study of French Socialism* (Paris, 1905) p. 107. M. Bourgin gives this reference without guaranteeing the place or date. These are, however, confirmed by Jullien de Paris, who states that the memorial was 'printed simultaneously in English, French and German tongues'. The contribution of Jullien de Paris to French Owenism is discussed later in the essay.

18. Ibid., p. 106. 'He was pleased to see Owen as a sort of precursor whom he would try to draw a little closer to himself.'

19. Ibid., pp. 110–11.

20. 'I was sent a very late note [8 July 1821] in which I see that in Paris there are some supporters of Association who want and are trying to discover an effective procedure: *the said note, signed Huard,* is to be found in the *Mémorial Universel de l'Industrie Française*, June 5 4th instalment. It contains a description of Mr Owen's establishment at New Lanark.' Charles Fourier, *Théorie de l'Unité Universelle*, vol. 2, in *Complete works*, III 7.

21. Charles Fourier, *Treatise on Domestic Agricultural Association*, 1st ed. (Paris and London, 1822); 2nd ed., entitled *Theory of Universal Unity* (1834) 4 vols. See vols II to V of the *Complete Works* (Éditions Anthropos, Paris, 1966). In other words, Owen was searching for what Fourier believed himself to have found: 'The article mentioned designates by name several distinguished personages living in Paris, who are working to spread the spirit of Association and to support those establishments which appear conducive to it: they should be happy to learn that the secret the two nations were searching for in vain has been discovered. It remains to be seen which of the two will outstrip the other in this new orbit and bear away the palm . . .' (III 7–9).

22. Ibid., p. 42. The same sentiments to a pioneer settlement are found: 'We were not thinking of undertaking such experiments: Mr Owen's institution is the first which is visibly conducive to this goal' (p. 43).

23. Manuscript draft reproduced in *Gans 46*, p. 110, and dated 1827 by M. Gans. My italics.

24. My italics. The *Revue* had already presented the translation of the work of H. G. Macnab by Ladébat. Jullien de Paris had also read de Lasteyrie's translation of Owen's *Memorial*.

25. *Gans 46*, p. 107.

26. J. Gans, 'Robert Owen in Paris in 1837: A Glance at an Owenite Group in Paris', *Le Mouvement Social* (Oct–Dec 1962) no. 41, pp. 35–45. This text will be referred to subsequently as *Gans 41*.

27. Bourgin, *Fourier*, p. 111.

28. Fourier's first letter is with a copy of one of his works. The reply (28 June 1824) is lodged in the Fourierist boxes in the Archives Nationales. Fourier's

second letter (17 September 1824) was found in the Archives and published. See *Gans 46*, pp. 108–9.

29. On Motherwell, see Harrison, *Robert Owen and the Owenites*, pp. 28–31, 153 n., 169–72ff.

30. Before returning to England, where she would distinguish herself by her zeal in arranging meetings between Owenites, Saint-Simonians and Fourierists (ibid., p. 113), Anna Wheeler had displayed the same zeal in Paris: 'In 1826 she was in touch with both Saint-Simonians and Fourier in France, and the Owenites in England. She does not seem to have distinguished very clearly between the three doctrines, but rather to have looked on them as three aspects of the same attitude towards society. *It was under her roof that Fourier met the Owenites. . . .*' *Gans 46*, pp. 110–11 (my italics). After attempting to 'Owenise' Fourier, she tried, on returning to England, to 'Fourierise' if not the Owenites at least English social opinion. M. Gans quotes several letters in support of this. Apart from her link with the editor of the *Crisis*, she seems to have been on intimate terms with Jeanne Désirée Véret. See R. K. Pankhurst, 'Anna Wheeler: A Pioneer Socialist and Feminist', *Political Quarterly*, XXV (1954) 132–43.

31. *Gans 41*, p. 35. Among the members of this society were Owen's translator, de Lasteyrie, Radiguet, 'the correspondent of the London Co-operative Society' and most likely secretary of that in Paris, in the name of which he would badger Fourier. The files of this organisation are in the Joseph Rey records in the Archives de Grenoble.

*Le Producteur* was the first Saint-Simonian journal to be founded after Saint-Simon's death, which took place in 1825. Two issues of the journal contained the first two of Rey's letters; the third remained in abeyance when the journal ceased publication. It was published in 1828, together with the first two.

32. See Bourgin, *Fourier*, p. 107; *Gans 41*, p. 35; *Gans 46*, p. 110.

33. Bourgin gives the date as 14 April, Gans as 4 April 1827.

34. *Gans 46*, p. 111. An analysis and commentary appears in F. Rude, 'A Forgotten Utopian Socialist: Joseph Rey', *Annales des Lettres de l'Université de Grenoble*, XX (1944), offprinted (Grenoble, 1944) 32 pp. H. Bourgin represents Rey as 'one of the main followers and propagandists of Owenism in France'. It would be truer to say *the* main follower. In fact it can be asserted that it was Rey who actually introduced into our country the doctrine of the reformer from across the Channel. One English Owenite, Thornton, sent the assurance of his respect and esteem to him who (he said) 'has done most to make known in France the ideas of our venerable reformer . . .'. Rude, op. cit., p. 31.

35. F. Rude stresses the sustained friendly relations of the two writers.

36. 'Perhaps because of the failure of the Owenite experiments'. See *Gans 46*, p. 106.

37. *Gans 41*, p. 35. On the Society for Christian Morality, see J. B. Duroselle, *Origines du Catholicisme Social*.

38. See Pankhurst, *The Saint-Simonians, Mill and Carlyle*, pp. 6ff.

39. *Gans 41*, p. 36.

40. Rude, op. cit., p. 19.

41. For background, see Pankhurst, *The Saint-Simonians, Mill and Carlyle*, pp. 45–6. This account remedies the deficiencies of H. d'Allemagne, *Les Saint-Simoniens*, pp. 155–6.

42. *Gans 46*, p. 113.

43. Pankhurst, *The Saint-Simonians, Mill and Carlyle*, p. 59.

44. d'Allemagne, *Les Saint-Simoniens*, p. 156.

45. The letter quoted is of 11 April 1832. *Gans 46*, p. 112.

46. Ibid., p. 111. A number of extracts are quoted.

47. Ibid., p. 112, letter to Fourier. The same note is sounded in *La Tribune des Femmes* (Oct 1833).

48. Pankhurst, *The Saint-Simonians, Mill and Carlyle*, pp. 101ff.

49. On Smith, see Harrison, *Robert Owen and the Owenites*, passim (see index, p. 578).

50. *Gans 46*, p. 113. This contains extracts.

51. Ibid., p. 113.

52. Ibid., p. 114.

53. Ibid., p. 113. M. Gans dates the letter 'from this period'.

54. Prudhommeaux, *Icarie and its Founder*.

55. Pierre Leroux, *La Grève de Samarez*, tome 2.

56. Prudhommeaux, *Icarie and its Founder*, pp. 136–7.

57. *Gans 46*, p. 114.

58. In the Archives Sociétaires.

59. Prudhommeaux, *Icarie and its Founder*, p. 139n. On the Texas project, see C. H. Johnson, 'Étienne Cabet and the Icarian Movement in France, 1839–1948', thesis (University of Wisconsin, 1968) pp. 558ff.

60. *Gans 41*, p. 37.

61. Ibid.

62. Exchanges in detail given in *Gans 41*, pp. 37–8.

63. M. Gans unfortunately provides conflicting evidence. In 1962 he opines (*Gans 41*, p. 38): 'It seems unlikely that the two reformers took the opportunity offered in this first and probably unique encounter to talk things over. There could be no more, as Fourier died three months later.' Yet in 1964 the writer seems to affirm the meetings (*Gans 46*, p. 110): 'During a visit to Paris in 1837, *Owen was taken to see Fourier*, who was to die a few weeks later.'

64. *Gans 41*, p. 44.

65. From the Archives Sociétaires. See *Gans 41*, p. 42.

66. *Gans 41*, p. 45.

67. Leroux, *La Grève de Samarez*, p. 38; V. Considérant in a note in records mentioned in *Gans 46*, p. 115.

68. *Gans 41*, p. 45.

69. Rude, op. cit., p. 26.

70. Prudhommeaux, *Icarie and its Founder*, p. 137.

71. *Gans 46*, p. 115.

72. Letter reproduced in *Gans 46*, pp. 116–17.

73. Letter from the Owen Archives, Manchester. Quoted in *Gans 46*, p. 116.

74. Owen's own plans regarding Texas have been discussed elsewhere. See Wilbert H. Timmons, 'Robert Owen's Texas Project', *Southwestern Historical Quarterly*, 11 Jan 1949.

75. M. Rubel, 'Robert Owen's Visit to Paris in 1848', *Actualité de l'Histoire* (Jan–Mar 1960) no. 60, p. 1. The text is reprinted in E. Dolléans, *Robert Owen, 1771–1858* (1st ed., Paris, 1905; revised and augmented ed., 1907) pp. 353–6.

76. Rubel, op. cit., pp. 2–3.

77. Dolléans, *Robert Owen*, p. 107.

78. The whole text is given in M. Rubel, 'Robert Owen in Paris, February and August 1848', *Archives Internationales de Sociologie de la Coopération*, VI (1959) 19–20.

79. 1868 ed., pp. 79–80.

80. Leroux, *Le Grève de Samarez*, I 380.

81. Quoted in *Gans 46*, p. 114.

82. Ibid., pp. 114–15.

83. The reference is to Judi Bullerwell, 'Cabet's Thought and his Relations with Robert Owen'.

84. Dolléans, *Robert Owen*, p. 276.

85. Charles Gide also wrote *Communistic and Co-operative Settlements* (Paris, 1927–8). On Owen, he wrote: 'Owen had brought into being [at New Lanark] almost every kind of patronal institution and had sketched out the entire work of labour legislation in the nineteenth century. One appreciates these reforms all the more when one realises that they were brought into being at the darkest moment in the history of labour' (p. 123).

On the likenesses between Owen and Fourier, Gide writes on pp. 124–6. On their antagonism, he declares: 'Owen, who was rich and famous, was profoundly ignorant of this petty clerk and never attached the slightest importance to his lucubrations. As for Fourier, he had many reasons for hating Owen: firstly, because Owen was an Englishman and, like all good Frenchmen in the first half of the nineteenth century, Fourier loathed perfidious Albion; but also because Fourier hated businessmen, and to him England was a land of businessmen' (pp. 126–7).

'. . . the real communist of the two was Owen, the great industrial capitalist, while Fourier, contrary to what one might think, was never a communist at all, but simply a partisan of co-operatives' (p. 127). The Owenite colonies in the United States are discussed on pp. 127–30 of Gide's work.

# CHAPTER TWELVE

# The Impact of Owen's Ideas on German Social and Co-operative Thought during the Nineteenth Century

## E. HASSELMANN

IN 1840 there appeared a small volume with a long title, published by Ernst Friedrich Fürst in Nordhausen. It was the *Book of the New Moral World* by Robert Owen, translated from the eighth English edition. The German title ran as follows: *Das Buch der Neuen Moralischen Welt, enthaltend die Grundsätze eines vernünftigen Systems der Gesellschaft, auf beweisbaren Thatsachen begründet, die Constitution und Gesetze der menschlichen Natur und der Gesellschaft enthüllend, der Wahrheit gewidmet, ohne Geheimnisse, ohne Beimischung von Irrthum, ohne Furcht vor Menschen.*[1] No details are known of the fate of this book, which certainly represents the first effort to make the German public acquainted with the ideas of Robert Owen. It was not a large publishing house which stood behind this venture, and it did not appear to have had a large success either, for evidently this first try-out did not find an imitator.

Perhaps we may say that this book appeared too early to find a fertile soil in Germany for the thoughts of Owen. The great social movements, the trade union movement, the co-operative movement and the varied socialist groupings had not yet appeared in 1840, and they did not even exist in embryo.

To be sure, a labour question did exist in Germany in 1840, as well as exploitation of labour and workers' misery. But factory labour was not yet the mass phenomenon in Germany that it had become in England and Scotland. Germany was still predominantly an agrarian country, and handicrafts were controlled by the guilds. German manufacturing industry was still so small that it could not even supply the home market. The products of British industry flooded the German market which remained without adequate tariff protection even after the foundation of the German Customs Union in 1833. It was only towards the end of the 1840s and in the 1850s that capitalist firms appeared in larger numbers, made possible by the financing of industrial and transport undertakings by the banks or similar financial institutions, and by the rise of joint-stock companies. That was the period in which a dynamic spirit of enterprise, and with it speculation and the seeking after profit, established themselves in the German economy.

That was the period also which saw the first deliberate defensive action of the labouring classes, following scattered earlier strikes and, in 1844, the year of the foundation of the Rochdale Pioneers' Society, the weavers' revolt in Silesia.

It was in that period that the first co-operative ideas make their appearance in Germany. The first attempts at trade union – co-operative organisation, in which something like a self-consciousness and a sense of mission of the German working class are evinced, occur in 1848, the year of revolution. Even before these revolutionary events, there had appeared early in 1848 in London the *Communist Manifesto*, in the German language, written by Karl Marx and Friedrich Engels who had been given this task in November 1847 by a meeting of the secret 'League of Communists'. This *Communist Manifesto* was destined later to exert an extraordinary influence on the working classes – and not only on them. The historical interpretation of dialectical materialism contained in it became the foundation of an ideology of the class struggle among major political movements and later, in a vulgarised form, of the 'scientific' ideology of totalitarian political systems and social organisations.

In the *Communist Manifesto* we meet for the first time a German critique of Robert Owen, or at any rate a critique expressed by Germans in the German language, that was to have important consequences. Although it pretends to be an understanding and explanatory critique, it has in fact contributed more than any other critical expression to the condemnation of Robert Owen's ideas *in toto* as 'utopian'. Since the opinion expressed in this critique became quasi-official as soon as the labour movement became 'Marxian', it became a barrier which prevented the thinking of the majority of German workers from reaching a just appreciation of the ideas and social achievements of Robert Owen.

There have been more severe criticisms of Robert Owen than those of Marx, but no other had the same devastating effect. The branding of Robert Owen as a utopian was taken over by many economists who in other respects rejected Marx. And certainly this branding has contributed to the fact that other economists did not think it important, and even today do not think it important, to concern themselves seriously with Robert Owen and his ideas. What, for example, can be said of a *History of Economic Theory* by L. J. Zimmermann, translated from the Dutch and published by the trade-union-owned 'Bund' publishing firm in Cologne-Deutz in 1954 which does 'justice' to Robert Owen in the following manner: 'Many of Bellers' (*sic*) ideas reappear in Robert Owen. Owen advocated the foundation of consumers' co-operatives. The first English consumers' co-operative society, the 'Rochdale Equitable Pioneers' Society', owed its foundation to his influence.' That is all – and not a single statement in it is correct. (Even the suggestion that Owen derived his ideas from John Bellers appears to be misleading, for according to Margaret Cole, Owen's ideas were already 'firmly formulated' before he had read Bellers' *Proposals for Raising a College of Industry*.)[2]

The critique contained in the *Communist Manifesto* of the 'socialist and communist systems' of Saint-Simon, Fourier and Owen furnishes a good example of the havoc which a correct heuristic principle can cause when it is put in absolute terms and is used with a political motive. Nobody will dispute today that there is a connection between conditions of production, social relationships and the superstructure of ideas. But to characterise out of existence the ideas of Owen and of the other 'utopian' socialists because of their origin in the 'undeveloped period of the struggle between the proletariat and the bourgeoisie' is a terrible oversimplification – and it is doubly terrible because it did not derive from honest motives, but from the intention to kill off intellectual competition as politically impotent before it could get going. However much we may admire Karl Marx's achievements in other respects, this was not something to be proud of.

Of course, it may be said that the *Communist Manifesto* was deliberately designed for its political impact and therefore had to simplify and, no doubt, be reduced to crudeness also. But as far as Robert Owen was concerned, Marx did not apparently at any later time find any opportunity of re-examining his attitude towards Robert Owen either, or even to explain it. At any rate, this much may be said: Marx without a doubt considers Owen to have been the most significant among the utopian socialists. Thus, in the third volume of *Capital*, he explains after a sharp criticism of Saint-Simon's writings: 'What difference compared with the contemporary writings of Owen!'[3] In a footnote, Friedrich Engels then mitigates the criticism of Saint-Simon and explains why Owen could 'see further' than Saint-Simon, on the grounds of living 'in the midst of the Industrial Revolution and of class antagonism coming sharply to a head'. Much later, in 1891, Engels was to claim Owen as a precursor of German socialism in an oft-quoted passage. 'We German socialists', he said, 'are proud to derive not only from Fourier, Saint-Simon and Owen, but also from Kant, Fichte and Hegel.' However, with the best will in the world it cannot be said that the German socialists have taken great care over the inheritance which has come down to them from these ancestors. What is astonishing is that Marx does not mention once in all his detailed description of the struggle for shorter hours in England and the British factory legislation, to be found in *Capital*, Robert Owen's internal factory reforms at New Lanark and Owen's initiative in the legal limitation of the working day and regulation of child labour. Evidently he was ignorant of it. He knew apparently only Robert Owen the utopian. He does not recognise that this 'utopian' developed lines of thought on labour value and surplus value similar to Marx's own in many respects. Owen – just like Marx – had drawn social conclusions from these lines of thinking, which, however, were very different from those drawn by Marx. Their views on the class struggle differed quite fundamentally, though this cannot be treated in any detail here. But there is no doubt that it is in this very different judgement on the class struggle that we have to look for the cause of Marx's low esteem for Robert Owen.

The first labour movement possessing social aims in Germany, which began with the General German Workers' Congress in 1848, was not under any noticeable influence of Marxist ideas. This congress took place in Berlin from 23 August until 3 September. It resulted in the foundation of a labour organisation under the title of the 'Labour Brotherhood' (*Arbeiter-Verbrüderung*). The leading light of this movement was Stephen Born, who had met Marx and Engels but had not become a Marxist. The much-travelled, well-read, thoughtful and talented Born, a typographer who later became Professor of Philosophy at Basle, did without doubt know something of Owen. The programme of the 'Labour Brotherhood' was an amalgam of concepts derived from producers' co-operatives, consumers' co-operatives and trade unions. The members of the Brotherhood were to join together in 'associations', to produce collectively, to exchange their products according to their 'true value' – i.e. according to their labour value at the lowest costs of production – and jointly to purchase or produce their required consumption goods. The programme even included the purchase of landed settlements for the purpose of joint cultivation by the members, as well as social welfare provisions, the satisfaction of their educational needs and representation of the labour interests of the members of these associations against their employers. This was not a pure Owenite programme, but several of its items are strongly reminiscent of Owenite concepts and demands. Unfortunately, the Labour Brotherhood was able to realise very little of its ambition. It spread quickly across Germany, and in its heyday it had about 250 local branches, but the stronger it became, and the more insistent in its demand for better conditions of labour for the workers, the more suspect it became to the authorities and the police. Born had to flee in May 1849; he had, together with Richard Wagner, taken part in the revolt in Dresden. The Labour Brotherhood was prohibited or closed down by the police in one Federal state after another; finally it was dissolved in 1854 over the territory of the Confederation as a whole. Whether the Labour Brotherhood would have developed, had it not been persecuted, in different directions, towards co-operation, trade unionism or perhaps even politics, is an open question. In that case it would certainly have been subject to a transformation of its body of ideas similar to the transformation which Owenite ideas underwent in England inside the trade union and co-operative movements. However that may be, the Labour Brotherhood seems to have been the sole social movement in Germany in which it is possible to recognise an undoubted intellectual kinship with Robert Owen. A direct influence of Robert Owen or of Owenite ideas can, however, not be proved. In the year in which the Labour Brotherhood was founded, Robert Owen did visit France, where after the outbreak of the Paris Revolution there existed a strongly marked readiness to try productive co-operative experiments. He had conversations with Louis Blanc, one of the leaders of the co-operative socialist labour movement. He lectured in Paris to the Comité du Travail on his system, and had some of his writings translated into French. Similar direct contacts never existed between Owen and Germany.

Possibly the experiences which Owen met with on his continental tour of 1818 in Germany may be held responsible for this. On that occasion he visited Frankfurt and Aachen (Aix-la-Chapelle), and he came into contact with many influential personalities, since the German Federal Diet sat in Frankfurt, and the Congress of the European powers was taking place in Aix-la-Chapelle. There, Owen handed to the British representative two memorials dealing with the creation of a lasting peace and the introduction of new economic principles. The British representative promised to put these memorials before the

Congress. Owen was told that these memorials had been 'recognised' – but they had no practical effects whatever. In Frankfurt, Owen met at a dinner given by the banker, Bethman, the Austrian diplomat, Friedrich von Gentz, and got involved in a dispute with him. This did him no good. Gentz, described by Golo Mann, one of the most acute present-day German historians, as 'the assistant and intellectual mentor of Metternich',[4] was as an individual the almost exact opposite of Robert Owen. He was an adaptable diplomatist of great ability, and a quick-witted political writer, who was always concerned with the rulers and their positions of power, while the 'people', those that were being ruled, held for him no interest whatever. It is therefore not surprising that Owen and Gentz found themselves in total opposition in their discussion. When Owen voiced his opinion that there was a good chance of a general improvement in the condition of the working population, Gentz replied, according to Owen's autobiography: 'We know that very well, but we do not like to see the masses comfortable and independent. How would we rule them otherwise?' Such an attitude must have shocked Owen deeply. He admits later that it opened his eyes to the relation of rulers and ruled. Perhaps no one had ever told him in Great Britain with such clarity what Gentz expressed. But in the end he did come to see that Gentz only expressed in words what many ruling sections in all countries thought – and practised.

Owen did not make contact with the lower strata of the population, to whom, after all, his efforts were devoted, nor with the democratic tendencies which already existed then in Germany (the 'Wartburg Festival' of the German students had taken place a year before Owen's visit, and the persecution of the 'demagogues' began the year after). They would have been more accessible to new ideas than the ruling circles that were intent merely to preserve intact the traditional systems of government that were already in part ossified and out of date.

Thus this first visit of Owen to Germany may have left a mark on Owen's ideas, but made no mark whatever on Germany. This may be the explanation for the fact that after that time Owen did not seem to have had any great hopes for Germany, though he did send his two sons to Hofwyl in Switzerland to go to Fellenberg's school, and made them learn German.

For three or four decades afterwards no Owenite influence can be discerned in Germany. Only when the German theories of co-operation begin to show signs of life and development around the middle of the century is there renewed interest in Robert Owen. At the same time the first co-operative societies were also being formed in Germany. It might have been supposed that these first co-operatives might have taken an interest at least in that part of Owen's heritage which had found its way into the administration of the Rochdale Pioneers. But this was not the case, at least until the first half of the 1860s. The reason for this was that those German co-operative societies which had some success and survived for any length of time were of a very different nature from the Rochdale Pioneers' Society, even where they were consumers' societies (and there were not many of those). Nearly all the co-operative societies founded in the 1850s were handicraft producers' co-operatives (the farmers followed a little later), most of them being 'loan societies', i.e. credit co-operatives, or, to a much smaller extent, 'raw-material societies', i.e. supply co-operatives for handicraftsmen. The few consumers' societies that did exist also had a petit-bourgeois character, their leaders and most of their members being craftsmen and office workers. These consumers' co-operatives had no wider co-operative ideas and aims beyond the cheapening of their cost of living, and for that reason they did not become a movement and did not grow into a community, but remained the odd men out in the handicraft co-operative movement.

The leading light of this movement was Hermann Schulze of Delitzsch (1808–83). He was a social-liberal in politics, a member of the Progressive Party which he represented first in the Prussian Diet and later in the German Parliament (Reichstag). He recognised, like Robert Owen, the devastating social consequences of the unrestricted development of capitalism. But he drew different conclusions from this recognition. He was not a revolutionary, and was not impelled by the vision of a new society. He wanted to preserve in existing society what he considered to be healthy and, despite all the dangers, to be capable of survival and development: this was for him, above all, the independent middle strata of society, and particularly the handicraftsmen. Co-operation seemed to him the best means for preserving and developing the small independent economic units in which he saw the chief supports for state and society. While he once described the productive co-operative as the 'glory' of his co-operative system, he did not conceive of it as a workers' co-operative, but as a co-operative of independent handicraftsmen, a combination of tradesmen's enterprises. He was involved in a most bitter dispute with the one political leader who was in favour of the wage worker's productive co-operative (supported by the state) as a possible solution of the social question

- Ferdinand Lassalle. Of consumers' co-operatives Schulze-Delitzsch thought little and Lassalle nothing at all: Lassalle, in fact, was strongly opposed to them. They did not fit easily into the Schulze-Delitzsch system of co-operation, and could not be squared in any sense with Lassalle's iron law of wages.

Although Schulze-Delitzsch allowed the consumer co-operative a certain limited right of existence, he neither approved of the highest flights of consumer co-operative aspirations derived from Owenite concepts, not did he ever fully accept the purely practical principles of Rochdale. Neither do his productive co-operative ideas make contact anywhere with the community ideas of Robert Owen. One will look in vain in the five volumes of collected works of the first great German co-operative leader, Hermann Schulze-Delitzsch, for a single mention of the name of Robert Owen in all its thousands of pages. Even in the chapter on associations in England and France in his book of associations for German handicraftsmen and workers which appeared in 1853, a chapter which incidentally shows but a superficial knowledge of the British co-operative movement, there is no reference to Robert Owen.

Much the same can be said in the case of Ferdinand Lassalle, the first great political leader of the German labour movement (if we except Marx and Engels). Although Lassalle has more points of contact, in his ideas of producers' co-operatives, with the thought system of Owen than had Schulze-Delitzsch, there is still nothing in his writings which would lead one to believe that he had given any thought to Robert Owen.

The pioneer of the German agricultural co-operative movement, Friedrich Wilhelm Raiffeisen (1818–88), had as the starting-point for his work for the suffering peasantry, the idea of the Christian love of one's neighbour; he originally tried to reduce the misery of the people on the land by charitable aid associations, until he found his way to co-operative self-help. He was in his whole system of thought a thorough conservative. He had little time for grand plans of social reform and was far more interested in directly effective small-scale operation. In his system of ideas there is virtually no link at all with Robert Owen, but he was not unlike the latter in his love of humanity and in his desire to help people to overcome their poverty and misery. Of course, Raiffeisen could never become a bridge for Owenite thought, since that system of thought, even had he known it, would have been alien to him.

This is the picture of the most prominent leaders of the organisations

of the first German co-operative movement, and the first labour movement of any size, as transmitters of Owenite ideas. They did not even
trouble to study him.

This does not, however, mean that there was no discussion at all of
Robert Owen in the early days of the German co-operative movement.
The first German co-operative theoretician, Victor Aimé Huber
(1800–69), not only knew the work of Robert Owen, he also took it
seriously and studied it in detail. Huber was a younger contemporary
of Robert Owen. Like Robert Owen, he was deeply affected by the
social consequences of the Industrial Revolution, and like Robert Owen
he was looking for a way out of the misery, the uprooting and the
isolation of the *worker*, and this search led him to co-operative thoughts.
Huber's co-operative thoughts had in certain detailed aspects some
similarity with the thoughts of Robert Owen. Huber also collected his
thoughts into a system. Here, however, the parallel ends and the lines
part company from each other, running on in opposite directions. The
chief reason for this lies in the respective personalities of the two men,
who were basically different despite their common traits. Without
attempting to describe fully the character of these two great figures of
British and German social history, we may indicate here in a few
headings the contrasts, and the points of contact, between these two
characters.

Victor Aimé Huber got to know Owen personally, probably without
being noticed by him. During his first journey to the Continent, Owen
had visited Switzerland and the school of Philippe Emanuel von
Fellenberg, conducted at Hofwyl in the spirit of Pestalozzi. One of the
scholars there was Victor Aimé Huber. Dr Helmut Faust, in his
*Geschichte der Genossenschaftsbewegung*,[5] mentions this early meeting of
Owen and Huber: 'The young Huber did not suspect that one day in
his later years he would follow in the footsteps of that great philanthropist, propagating the idea of co-operation. But when he later
looked back on his life, he nevertheless felt this meeting to have been
portentous. . . .'[6] Huber was then at a very impressionable age and it
is certainly feasible – even though not subject to proof – that it was
Owen who turned Huber's thoughts in the direction of the social
question. That he followed in Owen's 'footsteps' is, however, true in
only a very general sense. Huber could never have become a disciple
of Owen, but he had a high esteem for him as a human being, and he
took his ideas seriously even when he rejected them in the end.

His necessary rejection of Owen's principles derives from his own fundamental attitude to his surroundings, to society, and to history and its driving force. Huber was a conservative and a traditionalist by character. His critique of the new industrial society was not a revolutionary critique; on the contrary, he wanted to preserve whatever could be preserved of the pre-existing social ties, and create new communities having strongly authoritarian traits as guardians of Christian morality. He rejected the revolutionary and democratic demands of labour, he saw in them only the negative aspect and failed to understand what was positive in them. Therefore he was not understood by labour in turn, even though his social reformist thoughts were constantly devoted to the problems of industrial labour. In this respect he was more progressive than Schulze-Delitzsch, who never grasped what was specifically new in wage-labour relations – the degrading inhumanity and the atomising explosive power – and consequently never distinguished clearly between independent handicraftsmen and wage workers. Like Owen, Huber saw the effects of the Industrial Revolution in destroying the community, and like him, he was convinced that it was impossible to 'laisser passer' these social ill-effects, that one had to do something about them. Like Owen, he also saw in association the community-creating countervailing force. Thus Huber's co-operative ideas show a certain similarity with the ideas of Owen. This is not to be wondered at. For it was in England that Huber received the decisive impetus to a thorough preoccupation with the social question. In 1844 he visited England and became acquainted there with the concentrated misery of the new industrial towns and of their inhabitants. He recognised that industry threatened not only the outer aspects of life, but also the worker's inner existence and with it the survival of society itself. To be sure, he did not think that the causes were to be found in the conditions, but in the attitude of the employers. In this he differed from Owen, who believed in the power of circumstances and therefore wanted to change them first. Huber, on the contrary, expected everything from man's attitude, which could be changed only by educative example. Admittedly, he also wanted to create the preconditions for ensuring that the example should develop its full effect: the co-operative community. It is probable that the Christian Socialists, Frederick D. Maurice and Charles Kingsley, with whom, as a practising Christian, he was much in sympathy (and whom he had met during his first journey to England in 1844), had much greater influence on Huber than had Owen. But Huber later became acquainted with the Rochdale Pioneers' Society also and reported most positively about it in Germany, including their long-term aims inspired by Owenite thought.

Before that, however, in 1845, he had developed the idea of 'inner colonisation' from which he was never thereafter to depart. By inner colonisation he meant the foundation of workers' settlements, which were not quite to become the self-supporting communities in Owen's sense, but nevertheless were to be communal settlements, making common purchases for their members and possessing a central large building in which all the functions of the communal household and the communal life should be concentrated: store and shop, grain mill, bakehouse, abattoir, brewery, office and assembly rooms. If conditions were favourable, he even proposed to combine agricultural cultivation with the settlement. In 1848 Huber published his volume *Die Selbsthilfe der arbeitenden Klassen durch Wirtschaftsvereine und innere Ansiedlung*,[7] in which he propagated his thoughts of working-class settlements. It could not be said that his ideas had much success. A 'community-building society', founded in Berlin with his participation, collapsed again after a few years. Even then, it was merely intended to develop the communal building component of Huber's plan; the whole plan was never – at least at that time – put into practice. Even if this plan recalls in many details the Owenite communal settlement, it yet lacks the core of the Owenite community, the productive co-operative. Huber did not want to create 'self-supporting colonies', he merely wanted to improve the living conditions of the workers, without removing the labourer himself out of the capitalist system. Thus the Huber settlements would never become nuclei of a new economic order, and it is therefore not surprising that no missionary zeal and no revolutionary *élan* ever attached themselves to Huber's ideas, and that they did not become the programme of a movement. There is no doubt that Huber, as the first German co-operative theoretician, smoothed the way for the idea of co-operation in Germany around the middle of the last century: Helmut Faust calls him the 'theoretical initiator of the German co-operative movement'.[8] As far as we know, he was also the first to have drawn the attention of the German co-operatives to Owen, but he had no decisive influence on the direction of development of the German co-operative movement.

He introduced Owen to the Germans – but he gave them a very one-sided picture of Owen. At the same time we must not forget that all this took place at a period when all the communal experiments of Owen had already failed.

In his *Letters from a Journey in England in the Summer of 1854* which appeared in Hamburg in 1855, a great deal of space is devoted to a discussion of Owen and Owenism. He introduced a long disquisition on Owen with these words:

> It is unfortunately not possible to discuss the foundation of co-operative societies in England without referring to this man and his socialist system. I have to admit that I have tried in vain to discover a second *definite* source of this fruitful and significant line of development, or even a positive and independent subsidiary influence on the definition and growth of the principle of association. It has only *one* real source: Robert Owen.[9]

Huber has to recognise, honestly if unwillingly, that it was Robert Owen who was the intellectual progenitor of the British co-operative movement. Having done that, he immediately brings along his big guns: 'The Owenite system', he declares, 'is as wholly anti-Christian and democratic-socialist as any that have been spawned within the past half century.' As a Christian, Huber is particularly opposed to Owen's doctrine that it is circumstances which determine the character of man, and which leave no room for the idea of original sin, of guilt and of free will. He accuses the thought structure of Owen, which he calls a 'tower of Babel', of 'incredible triviality and stupidity', and its architect of the 'most incalculable and naïve vainglory'. However, this bombardment is followed by the statement of the

> fact that Owen, apart from his system and all that is necessarily and immediately connected with it, and apart from his vanity, is one of the most honourable men known to me. We cannot doubt his love of humanity, his truly fanatical philanthropy, his rare moral and intellectual as well as physical and practical business ability, to which have to be added a tireless persistence, an inexhaustible energy and a total fearlessness, a rare agility and acuteness of mind especially as regards arithmetical and mathematical relationships, and a wealth of practical common sense and varied experience of life, of business and of humanity.

Rarely can a man have been lauded so fulsomely while his work is being totally damned in the same breath. This may perhaps be explained by the fact that Owen and Huber started out in their endeavours from the same basic motive – the love of humanity – but were totally at opposite poles in their judgement of man whom they want to help: Owen considered man to be good by nature, but threatened by his circumstances, while Huber considered him to be weighed down by original sin. Owen was therefore engaged in removing the harmful influence of circumstances and replacing them by something better. Huber wanted to make men capable of leading the good life within those circumstances. All systems of improving the world were rejected by him in principle as such. But he was honest enough to admit that the co-operative movement had been inspired by such a system and some of it could be made valuable. He put his idea of the relation between world-improving Utopia and co-operative reality into the following metaphorical formula: 'In view of that catharsis, such original kinship or descent, particularly of the British co-operative movement, from Robert Owen needs to be denied all the less since, on the contrary, . . . it is no small merit to have picked out the real gold nuggets from a heap of false or valueless metal, and to have made use of them by coining them into valid money.'[10] It is Huber's merit to have drawn attention to these 'nuggets of gold'. Huber was an enthusiastic admirer of the Rochdale Pioneers' Society. It is indeed Huber who made the Rochdale Co-operative Society known in German Co-operative circles. If Schulze-Delitzsch, with whom Huber was friendly for a time, had had any sympathy for consumers' co-operation and had given his support to Huber, the consumers' co-operatives would not have remained the Cinderella of the German co-operative movement for so many decades.

But Huber was not interested in the 'gold nuggets' of Owen's system. He gave due credit to Owen's work in New Lanark, to his initiatives in social policy and to his educational experiments. Owen, he wrote, had besides 'the undoubted merit to have been the *first* to have [presented] the conditions of the working classes as the result of the development of modern capitalism . . . with a full and warm heart for humanity'.

There is a startling, not to say amusing, postscript to be added to Huber's critique of Owen's utopianism, the critique by a conservative of an optimist who believed in humanity and progress, and of his no doubt premature and in many respects one-sidedly dogmatising and unrealisable lines of thought: that is the fact that the anti-utopian Huber landed, by means of a speculative somersault, in a truly superlative Utopia which is too typical to be omitted here. Let us state it in Huber's own words (in the above-mentioned essay):

> What would have been the result if the British aristocracy had treated its calling in a truly aristocratic spirit and had applied its then existing material means, its power and position in state, church and society with all its energy to separating in the Owenite system the poison

from the medicine, the wheat from the chaff, by rejecting unconditionally the revolutionary and anti-Christian doctrines and, as long as he still propagated them, the man himself – but adopting the practical core of his plans of inner colonisation into its mighty aristocratic hands, and had carried it into effect under the discipline, control and dedication of the conservative powers and in organic unity with the total organism and on the grand scale? There is no doubt that in that case England would now possess, distributed all over the country, a healthy labouring population, anchored in cooperative property and settled in affluent communities, in place of the millions of her proletariat either sunk in pauperism or declining into it or otherwise brutalised; in other words, in place of the whole social question which is casting an ever-increasing dark shadow over all the power and the glory of the island queen.

   And the means, the money? – Only half of the millions swallowed up in the bottomless morass of pauperism, invested instead in appropriate form at 4 per cent over the past thirty years, would have been sufficient to cover not only Great Britain and Ireland, but also a good part of the colonies, with such settlements, to raise the value of the land three- and fourfold, to enlarge the circulating medium by millions of a soundly backed paper, etc. Indeed, the sums wasted in the senseless strikes of the workmen over this period alone, would, if used in this way, have by themselves solved a good part of the problem and have removed the causes of the strikes.[11]

If this thought had not been meant to be taken seriously, one could have assumed that Huber had wanted to drive Robert Owen *ad absurdum* with it.

About ten years after Huber's discussion of Robert Owen, another leading German co-operator took him up. This was Dr Eduard Pfeiffer of Stuttgart (1835–1921), the first great figure on the stage of the history of German consumers' co-operation. In contrast to Huber, who was by nature an academic, there was in Pfeiffer a combination of a practical realism with an idealism looking to the future. Pfeiffer was at the same time a thinker and a man of action. He himself was not born into the working class – his father was, as the general manager of the Royal Württemberg Bank, one of the most influential and one of the richest men in the then still independent state of Württemberg – but he made the cause of labour his own. Like Owen, he was one of those very rare individuals who recognised even then that the social question, the labour question, was the key question of modern industrial society, and that without a solution of this question social revolution and the collapse of the social order would become inevitable. Like Owen, he took his place on the side of the oppressed. Like Owen, he did not confine himself to a critique of the existing order and to sketches of a new order, but insisted on doing something practical. But quite unlike the older Owen, he approached his work both cautiously and energetically, both carefully and courageously; even when taking circumspect small steps he did not lose sight of his major aim.

Pfeiffer, like Huber, had been to England, and like him had made similar observations. Probably the deep impression which the social devastations of the Industrial Revolution in England made upon him formed the beginning of his socially critical thoughts. He visited the Pioneers' Society in Rochdale in 1862, and this visit was possibly the genesis of his thoughts on social reform. In the co-operative society Pfeiffer saw a way out of the workers' misery, a path to a share in decision-making and with it to reform of capitalist society. By 1863 he had published his book which was both an accusation and a signpost, *Über Genossenschaftswesen* (*On Co-operation*), with the descriptive sub-title: 'What is the labouring estate in present society? And what may it expect?'

This book contains a long chapter on working-class associations in England, in which the author describes, above all, the Rochdale Pioneers' Society and its principles. A separate chapter is devoted to the 'Doctrines of the Communists and Socialists'. And in this chapter the discussion of Robert Owen occupies a large space. The effectiveness of Robert Owen in New Lanark is fully recognised by Pfeiffer: 'By following this system, setting everywhere an example himself, always anxious to pull the worker up to him, he achieved marvels in a short space of time. . . . In less than four years he succeeded in making out of the miserable and degraded population of New Lanark one which was happy and working efficiently.'[12] We learn, incidentally, from Pfeiffer that New Lanark had found a disciple also in Germany. There existed, in Reutlingen in Württemberg, a very large enterprise for that time which had taken New Lanark as its model. Pfeiffer writes about it:

The fraternity at Reutlingen, under the direction of Herr Werner, which has existed and flourished for some years, and operates a large paper mill, besides engineering and carriage-making, agriculture and a host of smaller industries, is wholly founded on the scheme of the colony of New Lanark and directed by Herr Werner, a former minister of religion. It is striking that this institution has not so far acquired more fame. . . .[13]

However, as far as Owen's 'ideal society', his concept of a self-supporting colony and his social reformist ideas were concerned, Pfeiffer found a great deal to object to. He saw in them communistic levelling-down. After inquiring into the causes of the failure of New Harmony, he came to the conclusion that 'practice had pronounced a damning sentence on Owenite communism'. The basic mistake of Owen, according to Pfeiffer, was to attempt the erection of 'an absolute equality on the basis of the inequality created by nature'. He summarises his judgement on Owen in the following sentence: 'However perfect the leading idea of Owen might be, to wish to suppress individualism as totally as he does still represents a failure to recognise the highest and noblest traits of man; it means to command the progress of mankind suddenly to come to a halt and, by ordering all and everyone to stay at the same level, to banish from society all that is great and exalted.'[14]

Pfeiffer's generalising judgment on Owen's 'leading idea' may be unjust, but we cannot deny a certain justice to its central core. Doubtless Owen relied too trustingly on the belief that a new environment together with the proper educational support would ensure that the common humanity, with its potential for 'the good' in man, would become apparent, securing the unfolding of all good human potentialities and the development of man into communal man. We know today that this is in *every* social order and in *every* environment the most difficult problem facing humanity – and we also know, after the terrifying experiences of this century, the demoniacal powers of evil that are latent in man and what mischief they can do when they are unchained.

Even if Pfeiffer's judgment on Owen had been different, it would have had no practical significance. Pfeiffer had the great merit of having founded consumers' co-operatives on the Rochdale model in Germany, or of having inspired their foundation. He built a social ideal into their ultimate aim which may not have been Owenite, but was no less based on a social critique than the ultimate Owenite aims of the Rochdale Pioneers. By that time the Owenite community ideal was no longer predominant even in Great Britain – either in co-operative practice or in co-operative theory.

In the nineties of the last century the idea of communal settlement was taken up once more in Germany, studied scientifically in all its relationships and consequences, and presented systematically in an economic and co-operative framework. This was the work of Franz

Oppenheimer, an economist and sociologist and an independent, consistent and uncompromising thinker. His motif was economico- and socio-political. He wanted not only to destroy the strongest bastion of feudalism in Germany, the monopoly of land of the big landlord, but also to contribute materially to the solution of the social question. He wanted to reach this goal by means of large-scale inner colonisation and the creation of a network of co-operative settlements. In his book which appeared in 1896, entitled *Die Siedlungsgenossenschaft, Versuch einer positiven Überwindung des Kommunismus durch Lösung des Gesellschaftsproblems und der Agrarfrage,*[15] he developed a new theory of co-operation which cannot be discussed here in detail. As far as the land was concerned, 'agricultural workers' productive co-operatives' should become the foundation of inner colonisation. His picture of a productive co-operative appeared to be roughly as follows: there is a large scale co-operative enterprise in the centre, surrounded by numerous smaller enterprises which are linked among themselves in various co-operative ways, and whose owners are also partners and co-workers of the central enterprise. A system of accounting carefully tailored for such a complex ensures that every effort receives its just reward. The agricultural workers' productive co-operative should not be the final goal. But Oppenheimer thought it was the only path to a truly co-operative system. The decisive step in that direction would be made by a special form of co-operative, the communal settlement, 'which is no longer an economic co-operative, but co-operative economics, combining agriculture and industry in one body'.[16] Needless to say, such a far-reaching inner colonisation could not be achieved without the assistance of the state, above all by the acquisition of the large estates. The state was to buy up the large estates and hand them over to the workers. This particular brainchild seems, however, to have come to Oppenheimer only somewhat later. We do not find it until we get to his most important work, which appeared in 1910: *Theorie der reinen und politischen Ökonomie.*[17] In 1896, when criticising Huber's hesitation regarding practical attempts at settlement, he expressed the view that it 'is wholly sufficient to make a single co-operative settlement blossom forth; he [sc. Huber] could not see that as soon as the first fertile seed of a perfect social order which combines the whole system of co-operation in one economic organism, is put side by side with the present order, there must ensue such a strikingly rapid growth of the co-operative organism that it will mop up the old social order on its own and without outside aid'.[18]

Oppenheimer's theory of the co-operative settlement is a mental concept which is wholly new both in design and structure. It is not possible to derive the whole or its parts from one or the other 'forerunner'. Of course there are connections and similarities between Oppenheimer and the other social critics, co-operative thinkers, political economists, sociologists and psychologists. Oppenheimer studied in great detail all co-operative settlement ideas, experiments and data that he could find, described them, analysed them and used out of them what was to his purpose.

It goes without saying that he made a detailed study of Owen. And it is certain that his preoccupation with Owen must have influenced his own thinking. His judgment on Owen is mixed, but the positive side predominates. Thus in contrast to Huber, he wholly agrees with Robert Owen's thesis that it is basically circumstances which determine human character. At the conclusion of a very long chapter on the influence of economic conditions on the morals of men, he states: 'we know quite well that the basic thought, the dependence of morals on the economic circumstances of men, has become the intellectual property of socialism ever since Robert Owen's doctrine, particularly appertaining to this point, and especially since the world-renowned *proof* of these doctrines in New Lanark.'[19]

However, Oppenheimer has a series of reservations about the Owenite idea of 'communities'. Owen's colonies, he alleges, were *mechanisms* rather then *organisms*. 'Fourier, Cabet and Owen', he writes, '. . . failed in their hopeless attempts to turn the image of their dreams at once and completely into reality. They refused to plant and tend the fruit tree until it would bear fruit, but wanted to *make* it all complete.'[20] But like Huber he pays tribute to the 'justified central core of the Owenite settlement proposals'. Indeed, in spite of all the criticism he remains in favour of the Owenite 'concept' of settlements: 'In England, Robert Owen forms the point at which co-operation parts company with communism. We have seen how closely his concept of communities corresponds with the ideal of the co-operative settlement.'[21] One of the Owenite communities is altogether exempt from all criticism: Ralahine. He describes the constitution and history of this community with full approval, not to say admiration, in all its details .'This successful experiment, succeeding more day by day', this colony, which as a 'flourishing and strong organism' was destroyed by a 'mishap for which it bore not the slightest responsibility', could be described as a true agricultural producers' co-operative in transition to a co-operative settlement. The experiment was 'a wonderful success both in material and ethical respects'.[22]

There is no doubt that few attempts at settlement fascinated Oppenheimer as much as Ralahine. And equally there is no doubt that he was much stimulated by Owenite ideas. Some of them were woven into the fabric of Oppenheimer's co-operative settlement.

Oppenheimer's book received much attention and ran through several editions. He obtained a great deal of support, but also met much opposition. In Germany there were scarcely any practical consequences of Oppenheimer's ideas, though one attempt of his to set up a communal co-operative settlement was wholly successful and survived for many years. In Israel, however, the *kibbutzim* may be said to have turned a good part of his ideas into reality.

Huber, Pfeiffer and Oppenheimer were the German co-operative theoreticians who really took Owen seriously. The later theoreticians of the co-operative movement showed no great interest in Owen. They usually dismissed him in a few sentences – either as forerunner of a consumers' co-operative socialism (e.g. Eduard Jacob, *Volkswirtschaftliche Theorie der Genossenschaften*,[23] 1913) or of a productive co-operative socialism (e.g. W. Kulemann, *Die Genossenschaftsbewegung*,[24] 1922, 2 vols). In 1905 there appeared in Jena a major biographical work on Robert Owen by Helene Simon, *Robert Owen, Sein Leben und seine Bedeutung für die Gegenwart*.[25] Apart from this very thorough study, there are only two other books on Owen in the German language as far as we know, namely a novel by Richard Robert Wagner, *Robert Owen, Lebensroman eines Menschengläubigen*[26] (Zürich, 1942), and a small contribution by the author of this essay, published in Hamburg in 1958 under the title *Robert Owen, Sturm und Drang des sozialen Gewissens in der Frühzeit des Kapitalismus*,[27] which achieved two editions.

Of course, the economists and sociologists have always considered Robert Owen – but mostly in the above-mentioned sense of rubber-stamping him as a 'utopian socialist.' One of the few exceptions is the well-known economist Gerhart von Schulze-Gävernitz, who published in 1890 a work in two volumes, *Zum sozialen Frieden*,[28] in which he referred to co-operation. He calls Owen one of the 'great prophets of socialism . . . whose so-called Utopia has kindled in many younger minds the desire for social reform'.

On another occasion Schulze-Gävernitz discusses the 'foundations' of co-operation, 'laid long ago by Owen whose influence is still felt today'. This was eight decades ago. Is it still valid today? Does anything of the old community spirit, which after all was what mattered to Owen, still survive in the co-operative movement? If we were to believe co-operative speechmaking, we should say that it does. But practice speaks a different tongue. The inner relationship between the members of co-operative societies has largely disappeared, and the managers seem to have taken over control.

This is a challenge to the co-operator. As Owen in his own day, so we today likewise face strong 'atomising tendencies' in society. Owen had one powerful ally, *misery*, and we today have an additional enemy, *the self-satisfaction of the welfare society*. But even this self-satisfaction is about to produce its antidote: discomfort, unrest and *inner misery*, and, in the best sections of our youth, a 'burning desire' for community.

## NOTES AND REFERENCES

1. *The Book of the New Moral World containing the Rational System of Society Founded in Demonstrable Facts, developing the Constitution and Laws of Human Nature and of Society. Sacred to Truth, without Mystery, Mixture of Error, or Fear of Man* (trans.).
2. M. Cole, *Robert Owen of New Lanark* (London, 1953) p. 117n.
3. *Capital*, vol. III pt 2, p. 144 (German ed.).
4. In a contribution to the *Propyläen World History*, VIII 405.
5. Frankfurt, 1965, p. 148.
6. There is some doubt about the year and date of this meeting. The first continental tour of Owen is usually said by his biographers to have taken place in 1818. Margaret Cole (*Robert Owen of New Lanark*, p. 127) adds that 'it was the first occasion, so far as we know, that he had set foot outside his own country'. Yet we also know that Huber left Hofwyl in October 1816, never to return to it. That Huber saw Owen in Hofwyl is beyond doubt, since Huber mentions this himself, and it is to him also that we owe the phrase that he had later 'followed in Owen's footsteps' (V. A. Huber, *Ausgewählte Schriften* (Berlin, 1894) p. xxxi). We therefore have to assume that Owen's continental tour of 1818 was after all not his first. Could he possibly have visited Switzerland and Hofwyl in 1816?
7. *Self-help for the Working Classes through Economic Associations and Inner Colonisation* (trans.).
8. *Geschichte der Genossenschaftsbewegung*, p. 163.
9. The quotations are from the essay on Robert Owen in V. A. Huber, *Selected Works* (in German), pp. 958–77.
10. Ibid., p. 739.
11. Ibid., p. 968.
12. *Über Genossenschaftswesen*, p. 48.

13. Ibid., p. 52.

14. Ibid., p. 53.

15. *The Co-operative Settlement, an Attempt at a Positive Defeat of Communism by the Solution of the Social Problem and the Agrarian Question* (trans.).

16. Ibid., p. 413.

17. *Theory of Pure and Political Economy*, p. 603 (trans.).

18. Ibid., p. 455.

19. Ibid., p. 626.

20. Ibid., p. 432. Martin Buber took a similar view half a century later. On New Harmony he wrote: 'That, for example, is a settlement which failed, not because of its dogmas, but . . . because of the lack of a deeper *organic* relationship between the members.' *Der Utopische Sozialismus*, extract reproduced in Helmut Faust (ed.), *Genossenschaftliches Lesebuch* (1967) p. 37.

21. *Theorie der reinen und politischen Ökonomie*, p. 452.

22. Ibid., p. 412.

23. *Economic Theory of the Co-operatives* (trans.).

24. *The Co-operative Movement* (trans.).

25. *Robert Owen, His Life and His Significance for the Present Time* (trans.).

26. *Robert Owen, A Biographical Novel of One Who Believed in Humanity* (trans.).

27. *Robert Owen, Storm and Stress of the Social Conscience in Early Capitalism* (trans.).

28. *Social Peace* (trans.).

# The Authors

W. H. G. ARMYTAGE ('Owen and America') is Professor of Education at the University of Sheffield. Married to an American and a frequent visitor to the United States (where he has held visiting lectureships at the University of Michigan), he is a prolific writer on historical and educational themes. His books include *The Civic Universities* (Benn, 1955), *Heavens Below* (Routledge & Kegan Paul, 1962) and *Four Hundred Years of English Education* (C.U.P., 1964).

MARGARET COLE ('Owen's Mind and Methods') is the widow of G. D. H. Cole, himself a major biographer of Owen. A Fabian of distinction, her many published works include *Makers of the Labour Movement* (1848), *Robert Owen of New Lanark* (1953) and *The Story of Fabian Socialism* (1961).

HENRI DESROCHE ('Images and Echoes of Owenism in Nineteenth-century France') is Directeur de Centre de Recherches Coopératives at the Sorbonne. His many writings on the subject of co-operation and its history include studies of the important French socialist, Fourier. In 1965 he published *Socialismes et Sociologie Religieuse*. Professeur Desroche is a leading member of a team of scholars who with the help of English colleagues are engaged in producing a definitive statement of the sources for study of aspects of the history of European socialist thought.

R. G. GARNETT ('Robert Owen and Community Experiments') is Principal of the Hendon College of Technology. Apart from articles and monographs, he has published *A Century of Co-operative Insurance* (Allen & Unwin, 1968). A study of Owenite communities by Mr Garnett resulted in the award of a Ph.D. degree by the University of London.

J. F. C. HARRISON ('A New View of Mr Owen') is Professor of History at the University of Sussex and formerly held a chair at the University of Wisconsin, Madison, U.S.A. His book *Quest for the New Moral World: Robert Owen and the Owenites in Britain and America* was awarded the Walter D. Love Memorial Prize of the Conference of British Studies, U.S.A. Other publications include *Utopianism and Education: Robert Owen and the Owenites*, ed. with introductory essay (New York, 1968), and *Learning and Living, 1790–1960* (London and Toronto, 1961).

ERWIN HASSELMANN ('The Impact of Owen's Ideas on German Social and Co-operative Thought in the Nineteenth Century') is a Dr.Phil. of the University of Marburg. He left Germany, where he had been Secretary of the Civil Servants' trade union, but returned from Britain in 1948 to become editor of *Der Verbraucher*. Dr Hasselmann's numerous publications include *Robert Owen: Sturm und Drang des sozialen Gewissens in der Frühzeit des Kapitalismus* (Hamburg, 1958 and 1959, two eds). Among his publications in English are *Consumers' Co-operation in Germany* (Hamburg, 1953–61, three eds).

W. H. OLIVER ('Owen in 1817: The Millennialist Moment') is a New Zealander who has undertaken research at Oxford. From 1964 he has been Professor of History at Massey University, New Zealand. In 1960 he published his *Story of New Zealand* (Faber). A Canadian Commonwealth Research Fellow in 1970, he is currently preparing a book on millennialism in English thought from the 1790s to the 1840s.

SIDNEY POLLARD (co-editor) is Professor of Economic History in the University of Sheffield. His books include *A History of Labour in Sheffield* and *The Genesis of Modern Management*, and he has taken an interest for many years in the Co-operative movement. He is at present working on a study of British Labour in the Industrial Revolution.

A. J. ROBERTSON ('Robert Owen, Cotton Spinner: New Lanark, 1800–1825') is Lecturer in Economic History at the University of Manchester. He has also taught in the Universities of British Columbia and Glasgow. He is currently preparing a book for B. T. Batsford on *The British Cotton Industry, 1780–1870*.

JOHN SALT (co-editor) is Head of the Department of Modern Arts at Sheffield Polytechnic. He has published a wide range of articles in the fields of education and social history, being particularly interested in the provincial aspects of socialist and anarchist movements in the nineteenth century. The first volume of his *Discovering History* (with F. Purnell as co-author) was published by Oliver & Boyd in 1970.

JOHN SAVILLE ('J. E. Smith and the Owenite Movement, 1833–1834') is Reader in Economic History at the University of Hull. He is author of *Ernest Jones, Chartist* and *Rural Depopulation in England and Wales 1851–1951*, and co-editor (with Asa Briggs) of *Essays in Labour History* and (with Dr Joyce Bellamy) of a forthcoming *Dictionary of Labour Biography*.

HAROLD SILVER ('Owen's Reputation as an Educationist') is Senior Lecturer at the Centre for Science Education, Chelsea College, London University. He is author of *The Concept of Popular Education* (London, 1965) and *Robert Owen on Education* (Cambridge, 1969).

CHUSHICHI TSUZUKI ('Robert Owen and Revolutionary Politics') was born in 1926 in Japan and educated at Hitotsubashi (Tokyo), Wisconsin and Oxford Universities. He is at present Professor of Social Thought at Hitotsubashi, although he spent the session 1969–70 as Visiting Professor at the University of Sheffield. His publications include *H. M. Hyndman and British Socialism* (1961) and *The Life of Eleanor Marx* (1967).

EILEEN YEO ('Robert Owen and Radical Culture') worked with J. F. C. Harrison at the University of Wisconsin on 'Changing Patterns of Owenite Thought'. Transferring to the University of Sussex, she has maintained her interest in social history and, apart from her research into aspects of Owenism, is currently producing a book on Henry Mayhew.

# Index